BARRY UNIVERSITY

DATE DUE

GAYLORD		PRINTED IN U.S.A.

Headquarters in the Brush

Headquarters

Blazer's Independent Union Scouts

DARL L. STEPHENSON

Foreword by Brian C. Pohanka

OHIO UNIVERSITY PRESS

Athens

in the Brush

Ohio University Press, Athens, Ohio 45701
© 2001 by Ohio University Press
Printed in the United States of America
All rights reserved

Ohio University Press books are printed on acid-free paper ⊗ ™

09 08 07 06 05 04 03 02 01   5 4 3 2 1

Library of Congress Cataloging-in-Publication Data

Stephenson, Darl L., 1946–
  Headquarters in the brush : Blazer's Independent Union Scouts / Darl L.
Stephenson.
      p. cm.
  Includes bibliographical references and index.
  ISBN 0-8214-1381-3
  1. United States. Army. Blazer's Independent Union Scouts (1863–1865). 2. United
States—History—Civil War, 1861–1865—Scouts and scouting. 3. Scouts and
scouting—United States—History—19th century. I. Title.

  E608 .S74 2001
  973.7'41—dc21

                                                            2001016343

In memory of James E. Edwards
and to my late aunt, Elsie Ellinger,
and my mother, Lena Stephenson,
who gave me my love of history

Contents

Illustrations

Chapter 9

Roster

Maps

Foreword

The vast and stirring saga of the Civil War has generated more printed material and stimulated more interest than any other period in our country's history. Not only does the copious outpouring of books, magazine articles, scholarly tomes, documentaries—and in this computer age, a plethora of Internet sites—continue unabated, but recent years have seen a marked increase in the public's fascination with that bloodiest of American conflicts. But for all the attention it has received in the 135 years since the guns fell silent, the Civil War remains fertile ground for students and historians precisely because the entire story has not been told, indeed, can never be told. And the challenge of investigation, of reassessment—the historical detective work that fires the scholarly passions of so many researchers—is a great part of the appeal that era holds for us.

Historians willing to look beyond the oft-told stories of famous commanders and epic battles have found promising fields for their endeavors in reconstructing the lives of the common soldiers and recounting those collective experiences in unit histories. It is one of the most worthwhile of all historical projects, as it speaks to an inherently personal aspect of the great conflict. If, as Emerson said, "there is properly no history, only biography," battalions, regiments, and brigades were, in the interplay of diverse personalities, very much like extended families—bound together not by blood, but by a willingness to shed their blood for cherished ideals.

Despite the inevitable loss of potentially important documents, prodigious resources remain available for scholars willing to seek out and sift through those archival treasure troves. It can be time-consuming and laborious work, but the rewards are immeasurable. The challenge of crafting a unit history of even the most celebrated Union or Confederate organization is daunting enough. But in the case of Capt. Richard Blazer's Independent Scouts—an unorthodox unit comprising soldiers drawn from many different regiments—it would have been impossible without the diligence and commitment Darl L. Stephenson has brought to his task.

The story of Blazer's command has long been overshadowed by the legendary status of Col. John Singleton Mosby's Partisan Rangers, whose daring exploits, if at times embellished and invariably romanticized, have inspired generations of Civil War buffs. While generally granted a degree of credit as formidable foes, Blazer and his men have traditionally been portrayed as foils to the Gray Ghost's intrepid band—rather like the armor-clad underlings of the Sheriff of Nottingham, who marched into Sherwood Forest looking for Robin Hood and his Merry Men. In other words, Blazer's Scouts have remained faceless and anonymous, their commander something of a cipher, their full story untold.

Thanks to Darl Stephenson's research, in particular his careful examination of the military service and pension files of Blazer's soldiers at the National Archives, we now have a sense of just who those warriors were. We know each scout's name, age, appearance, and background, and through the author's perusal of a vast quantity of previously neglected sources, we learn how those soldiers met and endured their often tragic fates in the stern exigencies of war. Handpicked men of various units, they were brought together in a most unusual organization: one intended to locate, engage, and destroy the Southern guerrilla and partisan bands that were a perpetual thorn in the side of the Federal war effort. Blazer's headquarters would quite literally be in the brush. Initially pursuing and clashing with parties of Rebel irregulars in one of the war's most rugged theaters of conflict—the wooded and mountainous terrain of western Virginia—in the summer of 1864 Blazer's Scouts found themselves assigned an even more challenging task: "to clean out Mosby's gang."

Captain Blazer in fact shared many of those qualities of leadership that characterized his famous opponent. While nondescript in his physical appearance, he displayed great force of character; he was gritty, determined, strong-willed, and tireless. Like John Mosby, Blazer was well suited for command of a volunteer unit composed of tough individualists waging a type of warfare far removed from the more traditional set-piece structure of the nineteenth-century battlefield. Borrowing the tactics of their foe, Blazer's troops often garbed themselves in Confederate uniforms and infiltrated enemy formations.

Sometimes the hunter and sometimes the hunted, they moved quickly and struck the enemy hard, without warning, neither expecting nor giving quarter. With experience came success, and the ability, as one Scout put it, to "whip our weight in wildcats."

Though fielding no more than a hundred men—and usually fewer than that—Blazer's Scouts were armed with Spencer "seven-shooters" along with braces of pistols, and mounted on the best horseflesh they could obtain. They were thus a force to be reckoned with, and managed to win some rare victories over elements of the famed Partisan Rangers. Their freewheeling style for a time presented a very real threat to Mosby's operations, compelling the Rangers to concentrate in larger than usual numbers. Blazer's troopers thus brought a margin of relief to the Yankee outposts and convoys that were so often the targets of Mosby's band during the Shenandoah Valley campaign.

On November 18, 1864, fate caught up with the Independent Scouts in the form of a partisan force commanded by Mosby's trusted subordinate Maj. "Dolly" Richards. The Rangers were out for vengeance, and with the benefit of superior numbers the climactic confrontation at Kabletown resulted in the virtual destruction of Blazer's outfit. Carefully examining the often conflicting accounts of that brutal clash, Stephenson strips away layers of myth that have obscured the full story and for the first time presents an accurate record of the casualties.

The postwar legacy of Blazer's command is an equally fascinating part of the story of this remarkable group of fighting men, each of whom is profiled here in a detailed unit roster. Humble farmer or publishing magnate, from the violent Arizona frontier to the sweltering jungles of the Philippines, Blazer's Scouts left their mark on the pages of our nation's tumultuous history. *Headquarters in the Brush* is a worthy tribute to their memory.

BRIAN C. POHANKA
Alexandria, Virginia

Preface

On November 18, 1864, a unit of Union Army scouts commanded by Capt. Richard Blazer was attacked and defeated by at least two companies under Col. John Mosby's command near Kabletown, West Virginia. That defeat, the myths that have arisen because of it, and the egotistical intrigues of Gen. Philip Sheridan have obscured the true history of what may have been the most unusual unit of the American Civil War.

By the fall of 1864 this little unit led by a captain had achieved significant fame. Their exploits had been told on the pages of not just the most prestigious regional newspapers but also the leading Eastern newspapers. They were called celebrated and famous. After the war, their fame continued to be praised in the reunions of the Army of West Virginia and soldier newspapers such as the *Ohio Soldier* and the *National Tribune*.

However, Blazer's men never established a national audience for their adventures, as did Mosby's Rangers. Asbe Montgomery's little book about the Scouts was published in limited quantities for a local audience. By the late nineteenth century the unit was largely forgotten and its influence on American military operations unrecognized.

There are two important reasons why Blazer's Scouts never received the continued fame they deserved. First, General Sheridan, under whom they served, failed to give them credit. Instead of recognizing their total service to his army, Sheridan probably perceived the defeat at Kabletown as a mark of dishonor. He did shower significant praise on the unit of scouts which he founded, led by his favorite, Maj. Henry Young. Young's success in capturing Harry Gilmore was a feather Sheridan could put in his hat while Blazer's defeat at Kabletown was a failure with which Sheridan did not want to be associated.

Second, while given a measure of respect in the accounts of Mosby's

Rangers, the Scouts become a faceless enemy and in the case of Lt. Tom Coles are even demonized as cruel and unchivalrous. The Scouts, in these accounts, are just one more Union unit outwitted by the cunning men of Mosby's command. At the same time, layer upon layer of myth has been added by other authors to the already distorted accounts of the actions between Mosby's and Blazer's units written by earlier chroniclers of the Gray Ghost.

The research for this book involved extensive use of sources not normally consulted for Civil War books. Because the men were detailed from different regiments, I had to go through the compiled service records (CSRs) of each regiment to build a roster of the men who served in the Scouts. I also made extensive use of pension records.

Pension records have rarely been used as a source of information for Civil War research, but they do provide valuable information, particularly on units for which little other information is available. Pension records must be used judiciously by the researcher, because this was a welfare system, and the soldiers and their families did abuse it to obtain money from the government. That said, pension records are valuable for several reasons. Pension applications filed by mothers or fathers may contain original letters written by the soldier or sometimes an officer. These letters helped establish the bona fides of the relative as deserving a pension. The medical testimony contained in pension records also corroborates the stories of soldiers who were wounded or prisoners of war. Pension records filed late in life are the least valuable as military history sources, because they involve predominantly claims that make it difficult to distinguish between service-related causes and the normal infirmities of old age.

This book also documents many of the errors, distortions, and embellishments of Colonel Mosby's command written by his men and others after the Civil War. These accounts in many cases are not history at all but reminiscences. Some of them were written many years after the war and are real embellishments of stories that were probably told over several decades with varying degrees of accuracy. Unfortunately, many authors have used these sources without much critical evaluation.

Lest I be accused of being too partisan on the Union side, my research also uncovers more of the darker side of General Sheridan. It has long been known that Sheridan took credit for his subordinates' accomplishments and avoided being associated with operations that were not entirely successful.

Blazer's little command also appears to have been a victim of the ego of Sheridan, who would forget the valuable service rendered by Blazer. Later in life, Gen. George Crook, who had been a longtime friend of "Little Phil," used some very bitter words about Sheridan.

Finally, and most important, I hope this book will acquaint readers and historians with the forgotten legacy Blazer's Scouts may have left for American military operations, particularly in unconventional warfare. Blazer's unit may very well have had an influence on counterinsurgency operations during the Philippine Insurrection. It also probably influenced the operations of General Crook in the Indian Wars. Crook was arguably the most successful Indian fighter in American history because of his use of organized units of Indian scouts. A real case can be made that General Crook learned how to fight Indians in the mountains of West Virginia.

This book contains much new material taken from original sources. To preserve the flavor of the Civil War–era writing, for the most part I have retained idiosyncrasies in spelling, grammar, and punctuation as they occurred in original letters and documents. These sources were obtained from relatives of members of Blazer's Scouts as well as from private collectors. Without the help of many individuals over the years this book would not have been possible.

First, I thank my wife, Susan, and my children, Susanna and James, for their patience, love, and encouragement during this effort. Susan and her father, James Edwards, also edited early versions of my manuscript. I am also grateful to the many words of encouragement from friends, colleagues, and members of Company E of the 20th Maine, the reenactment unit to which I belong.

My thanks to the staff of the Ohio University Press for their patience and understanding during the production of this work. In particular I would like to thank Bob Furnish and the editorial staff for the careful editorial work on this book.

Two individuals gave generously of their time and effort to read my manuscript and provide critical comments and suggestions for improvements. Dr. Max Gross, a former colleague from the Defense Intelligence Agency who is Dean of Faculty at the Joint Military Intelligence College, edited my manuscript and provided valuable suggestions. Over the years I have discussed my project with Brian Pohanka, who always displayed an interest in my work, provided encouragement to me, and suggested sources. Brian graciously accepted the task of reading my manuscript and writing the foreword. My heartfelt thanks to him.

I would also like to express my appreciation to Woody West and the *Washington Times* for giving me my first opportunity to publish Civil War articles. Excerpts about the lives of Harrison Gray Otis and Samuel Harrop were published in the newspaper's regular Saturday Civil War page.

Among many archivists and institution staff members, I especially wish to mention the following individuals. I could never have accomplished this project without the kind help and knowledge of the archivists in the research branch of the National Archives. William Lind, Michael Musick, Rebecca Livingston, Dee Ann Blanton, Mike Meier, and others have all helped me find material and answer questions about possible leads to more information.

Nan Card of the Rutherford B. Hayes Presidential Center in Fremont, Ohio, was especially helpful in finding material in the Hayes Library and has always expressed great interest in my work and my comings and goings between Virginia and Ohio.

The extensive holdings of the Ohio Historical Center in Columbus provided valuable material, including several relevant diaries, materials from Ohio County histories, and other reference material. In particular, their holdings of major Ohio city and local newspapers from the Civil War era provided several pertinent articles and letters.

Sheri Pettit of the Boyd County Public Library in Ashland, Kentucky, made me aware of the narrow escape related by Henry Pancake of the 5th West Virginia Infantry, who provided the only complete account of the skirmish at Kabletown from the perspective of one of the survivors of Blazer's Scouts.

I am especially grateful for the help of family members of Blazer's Scouts who have provided so much valuable assistance and source material. Without their help I would not have been able to tell the tale of their ancestors in so much detail. In particular, I greatly appreciate the aid and friendship of the late Richard E. Blazer, a grandson of Richard Blazer and great-grandson Cy R. Blazer, who allowed me to use materials belonging to Captain Blazer.

My sincere appreciation to Alice Ann Harrop of Quincy, Illinois, who made available to me the *Memorials and Poems* of Samuel Harrop.

I owe a real debt of gratitude to the descendants and members of the Wass family, who provided much valuable material on William Wass of the 14th West Virginia Infantry. My thanks to Mary Lucille DeBerry for her help, interest, and friendship in exploring the wonderful story of the Wass family and allowing me to use portions of her poetry. She also graciously edited the manuscript entries about Bill Wass.

Gwen Babcock, the great-granddaughter of Harrison Gray Otis, put me in touch with the late Ann Gorman Condon, who has edited the diary and correspondence of Harrison Gray Otis and the diary of Eliza Ann Otis. I am grateful Ann allowed me to use this material from her book.

I am very grateful to Journalist Chief Petty Officer (JOC) Art Frith, USN (Ret.), who made a wonderful photo of Joseph Frith available on the Internet site for the 34th Ohio Infantry. Art also had Joseph's Spencer repeating rifle photographed for me.

Other relatives too numerous to name here have provided valuable information to this project. My heartfelt thanks to all of them for their contributions.

Headquarters in the Brush

1

Guerrilla Warfare in West Virginia

The Early Stages of the Civil War

WHEN the American Civil War began, most people believed it would be a short, nearly bloodless conflict. As the nation proceeded to move toward confrontation and the Southern states began voting for secession, the two halves of the nation began preparing for war. In the mountains of western Virginia, a relaxed atmosphere still reigned. Men began to join local militia units North and South. Taylor Hogg, a resident of Point Pleasant, Virginia, joined a militia unit of loyal Union men. War was still an act of posturing on both sides. Taylor noted that his unit "drilled in a field with Confederates on one side and Union men on the other side."[1]

After Fort Sumter, real war would soon start in western Virginia. Virginia passed its secession ordinance on April 17, 1861. Following the approval of the ordinance by the constitutional convention at Richmond on May 23, the governor of Virginia ordered forces into western Virginia to encourage enlistments and to guard the Ohio-Pennsylvania frontier. Union authorities immediately recognized the danger of letting the western portion of Virginia fall into the control of the Confederacy. First, most of the inhabitants west of the Allegheny Mountains were loyal to the Union. Their rights would have to be protected by Federal authorities. In fact, the secessionists underestimated the strength of the opposition which the people of northwestern Virginia would offer to the attempt to join them to the Confederacy. Politically, Unionists eventually moved to separate thirty-four northwestern counties (later thirty-nine) from the rest of the state and lay the foundations for the founding of the state of West Virginia at the First Wheeling Convention on May 13, 1861. West Virginia would eventually become a state on June 20, 1863.[2]

Second, western Virginia was important for protection and control of the vital lines of communication reaching westward to the Ohio Valley. These were, from south to north: (1) the James River and Kanawha Turnpike, (2) the Parkersburg and Staunton Turnpike, (3) the route of present-day U.S. 50 from Winchester through Romney and Grafton, and Clarksburg to Parkersburg, and (4) the extremely important Baltimore and Ohio Railroad from Baltimore through western Maryland and northwestern Virginia to Wheeling.[3]

At the same time that control of western Virginia protected vital Union lines of communication, control of this area was a threat to communications that connected the eastern portion of the Confederacy with lines to the west, especially the vital Virginia and Tennessee Railroad.[4]

Military operations in western Virginia were some of the first campaigns of the Civil War. The success of Gen. George McClellan in these operations led to his prominence as a Northern military leader. McClellan was put in charge of the Department of the Ohio, and in response to Confederate threats on the Baltimore and Ohio Railway and the Kanawha Valley he eventually ordered Union forces into action to secure the territory. Units from Ohio and Indiana, as well as loyal Virginia units, moved into Virginia from the Ohio Valley at Wheeling and Parkersburg. Union forces under McClellan and Col. Benjamin F. Kelley routed Confederate forces at Philippi, which left the strategic Baltimore and Ohio Railroad in Union hands.[5]

Confederate forces under Robert Garnett and Col. John Pegram then attempted to hold positions in forts at Rich Mountain and Laurel Hill. McClellan moved to attack both positions at once. After a sharp fight, Union forces won a clear victory; the Confederate forces were destroyed. Garnett abandoned his Laurel Hill position without a fight. Garnett's retreating force was pressed strongly by the Federals, forcing him to fight an engagement at Corrick's Ford, on the Cheat River in Ford County. Garnett was killed in the Confederate defeat which followed, and the Confederate army once again fled, abandoning

Adapted from Cohen, *Civil War in West Virginia.*

wagons, guns, and their sick to Union forces. Before he left the Laurel Hill position, Garnett informed Gen. Robert E. Lee that "the lack of enlistments and aid to the Confederate cause indicated he was in a foreign country."[6]

Robert E. Lee Takes Command

Confederate commanders had not been cooperating well with each other and around August 1, 1861, General Lee arrived in western Virginia and assumed de facto control over Confederate forces. Under Lee's leadership, Confederate forces attempted to go on the offensive. They routed a Union regiment at

Cross Lanes, near the Gauley River, on August 26, 1861. Gen. John Floyd, commanding other Confederate forces, then established a strong position in front of Carnifex Ferry on the Gauley. Gen. William S. Rosecrans, who had succeeded McClellan as commander of the Department of the Ohio and the Army of Occupation of Western Virginia, advanced on the Confederate position. Initially checked by the Confederates, Floyd was eventually pushed out of his position and forced to recross the Gauley River.

Union forces continued to prosecute their efforts against the Confederates, repulsing Confederate attacks at Cheat Mountain and attacking Southern forces at the Greenbrier River. Confederate forces would continue to contest the Union hold on western Virginia through 1863 and threaten the vital communications links through the area. However, McClellan's operations and the efforts of other Union commanders such as Rosecrans did much to secure the region and the eventual state for the Union.[7]

By the fall of 1861, the trans-Allegheny region of western Virginia was firmly in Union control and the Southern government never made a serious attempt to recover or hold this area, despite the belief of some Southern politicians and generals that the majority of the population was sympathetic to their cause. In fact, these Southerners should have heeded the words of Gen. Henry Wise, who left the region for the eastern theater after the fall of 1861: "The Kanawha Valley is wholly disaffected and traitorous. . . . you cannot persuade these people that Virginia can or will ever reconquer the northwest, and they are submitting, subdued, and debased."[8]

The Confederates were forced to resort to raids which could not strategically change the situation in the Kanawha, but could at least gain supplies for the Confederates and recruits, as some Southern politicians still hoped. In August 1862, Gen. Albert Jenkins conducted a raid through the state and crossed into Ohio near Ripley, Virginia, becoming the first Confederate commander to enter that state. He recrossed into West Virginia below Point Pleasant, in Mason County, and proceeded to Guyandotte (now Huntington) and Raleigh Courthouse. The raid demonstrated Union vulnerabilities in the Kanawha Valley, which had been weakened by the dispatch of five thousand troops to bolster Gen. John Pope's command in Virginia. This led the Confederate high command to send Gen. William W. Loring in September to retake the valley.[9]

Gen. Joseph A. J. Lightburn commanded Union forces in the valley, although he also had troops that had been transferred to Virginia. There were forts at Fayetteville and other points and a large supply depot at Gauley Bridge. General Lee directed Loring, the Confederate commander at Pearlsburg, to again invade the area to capture the Kanawha Valley and restore the trans-Allegheny area to the Confederacy.[10]

Loring left on September 1, 1862, with four thousand troops and marched to Fayetteville. The battle that took place there on September 11 led to an unexpected Union rout. General Lightburn ordered a general retreat and opened up the entire Kanawha Valley to the Confederates. His troops retreated in two columns, eventually linking up at Charleston for the defense of that city. In the early morning of September 13, Loring's advance units arrived in Charleston in the vicinity of the present university campus. After an all-day battle, Lightburn retreated toward the Ohio River, cutting the cables over the Elk River at Charleston. Loring did not pursue him and the Confederate occupation was short-lived. Concentrations of Federal troops at Clarksburg and Point Pleasant forced Loring to abandon the valley and retreat toward Lewisburg on October 8. Loring was replaced on October 16 by Gen. John Echols of Monroe County, who moved back into Charleston for a short time, but on October 29 he was also forced to retreat and the Kanawha Valley was permanently in Union hands.[11]

Confederate gains for the campaign included moving salt out of the valley to eastern Virginia and the corrosive effect Lightburn's Retreat, as it came to be called, had on Union morale. Desertions ran very high in the regiments involved, but commanders—recognizing the reasons for the wholesale desertions —often did not severely punish the men for their absences.[12]

Although Confederate fortunes were at a high point overall in early 1863, Union forces had consolidated their positions in western Virginia. The situation led to a series of Union raids to cut the strategically important Virginia and Tennessee Railroad. Confederate forces, on the other hand, had to content themselves with a series of raids to obtain supplies, keep Union forces off guard, and disrupt communications and transportation, particularly the Baltimore and Ohio Railroad.[13]

The great Jones-Imboden Raid in late April 1863 was one of the most ambitious undertakings in this period. The raid resulted from a strategy outlined by General Lee for war in western Virginia and communicated to Gen. John D. Imboden. One of the Confederacy's goals was to harass the Reorganized

Government of Virginia, an illegitimate creature in Confederate eyes. Besides raids, orders such as this undoubtedly contributed to the guerrilla warfare which was to rage in the state until the end of the war.[14]

Imboden's plan was to destroy the B&O from Oakland, Maryland, to Grafton, West Virginia; defeat the Union forces at Beverly, Philippi, and Buckhannon; recruit for the Confederacy; and control the northwest section of the state so the residents could take part in the Virginia state elections in May. However, except for the partial destruction of the railroad, the burning of thousands of barrels of oil, and the capture of thousands of horses and cattle, the raid was of little use to the Confederacy. The destruction from this raid as well as others by both sides helped impoverish the state and led to the wholesale exodus of refugees.[15]

The Origin of the Partisan Rangers

Another expedient the Confederates used to carry the war to the Union was the formation of partisan rangers. Home guard units had sprung up early in the war and bushwhacking and other forms of guerrilla warfare probably occurred from the beginning of the war as Federal forces attempted to secure the state for the Union. On April 26, 1861, an article in the *Kanawha Valley Star* boasted:

> The mountains of Transalleghany [*sic*] Virginia are filled with able-bodied men—accustomed from their youth to bear arms, every one of whom has one or more rifles in his cabin, and all of them are first rate marksmen.
>
> Should the abolitionists of Ohio send an invading army into Western Virginia, not a soldier of them will ever return alive. The mountain boys would shoot them down as dogs.[16]

However, a major impetus for guerrilla war was the Confederate passage of the Partisan Ranger Law, authored by John Scott on March 27, 1862. This law authorized the recruiting of ten to twenty companies of partisan rangers, composed exclusively of men whose homes were in western Virginia, which was held by Federal authorities. Each company was to consist of seventy-five men, with a captain in command, a first lieutenant, and a second lieutenant. For the most part these companies would act independently, although they were to cooperate with regular forces when they operated in the same area.[17]

The partisan rangers had a checkered reputation with Northerners and

Southerners alike. Although meant to be protection against an invading Northern army, their actions often brought great hardship to those with Southern sympathies as well. No less an authority than Robert E. Lee offered his objection to these organizations: "Experience has convinced me that it is almost impossible . . . to have discipline in these bands of partisan rangers, or to prevent them from becoming an injury instead of benefit to the service, and even where this is accomplished the system gives license to many deserters and marauders, who assume to belong to these authorized companies and commit depredations on friend and foe alike." Lee urged the disbandment of such groups with the exception of John Singleton Mosby's command in northern Virginia, which at least the Confederate high command considered in a different category.[18]

The depredations of some of these bands were notorious. Under a veneer of military organization, these men often used the opportunity to settle old scores, indulge in simple thievery, and, perhaps most important, engage in semilegitimate stealing to obtain horses for "military operations." The horse thievery was practiced by rangers, militiamen, and regular horse thieves. Horses were often stolen by men who wanted to join the Confederate cavalry and knew they must furnish their own mounts. Although the Confederates were undoubtedly the greatest culprits, the U.S. government also contributed to the problem both officially and unofficially. Due to the war, demand for horses skyrocketed, which probably led to thefts to obtain horses for the government. Union units were authorized to take horses from "disloyal citizens," and officers and probably others engaged in flimflammery to obtain money for captured horses.[19]

Of much more tragic consequence was the creation of thousands of destitute refugees who had to flee their homes because their loyalties were with the opposite side. In 1862 refugees packed Parkersburg from Wirt, Roane, and Jackson Counties: "the Ohio border is lined with refugees from western Virginia . . . their property of every kind is being taken by the guerrillas— their persons are unsafe."[20] Sometimes the refugees were uprooted by major military operations as when in September 1862, in response to Lightburn's Retreat, the orderly sergeant of Company A, 91st Ohio Volunteer Infantry, noted "the Kanawha jammed with refugees black and white."[21] But often, people became refugees simply because they were in an area occupied by "home guard," wearing the wrong uniform, or whatever passed as a uniform.

Telling friend from foe was often not easy in an area where loyalties were not only divided, but also elastic, depending on which side was in control of the area. One observer described the various "classes" of people who inhabited the mountain regions:

> When you see a man here, dressed in the "homespun" of our ancestors, wearing deer skin moccasins and a black, lop-rimmed, felt hat, with a piece of red flannel tucked under the band, you may swear he is a "Grey-back," or as denominated by himself, a "Home Guard."
>
> My opinion of this sect is this; when Federal troops occupy the country, they are good, sound, Union loving citizen[s], but when Floyd or Wise is here, they are as good secessionists, and, in the elegant vernacular of the Western Virginia secesh, believe in "hanging every d———d Yankee and abolitionist this side of h-ll."[22]

A little girl of the Kanawha Valley put it honestly and simply when asked if she was a good little Union girl. "O, we'se Union when the Union soldier is here, but we'se Secesh when the Secesh soldiers came."[23]

The bushwhacker was particularly feared by both soldier and citizen and was described as coming "mostly of the poorer classes. The richer people disdaining to fight much after the fashion of savages, joined the regulars."[24] He was probably a member of a partisan ranger group—but often as not just somebody out to settle a score. Bushwhackers were the scourge of the roads in the mountains. Capt. Charles Leib commented on the appearance and habits of the West Virginia bushwhacker:

> The bushwhackers are composed of a class of men who are noted for their ignorance, indolence, duplicity, and dishonesty; whose vices and passions peculiarly fit them for the warfare in which they are engaged, and upon which the civilized world looks with horror. Imagine a stolid, vicious-looking countenance, an ungainly figure, and an awkward, if not ungraceful spinal curve in the dorsal region, acquired by laziness and indifference to maintaining an erect posture; a garb of the coarsest texture of homespun linen, or "Linsey-woolsey," tattered and torn, and so covered with dirt as not to enable one to guess its original color; a dilapidated, rimless hat, or cap of some wild animal's skin, covering his head, the hair on which had not been combed for months; his feet covered with moccasins, and a rifle by his side, a powderhorn and shot-pouch slung around his neck, and you have the beau ideal of the West Virginia bushwhacker.

Thus equipped he sallies forth with the stealth of the panther, and lies in wait for a straggling soldier, courier, or loyal citizen, to whom the only warning given of his presence is the sharp click of his deadly rifle. He kills for the sake of killing and plunders for the sake of gain. Parties of these ferocious beasts, under the cover of darkness, frequently steal into a neighborhood, burn the residences of loyal citizens, rob stores, and farmhouses of everything they can put to use.[25]

Leib describes one of the leaders of such a group, whom he does not regard in any greater esteem than their followers: "A notorious bushwhacker is Bill Parsons, or 'Devil Bill,' as he is called. Bill is filthy in appearance, and, like the rest of his class, has low instincts, and is as ferocious as a hyena. It is said he has eleven wives, and it is a fact well known that one of them is his own daughter. He resides in Roane County, where he has been guilty of many gross outrages."[26]

Even organizers of such guerrilla groups became disgusted with their marauding and thieving. The founders of the Moccasin Rangers, for example, deserted the group because of its lawless ways.[27]

Another group that was notorious in the eyes of Northern soldiers, and probably many civilian inhabitants as well, were the two companies known as Thurmond's Partisan Rangers, named after the units' leaders, William D. and Philip J. Thurmond (sometimes spelled Thurman). One of George Crook's Federal cavalry characterized the Rangers as a

celebrated gang of mountain guerrillas, an independent organization, famous throughout West Virginia for keeping whatever they captured for private purposes. They were knights of ravines and caves . . . a terror to the country. Noted for deeds of daring from behind rocks, lying behind logs like other venomous reptiles, only more certain death when they drew a bead on a man. Besides blocking the roads in every possible way, annoying the advance guard and pioneers, they would lurk along the rear of a column and shoot worn out, footsore, sick, exhausted, and helpless soldiers, who fell an easy prey to these fiendish, barbarous bushwhackers.[28]

Despite their fierce reputation among Union men, the case has been made that the Thurmonds' companies were probably more disciplined and better behaved than most of the partisan ranger units. They certainly were at least above the level of groups such as the Moccasin Rangers. Brig. Gen. Henry

"Devil Bill" Parsons, the bushwhacker

William Thurmond after the war
Thurmond was the guerrilla leader
who harassed Union forces in the
Sewell Mountain region of West
Virginia.
Courtesy Tim McKinney

Heth objected to other partisan groups in western Virginia but did not mention the Thurmonds by name. In the departments of western Virginia and Tennessee, the Thurmonds' companies were viewed favorably and were never ordered broken up. Besides harassment of Federal units, probably the most important military contribution of such units was reconnaissance, which was usually reliable and always appreciated by the departmental commanders.[29]

Coping with the Partisan Rangers

The response to the guerrilla threat was often ad hoc scouting parties, retribution in the form of hostage taking, or other retaliation against those thought to be supporting the guerrillas. It is a story that existed in previous wars and would touch Americans in places such as Vietnam and Bosnia. But the situation in western Virginia in the Civil War was as ugly as could be imagined, although the guerrilla warfare there probably did not reach the level of ferocity evident in theaters such as Arkansas.

The most successful military stratagem against the guerrillas was constant scouting and maintaining discipline in the units to keep straggling down as much as possible. Commanders were urged to keep men in the woods at all times. Most scouting parties were small, and both cavalry and infantry units took part in these actions. The duty was treacherous and one for which little recognition was obtained, unlike the soldier's participation in such heroic struggles as Antietam or Gettysburg. In these battles, the men who participated realized almost immediately that they had been a part of history.

Lt. James Abraham of the Pennsylvania Dragoons, a company of the 1st West Virginia Cavalry, describes how his unit was engaged in constant scouting in the area below Charleston, West Virginia, where "the rebels seemed to strike our lines more frequently than any other. The conformation of the country in that immediate neighborhood is peculiarly adapted to predatory bands —the mountains coming close to the mouth of the river and furnishing excellent protection and hiding places for small bands, whose highest aims seemed to be in despoiling some luckless Jew of his goods, capturing a wagon or two loaded with commissary stores, or plundering an unguarded steamboat and then fleeing to the mountains where they could lay up in comparative security."[30]

Abraham notes that these raids were usually followed by a "profitless scout, as the spoils men were always secure in the mountains before we could reach the scene of their depredations." However, persistence in following raiders, particularly if the pursuit was continued at night, often led to the entrapment of guerrilla bands in houses and other hiding places they considered secure. Abraham goes on to describe such a successful endeavor. He notes that about the first of November, with detachments of fifteen men from each company of the regiment, they were ordered to Coal's Mouth, south of Charleston, to pursue just such a band of raiders. They moved off in "no very amiable mood," and found that the raiders had indeed departed. However, they were determined to follow them. "The night was intensely dark, and the road over which we must pass, only a bridle path, obstructed with rocks and fallen timber." With torches made from pine knots, they followed the Rebels and captured ten at the house of "a noted bushwhacker named May." Proceeding with these prisoners, they then continued on to capture another dozen at the house of a man named Bragg.[31]

Even on so hazardous a mission, the U.S. cavalryman could find something amusing to write, particularly a couple of years later. Abraham narrates that he and his men had been following a creek in pursuit of a rebel:

A scout on Big Sewell Mountain in 1861
This scene was drawn by Kip Roesler of the 12th Ohio Infantry.
Courtesy West Virginia State Archives

From some cause two horses and three riders were precipitated down the steep bank into the creek, unfortunately at a place where the water was deep enough to take the horses off their feet. This created something of a panic, especially among those who had gone overboard, and somewhat demoralized our column. One of the unfortunates was a torchbearer and as he foundered in the water his light went out, as also the prisoner who rode behind the other fellow. Gathering themselves out of the water and mounting their wet and chafing steeds, they gave chase to the fugacious rebel, with affectionate and yearning entreaties to return, which he strangely did not heed. That rebel was hopelessly lost in the darkness and woods.[32]

The party continued on, eventually capturing several more guerrillas, including their captain. The unit made a march of ninety miles in less than thirty hours and claimed to capture the entire force of Rebels that had taken part in the raid. Abraham thinks that, from reading such an account with its tragicomic quality, most readers would not truly appreciate "the fatigue or danger attending such expeditions of the scout, or the earnest bravery that led him to confront them all in the service of his country."[33]

Abraham then contrasts the repetitive, lonely life of the scout, who may die unnoticed in the mountain wilderness, with the death of those in the grand encounters of the war:

> Who knows from behind what tree, or fence, or bush, or rock, may hurtle the assassin's bullet to topple him from his horse without the slightest chance to clutch his carbine, or even to leap from the saddle and grapple his sneaking foe and measure strength with strength? How it galls the proud soul of a spirited man that he cannot even so much as see the villain that shoots him down in the gutter like a dog. Give him but one sure glance along the sights of his trusty gun, or one swift thrust with the bayonet, and then if he must die, he dies content. The soldier at South Mountain or Antietam had all these; he heard the long thundering roll of the cannon, the soul stirring clangor of the bugle and drum and the wild ringing cheer of his comrades; all about him were the thick rushing masses of the charging columns, and above him "the glorious ensign, still full high advanced, its arms and trophies streaming in all their original luster" and even the weakest becomes brave; and the historian, and the poet, and all mankind together call it "glorious." But the lonely wandering scout in the trackless forest of West Va., who was there to notice his fall or drop a friendly tear upon the little mound that covers him? "and what if thou shalt fall unnoticed by the living and no friend / Take note of thy departure." is beautiful and eloquent poetry but it gave poor consolation to the soldier when he felt his end drawing near to reflect that there was no one to bestow on him even the poor boon of a handful of earth sprinkled upon his bones.[34]

Such missions as Abraham's comprised the majority of actions against guerrillas. Scouting also helped guard against raids into West Virginia by larger forces. Many young officers gained hard experience leading such scouts during the course of the war.

The Role of George Crook

Sometimes larger expeditions were put together. Such an expedition was organized by one of the most successful irregular warfare officers in American history, Col. George Crook of the 36th Ohio Volunteer Infantry. Crook was a regular army officer who before the Civil War had seen service in the West, where he had fought Indians in the Oregon country in the Rogue River War. It was in this service that George Crook gained experience against a wily foe who did not fight by European standards. Crook had an incredible ability to appreciate geography and understand the thoughts of his prey, whether man or beast. He was an accomplished hunter who often amazed others with his ability in the brush. During the Rogue River War, Crook "took a mule, a frying pan, a bag of salt and one of flour, a rifle and shotgun, and sallied out into the wilderness," where he kept the mess supplied with game and even earned a dividend for his messmates by selling excess meat to miners and others. In this manner Crook developed an uncanny woods sense and ability to read a tactical situation that made him an exceptionally good general. It certainly was not his excellence in formal military training.[35]

George Crook was born on September 8, 1828, on a farm near Taylorsville, Ohio, not far from Dayton. He was the ninth of ten children born to Thomas Crook and Elizabeth Matthews. He received a nomination to the U.S. Military Academy at West Point from Robert P. Schenk, a Whig member of Congress. George Crook seemed at the time an unlikely candidate for a soldier. He was "exceedingly non-communicative. He hadn't a stupid look, but was quiet to reticence." When asked whether he could handle the rigors of military school, Crook replied laconically, "I'll try." To prepare for West Point he attended Dayton Academy. The superintendent there noted progress in Crook and wrote Schenk that he had the mental ability to take on the course of study at West Point.[36]

Despite being a poor student, he eventually graduated from West Point in 1852, ranking near the bottom of his class (thirty-eighth), and became the lowest-ranking cadet ever to attain the rank of major general. Crook did rank consistently high in conduct. He was still reticent and received little attention from the other cadets, but did become friendly with Phil Sheridan and a few others. His quiet character was his hallmark all his life. He issued few orders and directives, preferring to set the mark through his own demeanor. He would never issue an order that he was not personally willing to carry out. "Example is always the best general order," he felt.[37]

Crook was a big man, slightly over six feet tall, "straight as a lance, broad and square shouldered." He did not appear overly muscular at the time of the Civil War, but had already attained a "sinewiness of limb" through constant exercise in the hills and mountains of the West.[38]

Gen. George Crook

As colonel of the 36th Ohio Infantry, Crook led early successful expeditions against West Virginia guerrillas.

Courtesy National Archives

When the Civil War broke out, Crook headed east and gained the colonelcy of the 36th Ohio Volunteer Infantry with the help of now General Schenk. Crook was a good organizer and was already much admired by officers and men alike. During much of 1862, the war in the Kanawha Valley meant garrison duty, which was boring and could lead to morale problems. Crook, like most good commanders, knew that keeping the troops busy was the best antidote for boredom: "The colonel keeps the men of the 36th busy drilling so they don't have their minds on home and comrades lying in the hospital. 'Nostalgia,—' Homesickness—, is working havoc among the boys and men, the large majority of whom had never been so far and so long away from home at a time, certainly, never before, where continued absence was compulsory. To obviate this condition, so far as may be possible, he subjects those of us fit for duty, four times daily to that fearsome passage to and from the drill house."[39] Thus, under his leadership, the 36th Ohio was becoming a very good regiment. It was even nicknamed the Thirty-sixth Regulars by the other regiments in the division. George Crook was setting an example of leadership which would elicit praise from both enlisted men and officers throughout his career. Superiors, subordinates, and peers give him a nearly unrivaled admiration throughout his career, with only minimal criticism. The comments of John Booth are typical: "Colonel George Crook is a military man all over, possessing all the good qualities of a military man, without tyranny and red tapeism that belong to most West Point men, while he is firm and [with] as much decision as any man ought to have, yet he is agreeable and pleasant to his officers and men."[40]

While posted to the Department of West Virginia, he would use his unique ability in irregular warfare to fight the guerrilla threat. A prime example is an operation carried out in 1862 by regular forces under his command.[41] In the area of Summersville, Crook and his regiment were

> in the very midst of the bushwhacker. . . . This country was the home of counterfeiters and cut-throats before the war, and it was the headquarters of the bushwhackers. It was well adapted for their operations, for, with the exception of a small clearing here and there for the cabins of the poor people who inhabited it, it was heavily timbered, with thick underbrush, rocky and broken, with dense laurel thickets here and there. The thoroughfares and country roads that traversed this country were like traveling through a box canyon with the forest and underbrush for walls.

It was here that the cowardly bushwhackers would waylay the unsuspecting traveler, and shoot him down with impunity. Their suppression became a military necessity, as they caused us to detach much of our active force for escorts, and even then no one was safe.[42]

The bushwhackers would be caught and sent to Camp Chase (Ohio) only to come back

fat, saucy, with good clothes, and returned to their old occupations with renewed vigor. In a short time no more prisoners were brought in. By this time every bushwhacker in the country was known, and when an officer returned from a scout he would report that they had slipped off a log while crossing a stream and broke his neck, or that he was killed by an accidental discharge of one of the men's guns, and many like reports. But they never brought in any more prisoners. . . .[43]

Being fresh from the Indian Country where I had more or less experience with that kind of warfare, I set to work organizing for the task. I selected some of the most apt officers, and scattered them through the country to learn it and all the people in it, and particularly the bushwhackers, their haunts etc.[44]

Webster County, which adjoined Nicholas County, whose county seat was Summersville, was "the nest of bushwhackers nearest to us . . . about forty miles up the Gauley River." The bushwhacker's depredations consisted "chiefly in horse stealing, cow stealing and robbing defenseless women of their means of subsistence and occasionally, firing from the mountain sides on our men as they pass." Crook noted that the area was "so bad that we had to burn out the entire country to prevent people from harboring them. Towards spring about all of them had either been killed or run off within reach of our headquarters."[45]

Crook set up an ambush by placing companies in the passes going into Greenbrier County, where the raiders would try to fly. He then took companies to scour the countryside and drive them through the passes, where they were ambushed. "I believe Colonel Crook could give cards and spades and then learn them something in line of 'surprising,' in 'bushwhacking,' he having been practicing those warlike arts for over ten years among the Indians on our western frontiers, their plains and mountains."[46]

Despite the efforts of scouts like Abraham and resourceful commanders like Crook, the scourge of bushwhackers would persist throughout the war.

However, in the fall of 1863 a group of men was organized that dealt with the guerrillas in a new way. This unit eventually became known as Blazer's Scouts, after their commander, Capt. Richard Blazer of the 91st Ohio Volunteer Infantry. The Scouts may be most the extraordinary group of men to have emerged from the Civil War, and their leader years ahead of his time in his conduct of counterinsurgency warfare.

2

The Independent Scouts

Scouts and Spies

S COUTS may be nearly as old as military operations themselves. Certainly scouting operations go back to biblical times, when Joshua sent men to scout out the land of Canaan. Joshua's men were deemed spies and it may be well to establish the definition of spies and scouts. A spy is "one who acts in a clandestine manner or on false pretenses to obtain information in the zone of operations of a belligerent." A scout on the other hand is "one sent to obtain information, especially a soldier . . . sent out in war to reconnoiter."[1] Sometimes the distinction between these two is blurred, but in general the first acts clandestinely, often wearing the uniform of the opposing side or posing as a civilian. The second usually operates in his own uniform, much as cavalry, to obtain reconnaissance information about the enemy.

In the American Civil War, scouts on both sides often doubled as spies, with all the perils that entailed:

> There is a description of invaluable service requiring the coolest courage, and the clearest head and the quickest wit of any soldierly duty. . . . I refer to the achievements of the scout. He passes the enemy's lines, sits at his camp-fire, penetrates even into the presence of the commanding General. . . . The

scout voluntarily signs away his right to be treated as a prisoner of war. If he is detailed from the ranks to render this special service, he is denounced as a deserter by his comrades and as a spy by the enemy. He takes his life in one hand and seeming dishonor in the other.[2]

Capt. H. J. McKinney of the 12th U.S. Cavalry, in his *Handbook of Scouts* (1912), spells out the information most necessary to a commander.

1. The strength, intentions, position, resources, morale, etc. of the enemy
2. The topography of the land
3. The resources of the country.

McKinney also outlines the characteristics of a scout: "These men in his opinion, must be paragons of soldierly virtue: They must be physically strong; they must have good moral habits; they need to be well versed in reading, writing, and arithmetic; they must have good memories; they must be determined to carry out their mission against seemingly insurmountable odds; and their fidelity, truthfulness, and physical courage must be unquestioned." They must be aware, he adds, that a dead scout is of no value to anyone. Their mission has failed if they do not return alive with the desired information. It is uncanny that McKinney's description, written so long after the Civil War, describes the qualities that would be found in the unit commonly known as Blazer's Scouts. "Scouts do not always act alone. More frequently they operate in small groups to provide security and to effect a fighting withdrawal if necessary. The mission is nevertheless the same—to obtain the information and get it back to the commander."[3]

In the Civil War, both sides carried out extensive scouting operations. For the most part they were to obtain reconnaissance information in the classic sense described above. For Union forces, however, the scout often was part of a counterinsurgency effort, in modern military parlance. Scouts of this nature were much like those described by Lieutenant Abraham in the preceding chapter.

Carr B. White Forms the Independent Scouts

As part of these counterinsurgency operations, ad hoc scouting expeditions, sweeps against the guerrillas, and retaliation were all methods that worked with some degree of success against the guerrillas in West Virginia. However, in

the fall of 1863, a new, unique organization was formed. The exact impetus
for the formation of this unit is not known from the records available. However, some information can be gleaned from previous efforts at the formation
of special units in West Virginia and from biographical information about the
man who first detailed the Independent Scouts, as they were most commonly
called.

On September 5, 1863, Col. Carr B. White of the 2nd Brigade, 3rd Division, 8th Army Corps, signed order no. 49 forming a unit of independent
scouts.

Three (3) Lieutenants, eight (8) Sergeants, eight (8) corporals and one-
hundred (100) privates will be received as volunteers to form an independent scouting company for this brigade.

The company will be relieved from guard, fatigue and other camp duties
during the continuance of its organization. At least one half of the company
will be expected to be on the scout all the time. Its headquarters will be in the
woods. None but experienced woodsmen and good shots will be accepted.
Commanders of regiments are directed to receive and report the names of
suitable men volunteering for this service.[4]

Colonel White was a physician and a veteran soldier, "brave as a lion, but
gentle as a woman, with the honors of Mexico upon him." While visiting her
husband Harrison's 12th Ohio Regiment, Eliza Otis described the brigade commander who had formerly been the regiment commander of the 12th Ohio.
"He is a man whom one instinctively likes. There's something about him which
makes you feel his *manhood,* although he is plain, and unpretending in his
manners, wholly free from ostentation or display, and talks to you as if he had
known you always."[5]

Carr B. White was born February 8, 1823, in Mason County, Kentucky.
He was named after old Capt. Carr Bailey, who was seven years a captain
of a Virginia volunteer company during the Revolutionary War. He was the
son of John D. and Margaret R. (Baker) White, who were natives of the Old
Dominion of Virginia. He accompanied his parents to Ohio when he was two
and was reared and educated in Georgetown, in Brown County. He studied
medicine and graduated from the Jefferson Medical College in Philadelphia
about 1848. He practiced the profession at Point Isabel, in Clermont County,
Ohio, and later moved his practice to Brown County. Carr's father was the

Col. Carr B. White
Colonel White organized the Independent Scouts in 1863. He probably also influenced the organization of the mounted unit of 1864.
Courtesy U.S. Army Military History Institute

teacher of General Grant when Grant was a boy in the old brick schoolhouse on "Dutch Hill" in Georgetown. Ulysses Grant was sent to West Point at the suggestion of Carr's father and the solicitation of Congressman Thomas L. Hamer. John White and Grant were firm friends and Grant appointed him assessor of internal revenue for the district in which he lived.[6]

Carr had served previously in the Mexican War with the 1st Ohio Volunteer Infantry. He enlisted as a private and rose through the ranks to become a sergeant. He was eventually appointed lieutenant and closed the war as a captain of volunteers.[7] Although a volunteer soldier, this experience probably enabled him to meet many West Point graduates with formal military training. As a member of the 1st Ohio Infantry he may have gained experience fighting Mexican guerrillas while that regiment was kept on garrison and train guard duty in the rear of the main American army. He probably also met Col. Samuel Ryan Curtis of the 3rd Ohio Infantry, who was a West Point graduate and had sent out scouts against Mexican guerrillas and personally led such forays.[8]

Later, during the Civil War, it was evident Carr White was well acquainted with intelligence-gathering techniques of the day. From the 8th Army Corps, Charleston, West Virginia, June 10, 1863, Brig. Gen. Eliakim P. Scammon reported the enemy's disposition of forces "compiled from reports of scouts, deserters, and refugees, furnished by Colonel [Carr B.] White, commanding the 2nd Brigade. Where the reports are given from personal observation, they corroborate each other; where they depend on here say, there is some conflict." This report placed Philip J. Thurmond's "bushwhackers" on the south side of the New River with a strength of eighty men. William D. Thurmond's "bushwhackers" were placed on the north side of the New River near Lewisburg with seventy men. This report is probably reasonably accurate and illustrates Carr White's attention to matters of intelligence in his front. White was also receiving a good deal of advice from his division commander, General Scammon. At one point Scammon admonished White, "You cannot be too careful or too bold in pushing forward reconnaissance on every road."[9]

Colonel White's contact with West Pointers may have acquainted him with military strategy, doctrine, and the military history of the American colonies and the United States. This included the service of a French and Indian War unit known as Rogers' Rangers. Robert Rogers was the first of the great American scouts. In early life he became an adept frontiersman, feeling uncomfortable in more settled circumstances. With the outbreak of the French and Indian War in 1754, he raised a company of infantry. Rogers and his men were often sent out on expeditions to obtain information about the French, reconnaissances which he terms scouts.[10]

Robert Rogers provided outstanding information to the British and was finally recognized on May 23, 1756, when William Shirley, governor of Massachusetts and commander of all British forces in North America, commissioned Rogers "to be Captain of an Independent Company of Rangers to be forthwith raised and Employ'd."[11] This was the first use of the term *Ranger* in American military history.

Ten years earlier the Assembly of New York had raised "new levies to range the woods," and the next year, 1747, the New York assembly passed a bill providing for one hundred rangers to be used in protecting the settlements. Rogers was authorized to enlist sixty privates, four sergeants, and an ensign or junior lieutenant.[12]

There certainly appears to be a similarity between the way Rogers operated and the scout group that was established by Carr White. Certainly, the organization was company-sized, about a hundred men. Second, they were authorized to act independently, as denoted by their name. The primary difference between the two units was the emphasis on a counterinsurgency mission for Blazer's unit, whereas Rogers' Rangers were noted more as an offensive striking force.

During the American Civil War, there were numerous units known as independent scouts, particularly in the western theater, and especially in Arkansas. Many of these units, particularly on the Confederate side, were as ill disciplined as the partisan rangers of the eastern theater. At one point General Beauregard informed General Hood, "The system of roving or independent scouts he [Beauregard] regards as detrimental and should be abandoned." Notably, a couple of Union independent scout units appear to have been fairly well disciplined and probably rendered valuable service.[13]

Another inspiration for the Independent Scouts may have been a unit of sharpshooters serving with Gen. Robert Milroy. Little is available about the organization of this unit, but it was made up of detailed men picked for special qualities, especially marksmanship. It existed between the fall of 1862 and the spring of 1863. A young man named Jesse Middaugh of the 5th (West) Virginia Infantry was a member of the unit, as were scouts William Toppin, Samuel Burdett, and James Webb of the 9th (West) Virginia Infantry. This unit of sharpshooters could have been the scouts organized by Gen. John C. Fremont early in the war and which were associated with General Milroy after Fremont resigned.[14]

In any case, it is likely that Carr White staffed his ideas up through military channels. In an intriguing letter from Charleston, September 13, 1863, addressed to Col. C. B. White at Fayetteville, West Virginia, Brig. Gen. E. P. Scammon writes, "Yours of 13th rec'd. Am making all efforts to get axes, will be up by first boat. . . . *Like your organized scouts.* Glad you are at Fayette." It is clear from this letter that Colonel White had given General Scammon the details of his idea for a company of independent scouts and that Scammon approved.[15]

The Organization of the Scouts

Although Carr White's order authorized three lieutenants to be in charge of the company, Capt. John W. Spencer of the 9th West Virginia Infantry became the actual commander. This was probably done in the realization that a company-sized unit needed to be commanded by a single individual to preserve unity

Capt. John White Spencer
Spencer was the first commander
of the Independent Scouts.
Courtesy James M. Conley

of command. Captain Spencer's role in this unit appears to have been eclipsed by Lieutenant (later Captain) Blazer. Asbe Montgomery notes that Captain Spencer took part of the unit to Roane County, while Lieutenants Blazer of the 91st Ohio and Otis of the 12th Ohio operated with the rest of the Scouts. There is little to note about Spencer's operations in Roane County. He did suffer some losses, but he was not where the main part of the action would be for the Scouts in opposing the Thurmond brothers.[16]

John White Spencer

John White Spencer was born March 11, 1817, in Massachusetts. The family history goes back to Robert De Le Spencer, a steward to William the Conqueror. From him descended the Spencers of Savannah Mills, England. In 1634 Jared Spencer and his five sons immigrated to America and settled in Massachusetts. Several generations later, John White Spencer was born to this long lineage.

Around 1850, John moved to Gilmer County, Virginia, part of which became Roane County, West Virginia. On May 24, 1850, before he left Massachusetts, he married Permelia Andrews, who was born December 16, 1827. John bought one thousand acres of land on Brush Run on Upper Henry's Fork, paying twenty-five cents per acre. John was trained as a physician, probably

Special Order no. 3
The order was signed
by Lieutenant Blazer of
Spencer's Independent
Scouts, dismissing men
from the unit.
*Courtesy Richard E. and
Cy R. Blazer*

before he left Massachusetts. He attended premedical school at William &
Mary and may have attended medical school in the east also. After the beginning of the Civil War, John W. Spencer was mustered into Company B of the
9th West Virginia Infantry as its captain.[17]

In existing documents, Capt. Spencer is noted only three times in connection with the Independent Scouts. Asbe Montgomery, a sergeant of the 9th
West Virginia, lists Captain Spencer as the original commander in his book
published in 1865. Sgt. Edward Davis of the 9th West Virginia Infantry notes
in a September 12, 1863, diary entry, "Captain Spencer's Scouts went out this
morning to be gone several days." In the most authoritative record specifying
Captain Spencer as the commander, Lt. Richard Blazer writes in Special Order
no. 3 that he is sending several men back to their companies "for drunkenness
in the face of the enemy." He signs the order, "Lt. Blazer, Comdg, Scouts." In
what appears to be an afterthought, the lieutenant writes *Spencer's Indp't* between *Comdg* and *Scouts*.[18]

Hd Qtrs. Spencer's Ind Scouts
Bowyer's Ferry Va.
Oct. 25, 1863.

Special Order No. 3.

Privates John W. Fenner, Milton Terwilliger and G. A. Loyd, 12th Regt Ohio Vols; John W. Moore, 91st Reg't Ohio Vols, and James D. Cremeens, 9th Reg't Va Vols. are hereby dismissed from this command for drunkenness on duty in the face of the enemy and will forthwith report to their respective Regiments.

The Officer commanding is surprised and mortified to know that there are men in the command who are so far forgetful of their duty and their personal safety as to become intoxicated in the midst of the enemy and more than thirty miles from camp, thus jeopardizing their own lives and the lives of their comrades. He trusts that in future there may not be a recurrence of so grave and dangerous an offence.

By order of
Lieut. R. Blazer, Comdg
Spencer's Indp't Scouts[19]

Besides establishing Capt. John Spencer's association with the Independent Scouts, this order also illustrates the strict discipline of Lieutenant Blazer. The men selected for this unit were supposed to be the best in their respective units and Lieutenants Blazer and Otis would not tolerate men who did not live up to the standards they set for this unit. This would apply both to the Scouts in 1863 and even more to the men who would serve in the unit in 1864.

Captain Spencer eventually disappears from the story of Blazer's Scouts. The most likely explanation is that after the formation of the Independent Scouts, Spencer was ordered by General Scammon, on September 29, 1863, to take two companies of the 9th West Virginia to Roane and Calhoun Counties. Although the officer selected for this mission is not specified, the record of a court-martial for absence without leave and neglect of duty against Captain Spencer places him in Calhoun County in charge of two companies of the 9th West Virginia during this time.[20] The charges and findings of the court were eventually dismissed by Gen. Alfred Duffie but this does explain Spencer's disappearance as the commander of the unit.[21]

In 1867, Maj. John Scott wrote a book called *Partisan Life with Col. John S. Mosby,* the source of some of the myth about Blazer's company of scouts that has been passed down as history, although there is no documentation to back it up. Scott mentions that Blazer's unit originated in West Virginia and became known as the Legion of Honor. In his book about the Scouts, Asbe Montgomery—surely the most credible firsthand source about Blazer's unit —never mentions such an organization. Nor does Harrison Gray Otis, in his "Recollections of the War," published in 1876.

As further, overwhelming evidence that this organization never existed, or at least that it was not Blazer's unit, not one of Blazer's men ever mentions it in a pension file. The Legion of Honor appears to be nothing more than a construct of John Scott to amplify Mosby's foe so that the eventual defeat of Blazer's unit at the hands of Mosby becomes even more heroic. Blazer's men were content to identify themselves as Blazer's Scouts, Brigade Scouts, Division Scouts, or Independent Scouts in expressing their association with the unit. None ever used the grandiose term Legion of Honor. The term is sometimes found in Union articles, but stems entirely from the Confederate sources. This is not the only example of this mythology surrounding Mosby's men, as will become evident throughout this account of Blazer's unit.[22]

The men who comprised Blazer's unit in the fall of 1863 were chosen from the three "old infantry regiments" that made up the 2nd Brigade, 3rd Division, 8th Army Corps: the 9th West Virginia Volunteer Infantry, 12th Ohio Volunteer Infantry, and 91st Ohio Volunteer Infantry. The 12th Ohio was one of the original three-month regiments formed in the initial call for volunteers, and a majority of its men had signed up to be three-year men when that call came. It was a veteran unit that had seen service at Bull Run, South Mountain, and Antietam, although it never became engaged at Bull Run. At South Mountain it had charged alongside another Ohio regiment, the 23rd Ohio, along the left of the pike, "routing by one irresistible onset the enemy in its front from the stone wall behind which he was posted." One of its officers selected for the Scouts was Lt. Harrison Gray Otis, a printer born in Washington County, Ohio, along the banks of the Ohio River. He was intellectual and well read, but he also had a no-nonsense attitude toward the war. He had already seen much action, having been slightly wounded in action at Antietam.[23]

The 9th West Virginia was something of a hard-luck regiment. Its service during the war did not have an auspicious start. Shortly after two initial companies had been raised for the unit, they had been captured nearly to a man in a raid by Col. Albert Jenkins at Guyandotte, Virginia (a suburb of present-day Huntington, West Virginia), on November 10, 1861. After capture, the men were horribly treated on their way to Libby and Salisbury Prisons, where they would spend some months until paroled. Even this early in the war, the prison camp experience was not a pleasant one, and many of these men would suffer the effects years after. However, many of them would go on to get revenge as members of the Independent Scouts. On May 9, 1864, the 9th West Virginia got its collective revenge against Jenkins when it charged the Confederate works at Cloyd's Mountain, capturing them and taking a leading role in defeating the force under Jenkins there. It even may have been a ball from the musket of a 9th (West) Virginia man that inflicted the wound on Jenkins that eventually proved fatal.[24]

The 91st Ohio was a somewhat newer, but veteran, unit that had seen duty primarily in western Virginia. It was organized in August 1862 at Camp Ironton, Ohio, along the Ohio River under Col. John A. Turley. The companies were raised from Adams, Scioto, Lawrence, Gallia, Jackson, and Pike Counties in southern and southeastern Ohio. Besides the usual majority of farmers, many of the men from this area worked in the coal mines and iron foundries and on the steamboats that plied the Ohio River. The 91st operated along the Ohio River and in the Kanawha Valley during the summer and fall of 1862 and was involved with Lightburn's advance and retreat in the fall of 1862. The unit participated in the pursuit of the Confederate raider John Morgan in July 1863 but only managed to round up about thirty prisoners, since Morgan had already been captured. One of the officers of this unit was Lt. Richard Blazer, a seemingly ordinary man for an officer, but one who would go on to become much admired as a military leader by enlisted men, his fellow officers, and senior leaders of the Union Army. He would also gain the respect of one of the most revered icons of Confederate military leaders and the men of his command, Col. John Singleton Mosby.[25]

Capt. Richard Blazer: The Leader of Blazer's Scouts

To some observers Richard Blazer did not make much of an impression as a military man and certainly not as a leader of an elite unit.

> He surely impressed no one with a martial bearing. He had a far away look in one eye, and a nearly sleepy look in the other. His vest was not always

Capt. Richard Blazer

Captain Blazer appears to have had vision defects, as described by those who knew him. Family oral history nevertheless indicates that he was a good shot.

Courtesy Cy R. Blazer

buttoned straight, nor his coat collar always turned down. If his boots were not made to shine as the picture on the blacking box is represented, he made no racket with his servant, for as like as any way he had no servant, or blacking either. If he undertook to drill his company he would give the wrong command, and at dress parade he rarely placed himself in the exact position required by the adjutant. He messed with the men or not, just as he felt disposed, and, straps apart, would not have seemed more fit to command than any of his fellows. He never stickled for red-tape. Indeed, he was indifferent both to its color and texture. He was jolly at times, at others silent and even morose. Some times he was cross, but in the latter particular he did not essentially differ from many others. In every action in which his command was engaged, he was there, and like the great majority did his duty, but displayed no conspicuous qualities, so that he became regarded as one upon whom dependence could be placed in an emergency. When the order came detailing him for this special service, all wondered what qualities he could bring to bear against the skillful Thurman, who had long been feared and with much reason.[26]

Neither had Richard Blazer's pursuits before the Civil War marked him as anyone who would excel at special service in the army. Before the war Blazer was a coal boatman and at his time of enlistment was driving a hack (horse-drawn carriage) between Gallipolis and Portland, the first station on the Cincinnati, Washington, and Baltimore branch of the B&O.[27] Assertions that he was a "hardened Indian fighter" seem to have no basis in fact and have become part of the mythology of Mosby's command. Richard Blazer was about thirty years old when the war began. Hostile Indians had been long vanquished from the Ohio Valley and there is no record that he ever went further west to encounter Indians. There is, after all, more glory in defeating a hardened Indian fighter than a man who before the war drove a hack along the Ohio.[28]

Lt. Harrison Gray Otis

Lt. Harrison Gray Otis of the 12th Ohio Infantry rounded out the three officers chosen to command the Independent Scouts. He was the youngest of the children of Stephen Otis and his second wife, Sarah Dyer Otis, of Marietta. Stephen was related to Senator Harrison Gray Otis of Massachusetts, after whom his boy was most likely named. The family had a military heritage,

Lt. Harrison Gray Otis
In this photo, taken when he had
been promoted to captain, Otis of
the 12th Ohio Volunteer Infantry
wears no epaulets, as authorized by
General Crook to make officers less
visible to bushwhackers.
Miller's Photographic History

since Stephen's father, Barnabas, had served thirteen months in the Connecticut line in 1775 and 1776. Besides the Otis family, most of the inhabitants of Marietta traced their families to New England. With its college and New England heritage, the town impressed those who visited it. The historian Henry Howe said of the Ohio town in 1846, "There are few places in our country that can compare with this in point of morality and intelligence—but few of its size that have so many cultivated and literary men."[29]

Otis lived on his father's farm and his early education was limited to three months each winter. The family's New England heritage and Methodist morality probably greatly influenced their political beliefs. His father was a member of the Liberty Party, and the Otis house was used as a station on the Underground Railroad. Marietta was a major southern terminal of the railroad and there were many strong abolitionists in the city. The antislavery townspeople were careful not to provoke their pro-slavery neighbors. Otis became part of a great cause and he probably enjoyed the suspense of the "conspiracy to which his family was dedicated."[30]

Young Harry became a printer's apprentice at the age of fourteen, working for his brother Charles, who published the *Sarahsville Courier*. Otis worked at other print jobs in Ohio and in 1855 worked on the *Courier* in Rock Island, Illinois. He quit after attempting unsuccessfully to unionize the paper. He

moved back to Marietta in 1856 and attended Wetherby's Academy in Lowell, Ohio, for five months in 1856 and 1857. While at Lowell, he met his future wife Eliza Wetherby, a native of New Hampshire. They were married on September 11, 1859. Otis later took a commercial course at Granger's College. Despite his limited formal education, Otis was quite literate and gifted in the English language. While living briefly in Louisville, Kentucky, he became an ardent Republican and attended the Republican convention that nominated Lincoln in 1860.[31]

The Character of Blazer's Scouts

Thus, an unlikely trio—physician, hack driver, printer—was chosen to lead a handpicked group of volunteer scouts against some of the shrewdest, wiliest veterans of the Confederacy. If the officers seemed unlikely leaders of scouts, what sorts of men were chosen for the Independent Scouts, besides "experienced woodsmen and good shots," as specified by general order no. 49? For the most part they were farmers from the wooded foothills of the Appalachians in southeastern Ohio and West Virginia. Most belonged to families who had been in the United States for a long time and were primarily of Anglo-Saxon stock; there were only a few more recent immigrants in their ranks.

They undoubtedly spoke in accents nearly indistinguishable from the Confederates of the western part of the Old Dominion. In many respects they resembled their Confederate opponents more than their Union brethren from farther north. They differed only in their motives for fighting the war and thus in the uniform they wore. Many of the men from the 9th West Virginia came from counties with large numbers of soldiers serving in the Confederacy. Many had become refugees, forced to flee their homes for fear of being burned out, bushwhacked, or lynched because their allegiance lay with the old flag of the Union. William R. Wilson of the 9th West Virginia was one of many who had their homes burned.[32]

Physically the men were a little taller than the average Civil War soldier, just a little over five foot nine inches, but there were a fair number over six feet. By 1863, the men most susceptible to disease and those least fit to bear up under the hardships of war had been weeded out. Even so, the men of Blazer's Scouts were healthier than the rest of their comrades in the regiments from which they had been drawn. Very few spent repeated stays in the hospital.

Lt. Milton Brown

Milton Brown of the 91st Ohio Infantry was a sergeant when he was detailed to the Scouts in 1863. He was later commissioned an officer in the regiment.

Courtesy L. M. Strayer Collection

A full complement of musicians was also detailed to the Scouts. Operating in the thick brush, difficult terrain, and spread out broadly in a skirmish line, drummers and buglers would have been an advantage once engaged. It is likely the musicians were silent before contact with guerrillas was made.[33]

Richard Blazer picked experienced and capable noncommissioned officers to serve as his sergeants. One of these was an older man named Asbe Montgomery of Company A of the 9th West Virginia Infantry. He was a tall man (6 ft., 2 in.) and already was showing the gray hair of his forty-three years. Like so many others, he was a farmer. He was born in Tyler County, Virginia, on January 3, 1820, and at the time of the Civil War was a resident of Wood County. Asbe had served a brief period as second lieutenant of the 113th Virginia Militia, also known as the Limestone Hill Company. He was captured at Summersville in the summer of 1862 in the second disaster of the 9th West Virginia, which had led to the wholesale capture of a great number of personnel of two companies of the regiment. He was paroled in September of 1863 and that same month was detailed to become one of the early members of the Independent Scouts.[34]

Adam Head was a farmer born in Ripley, in Brown County, Ohio. He was a tallish man with an imposing build. Like so many others of the region,

35

he had blue eyes, light hair, and a light complexion. He had been one of the first volunteers of the 12th Ohio Volunteer Infantry, signing up for the original three-month unit before enrolling for three years on June 19, 1861, at Camp Dennison, near Cincinnati. He clearly displayed leadership qualities and was appointed sergeant on June 4, 1861. A casualty sheet shows that he was wounded near Sharpsburg (Antietam Creek) on September 20, 1862.[35]

If any soldier epitomized the qualities of the men selected for the Scouts, it was Cpl. Samuel Harrop of Company B of the 91st Ohio. He was born in Allegheny County, Pennsylvania, the second oldest of four boys born to James and Mary Harrop. James and Mary were immigrants from England and James was a surgeon. Samuel was a man with the very look of deep intelligence. With his family's background, he probably could have become an officer if he had desired. However, Samuel was an unassuming man who shied away from exalted posts. He worked nearly his entire life as a skilled tradesman, employed at various times and places as an iron molder. He learned the trade in 1857 and was employed with other men who would join the 91st Ohio at the Torn Hills Foundry in Gallipolis.[36]

In 1866, Captain Blazer remembered Samuel as a soldier whose "loyalty was never doubted or questioned, that he was among the chosen soldiers selected by me to aid me in picket duty and all knew that he was a soldier of dauntless bravery and in point of moral and manly deportment no one excelled Samuel Harrop."[37] Capt. Blazer noted that Samuel "discharged his duty as a corporal, and at all times and on all occasions and at various times both in skirmishes and severe fighting with rebels he exhibited the bravery and presence of mind requisite in successful fighting and on all occasions his conduct received my cordial approbation. . . . he was not only respected by his fellow soldiers but was the idol of the whole company and anything I can say of him cannot be equal to his merits as a soldier and a worthy young man."[38]

Volunteers for the Scouts

There was no shortage of men willing to volunteer for the scouting company. Although it was officially not formed until general order no. 49 on September 5, 1863, the men in the units were already in the know about the formation of the company. James Ireland of the 12th Ohio notes in his diary for September 6, 1863, that the weather is "variable & quite warm. Soldiers scatter all over the country. A large mail. News of no importance except general activity in the army. Burnside in E. Tenn. Rosecrans at Chattanooga. Gilman at Charleston." He then writes, "A scouting company to be organized."[39]

Another incentive for volunteering for the Scouts was that the men of the scouting unit would be relieved from most other duties and it would probably relieve the tedium of ordinary camp life. "Clark Howard, Jas. Watkins, Ed Neader, R. J. Butler, and J. Hester volunteer to join the scouting Co. from our co." Harrison Otis spoke not only for himself but many of the other men when he wrote. "I suffered nothing from the lethargy of garrison life, but had free play to indulge my penchant for doing audacious things in war."[40]

For the most part the men who volunteered were the best in their companies and regiments. They were "the best shots, best woodsmen, best marchers and the most dashing fellows that could be found in the three old regiments."[41] Typical perhaps was John McMullen of Company G of the 9th West Virginia. He was a mere boy, having been born June 11, 1845, in Jackson County, Virginia. He lived on a hardscrabble farm, helping his sickly parents, Mathew and Sarah. He contributed to the support of his family in various ways, worked at home, and helped tend his farm—sixty-three acres of "poor nuff land" worth not more than three dollars an acre. His father was suffering from heart disease and could not do much work on his own. Like many other boys in the army, he sent money home to his family to help with expenses. He sent a letter to his sister Matilda from his camp at the mouth of the Coals River on June 9, 1863.

> Dear Sister Resume my pen in hand to let you no that I am well at Present hoping when those few lines comes to hand they may find you all well I am going to send you A Nice present and I send it to you for to remember me I want father to come And see me as soon as he gets time and then I can send you something else I Cant send you nothing much be cause Mr. riddle has so much to take through I am sending 25 dollars home we got paid off the other day Nothing more at present only remain your friend until Death.
>
> John Mcmullen
X This is my pen and ink

John has drawn a hand with an X on it. He seems to indicate his ink is his own blood. His vow to remain a friend until death would become tragically prophetic.[42]

Frederick Gandee of Company B of the 9th West Virginia was a descendant of a prominent family of Roane County, West Virginia, who were among its earliest settlers. Early Gandee ancestors were reported to be Indian fighters and defenders of the settlements of the Monongahela Valley. The family was also related to the Hughes family, which numbered among its members a Jesse Hughes, who was known as a "scout, guide, and single-handed slayer of Indians; hero of all historians of Border Warfare and Frontier settlements." The early historians relate that Martha, the daughter of Jesse and Grace, was captured by the Indians and held for a couple of years before being rescued by Jesse. For Frederick Gandee, scouting and the lore of the woods was in his blood.[43]

Frederick's father, William, was also prominent and had taken part in the organization of Roane County and sat as a member of the first county court. At the outbreak of the Civil War, he was pro-Union and against secession. He became a captain of the Home Guards and "led his men in defense of and keeping legal authority in the county during the five years of that awful turmoil, and so behaved as to hold the friendship and respect of even returned Confederates."[44]

William would eventually serve as a member of the West Virginia legislature in 1887. Frederick was also a Union sympathizer during the "War of the Secessions" and according to his biography, which he dictated to *Hardesty's* in 1882, he was in the "seven days battle at Spencer," the series of shootings, and the surrender of Col. Rathbone to Gen. Albert Jenkins. Frederick enlisted in Company B of the 9th West Virginia on October 15, 1861, at Spencer and was mustered into the regiment on December 9, 1861.[45]

Stephen Glaze also enlisted in Capt. John W. Spencer's Company B of the 9th West Virginia. He was the son of Henry and Sophia Glaze of Lewis County. His family had moved to the county sometime before the war and had a farm of about 150 acres there.

Stephen's older brother, Marshall, joined Company C of the 11th West Virginia Infantry. He had married Jane Wilt in 1858 and they had two small daughters, Mary and Henrietta. Marshall left the family with his parents when he went off to the war. In March 1863 he was admitted to the hospital at Parkersburg with chronic rheumatism and on June 27, Captain Simpson, his company commander, allowed him to go home on sick furlough. Another brother, Isaac, had just enlisted in Company K of the 14th West Virginia Infantry in early September 1863. Thus, the Glaze family was heavily committed to the Union. Stephen Glaze was a good soldier and would become a veteran volunteer in 1864.[46]

Patrick Collins of Company K of the 12th Ohio was a blacksmith born in Highland County, Ohio. He was a good and generous young man who cared very much about the welfare of his family. He was religious and believed in the guiding hand of God in the affairs of men. He often sent money home and was helping his father invest in a piece of land.

On April 27, 1863, Patrick wrote to his father from camp at Fayette Court House, Virginia, "You say you are getting old which I know must be the case and nobody feels it any Keener than I do therefore it will be my first thought to try to enable you to pass the remainder of your days as Easy as Possible and thank God that he spared me that I might comfort you in your old Days, but do not let that in fact trouble your Mind for if it is the will of God that you or I should be called away why you will have to put up with it." Alluding to his sentiments about the war, Patrick tells his father to ask his younger brother, Johnny, if he is "for the Union or a butternut [Confederate] for My Part I am for the union and against all its enemies whether in the field or not."[47]

With men such as these, Spencer's Independent Scouts prepared to take to the field against the guerrillas roaming the mountains of West Virginia.

3

Headquarters in the Brush

First Operations

A SBE Montgomery indicates that he joined the Independent Scouts in
September 1863. He was in fact detailed along with the other men in response to general order no. 49. Asbe writes, "They had several long and hard
marches, captured several rebs, quite a number of horses, and had divers engagements, before I joined them, which was in September 1863."[1] He is either
taking literary license or perhaps Captain Spencer or other 9th West Virginia
companies were involved in ad hoc scouting operations before September 1863.
It is clear from orders that all the men for the independent scouting company
were detailed at one time by one order from Colonel White.[2]

Asbe Montgomery, in writing his book on the Scouts, then makes a critical decision that will help keep this unit shrouded in mystery for over a century. Perhaps because he does not have a complete roster, or more important,
because feelings between the Scouts and the men they fought were so high, he
purposely does not include a roster of the men detailed for the Scouts. Even
in his narrative, he mentions only the officers and himself: "I think it proper
and prudent to withhold the names and number of killed—as many of our
comrades and our regiment are so well acquainted with our raids, and how we

put to flight the rebs, not only in West Va., and on the great Lynchburg Raid, but in the Shenandoah Valley, and Loudoun Valley."[3]

Although the order detailing men to the Scouts was issued on September 5, 1863, the planning for this organization probably occurred sometime before; perhaps it took several weeks. It is likely that intelligence on Confederate forces was obtained well before the Scouts took to the field. After September 5, it appears that the unit went into camp at once and prepared to operate against the local partisans. There was no special drill for this unit. The men had been chosen for individual traits. As was typical with scouting expeditions or other Civil War military expeditions, three days' rations were issued. As per orders, this new command then went to the woods in pursuit of the Thurmonds. "Where he [William or Phil Thurmond] was none knew, as he had seemed to be everywhere we sent a scouting party, or established an isolated outpost."[4]

The Scouts took to the field almost immediately. The company moved out into the convoluted country of the Gauley and New Rivers, some of the most difficult terrain in the eastern United States. They "boldly entered the hostile country in our front, marching on foot where cavalry could not go, moving with secrecy and celerity, often at night." As reported in the previous chapter, Sergeant Davis noted that Spencer's Scouts went out on September 12. William Newton, the surgeon of the 91st Ohio, noted in a letter to his wife on September 14 that "The pickets over at Gauley were fired on & driven in last evening. The report is they are advancing on us, through Lewisburg & Raleigh both. We are incredulous. But may have a fight."

In what is almost surely a reference to the intelligence being supplied by Spencer's Scouts under Lieutenants Blazer and Otis, he writes, "Scouts report eight or ten regiments of Rebs at Princeton, if so, no doubt a movement against us is intended."[5]

The Scouts started taking casualties almost immediately. Some of the Scouts under the command of Capt. Spencer were ordered into Roane County to scout out the area around the headwaters of Spring Creek. This area happened to be near the homes of some of the Scouts. On the night of September 14, a group of the Scouts was invited by Stephen Glaze to visit his family's house. Among them were John McMullen, Eli Rogers, and Jacob Argobrite. Also present was Stephen's brother Marshall, home on leave from the 11th West Virginia Infantry. The soldiers shared the hospitality of the Glaze family and some friends. About nine o'clock Alexander Donalson, one of the family friends, left the house for home. He had gone about a quarter of a mile when he came upon a group of eight to ten soldiers dressed in the uniform of the Confederacy. It is unknown to which unit this group belonged, but they could have been part of the band to which "Devil Bill" Parsons belonged. They took Donalson captive and placed a guard on him and proceeded to the home of Henry Glaze.[6]

Within a few minutes gunshots were heard. There was a considerable firefight but after a few minutes, the five or six Union soldiers were forced to retreat from the house, leaving Marshall Glaze and John McMullen mortally wounded. The Rebels also soon retired and released Donalson before they left the area. Glaze lived for about a day before dying of his wounds. McMullen died two days later. He was the Scouts' only casualty during September, remembered as "a meritorious soldier."[7]

The area in which the Independent Scouts would operate contained some of the most spectacular and rugged terrain in the eastern United States. Here the New and Gauley Rivers meet to form the Great Kanawha River, above Charleston. Eliza Otis, who had come to West Virginia to be with Harrison, aptly describes some of the terrain: "The mountains were suggestive of Alpine heights—vast, frowning, and majestic—just the place where mythologists might dream, and people their caverns, and rock-ribbed, heaven-reaching cliffs with Gods and demons—and the Druids that lived in the forest of old . . . grand magnificence of mountains, their tops kissing the clouds and the blue sky touching them softly like a mothers hand." The mountains and forest showed "waves of hues . . . huge precipices, and yawning chasms . . . valleys so deep it seemed as if they belonged to a world below . . . unchanged by time, untouched by man . . . vast and changeless." New River roars along in its gorge, the sound echoing through the aisles of the forest, "its waters dashing with musical rhythms and cadences over the rocks where the ripples chased each other in eternal laughter."[8]

The following account by one of Blazer's men of a scouting expedition demonstrates his attention to obtaining precise intelligence about enemy forces before taking the field against them.

Captain [*sic*] Blazer revealed no sign of his plans and the boys soon began to respect his silence. He questioned every women [*sic*] and child he saw and still held his peace. The first day was uneventful only that when night came the boys discussed their commander in whispers, as absolute silence had

Pvt. Stephen Glaze
Stephen Glaze of the 9th West
Virginia Infantry was a very good
soldier and was typical of the scouts
selected by Col. Carr B. White.
Courtesy Blanche M. Bartlett, Bette Butcher
Topp, Jim Bartlett

Pvt. Marshall Glaze
Marshall Glaze was killed along with
Scout John McMullen at the home of
Henry Glaze.
Courtesy Blanche M. Bartlett, Bette Butcher
Topp, Jim Bartlett

been enjoined from the very start, not only enjoined but enforced, and the man of little camp drill and less tactics as per books, had already proved himself an excellent disciplinarian. Next morning at early dawn they were again threading the mountain by-paths in silence—no word above a whisper dared any man to speak. None knew where they were. They were treading upon strange ground, but every man was enjoined to observe closely every feature of the country, as a knowledge might stand them all in good stead.

Another uneventful day passed, only so far as it was the repetition of the first, Captain Blazer still taking it upon himself to do all the talking with the natives and keeping to himself the information obtained, as well as his conclusions. At the close of the day the boys were much surprised when they were ordered to prepare torches of pine that grew in great abundance all about them, and more surprised still then, with a lighted torch in hand, he led off over the mountain path unknown to all of them, the command following in single file through the tangled way, with a lighted torch here and there along the line, and each man carrying one ready to light when it should be needed.[9]

Traveling about in the tangled underbrush in mountainous West Virginia probably led the boys to derisively parody the order that had sent them out. Good old Colonel White might wish they would make their headquarters in the woods, but to them, their headquarters was in the brush. Even Eliza Otis mentioned the seemingly endless "dense pathless" thickets, often of laurel and underbrush, that they encountered on journeys around the camps. Harrison Gray Otis noted, "We speedily acquired an intimate knowledge of that most difficult country to conduct military operations in, so that we could easily beat the rebel bushwhackers on their own ground."[10]

In early October, Blazer captured a cavalry picket near Blue Sulphur Springs and then attacked one of the Thurmonds in his camp above Pack's Ferry. The attack came as a complete surprise. They approached with stealth, then struck fast as lightning.

About midnight a halt was made and the torches extinguished and too weary even to compare notes in a whisper, the boys were soon sound asleep except those who stood guard and the captain himself, who possessed with a hardy constitution and all his life inured to hardships, kept watch with the sentinel until morning was close at hand, when all were once more aroused and quietly took up the line of march. In a very short time word was passed along the line for every man to be sure that his piece was in condition for use, and

Eliza Otis

Eliza Otis visited her
husband just before he
became a Scout and wrote
wonderfully descriptive
diary entries about the
mountains of West
Virginia.
Harrison G. Otis, *Where
Sets the Sun*

then another halt to make sure that every man was ready for action, then a few more quiet paces brought them in view of the bivouac of Thurman, whose men were disposed in slumber just as they committed themselves to the drowsy goddess the night before, when they not as much as dream that there was a foe within twenty miles of them.

Capt. Blazer made quick work of it and first sending a volley into their camp, he charged them with a yell, and capturing many prisoners, several horses and all their camp outfit, with which he returned to Fayetteville, and once more entering into his own camp not having lost a man or sustained a scratch. The boys made visits to their comrades in the companies to which they belonged, and told the marvelous tales that caused all to wonder, and to invest Blazer with a character hitherto unsuspected.[11]

Colonel White reports that Blazer captured the camp and equipment with a quantity of commissary stores. "Thurman skedaddled leaving a cooked supper which our boys ate—then destroyed the property and brought in 13 horses —13 prisoners & 23 head beef cattle."[12]

Asbe Montgomery describes an action against one of the Thurmonds in his little book on the Scouts:

> We learned that Thurman, with part of his men, was raiding in the Big and Little Sewell Mountains, not only disturbing what few Union men there were, but waylaying all roads, and causing terror to prevail in the neighborhood. It did not suit such men as we were to have any cut-throats within our range. Off we started, marched by night, and in the day time lay still, until within reach of him we wished to find, and then pounce upon him "like a cat on a rabbit," and use him up "like string beans." Fortunately, near Little Sewell, we routed the fellow, and after a few center shots, old Phil thought that no place for him, so off he put as hard as he could; but some of his clan did not go, as they got their "rights," and stopped troubling better people. We gathered up what we could around his camp, which was of little use to us—such bands of starving villains not usually having anything that brave and well-fed soldiers desire, only some trinkets to laugh over and make pastime.[13]

After "receiving from the few Union men their warmest thanks and words of assurance of all news they could convey to us," Blazer's men returned to camp "and found all things safe."[14]

The Scouts were always aggressive—striving "to light down upon 'em like a hawk on a chicken or like a clap of thunder out of a clear sky." They had become a "besom [broom] of destruction," surprising the Confederates behind their lines time after time and keeping Rebel commanders "constantly confused and perplexed." Other soldiers of the regiments were taking note of the activities of the Scouts. James Ireland notes on Sunday, September 20, "Our scouting Co. has been doing some good scouting."[15] On October 7 he records, "Jonathan Miller volunteers in the scouting Co. & Wm Shields is detailed for the same." Entries in his journal also record indications of poor morale in the Confederate army. On Thursday, September 24, he reports, "Several deserters in from the rebels." On Sunday, September 27, after noting that the area has had "[a] very heavy frost. Has an appearance of a very early fall," and that the weather is "[m]oderate through the day," his journal continues to indicate things are going badly for the Confederates in the mountains: "Prisoners coming in daily & many deserters from the rebel army."[16]

The fighting in the mountains and valleys also displaced numerous residents of the region. On October 6, Ireland reports, "Refugees coming in daily

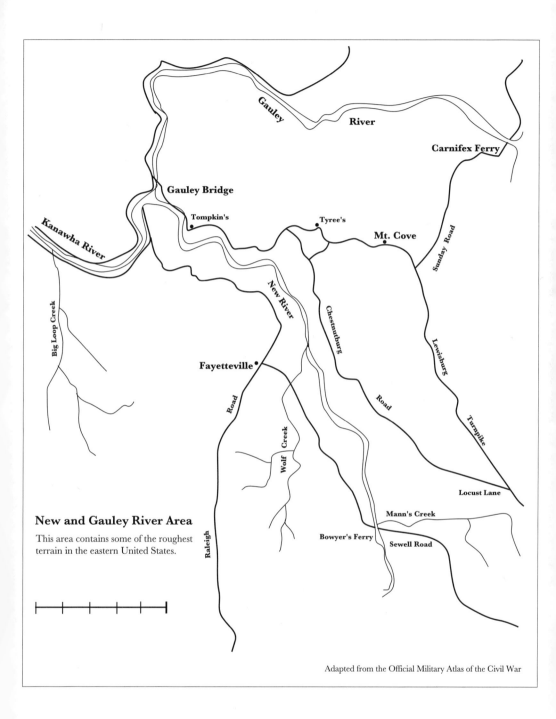

New and Gauley River Area

This area contains some of the roughest terrain in the eastern United States.

Adapted from the Official Military Atlas of the Civil War

from the rebel lines who report they are starving. Some women have walked the distance of 100 miles & brought small children with them."[17]

During one of their expeditions in September on Big Sewell Mountain, some of the Scouts approached a mountain house to forage for vittles and information. They were told a strange tale by the women of the house for the men were all away in the Rebel army. The women believed the war would soon be over and the South conquered.

> In their peculiar mountain dialect these simple natives exposed their conviction of the coming calamity, showing firmer faith in the downfall of the Confederacy, not because of its disasters on land and sea nor yet because of its depleted resources in men and *material,* but for that they had beheld "a vision"—a vision most convincing to their untutored minds than battles or blockades, death or desperation? They declared they could frequently see in broad daylight endless masses of Confederate infantry, and artillery without arms—moving northward all day long over the Lewisburg and Charleston pike, a shadowy spectral, ghastly host, sad, solemn, silent, tireless, unceasing! Northward, ever northward!

The women's story was that the marching host seemed to be clad in the Confederate gray, only their robes were more sepulchral, impalpable, shadowy, than those of the living rebs. The line of march of the ghost army would have led them from southwest Virginia, where they surrendered at Appomattox, back west to West Virginia, Kentucky, and even as far as Missouri. Did the women truly see a vision of the end of the Confederacy or were they merely partaking of the stocks of corn whiskey their menfolk may have left behind?[18]

Confederate Reactions

Confederate accounts of Captain Blazer and his men paint a picture of a unit that was "the terror of the Lick Creek region of country" in lower Summers County. Blazer himself was described as a "cruel, relentless soldier, not disposed to ameliorate the necessary hardships always incident to war." Blazer certainly was relentless, but the charge that he was cruel is contradicted by both Union and Confederate accounts of his operations in West Virginia and the Shenandoah Valley.[19]

One account tells of Captain Blazer's men surrounding the house of a

William Holcomb, reported to be home on furlough from the Confederate army. It was said Holcomb was arrested in bed, dragged from his house, and shot in the neck on the orders of the commander, for no other reason than that he was in the Confederate army. The first shot not being fatal, he was taken down the road a few hundred yards, where he was shot in the back and killed. Although quarter was often not given to bushwhackers, this account seems out of character for Captain Blazer if the man was indeed merely a soldier on furlough.[20]

More representative is a desultory encounter between Blazer's men and the Thurmonds in the Mill Creek neighborhood of the Green Sulphur district of Summers County. A squad of the Thurmonds' men was temporarily camped at the residence of the Widow Crotty at Long Bridge, about a mile below Hutchinson's Mill. It was a surprise engagement, "Neither party expected the other; neither party whipping the other." Green Rodes, a member of William Thurmond's company, was seriously wounded. Marion Gwinn had his belt shot apart in the fight. A legend of the area recounts that a Yankee was killed at the bridge and afterward haunted the area, but Blazer's men apparently suffered no casualties in this affair.[21]

The Scouts even got the attention of Confederate general John Echols after Lieutenant Otis burned two buildings near Blue Sulphur Springs. On November 30, General Scammon telegraphed Carr White, "Who was the officer who burned a Baptist Church at Blue Sulphur. Why was it done. I wish to reply to Gen. Echols." White replied that Otis had burned the buildings on reports by citizens that one had been used for keeping stolen cavalry horses and the other had been used only two nights before the burning as quarters by Bill Thurmond's company. Otis reported to White that the house had contained scant furniture, some soldiers' clothing scattered about, and graffiti indicating the 36th Virginia had used the house. There were no pews or seats indicating it had ever been used as a place of worship. Otis said it was a large two-story brick building designed for accommodating visitors.[22]

Besides combating the guerrillas, Blazer also detained citizens who were deemed disloyal and possibly aiding the Southern cause. One such group of prisoners was released by the provost marshal at Charleston. A man named Hutchison was reported to be buying cattle for the Southern army. "Wood is a blacksmith & a noisy Secesh & has certificate of exemption also that he may do the work of the neighborhood." White asked Scammon, "If these men do not give aid to the enemy, who does?" White informed Scammon that he would rearrest them in the morning and await orders. Blazer seemed to be everywhere and caught the attention of General Scammon. About October 10, 1863, he telegraphed White, "Thank Lieut. Blazer. He is alive [active or alert]."[23]

Everyday Life with the Scouts

Asbe Montgomery reports that at one point the men felt "'wolfish,' time was dreary, and camp life did not suit these brave and hardy yeomen, who felt sure that every shot they fired counted one less to trouble the friends of our glorious land, that they were determined to stand and fight for in every emergency. I really believe some of them would travel and undergo any hardship to get a crack at a Johnny. And so sure was their aim that they could knock a squirrel out of any tree, every pop, and I have often watched them holding on a reb at long range, as steady as a marksman at a target, and seldom failed to bring him down."[24]

Asbe also describes camp life for the Scouts and the rest of the men in the regiments and the attitude of the Scouts toward their enemy.

> My mind runs back to the old camp built out of Lynn logs, covered with Lynn slabs, and the cracks stopped up with moss; in the thick woods, away from friends and only our Enfield rifles which we slept with, and considered our only source of trust in the days of such trouble as we were compelled to undergo, to put down such outlaws as Thurman, which we were determined to do or die. In fact, my reader, you who have never been in the habit of scouting cannot form an idea how daring a company becomes after being blessed with success for a time; and feeling that your all is at stake, your country, life, and dearest friends, one will rush forward to battle, with gun in hand, and firm nerves, not dread even death, though staring you in the face oftentimes. I have seen our brave boys, when in pursuit of the enemy, in full stretch, straining every nerve to see who would get the first shot at a Johnny—when bang goes the rifle with a yell enough to send a thrill through the heart of the rebs. See the brave fellows bound forward, and oh! how quick death is dealt out to some of the scattering and flying scoundrels! Sometimes the foremost of our boys would bring a gun back, or something in token of what they had done.[25]

In the meantime, Asbe has been out with Lieutenant Otis and reports that Blazer is at Fayetteville. The command was probably split at this time, in accordance with orders that half of the command should be "in the woods" at all times.

After joining the company at Bowyer's Ferry, we lay there to rest a few days as they had just come from a hard march. One evening, when we were all quiet, with our pickets out, all of a sudden a lady came running down the river hill, saying Thurman was at their house, with a large body of men, and had captured one of our men, killed one, and were coming down on us "like a thousand of brick," were going to use us up like salt. Lieut. Blazer had gone to Fayetteville. We were not very well prepared to engage so large a force as this was represented to be. Lieutenant Otis being at the river, obtained the word from the young lady, and sent word to me to have the men fall in immediately, and march down to the river. I did it, double-quick, thinking something was not just right.

When we came to the ford, Lieut. Otis ordered myself, in charge of ten men to cross the river and go up the hill to the first forks of the road, and remain till he crossed the rest of the men in canoes. As soon as my squad was over, we started up the hill, two miles long, quick time, it being near sundown. We advanced without a word to break the silence, each one—once in a while looking at his comrades, showing determination to stand by each other. . . . As I had not had command in the company long, I thought it best to see how they felt. In a low voice I halted them, and addressed them in this wise:

"Now, my brave boys, perhaps we may soon hear a shot from that cruel wretch, and I don't want a man to flinch. Just stand to me and I will take you through or die with you. We can check them till the rest of the men come up."

"All right!" was the reply.

"In two ranks, right face, forward, march!" I commanded.

So on we marched, watching for a volley from the brush, till we gained the road where we were to halt. We carefully looked around and saw no one nigh. Dark was approaching and we saw the Lieutenant and the rest of the company coming, when we left part of the company on one of the roads, then started out to reconnoiter—traveled several miles in the dark, but found no one, so we returned for camp, crossing New River, and putting out a strong picket. In the morning, as soon as we could get a bite of breakfast, we fell in, crossed the river again, and started to find our wounded comrade, and hear from him all about the number of the enemy, as we were rather dubious about going to him in the dark, the night before. We came to the house where they had been and posted one half of the company on the road on which they came, for fear of a surprise. Suddenly we heard the fun commence. Looking

out on the road, we could see the rebs coming double-quick. We flew to arms.
Our outpost men fell back, and reported about 600 rebs. As soon as in nice
range we commenced firing, and they poured a heavy volley at us. Fortunately
none of us were hit. We soon found they were surrounding us so we broke
for New River hills, and had to fight our way through, they having the advantage of ground. But we poured the shots into them so hotly that they gave
way, so we all got outside of their line; and such skedaddling as we did was
not pleasant, over logs, rocks and through briers for the Ferry. We found that
they had the road and could make the river first. So nothing was left for us
but to wade Man's [Mann's] Creek at its mouth, hot, tired, and torn with
greenbriers. We plunged through and gained a desirable place behind some
rocks, where we could have whipped old Phil and all his crew.[26]

Asbe reports that Lieutenant Blazer had heard of this attack and General
White sent some men to their relief. He notes that only two men had been lost
—one dying of his wounds, the other captured. "This only set our faces hard,
and men in Thurman's gang suffered every week till Gen. White determined
to put things in motion." This part of Asbe's narrative appears to be corrob-
orated by James Ireland's diary. On October 31 he notes, "Our scouting Co.
are troubled with bushwhackers." He then notes, "Co. F. and others are ordered out to them." The next day he reports, "Find the company gone to the
relief of our scouts. The co. Returns from the scout. No damage done."[27] This
affair near Bowyer's Ferry (some records say Boyce's Ferry, which is incorrect)
resulted in several men killed or captured. Sgt. Charles G. Painter of Company F of the 9th West Virginia was captured there, as was Joseph Redden of
Company H of the 9th. Both eventually died in Andersonville Prison. Private
Samuel Irwin (Irvine) of company D of the 12th Ohio was also captured, sent
to Andersonville, but survived the ordeal. Corporal Joseph Blair of Company
F of the 12th Ohio was wounded through the lung. He died November 10 of
severe pneumonia complicated with a slight inflammation of the brain, which
may have been due to falling when he was hit.[28]

Pvt. Milton Terwilliger of Company C of the 12th Ohio was also among
the brave men captured in this fight. He had previously been a corporal and
the orderly sergeant of his company but had been reduced to the ranks by
order of Col. J. D. Hines for using abusive language. It was apparently a matter important enough that the sergeant was not willing to compromise his
integrity to save his rank. "I told my opinion to Col. Hines and Lt. Hiltz and

if they don't like it they can reduce me to the ranks. I can carry a musket for ten months longer." The ex-sergeant may have been out of favor with his regimental commander, but he was precisely the kind of man wanted for the Scouts.[29]

Pvt. Warren Thomas Timberlake of Company D was also among those captured. He too had been a former sergeant who had been reduced to the ranks. Also sent to Andersonville, he survived, was mustered out with his company, and lived until 1924. The boys of the 91st Ohio, possibly because they were with Captain Blazer, did not suffer any casualties.[30]

Shortly before this movement Sgt. Adam R. Head of the 12th Ohio was captured about the end of October while several miles outside the lines. The circumstances surrounding his capture are murky. He may indeed have been out scouting. However, the big, handsome sergeant may have had romance in mind. Years later Sgt. Samuel Pangburn of Company H of the 12th Ohio reported that Head was "dishonorably discharged for going outside of the lines *without permission* and while out being captured." Pangburn attested that the colonel of the regiment did not like Head and that he "had a woman outside of camp and was running her strong and he had about one-half Captain's permission and he took the bull by the horns and run his woman any how orders or no orders and when he was captured Capt. and the officers wanted to shield him and we wanted to mark him just captured and the Colonel wouldn't allow it and made us report him outside of the lines when captured. That's plain facts." No matter what the circumstances, Adam R. Head was on his way to Andersonville, Georgia, as a prisoner of war.[31]

The First Lewisburg Campaign

Shortly after this affair, and possibly writing as one who supported it, Asbe recounts the Scouts' part in the Droop Mountain campaign when "Gen. [William Woods] Averell marched to Droop Mountain, and whipped the Johnnies."[32] This expedition led to the last large-scale battle of the Civil War in West Virginia. Colonel White's brigade was part of a column of infantry supporting Averell's movement. The infantry started out on November 4, 1863, a day that was "warm and pleasant for the season," as Ireland notes. Cornelius Cottrell of the Independent Scouts was captured that day near Blue Sulphur Springs.

The column crosses over the New River on a "poor temporary pontoon raft & camp on the banks of the river. Witness the drowning of two horses through the recklessness of their master." The Scouts themselves cross New River on a raft "extemporized" from a mountain house. The next day continues warm but cloudy and rain threatens all day. The infantry makes do with breakfast cooked in tin cups, for want of other utensils. They "ascend an uncommon & rough & difficult hill," then continue on "a very bad road which hinders us very much." The column then strikes the turnpike between Gauley and Lewisburg. Camp is made at the foot of Big Sewell Mountain on the farm of "old Tyree—an old secesh bushwhacker. The boys go for poultry & apples." Here the infantry is joined by General Duffie's forces, consisting of two mounted regiments and one section of artillery. All along the weather has been deteriorating and probably vexes both the Scouts and the main infantry column. On November 6 everyone passes a sleepless night. "It rained until two o'clock A.M. making it very disagreeable having no shelter but our blankets." The column is on the march by daylight and the weather clears up and turns cool.[33]

The Union Forces enter Lewisburg on November 7:

A very windy night & quite cold. Get but little sleep. Camp aroused by two o'clock A.M. Get breakfast & start for Lewisburg by three o'clock. Our out pickets [possibly the Scouts] were attacked fiercely during the night. Move on rapidly. Pass through a beautiful country and & healthy people. Arrived Lewisburg by 11 o'clock A.M. having marched 17 miles. . . . Town in our possession without a fight. They had gone out to meet Genl. Averell on the Frankford Road, who engaged them. Defeated them badly, putting them to flight in all directions. Killed, wound & captured 1000 of them. Taking a portion of their artillery & train. Bivouac just beyond Lewisburg.[34]

The Scouts marched from Bowyer's Ferry to Lewisburg to assist the infantry column. With pride, Asbe notes, "It fell to our lot to take the advance all the way, which was just to our hands." They distinguished themselves by marching, and routing [Bill] Thurmond, taking several prisoners and being in advance several miles, charging into Lewisburg yelling in advance of even the cavalry. The place was defended by a small mounted force. The Scouts took several prisoners, "besides compelling the enemy to abandon a piece of artillery, and property of considerable value to them."[35]

The brigade stayed in Lewisburg for about a day. The behavior of many of the troops was not admirable. James Ireland notes with dismay, "The town of Lewisburg ransacked by the soldiers for forage. . . . Some soldiers act very disgracefully taking things which do them no good. The disgraceful plunder of the Caldwell or North House—burning of barn etc." Ireland had previously noted that at Meadow Bluff, "Boys take more liberty than I ever saw them before. Some houses are almost stripped of almost everything."[36]

On November 7, General Averell's forces joined the column at Lewisburg. Gen. J. A. Mulligan moved toward Covington and the Union forces marched toward White Sulphur Springs. The Greenbrier River was crossed on flatboats. The Union forces, however, found "the enemy have made a disorderly retreat leaving any amount of forage on the road—flour etc. which is destroyed." They marched some eight miles further and countermarched back across the river again and camped on the side of Lewisburg. By this time the weather was turning more and more disagreeable and may have been a major factor in the commander's decision to retreat when they faced almost no enemy opposition.[37]

For the Scouts, as for the rest of the column, the retreat from Lewisburg on Monday, November 9, was an ordeal. The weather turned quite cold and windy. Every now and then there were snow squalls. Ireland notes, "Many contrabands follow us." All in all it was "A very disagreeable day." After lunch the column marched over Little Sewell Mountain and camped between it and Big Sewell. In the afternoon there was a heavy snowstorm and it snowed another three or four inches during the night. "An uncommon hard night on the soldiers who have no way of sleeping. As disagreeable a night as I have ever passed," was how Ireland described the experience. During the day they had marched an incredible twenty-six miles in foul weather and over narrow mountain tracks.[38]

The 10th was also a cold snowy morning. "The column was all ready to move by daylight—boys anxious to reach camp which is 30 miles," Ireland notes. "Slowish traveling cross big Sewell Mt." The column finally reached camp, the "boys never more anxious being [illegible] and having but little sleep during the whole trip. Many of them worn out their shoes & are barefooted."[39]

Surgeon Newton watched the column return. In a letter to his wife from the hospital of the 2nd West Virginia Cavalry in Charleston, November 24, 1863, he noted the spectacle of its arrival:

Our brigade came in today. Fatigued and worn out, with some fifteen prisoners, a lot of refugees! They drove the Rebs out of Lewisburg, captured their train, burned their stores, and brought away over one hundred head of cattle.

They captured two Reb Flags, one of which they trailed in the dust, while marching into town. It looked real provoking & I suppose, many of the Secesh were mad enough to bite.[40]

Asbe Montgomery noted that such missions were almost daily occurrences "from the time we camped at Boyer's Ferry till it became too cold to stand the severity of the winter when we were ordered into camp at Fayetteville by Gen. White. He highly complimented all the men and the officers for their service and bravery, who had not only driven all the Johnnies out of Fayette County, by this time, clear over the Greenbrier River, but also had captured and destroyed a large portion of the guerrillas."[41]

Indeed Colonel White had been highly complimentary of the unit, as evidenced by the following order signed by him at the headquarters of the 2nd Brigade, 3rd Division, Department of West Virginia:

The company of detached men acting as scouts under command of Lieutenants Blazer and Otis having accomplished the ends for which it was formed is hereby disbanded and the men will be returned to their various Regiments and Companies for duty. . . . The Col. Commanding desires to return his thanks to the Officers and men composing the Company for the very efficient service, they have rendered in keeping the country in our immediate front clear of rebel guerrillas and in furnishing the commanding officer with much valuable information regarding the movements and intentions of the enemy.[42]

Colonel White informed his superiors of the efforts of the Independent Scouts as well. Edwin Stanton, the secretary of war, was told of the operations of this independent scouting unit and its successes. The following undated communication was published in the *Santa Barbara Daily Press* in 1876:

They engaged these [Rebel] companies frequently, and drove them back under cover of the enemy's lines at Lewisburg and Raleigh Court House, after which our front and rear were relieved of further molestations. In some of these skirmishes the display of individual bravery was as great as in the severest contested battles of the rebellion. He [Blazer?] made frequent captures of the enemy's pickets, patrols and scouts, and gave me valuable and reliable information of the enemy's movements.[43]

The order disbanding the Independent Scouts makes it clear that by this time actual command of the Scouts was entrusted to Lieutenants Blazer and Otis. No mention is made of Captain Spencer. His assignment in Roane and Calhoun Counties had probably become more one of maintaining order than active scouting. Also, charges brought against him and the resulting court-martial also worked to tie him down. The charges against Spencer seem to have been brought by someone who bore a grudge against him. Although the court found him guilty, the sentence of the court-martial was put aside by General Scammon.

The Second Lewisburg Expedition

Although the Independent Scouts were officially disbanded in November, a second Lewisburg expedition would put some of Blazer's men in the field again after special orders from headquarters. The second Lewisburg move involved only the men of the 12th and 91st Ohio, with the 9th West Virginia Regiment left in camp. However, men of the 9th West Virginia were picked by Blazer as scouts for this action. Harrison Gray Otis did not accompany the Scouts but commanded his own company. On December 2, 1863, from Charleston, General Scammon ordered Lieutenant Blazer to once again take to the field in charge of the Scouts: "Send Lieut Blazer to Lewisburg to learn the enemy's force and position. Let him take such men as he wants & do the work quickly and thoroughly—If he succeeds he shall be rewarded."[44]

Brig. Gen. Benjamin F. Kelley, the department commander, was determined that the Confederates would not reoccupy Lewisburg during the winter. He sent General Scammon a telegram on November 9 from Clarksburg even before the November expedition to Lewisburg had returned. He also asked for the general's advice.

> I am at a loss to determine what is best to do in regard to holding Meadow Bluff this Winter. Please give me your views fully by letter on this subject. It may be our true policy to place most of your infantry on the river during the winter, Say a regiment at Loup Creek and one at Candelton and one at the falls [of the Kanawha] or Gauley and hold Fayetteville with one regiment and a battery. I am determined, however that the enemy shall not occupy Lewisburg.[45]

At the same time Gen. Jeremiah C. Sullivan in Harpers Ferry is ordered to move up the Shenandoah to Harrisonburg and to threaten Staunton, twenty-five miles to the southwest, with cavalry. This movement is also in support of General Averell's Salem Raid, when Averell left New Creek (Keyser) on December 8, marching on Monterey and then down to Sweet Springs and New Castle, just over the Virginia line.[46]

Blazer's Scouts once again took the lead as advance guard for the infantry. They had a particularly severe fight with Philip Thurmond's men on Big Sewell Mountain. On the night of December 11, the Scouts were attacked by Thurmond's men while acting as advance scouts and pickets for the army. The main force was camped at the foot of the Sewell Mountains after marching across muddy roads. The men in the line infantry units settled down for coffee while the Scouts kept watch. Early that morning, Ireland reports, "Scouting Co. attacked. One wounded & two captured. The boys lose their haversacks. The rebels make a rush for coffee. Wm Shields makes a narrow escape of being captured. One rebel mortally wounded." Ireland also reports that "Lin's guerrillas" fired into Company E of the 12th Ohio and wounded two stationed as rear guards.[47]

In the fighting on Big Sewell Mountain, William Bishop of Company A of the 91st Ohio was severely wounded in the left leg. Salathiel Boldman of Company I of the 91st was captured. Bishop spent several months in the hospital and was finally dismissed for disability on July 14, 1864. Though severely wounded, he was lucky in the timing of the wound. Since casualties coming into Union hospitals were relatively light, surgeons had time for surgery and the leg was saved. Boldman was imprisoned at Richmond and sent to Andersonville on February 10, 1864. There is no further record. He is probably one of the many unknowns buried at Andersonville. Henry Fisher of Company H of the 12th Ohio was also captured by Thurmond's men and imprisoned at Richmond and Andersonville.[48]

Stephen P. Drake of the 2nd West Virginia Cavalry wrote a letter about the expedition to the *Ironton Register*. He mentions the affair on Big Sewell Mountain. "Here we came across Lt. Blazer of a 'bushwhacking' company from Fayetteville, who said that about midnight his company had been attacked by the rebels, and that two of his men had been wounded; also capturing all the blankets of his men. A rebel of the 22nd Virginia was wounded and died shortly afterward." In an irony of the war, this same Stephen P. Drake would be involved with Blazer's Scouts again a little less than a year later in the valley of the Shenandoah and against a more formidable foe, John S. Mosby.[49]

Thurmond's men had been part of an advance guard sent out by General Echols to warn of Union advances from the Kanawha. Echols claimed that Thurmond had dispersed the Yankees and killed, wounded, or captured several of the force they encountered. Thurmond quickly realized that the force he was facing was part of a larger body and reported this back to Echols. Indeed, it was the advance of General Scammon's forces which were heading to Salem on the Virginia and Tennessee Railroad.[50]

Saturday, December 12, was "cloudy & rainy at times." The Union men started early for Lewisburg. "Scouts in advance. Co. or part of it sent in to the ____ [probably *support* or *aid*] of the scouts. We soon commence to skirmish with rebel cavalry. We follow them for several miles. We send a few shells in Brush Hill & then the skirmish line advances. Wm. Bateman the first in the rebel ranks. We then fall into our co. & the column moves on Lewisburg. Some cannonading before we enter the city. The rebels skedaddle across the Greenbrier River. Heavy cannonading across the river. One hundred rounds fired. No damage done. Lay & guard the artillery all night in the rain. A long dreary night."[51]

The return march was a trying one for man and beast. "While crossing Little and Big Sewall Mountains a blinding snow storm drove into the faces of the troops, and a piercing cold wind chilled the very marrow of our bones. We bivouacked in the snow on the summit of Big Sewall Mountain, spending a miserable, sleepless night."[52]

Surgeon Newton summed up the affair once again to his wife after his return to the hospital on December 19.

This is Saturday evening. Have just returned from a twelve days raid 100 miles into Dixie, We have had a very fatiguing march, the weather was very fine until we reached Lewisburg. There after chasing the Rebels out, we stayed two days. Then we fell back slowly at first,—waiting till the Infantry Brigade, had got almost to Gauley & Fayette. The 12th & 91st Ohio, 6th Va & 23rd Ohio composed the Infantry. The 34th Ohio, 2nd Va & part of the 3rd Va., the mounted brigade. McMullens battery & part of Simmons were also along. These necessarily retarded our progress, especially on the return when the roads were bad, the weather worse, and the horses almost run down.[53]

The weather eventually did become too cold for active operations and the terms of enlistment were winding down for many of the men who had been in the conflict since 1861. Asbe Montgomery, like so many others, decided to enlist for another three years. With men like Montgomery, patriotism and the desire to see the thing through to the end probably played a large part. The men also received large bounties and attractive enlistment papers that enshrined their solemn oaths to defend the United States. Asbe noted that "we all pretty much went 'Veterans,' and left for home on a furlough of thirty days, and all enjoyed themselves well. At least I did so, time going on gaily and lively."[54]

Surgeon Newton, now with McMullen's Battery and ever the astute observer, notes an early indication of plans for the spring campaign of 1864. He writes on February 21, 1864:

> There is not much to disturb the monotony of our camp, Yet the sameness is to be disturbed, by the sending out of an hundred men, in three different directions. The 100 belonging to the 91st is under command of Capt. [James E.] Niday. Crosses New River and goes toward Lewisburg. The object is to press, or capture horses, these to be used, in mounting scouts for the spring campaign. Almost every day rebel deserters and refugees come into our lines anxious to take the oath, and be sent where they can obtain the necessities of life. They rarely enlist, but are very anxious to put as wide a space, between themselves and the rebel conscription officers as possible.[55]

The Impact of Gen. George Crook

The activity Surgeon Newton describes is in response to an order from Gen. George Crook, now in command. Crook has apparently heard of the exploits of the independent scouting company from the previous fall and now proceeds to improve on the concept by mounting the men and equipping them with carbines.

Headquarters, 3rd Division
Department of West Virginia
Charleston, WVA, Feb 16, 1864

General Order
No 2

The regimental commanders of this division will select one man from each company of their respective regiments to be organized into a body of Scouts to act under instructions hereafter to be given. One man from each regiment so selected to be a Non-Commissioned Officer who will be responsible for the scouts of his regiment. All these scouts when acting together will be under command of Commissioned officers hereafter to be designated. The names of the persons selected will be reported to these headquarters without delay.

Officers will be particular to select such persons only as are possessed of strong moral courage, personal bravery, and particularly adept for this kind of service. The scouts, when not acting under orders from this Division or Brigade Commanders, will remain with their regiments, but will be excused from fatigue duty and guard dutys.

The men selected who are not already mounted will mount themselves in the country by taking animals from disloyal persons in the proper manner. The regimental quartermaster giving conditional vouchers for the animals thus taken, provided however, that sufficient stock is left these people to attend their crops with. Commanders may send out expeditions for the purpose of obtaining these animals.

by order of Brigadier General George Crook[56]

Asbe Montgomery describes this turn of events:

About this time Gen. Crook took command in Kanawha Valley, headquarters at Charleston. Hearing of our services as scouts, he issued an order for a company of mounted men to be known as his Division Scouts, to be commanded by Lieut. R. R. Blazer, each regiment to have a detachment, making some eighty men, the sergeants to take charge, each of his squad, and be responsible for their good conduct. It fell to my lot to take charge of the old 9th Virginia boys, which I was proud of, as I could eat, fight, and if necessary, die with them. The details were made out of the 9th, 5th and 13th Virginia, 2d Va. cavalry, and the 12th, 23d, and 34th and 91st Ohio. The beauty of it was that we were to be mounted on such horses as we could get from the rebs, either citizens or soldiers. Well, you may guess it was not long before we were mounted.

It may be interesting to know how soon a company of eighty men could mount themselves.

We divided into squads of twenty, and started into Dixie, with hard faces, and as we traveled into Fayette, Raleigh and Logan counties, we told the citizens we were on the lookout for horses and as we met a good horse we would kindly invite the rider to get down, saying that Uncle Sam wanted us to have horses to drive Thurman's men, or those of other guerrillas, out of those parts. They would sigh and politely deliver the animal, when they saw no excuse would be taken. We soon had part of our men mounted and ready to take a trip of twenty-five or thirty miles. To finish mounting our eighty men we thought we must give old Phil's men a call, so we left Fayette, and started for Greenbrier county, swimming New River. But old Thurman got word of our approach, and rather than fight for the horses of that fine Southern neighborhood, he chose to leave, and Blazer and his men gobbled them up. In one day and night we collected twenty of the best horses in that county, and left old Phil Thurman and his sneaking, cowardly villains to spout about Blazer and his men, while we crossed the river and snugly rigged the horses for good purposes. All being mounted, we left to report to Gen. Crook, at Charleston, going off in high glee to the falls of the Kanawha, crossing at the Ferry, and reporting to the General the next day. We went into camp at the first old salt furnace, on the west side of the river. Here we commenced to feed and train our horses. But a short time was required to have them trained to the crack of the gun, etc. In a short time we left to try our luck as mounted scouts. With a commander at our head, a country at stake and such a General to instruct, you may suppose we felt sure of success and to break down and smash all guerrillas was our delight. We were sure of something to do, for Wicher [Witcher] and Canterbury[57] were raiding in Logan, and on the Guyandotte and Coal Rivers.[58]

Sometimes a citizen would attempt to get a horse returned. However, if the aggrieved party fit the profile of disloyal citizen these pleas were apt to fall on unsympathetic ears. Such was the case of one Thomas Atkeson. Col. William R. Brown of the 13th West Virginia had received an order from the provost marshal at Charleston to return Mr. Atkeson's horse. Colonel Brown replied to his superior,

> Dear Col. Mr. Atkeson has always been a rebel sympathizer and I question whether he can point out a single act of his own that he has voluntarily done for the support of our government service since the commencement of the rebellion. The horse in question is in the U.S. Service. One of the scouts sent up from this Regt. is now using him and therefore it is impossible for me to return the animal as I do not know where the scouts are. As regards the loyalty of Mr. Atkeson, I refer you to col A.R. Hall and many others.[59]

The idea for mounted scouts may not have originated with Crook alone; Carr B. White—always the innovator—may have had a hand in it. In a letter to Colonel White, General Scammon approves "mounting of thirty or forty men for brigade service."[60] It is certainly possible that these horses were meant for brigade scouts. In any case Crook decided to make the command a full company and he proposed to give it as much firepower as possible by requesting repeating weapons. On February 15, 1864, Crook sent a telegram from Charleston to the Department of West Virginia: "[General Crook] Wants one hundred Spencer Rifles as soon as possible to use to clean out guerrillas."

The department replied the next day, forwarding a telegram from the ordnance department: "There are no Spencer Rifles on hand and none being made." Crook, not satisfied with the answer, fired back a telegram on February 17 to General Kelley: "Cannot Government have these Spencer Rifles made expressly for the case. That is the way in the Army of the Cumberland. Please push this matter." A direct answer to this telegram was not received, but Crook persisted in getting as much firepower for his command as he could, not just the Scouts. He initially received a positive response. On March 24 he received a telegram from Maj. General Sigel that the ordnance depot at Harpers Ferry had been ordered to procure 2,500 Spencer carbines and 100 Henry carbines, among other ordnance stores, for Crook's division.[61]

Crook was probably pleased with the response but still wanted to refine the standard to which his men would be equipped. He replied to the department on March 25, "I would rather have the Henry guns to be rifles instead of carbines. Also two thousand of the Spencer guns to be rifles."[62] He probably wanted the rifles, as opposed to the shorter carbines, to get as much range and accuracy as possible. It is also interesting that he wanted 100 Henrys since the Scouts also would number 100 men. However, there is no evidence Crook's infantry as a whole or the Scouts were equipped with a large number of repeating weapons. The Scouts apparently were not equipped with Henrys or Spencers—with the possible exception of the 34th Ohio and probably the 2nd West Virginia Cavalry—until Sheridan ordered them equipped with the Spencer rifle in August 1864.

It is likely this order was not fulfilled once the ordnance department found out the weapons were meant for infantry regiments. Crook replied to Gen. Julius Stahel on April 17, "The Spencer Rifle is not a cavalry arm in the Army of the Cumberland. Infantry regiments are armed with them. Respectfully."[63]

Whatever may have been the status with the majority of Crook's forces, it is very likely that the 2nd West Virginia Cavalry and the 34th Mounted

Infantry were equipped with these weapons as mounted units. At any rate, Blazer's men were probably equipped with some sort of short weapons, possibly Smith or Linder carbines, already in the command.[64]

By the time they took the field, Crook had done all he could to insure he had a hard-hitting, well-equipped unit of scouts who were audacious and woods wise. They would soon get to prove themselves against the enemy because Crook already knew the spring campaign was at hand.

4

To Horse

The Scouts in 1864

THE regiments that now furnished men to Blazer's Scouts were a mixture of veteran units and ones that had seen less combat. The 23rd Ohio Volunteer Infantry was the most diverse unit that sent men to Blazer's Scouts, and its men probably stood out from most of the southeastern Ohio and West Virginia men as true Yankees. The 23rd was raised from counties in northern and northeastern Ohio, mostly from prosperous flatland farms and industrial cities like Cleveland. However, even this region contained hilly land, including part of the foothills of the Appalachians. The regiment counted ethnic Germans and even Canadians among its members as well as the usual mix of Anglo-Saxons and Irish common to many Northern regiments. (Of the three Canadians in the Scouts, two would remain in the United States after the war.) Many of the men served in industrial trades and other skilled occupations in addition to farming.[1]

The mountains of West Virginia and the poverty and lack of education of many of its inhabitants must have been a shock to many of the men of the 23rd Ohio. One derisively reported, "These western Virginians eat and sleep like pigs." The 23rd Ohio, which would be most famous for having two of its members become U.S. presidents, was a veteran combat unit that had seen service at South Mountain and Antietam. At Antietam, Lt. Col. Rutherford B. Hayes, leading the regiment in the advance, had an arm broken but refused to leave the field until he was carried off. The losses of the 23rd that day were indeed horrible, the unit suffering more than two hundred casualties. The 23rd also saw much service in West Virginia and was involved in the pursuit of John Morgan's raiders in July 1863.[2]

The 34th Ohio Infantry began the war as a dashing Zouave unit dressed in dark blue jackets and light blue pants with a red shirt and fez. Known as the Piatt Zouaves in honor of their colonel, they were mustered into service at Camp Dennison at Cincinnati. Like the 23rd Ohio, the 34th was a diverse unit whose men had a variety of occupations and nationalities. Many of the men were farmers from the good land of southwestern Ohio—flatter and more prosperous than the poor farms of most of the men from the southeastern Ohio and West Virginia regiments. Many of the men were Germans, reflecting the influence this group had in Cincinnati and its vicinity. The regiment saw duty in western Virginia in 1861 and 1862 in the Kanawha Valley, participating in many campaigns and actions, including defense against General Loring's advance in September 1862. In May 1863 the unit was furnished horses and became mounted rifles. In January 1864 nearly two-thirds of the men reenlisted as veterans. The regiment was divided into two detachments in April 1864, the mounted portion serving with General Averell and the dismounted portion, along with the 36th Ohio, serving in General Crook's division of infantry.[3]

Not mentioned by Asbe Montgomery but also providing detached men for the Scouts was the 36th Ohio Volunteer Infantry. The 36th was also primarily from southeastern Ohio, many of its men coming from nearly the same area as the 91st Ohio. The 36th Ohio was one of the very best combat units of the Civil War and one which saw some of the most diverse service. Most important, its first commander was George Crook. Its service ranged from early service in western Virginia to combat in the eastern theater of the war at South Mountain and Antietam to Chickamauga and Missionary Ridge in the west. A portion of the unit also participated in the general assault on Kennesaw Mountain with Gen. William Tecumseh Sherman. In the spring of 1864 the regiment returned to West Virginia and participated in the campaigns of 1864, including Hunter's Raid to Lynchburg and the entire Shenandoah Valley campaign.

Ohio counties with men in Blazer's scouts

These are the primary counties furnishing men to Blazer's Scouts. Most men, with the exception of the 23rd Ohio and a few men from the 34th Ohio, came from a band of counties in Appalachian Ohio.

George Crook personally wanted the 36th Ohio—his old unit—back in his command.[4]

The mounted scouts of 1864 also contained men from two newer West Virginia infantry regiments, the 13th and 14th West Virginia, and a cavalry regiment, the 2nd West Virginia. The 13th West Virginia was organized at Point Pleasant and Barboursville in October 1862. It participated in operations in West Virginia in 1862, 1863, and into 1864. It was on the Virginia and Tennessee Railroad Raid with Crook in May 1864, Hunter's Raid against Lynchburg, and the Shenandoah campaign of 1864. Compared to many other units, however, it had seen less service; nevertheless it contained some very good men.[5]

The 14th West Virginia was organized at Wheeling on August 25, 1862. The 14th participated in the various Lewisburg raids in November and December 1863, penetrating all the way to Covington, Virginia, on December 19, 1863. It also took part in the Virginia and Tennessee Raid in early May 1864 and was heavily engaged at Cloyd's Mountain. Like the other units, it would also participate in Sheridan's operations against Jubal Early in the Shenandoah Valley.[6]

The 2nd West Virginia Cavalry was a veteran regiment that had seen much action in the state. It had been organized at Parkersburg, Virginia, from September to November 1861. Only one company was composed primarily of West Virginians, however. Most of the men were from southeastern Ohio. A letter from Charleston, West Virginia, dated March 15, 1864, proudly informs readers of the *Zanesville Courier* of this fact: "We beg leave to inform all, who are not already acquainted with the fact, that although we are called a West Virginia regiment; that there are not over fifty Virginians among us. We belong to *Ohio*, we are buckeye boys, all the regiment except one company hail from the counties along the Ohio river." The 2nd West Virginia Cavalry had been on several campaigns in the Kanawha Valley and western Virginia, including several scouts and actions against bushwhackers.[7]

The men selected for this mounted unit were chosen in an even more rigorous manner than the Scouts of the fall of 1863. Now the Scouts were chosen from the first two brigades of the 2nd Division of the Army of West Virginia. Many of the men from the 12th and 91st Ohio and 9th West Virginia who had been Scouts in 1863 were chosen for this new unit. However, many were not and went back into the line to continue to serve as infantrymen. For the most

Pvt. Albert D. Shaffer

Shaffer was one of the boys detailed to the Scouts from the 36th Ohio Infantry. Note the sentiment written on the photograph.

Courtesy L. M. Strayer collection

Pvt. James M. G. Byers, 23rd Ohio Volunteer Infantry
Courtesy Hayes Presidential Center

part they carried out their duties with the same diligence and courage displayed earlier.

In addition to the other qualities specified by general order no. 2, these men also had to be good with horses. Since most were farmers, they at least knew how to handle a horse and care for one, although it may have been more common for the men to drive a horse rather than ride one. Some of the new Scouts were teamsters or had previous experience with horses. The men of the 34th Ohio had been mounted infantry and of course the 2nd West Virginia Cavalry was already mounted.

The Men of the 1864 Scouts

Pvt. Tobias Haught was a farm boy of the 14th West Virginia Infantry. He wrote to his parents about his horse from Meadow Bluff on May 27, 1864: "you Said you would pay for the pasture of my mair this sumer and if I would let you work her you can have her this sumer and if I never get back that I have entend for you and mother to have it."[8] There is no evidence that Tobias eventually brought his mare to serve in the army, but it is a possibility.

Jesse Able was a sergeant in the 2nd West Virginia Cavalry. In a board of survey ordered by General Crook on August 13, 1864, Jesse's horse was valued at $140, about $10 less than the going price for cavalry horses in 1864.[9] Although it is more generally known that Confederate cavalrymen furnished their own horses to the army, it was much more common than recognized in the Federal army as well. This was particularly so in western units, where men like Tobias Haught and Jesse Able often grew up on farms and were used to training and caring for their own horses.[10]

Some of these young boys had little childhood at all. Sylvester Keith of Company F of the 13th West Virginia Infantry worked as a miner in the coal banks of Mason City, West Virginia, hauling out coal by mule team for the firm of Lovell and Paine. He and many of his comrades had started to work at very early ages. Sylvester was only eight when he started in 1852. When he wasn't working in the mines, he was helping his widowed mother take care of the poor land they owned. The army must have provided relief from such tedious lives at home. Despite his hard life, with probably little time for formal schooling, Sylvester Keith was literate. He used his skill to write numerous letters home to family and friends and help pass the boredom of camp life.

The boys hungered for letters from home. Sylvester told his mother in one letter to "tell all my friends up about Coal Run if they ever expect to hear from me that I want them to write give them my address and if they dont write they may go to thunder."[11]

Samuel Harrop was one of the many former foot scouts who were chosen for the new mounted unit. These were men whose sterling qualities had recommended them for this even more elite scouting unit. Samuel's intelligence, wit, and gaiety undoubtedly made him a hit with the other men around the campfire and on the march. Samuel's qualities were well known to Captain Blazer since they both came from the same company.

Jesse Middaugh was an older, worldly-wise member of the 5th West Virginia Infantry with a keen sense of humor. He came to Blazer's unit with a great deal of scouting experience. Jesse was also an adventurer who had done a great deal of traveling and had been away from family and friends for a long time. Before the war, Jesse had been traveling around much of the United States. In 1862 he wrote to his sister Elizabeth about coming home to his family after his travels:

> I was in California and then I went to Central America and from there home to my wife and children. She has three of the pretiest you ever saw two boys and one girl The girl is seven and as fine a girl as you ever seen I have not bin home for seven months. I got a letter from her this morning She was well on the first of may She lives in ironton Lawrence, County, Ohio She is just about hansom As a picture her self and I am not so bad looking myself you must not think hard of my foolish talk I suppose that you would like to know who I married She is a Kentuckian her name was Vanhoose, of good stock I must bring this to a close my prayers be with you for ever and remain your Afectionate brother until death.[12]

Jesse met Mary Ann Vanhoose, a schoolteacher, while crossing a bridge in either Ironton, Ohio, or Ceredo, Virginia. After a whirlwind courtship of three months the two were married at Peach Orchard, Kentucky, on April 28, 1854. It is unclear why the Pennsylvania-born and well-traveled Middaugh came to the tri-border area of Kentucky, West Virginia, and Ohio. In any case, on September 2, 1862, he joined Company C of the 5th West Virginia Infantry, which was raised in this vicinity, as a sergeant.[13]

Jesse had been a member of a handpicked group of men known as Milroy's

Sharpshooters. In a letter dated June 25, 1862(?), from Camp Copperhead near Strasbourg, Shenandoah County, Virginia, he relates, "I am one of the western verginia Scouts and am not in Camp more than once a month so that I get no chance to rite to anybody much." On July 29 from camp near Woodville, Rappahannock County, he writes, "Dear Sister and brother After 10 day Scout and hard Scurmishing I came in camp today. . . . I can say that I am well myself but vary tired of this thing Cald [called] War it is fun for some but if they all had to do as I have to do they would not think it much fun I now belong to Milroys Sharp Shooters and perhaps I can have a little more rest than I have ben agitin for the last year I have bin A Scout Captain and now I shall stay in camp a little more than I have bin in the habit of doing."[14]

Jesse then describes the shrewdness that made such men prime candidates for Blazer's unit: "I have bin taken prisoner twice in the last two months and have had good luck to get away from them both times and return to camp." On December 29, Jesse writes from Ceredo, Wayne County, Virginia: "I have bin off on a Scout for ten days and when I came home I found my wife very sick but the rest of us are all well I have bin out in the rebel country about one hundred miles and just got back today I have bin alone and passed for a rebel major and got along first rate with the dear rebs."[15]

Passing for a Rebel was probably not very hard for Jesse. He was a master of disguise and had probably lost his Pennsylvania accent and picked up the more Southern tones of the tri-border area. He refers to himself as a Southern Yankee in another letter to his sister on March 9, 1864. Passing for Southern was probably quite easy for most of the men from West Virginia and southern Ohio.[16]

Jesse's prowess as a scout is amply illustrated by a description of an individual scout carried out to Greenbrier County. In a letter dated October 21, 1863, he tells the tale the night before he is to go out on another solo mission: "I just came from one vary hard Scout out in greenbryer County Va I had forty men with me we had two fights I lost one killed one Captured and he stripped of all his clothing and let go We killed 17 and wound four I burned two large flouring mills for them and Stole 21 horses from them and got to camp on the 28 of Sept My duty is Scouting altogether I have had a hard time in this rebelion."[17]

Jesse may have exaggerated some of his exploits in his letters home, but there is no doubt he was chosen for special and hazardous duties. Jesse is one of three men mentioned in special order 44 (March 1, 1864) who were paid money for "secret service." Jesse was paid $20 for his activities. Samuel Burdett, of Company I, 9th West Virginia Infantry, was paid the truly handsome sum of $260 for his secret work. By command of General Crook, Samuel was subsequently detailed for "special duty," along with Lt. James Ewing and James Webb of the 9th (special order 58, March 19, 1864). Since Webb and Ewing were all detailed to Blazer's unit during this same period, this detail could be for even more hazardous spying beyond their duties as regular scouts. The seriousness with which General Crook regarded these duties can be seen in his additional instructions: "These amounts are specified not to be put on quartermaster document Form No. 2 (report of persons and articles paid) in order to preserve better secrecy."[18]

William Wass was but a boy of sixteen who had to have his father's consent when he enlisted in the 14th West Virginia Infantry. His family was prominent in Ritchie County and had come into possession of land formerly belonging to Henry Purviance. Purviance had to return thousands of acres before 1816 because of delinquent taxes, and William's father, John, settled on part of the tract. After years of litigation, John acquired title to the land in 1851. John was born August 2, 1805, in Somerset County, Pennsylvania—not far from the Maryland and western Virginia border—the son of George Wass. In 1829 John married Barbara Boyer, of Pennsylvania Dutch descent. They migrated to West Virginia with their first five children and settled in a log cabin that would become the Wass homestead.[19]

The family had strong religious beliefs and William attended Pleasant Hill Methodist Episcopal Church. They were not just loyal to the Union but supported the root cause of the war, the effort by Northern abolitionists to free the slaves. According to family oral history, William's father, John, ran a station on the Underground Railroad, located in the family barn. Years after the Civil War, after attending a community church gathering in 1993, Mary Lucille DeBerry, the great-great-granddaughter of William's sister Elizabeth, described the scene affectingly: "The church was built after the War Between the States, long after Harrison and Elizabeth realized that the trips made from their remote barn, just down the road, back to German speaking Pennsylvania were directly linked to black faces hidden under hay."[20]

Like so many families loyal to the Union cause, William's family would suffer as a result. His father John, whose activities with the Underground

Pvt. William Wass

Bill Wass was one of Captain Blazer's "Southern Yankees," who wore the butternut and gray uniforms of the Confederacy.

Courtesy Patricia Ploehn and Margaret Wilson

Railroad, were probably known to neighbors with Confederate allegiances, was bushwhacked on July 21, 1863, as he was returning to his house. Even now, many years after the war, the scars remain. The following passage by DeBerry tells the tragedy of that event: "Joe Pyeweed blooms in clusters along the South Fork of the Hughes River where the cousins' great-great and my great-great-great grandfather John stopped to water his horses just before the Confederate grey sympathizer's bullet struck him in the back."[21] John Wass also raced horses and even sent some into Maryland, according to family tradition. William was exposed to horses from an early age. His slight form may have enabled him to be a jockey for his father in races around the country.[22]

Joseph A. Brown of the 23rd Ohio was born in Ashland, Ohio, on July 16, 1844, the son of James S. and Rebecca Zimmerman Brown. Joe was a clean-cut farm boy with fine features. He was raised to young manhood in his own county, where he benefited from the already good Ohio schools. When the war came he enlisted in Company G of the 23rd Ohio, as did his father. He was with his regiment on the banks of the Monongahela River when he made his first scout, in an action near Fort Pickens with some bushwhackers. After he returned to Camp Scott, his father, who was working as a teamster, was stricken with typhoid. He was moved to Camp Lookout where he died of the fever on October 1, 1861, at the home of a Negro family. Joseph had the hard task of making his own father's coffin, from boards torn off an old corncrib, and burying him in an old cemetery nearby.[23]

Joseph engaged in another scouting expedition in the winter of 1862 with a party of twenty that captured twenty prisoners and fired but three shots. Joseph then went East with the regiment to participate in South Mountain and Antietam, where he was wounded. His good record as a soldier and prior experience scouting made him a good candidate for the newly formed band of elite scouts under Lieutenant Blazer.

Operations around Charleston

George Crook was serious in his resolve that only the best men be detailed for the scouting company. A regimental commander was not in the good graces of the division commander if Captain Blazer had to send men back to the regiment because they were not up to his strict standards. Col. William R. Brown of the 13th West Virginia Infantry received a strong written rebuke on April

21, 1864. Special order 80 returned several men to the regiment, including Sgt. Philip Nicholson, who was reduced to the ranks for allowing a prisoner to escape: "It is desired that none but the best men be detailed to serve in this company, and you will be held personally responsible if other than good men be sent—your attention is called to the fact that this is the second time enlisted men from the scouting party have been sent back to your regiment. By order of Brig Genl Crook."[24]

The Scouts took the field early in March 1864 to pursue guerrillas infesting the area around Charleston. The men had had a couple of months of relative ease. They had been off to visit family and friends on their veteran's furloughs and otherwise had passed the time until the spring campaign would begin. Many had undoubtedly sampled the pleasures of Charleston, a rollicking city that contained many of the vices prevalent where large numbers of troops were camped during the Civil War. Charleston had more genteel charms as well. The city was said to have been settled by many families of refinement from New England. The outlying suburbs "contain a number of elegant residences, whose grounds are plotted and planted with taste." The banks of the Kanawha River could be beautiful when covered with vegetation and bathed in sunlight. "The summer and autumn scenery in this vicinity is said by those who have looked upon it in its full glory, to be enchanting; and the enthusiastic lady of one of the officers declared that the irregularly but gracefully winding chain of hills which skirt the river on either hand, while yet their ruggedness was hidden and just after the hand of the autumn frost had spread upon them its superbly mottled drapery of crimson and green and gold, appeared to her like nothing so much as immense bouquets."[25]

However, wartime Charleston in the winter of 1863 and 1864 had lost much of its charm. The overall impression of the place was gritty and grim, like a black-and-white photo which cannot convey even the gaudiest of autumn colors.

Mud, mules, and muleteers—such were my first impression of Charleston. But it would be a great injustice to conclude what the town once was from what it is now. A heavy fall of rain, which was well incorporated with the retentive soil by the careless poaching of hundreds of men, mules, and horses, together with the general desolation and dilapidation caused by the long occupation of even a friendly army, to say nothing of the damage caused by the recent fire, and the slashing of the rebels, have thrown a gloom and a damp over the whole city, which nothing but spring can soften, and peace and prosperity alone wholly dissipate.[26]

The city also was filled with a cast of characters that probably shocked those refined families from New England, if they happened into the downtown streets or in the areas of the army camps.

The presence of troops in and about Charleston attracted the attention of speculators, and the town swarmed with these characters, all of whom were in competition with a view to relieve the soldiers of their hard-earned money. Billiard saloons, eating and drinking establishments, groceries, clothing houses, and every conceivable business enterprise, soon gave an appearance of activity to everything which the place had never before known. But greatest among the numerous evils were the gambling establishments, the number of which could never be definitely ascertained. These managed to do a thriving business and many impoverished unlucky individuals can attribute their misfortunes to nothing else than a foolish indulgence in gaming.[27]

Charleston could indeed get even a good man in trouble. Thomas Connell of the 91st Ohio was apparently not feeling up to active scouting operations and Lieutenant Ewing of the 9th West Virginia gave him a duty that he could perform while recuperating. Tom Connell, however, managed to get himself into some very hot water. He attempted to get a wagon to clean up the camp gear as ordered by the lieutenant and may have indulged in some of the pleasures of Charleston while doing so. His misguided efforts ended in a wide variety of charges and specifications brought against him. He was accused of "grossly insulting and beating a peaceful citizen" on June 3, 1864. It was further charged that he "assaulted and maltreated a peaceful citizen without cause or provocation—striking him with a club and breaking his arm. Also striking him with a stone on the head until said citizen was insensible." It was alleged he also called the citizen a "God damned son of a bitch. You are a damned rebel." He was also charged with "Conduct subversive of good order and military discipline," specifically that he "kept and cohabited with a common Prostitute and appear with her in the street and public highway. Greatly to the detriment of the service and ridicule of the army. Thereby bringing the Army into disrepute."

The charges against Thomas now escalated into insubordination and physical threats against officers. It was alleged that "while in a state of intoxication" he used insulting language to his superior officers. He called Capt. Andrew Grubb of the 5th West Virginia Cavalry "a damned cowardly son of a bitch," and to Lt. H. W. Brazie, also of the 5th West Virginia, he said, "You are a damned old piss pot."

According to the charges, Connell disobeyed Brazie's order to desist from using abusive and disrespectful language to his superior officer. In the most serious charge of all, Brazie asserted that "while in discharge of his duty in arresting him that Connel attempted to strike him."

The charges and specifications were addressed to Colonel Wilson, commanding the brigade, and were witnessed by civilians, officers, and NCOs involved in the incidents. Tom Connell did not see things quite the way the army outlined them. The following explanation must surely have been the correct one:

While I was at Charleston, Va, where I was left behind in Charge of Some Horses, and Camp *Equippage* Lieut Ewing came there and got all the horses but four and what men were there except me. He told me to get a Wagon and to take what things were left and *"turn them over."*

I went to get a wagon, and they were all engaged, and the Major [presumably a quartermaster officer] told me to take any Wagon along the Road that I could find, the first one I found belonged to Mr. [Charles] Noyes, (A man by the name of Dickson was driving it), I told him I wanted the wagon, *"He said he had been sent to draw some Rails and that no Yankee could have the Wagon, and that one had been taken from his Brother, and that he would not give his up."* I told him that I had orders to get a Wagon, and that I must have it. "He told me that if I did not go away he would give me a thrashing." I got off of my Horse to take charge of the Wagon and he threw a *stone* at me. I then got a Stick about three feet long, and Struck him, then I went to the Wagon, and he *threw* another *stone* at me, then, I Picked up a Stone and threw it at him, and knocked him down. I then went and picked him up, then he Started across the Field to his home, leaving his Wagon in the Road. I took the Wagon to my Quarters, and got the things and turned them over, and then sent the Wagon Home. This about the 3rd of June 1864. I cannot say positively whether I did or did not call him [Dickson] "a *God Dammed Son of a Bitch*, or a D^d *Rebel*. There was a Woman by the name of Stewart, of a *Loose Character*, that used to Sleep with me in my *Quarters*. She was around the Quarters about one month. I never walked in the Street with her. She was there when I came away, on about the last of June. on the 10th of June, Capt. Grubb arrested me, and sent me to the Provost Marshal, but he was not in.

79

Additional Statement of Thos. Connell
Co E 91st O. Vol. Inf

While I was at Charlestown Va, where I was left behind in Charge of some Horses, and Camp Equippage Lieut Ewing came there and got all the Horses but Four, and what men were there except me. He told me to get a Wagon, and take what things were left, and turn them over, I went to get a Wagon, and they were all engaged, and the Major told me to take any Wagon, along the Road that I could find, the first one I found belonged to Mr. Norce, (a man by the name of Dickson was driving it, I told him I wanted the Wagon, He said he had been sent to draw some Rails and that no Yankee, could have the Wagon, and that one had been taken from his Brother, and that he would not give his up, I told him that I had orders to get a Wagon, and that I must have it, He told me if I did not go away, he would give me a Thrashing, I got off of my Horse, to take charge of the Wagon and he threw, a Stone at me, I then got a Stick about, Three Feet long, and struck him, then I went to the Wagon and he threw another Stone at me, then, I, Picked up a Stone and threw it at him, and knocked him down, I then went and picked, him up, then he Started, across, the Fields to his Home, leaving his Wagon, in the Road, I took the Wagon to my Quarters, and got the things and turned them over, and then sent the Wagon Home, this about the 3rd, of June 1864, I cannot say positively whether, I did or did not call him (Dickson) "a God Damned, Son of a Bitch, or a D.d Rebel

Statement of Thomas Connell

Thomas Connell signed this statement, as recorded by an army clerk, regarding charges against him for his actions at Charleston.

Courtesy National Archives

There was a Woman, by the name of Stewart, of a Loose Character, that used to Sleep with me in my Quarters. She was around the Quarters about one month. I never walked in the Street with her. She was there when I came away, on about the last of June.

On the 10th of June Capt. Grubb, arrested me, and sent me to the Provost Marshal, but he was not in. He then came in, in a few Moments after, and told me to go to my Quarters, and to stop on my way and tell Capt. Grubb that he had Released. I stopped and told the Capt. and he said He did not beleive me, and ordered a Guard, to take me to the Guard House, which they did, "I used some pretty Hard Language," I was drunk at the time, and do not remember what I did Say. It is more than probable that I used the Language with which I am Charged. There were Officers and Enlisted men Present, that heard all that was Said, I do not Know, Lieut. H. W. Brazie, and could not say, whether he gave me any orders or not, or whether I obeyed or disobeyed him, I have no Recollection of being arrested by Lt. Brazier, I was arrested, June 10th. by a Sergt. who was ordered to arrest me, by Capt. Grubb. I never knew a Lieut. by the name of H W Brazie. On the 12th of June when the Officer of the Day came around I asked him if there were any Charges against me, he Examined the Books, and found none. He then Released, me from the Guard House, and I went to my Quarters, where I staid about Six days. I was then sent by the Pro Marshal to go to my Regt, thence to Camp Distribution Va — and thence St. Mil Prison ————

Thos. Connell

He then came in, in a few moments, after, and told me to go to my quarter, and to stop on my way and tell Capt Grubb that he had released [me]. I stopped and told the Capt. and he Said He did not believe me, and ordered a Guard, to take me to the Guard House, which they did. "I used some pretty Hard Language" *I was drunk at the time,* and do not remember what I did say. It is more than probable that I used the language with which I am Charged. There were Officers and Enlisted men Present that heard all that was said. I do not know Lieut. H. W. Brazie, and could not say whether he gave me any orders or not, or whether I *obeyed* or *disobeyed him.* I have no Recollection of being arrested by Lt. Brazie. I was arrested June 10th by a Sergt, who was ordered to arrest me by Capt Grubb. I never knew a Lieut by the name of *H. W. Brazie.* On the 12th of June when the Officer of the Day came around I asked him if there were any charges against me, he examined the Books, and found none. He then Released me from the Guard House, and I went to my Quarters, where I staid about six days. I was then sent by the *Pro[vost] Marshal* to go to my Regt. . . . Thos Connell.[28]

Tom's statement was witnessed by officers at the Prince Street Military Prison in Alexandria. Despite the severity of the charges, there is no existing record of a court-martial against him. The charges and specifications had been initially routed to the wrong regiment. Also, he may have gotten off because the whole set of events actually started in the line of duty. Tom was, however, eventually released from scouting duty, possibly his punishment for his exploits in and about Charleston. In any case, the rest of the Scouts were preparing to take the field for active service against Confederate partisans.

Soon after their formation, General Crook reported to General Kelley that the Scouts had returned from Boone and Logan Counties. He reported that all Rebels had left that country and that the Scouts had killed several guerrillas and taken a few prisoners. The pathetic state of Rebel fortunes was also noted: "Deserters from the rebel army and refugees are coming in daily."[29]

Operations around Coal River

About March 10, 1864, the Scouts started for the mouth of Coal River, which empties into the Big Kanawha and has been described earlier as an area where guerrillas pestered the Union forces. After a ride of about twelve miles the Scouts halted at Coal's Mouth. They started up Coal River with a guide and proceeded a few miles and let the guide go as they were now sure of their route.

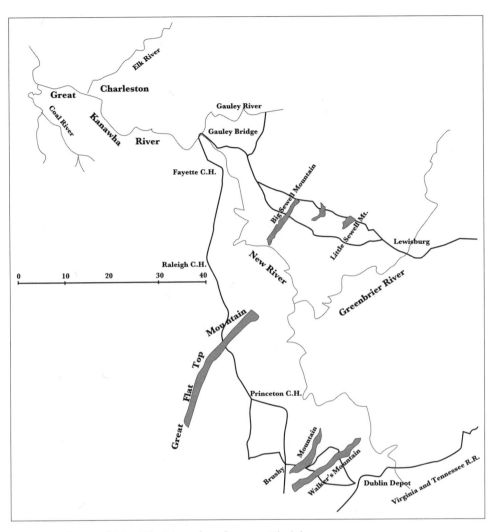

South-central West Virginia and southwestern Virginia
Many of the campaigns of the Army of West Virginia and Blazer's Scouts occurred in this area.
Adapted from *The Official Atlas of the Civil War*

We were now on a strange road and soon became very sure we were not among friends, as all we met looked shy; so no one knew anything about the road or anything else, in a word, all we met or saw were know-nothings. By evening the road became very dim and hard to follow, so at a late hour we halted at a farm house, found some rye straw which we fed our tired animals and struck a fire. After posting our pickets, we broiled and ate some meat and rested ourselves and horses for a short time. Long before day we saddled and started, so that we might be able to surprise anyone that was at Logan Court House. Just at daylight we crossed the Guyandotte. We put our horses to full speed, and before any of the inhabitants were apprized of us, the Yankees were thick in the splendid town of four or five houses, and not a reb soldier to boss them, or steal one chicken. We halted in the town on "Main Street," which was all the one there was; so the citizens need not thank us for not promenading in any other part of the town. One old sinner, was there, who was a blacksmith. We got him to fasten some of our horse shoes, and fed a good share of his corn to our animals, to save him feeding that much to guerrillas. After a short rest, and inquiring about the road and the rebs, which was of no use to us, our old friend could give us no information, he, too, being a know-nothing, we started on some distance up the stream, then took to the hills which were large and not a few. Finally we crossed a large range of mountains and wound our way to Wayne county. We found some rebs here and gave them some "Southern Rights." Some of them got away. We might have taken some prisoners, but we were too far from camp. We next went to the marshes of Coal River, and captured several prisoners. Then we went to Fayette county, and from that to camp at Charleston, having made a trip of two hundred miles, picking up several good horses along the route.[30]

Captain Blazer reported by telegram on March 28 that he had "found no enemy" on a raid through Boone, Logan, Wyoming, and Raleigh Counties. If this raid is the one described above, Asbe's account may be somewhat exaggerated.[31]

The Scouts continued to make forays against the Thurmonds and other partisan bands in southern and southwestern West Virginia, often making deep raids into areas where Southern partisanship was strong. Asbe Montgomery continues his vivid description of scouting operations.

Ready for another trip in a few days, and went up and left the river opposite Camp Piatt, crossed towering hills, and after a long, hard march found ourselves in Logan again. Being sure we were near some guerrillas we kept a sharp lookout. Not far from the marshes of Coal River, we captured several after a smart skirmish whom we saved on account of mercy. Returned by way of Flat-top Mountain and there run into one of the chief of bushwhackers with some reb soldiers with him. My reader need not enquire about their welfare. In we came to Raleigh Court House, thence to Fayetteville, wishing to meet old Phil, as by this time we had concluded we could fight on horse-back as well as any way. After a short halt at Fayetteville, we arrived safe in camp at Charleston, and were complimented by Gen. Crook.[32]

Captain Blazer reported this raid in a telegram he sent on April 15, 1864. Once again they had swept the region of Boone, Logan, Wyoming, and Raleigh Counties. "Had a skirmish with a company of Beckley's Battalion in Wyoming in which I routed him wounding one and capturing one. . . . I have captured fourteen prisoners and killed one man."[33]

On the same day that Blazer's command returned to Fayetteville (April 15), he was ordered to immediately move again against other guerrillas. Crook's telegram from Charleston demonstrates the intensity of the general's operations against the guerrillas.

> You will turn over your prisoners and what surplus horses you have to Col White to be sent here. If your horses can stand it move by the marshes of Coal to this place. There was some horses and men captured on Field's Creek the other day and taken over. Their force is said to be under the command of Crawford who is trying to raise a company about the marshes of Coal.[34]

It is clear from the official record that Asbe Montgomery is not just being fanciful about the number of prisoners and horses captured in their expeditions and that General Crook is well pleased with their activities.

Harrison Gray Otis remained with the line infantry and Lieutenant Blazer needed another officer to share the responsibilities of commanding the Scouts. Asbe describes his role in helping Blazer find a suitable replacement:

> While resting a few days, Lieut. Blazer wished a helper, and came to me and asked who would make a good scout in my regiment? I replied Lieut. Ewing had scouted some, and I had no doubt of his bravery, so he asked for him . . . to take command in the scouts, which seemed to be agreeable all around. Lieut. Ewing was a brave man, delighted in a horse, and believed in quick, active fighting, and a lively rough-and-ready life—could put spurs to his horse and make him "git" just as fast as anybody else; and his very soul and strength were all strung at full might at warring against the rebels.[35]

Lt. James Ewing of the 9th West Virginia was one of three men of the regiment who were detailed to the headquarters of the 3rd Division, 8th Army Corps, for special duty by order of General Crook (special order 58, March

19, 1864). The special duty referred to is quite likely "secret service" involving intelligence operations, for which Samuel Burdett had already been rewarded. Lt. Ewing is noted on detached duty starting in March 1864.[36]

Blazer's men remained only shortly in camp, many like Asbe Montgomery finding camp life "so tedious that a day seemed like a week." Men in the regiments would ask them if they got tired of so much riding. Asbe asserts, "Some of the boys some days would complain, but let a gun crack then they were ready for a fight."[37]

Blazer kept up the fast-paced operations against Confederate partisans. With large portions of many of these counties loyal to the South, it took skill and resourcefulness to conduct their operations.

> We left camp, and struck out for a grand raid, across Coal River, and then for the mountains, in the direction of the Guyandotte. After three or four days marching, over hills and across creeks, we struck the Guyandotte near a little village. We ran into a lot of rebs and caught some of them. We drove everything like guerrillas before us, or rather scattered them. By this time, in all the country, our name or the name of Blazer, was enough to start everything to flight. Every child and lady, if I may say "lady," was ready to fly with the word that Blazer and his company were coming, so it took skill and energy to keep up with the Female Telegrams. After some hard riding, one long day, as it seemed, for we were dogging some one all day, just about sundown, we routed Canterbury and his company. They had been, as they said, all day hunting for us, so we just met at the time to get acquainted. We saw them pouring out of a house. They saw us first and opened the ball, but it did not stop us. About half of our company were across the stream, and while the rest were crossing the foremost part charged at full speed to the horse, and while the balls were whizzing like hail, we sprang from our horses and began to give them Yankee thunder. But when they found that we had seen rebs before and were not going to be checked, they took to the mountain. After them we went making all the noise we could, both by shooting, and yelling like wild men. some of us followed them so closely that they had to leave guns, coats, and everything, except what they could get away within the quickest time. How many we killed, I leave for their neighbors to say. Some citizens told us a few days after that we gave several of them "Southern Rights."
>
> After traveling some days where we pleased, we returned to camp, with a lot of good horses, and a large number of prisoners. Landed in camp, and made several short trips successfully.

We came off victorious all the time, and I may say that while scouting hereabouts for two months, we found ourselves better mounted than when we first started—capturing in March and the first part of April 50 prisoners and 75 horses, or more.[38]

Blazer's efforts by the middle of May 1864 had reduced the guerrilla threat considerably. In a dispatch from correspondents of the *Cincinnati Commercial* dated May 17, Meadow Bluff, a reporter writes, "The general informed me last night that the bushwhackers have been entirely driven out of Kanawha Valley, owing to the skill of Lt. Blazer and a company of picked men. Travel from Gauley to here is now comparatively safe, and immense trains and supplies are continually coming in."[39]

Blazer's men had won considerable laurels for their efforts against the bushwhackers and their support of the operations of Union forces in West Virginia. Now, however, they were about to be thrown into even more momentous campaigns as the North prepared its most devastating blows against the Confederacy.

The Virginia and Tennessee Railroad Raid

Asbe now describes the part Blazer's Scouts played in the Virginia and Tennessee Railroad Raid. Crook's command was to take part in Grant's spring offensive of 1864. Crook's mission was to move up the Big Kanawha River and reach Dublin, on the New River, where he was to destroy as much track as possible and demolish the New River bridge, thus cutting the Virginia and Tennessee Railroad, a vital artery of the Confederacy. The main body of cavalry under General Averell was to destroy the salt works at Wytheville. Crook would take only a small force of cavalry with his main body.[40]

Crook's genius as a commander is exemplified by the mission he gave Blazer's unit, the 5th West Virginia Infantry, and most of his field music. They were to provide a diversion to draw off as many Confederate forces as possible from Crook's main body, operating deep in enemy country and probably unsure of just what force the Confederates could bring to bear against them. This little force marched out with much pomp and ceremony on the right bank of the New River along the Lewisburg Pike toward White Sulphur Springs. The bands were ordered to "make noise enough for an army of ten thousand men."

Each night at their halting places "each band bivouacked apart from the rest, built great camp fires and made the mountains echo with their martial music."[41]

Asbe Montgomery can best tell the story of the part Blazer's men played:

After resting a short time, we learned that the army was about to move. We were ordered to be ready, and on the 28th of April 1864, we started. Gen. Crook's division also moved up the valley of the Big Kanawha, and at the Falls [of the Kanawha] all the army marched in the direction of Fayetteville, except for the 5th Va. Infantry and the scouts. That regiment and ourselves lay at Gauley [Bridge] for a day or two [Otis reports the move was made simultaneously], and moved toward Lewisburg, Greenbrier Co., to make a feint and detain Gen. Echols, if possible, while Gen. Crook moved on Dublin Depot. This had the desired effect. On the march we had the Big and Little Sewell mountains to cross. When we started, the rebs learned of our coming, and blockaded the road over those mountains, so no wagon or horse could pass, as they supposed. But our horses were too well used to the woods to be stopped; so when we came to the blockade, after carefully looking out for the rebs, we cautiously advanced, and wound our way through the brush and over logs a short distance. Then we would halt to gain a view of some point on the road, expecting every tramp our horses made to hear a bang, bang from Thurman's men, as it was him and a lot of the 14th Va. reb cavalry that were detailed by Echols to block the road, with orders to waylay our forces and kill all they met, as we learned from some of the citizens. We had to be cautious ourselves from sunrise. The 5th Va., which was to support the scouts, by some mistake, had not come up, but lay at the Thompson farm [located at Hawk's Nest] on the hill south of Gauley River, leaving us in all danger, not only of small squads, but of being cut off from them who were to be our support. This, however, did not stop our operations. For several days we were between Big and Little Sewell, and had several brisk skirmishes. We would leave the main road late at night, and cautiously wind our way through the mountains, and when day would break, if not at a desirable point, we would secret ourselves and lay concealed perhaps all day. If no Johnnies made their appearance, when dark came off we started, for this was our time to work.[42]

Montgomery describes well the patience and woods sense that Blazer employed to accomplish his mission and avoid deadly mountain ambushes. However, even with the utmost care, the roving partisan bands would make their kills.

Asbe continues to describe the events of early May 1864. "Before the Fifth Va. came up we had done much, but we had not been so fortunate as usual,

James River and Kanawha Turnpike
The original route of the James River and Kanawha Turnpike, along which Blazer's men would have made their feint toward Lewisburg. This view is looking west, toward Little Sewell Mountain.

for we had lost some of our brave boys. But that had only fired our feelings." Andrew J. Long was captured on one of the Sewell peaks on May 4, as stated in a casualty report by Captain Blazer to Colonel Brown, commanding the 13th West Virginia Infantry. James Byers of the 2nd West Virginia Cavalry was captured May 8 at Locust Lane while carrying a dispatch. Louis Timberlake of the same regiment was killed May 9 by a bushwhacker at Brushy Ridge. Another "casualty" was Manassas Steel of the same regiment, who, Blazer reports, "deserted me on May 6 under the following circumstances, Having been placed under arrest and sent back to Gauley to be confined for sleeping on his post while on duty he escaped the guards and has not been heard from since." Judging from available records, Manassas Steel was one of the few men who deserted Blazer in the field.[43]

> When our support came we left for Lewisburg, which was just to our hands. After considerable work and fighting, we cleared the way so that our little regiment could pass—little I mean, in numbers, for they were large in hearts

as any regiment. We gained Meadow Bluffs [*sic*], well known to Western troops as a harbor for guerrillas and rebs, and where the brave Gen. Crook often gave the rebs to know that he was not their friend, while they were trying to break down a Government he loved so well.[44] Here we halted for a short time, and went to work in earnest, for we found the country alive with lawless robbers, such as old Phil and Bill Thurman, who had with them the 14th Va. rebel cavalry. The latter, however, were a source of comfort to us, for they had the name of the "Greenbrier Swifts," taken, perhaps, because they had the swiftest horses in all Dixie, and were willing to use spurs, as their horses were swift, at the first sight of a "Yank." You would hear from a dozen or more one or two shots, and then tails flying off, at the speed of an antelope, would be the next thing, to see no more of them until some high point was gained, and then they would face about and sit on their life preservers [their horses], looking like so many gray ticks, till you would come near enough to scare them by raising your piece, when off they would lope again, like wild hogs.[45]

Montgomery's disgust for Company K of the 14th Virginia Cavalry is hardly disguised. While speaking disparagingly of the Thurmonds, it is clear that although he might disapprove of their methods, he does regard them as fighters. In contrast, he has little respect for Company K of the 14th Virginia.

But we wanted some good horses and now was our time. We soon learned while lying here, that they had no idea of scouts. We taught them some things, however, but not till we made it cost them some fifteen or twenty of their best horses. How could that be you may ask? I will explain how we "sucked in" the Johnnies. Part of our company would start out late in the night, and go directly back from our camp, go around a large scope of country, and get entirely in rear of the rebs, and lay concealed. A small force would next start from camp, in front, and slowly advance and commence skirmishing and feel of them gently, for a time, till they would conclude we were surely afraid or intended no harm; when our men who were in the rear, would know by our guns we had them ripe, they would come yelling, like demons, wild Yanks, surely, and bang, bang, it would go—now begins the fun! At this moment every man would put his spurs to his horse, and with our Old Dick at the head, for so we called Blazer—he would shout, "Charge, boys, give them fits!"

Directly there would be Yanks all around them, and to the woods some of them would start, while others would surrender at first sight—some of them tearing off their hats in the brush, some being flung from their horses, and once in a while one would receive a shot from our unerring rifles, which would "compromise" with whoever it was. Then we would pick up the horses and off to camp, laughing over our fun. Coming into camp we would dismount, and examine who had the worst horse, change off for a better one; so all the time we were improving our company's condition in the way of swift and suitable horses for our arduous labors. But after some two or three such "Yankee tricks," the swift 14th reb Virginia cavalry left for a more healthy clime, and made their headquarters at Lewisburg. So we had a day or two to spare, and we concluded to pay old Phil Thurman a visit before moving to Lewisburg. Licking being his place of rendezvous, we had to go down there, and mounting, we were off.[46]

Lieutenant Ewing then left with a dispatch for Weston, West Virginia, "it being a very dangerous route, which weakened our company some; besides had lost some of our brave boys. Still with lucky Dick at our head, thought ourselves 'bully,' and not be scared at trifles."[47]

Once again the Scouts got into the saddle late in the evening to pursue Thurmond's men. Blazer made very good use of the night, a tactic that apparently not even the partisans used to good advantage, for Blazer seems to have used it time and again to get the advantage of guerrilla units. Asbe notes that they soon neared Little Meadows, hoping to find signs of Thurmond. Blazer also used his subtle methods to gain precise intelligence on the enemy so that when he did go into action, he could hit swiftly and fiercely with confidence he himself would not be surprised.

After resting awhile, it being dark, mounted, and the Captain, as usual, took the lead—I call him Captain, for he had been promoted by this time—going into the enemy's country, riding slowly, with not a word to break the silence. On we rode, each comrade holding his gun in hand, not knowing how soon we might need them, as all that country had in it more or less scouts of Thurman's men; and so used every means to avoid a surprise. Late in the night came to a house where a lady lived, we knew to profess some Union sentiment, and there halted. Here got some milk, and learned which way to go.

Remounted and a little daylight came, found ourselves in the Licking neighborhood. Saw some signs of the enemy, and moved slowly on to the place we intended to take dinner. Coming up to a large brick house, posted a strong picket, fed our horses, and ate some dinner. Rested and started. Had not rode over a mile, when bang, bang, bang, sounded the guns from the brush, some fifty shots being fired. We knew what they meant, having heard the like before. As some of them could be seen, being hid in the brush, off we dropped, and over a small creek, and up the bank, as if the "old Nick" had been up there, and so he was in human shape, but not to stay long, for they had made us mad.

Several of our boys had their hats and coats cut by balls, getting our "dander up" a little, for we did not allow a reb to insult us in any manner. Soon gained the brush and bank from which they fired, and gave them some "Yankee pills" wounding one, and off they scampered. Gave them hot chase for a short distance, but the brush being too thick to see them, returned and remounted, and going to a reb house, perhaps half a mile off, left our provisions, telling the lady reb to have us some supper cooked, hoping to show them another "Yankee Trick," and so it proved, as I'll tell in the proper place.

Then turning our course, left the neighborhood; and traveling in the direction of Little Meadows, seeing some citizens, made all inquiries, but they all being know-nothings, our breath might have been kept to "cool our broth." Coming to a large house, about 10 o'clock, our advance was fired on, but luckily no one hurt. All of us rushed up, dismounted, and surrounded the house, but the lads being a little too quick dodged out, and it being very dark they escaped, firing several shots at us at random as they ran. This put our boys in pretty good tune for the milk-house and smoke-house, so they helped themselves, and in feeding the horses cared not to count the ears very sparingly, for it took about forty bushels of corn. Rested in a short time, and heard the lying folks talk of their innocence. At a proper time started on to Little Meadows; then turned our course, and marched directly on our trail of the night before, near daylight finding us again down on Lick creek, close to the house where we left the provisions. Searched every house near the place, and turned out some of the good Johnnies. You may guess how they fared, as we had refused to take any more of Thurman's men prisoners, as they had shot some of our men.[48]

After making this settlement, we discovered the road blocked snugly close to the house our provisions had been left at, and to all appearance forces [were] lying and watching for us. Dismounted, and leaving a few men to guard the horses, and cautiously crept into the woods, deployed and moved up, hoping to pay them for their yesterday's fun. Exactly so; as it proved, for we took better aim than they did. Crawling up, I espied them just in time to get the first crack, so bang, bang, sounded our deadeners, myself being at the right of the company and the Captain on the left. I bawled out: "Here they are boys; shoot their hearts out; go for them; show no quarter!" It rang along the line, the Captain making his voice heard like homemade thunder: "Give it to them; don't spare one; remember bushwhackers have no quarter." After a nice little brush, we left some more to trouble no one.[49]

Giving no quarter was probably a necessity in deep scouting missions. The Scouts simply could not deal with prisoners. Also, Asbe's account shows the intense hatred of the troops, including the Independent Scouts, for the bushwhackers. It was deadly business on both sides. The bushwhacker truly gave no quarter, nor helped those he wounded, as his most immediate thought was to get away. If he did not, "justice" was sure and with no appeal. Asbe notes, "This closed our fun here. Thurman's men departed for the other side of the Greenbrier River, leaving the scouts 'bully' victors." The Scouts returned to camp, feeling themselves able to "whip our weight in wildcats."[50]

Losses at Cloyd's Mountain

The Scouts started the advance the next day, supported by the 5th West Virginia Infantry. "Not much to do, as Echols, the old coon, had left the day of our arrival, his signs being plenty of burning fragments of his dog-huts." Asbe reports the 5th West Virginia halted at Bunger's Mills, about four miles north of Lewisburg. According to Montgomery, "We had fine times foraging. We went where it pleased us, although the 14th Va. reb cavalry had been left to look after us."[51]

The feint had its desired effect. Absolute panic was thrown into Lewisburg, the citizens sure they were once again to be the target of the Union army. "Rumors that an army of five hundred men was approaching the town caused residents to fear the worst and cause many . . . to leave for places of safety." But the feint had a more concrete effect than to just spread fear and panic in residents who had seen enough of invading Yankee armies.[52]

The belief that Crook might have his main force on the James River and Kanawha Turnpike caused confusion in the Confederate command and compelled it to have forces in Greenbrier and Monroe counties equal to those that participated in the fight at Cloyd's Mountain. In fact, on the march from the Narrows of New River to Dublin, Gen. John McCausland's command met Battery E, 3rd Georgia Battalion, going the other way. General Lee himself, believing that Crook was on the Staunton and Parkersburg Pike, misread Crook's intentions. As a result, Crook met only token resistance to his main force, mostly scouting parties that "fled precipitately" when they met him.[53]

The good residents had some reason for trepidation for this region and its inhabitants were not liked by the Union men, who reckoned most citizens

Unidentified trooper

This unknown trooper could be close to what Blazer's Scouts looked like in the field.
He is well mounted, wears an oversized infantry sack coat, and has saddle pistols.
Unlike the Scouts, he is not carrying a rifle or carbine.
Courtesy William Elswick

irredeemable Secesh. Asbe reports that the "roads being well cleared out, gave us some of the best sport in Christendom, for as I told you, we had captured some twenty of the Swifts' horses, and could ride them as well as they, and every day had a race with them."[54]

The main body of Crook's army had now defeated General Jenkins's force of Confederates in the vicious fight at Cloyd's Mountain. Many of the Independent Scouts of the fall and winter of 1863 would fall in the infantry line at that fight. Crook then went on to destroy the New River bridge near Dublin. Unsure of the success of other elements of Grant's plan, deep within enemy territory, and with a force that had suffered horrible casualties, Crook decided to withdraw his army to West Virginia. It is, however, interesting to speculate on what Crook might have done had his force been equipped with repeating weapons, as he had wanted. He may well have continued the plan, figuring that his firepower could defeat almost anything thrown against him.

The retreat would be a hard one, with men suffering and dying from exhaustion and lack of food. In the meantime, Crook had sent a dispatch for Blazer and his men to forage in the vicinity of Lewisburg. The Scouts loaded ten wagons and sent the much-needed provisions to the army. They then marched to Meadow Bluff to join the main body, "after an absence of seventeen or eighteen days, the army having had a long march and some desperate fighting. Worn out by loss of sleep all lay here and rested a short time, there being also a rest for us a day or two. But it seemed, that summer, no rest was to be had long."[55]

George Crook congratulated the men of his command at Meadow Bluff for their great victory, but correctly predicted the hard times ahead for the Army of West Virginia:

> The General commanding congratulates the troops of this command on their brilliant achievement . . . having marched a distance of two hundred fifty four miles in nineteen days during which time you attacked and defeated the enemy at Cloyd's Mountain and New River Bridge routing him each time with severe loss. . . . You have conquered the enemy and the elements which opposed you enduring cold and hunger and fatigue without a murmur. . . . While we deplore the loss of many brave comrades, we have the consolation of knowing that the ground made sacred by their blood has been rendered untenable to the enemies of our government at least for a long time. The great Struggle is not ended: you must therefore be prepared for other and great efforts.[56]

5

The Main Tug-of-War

The Lynchburg Campaign

THE Cloyd's Mountain campaign had been a hard one for both the Army of West Virginia and Blazer's Scouts, but it was only the beginning of nearly constant campaigning over the next several months, as the Union army, under Grant, gave the Confederacy no rest. Asbe Montgomery called it "the main tug of war." Once again, rumors were probably rife in the camps that they would march again. "Looking for orders to march for several days, not having any idea in what direction, we did not know how nigh was one of the hardest marches ever any set of men endured. The time had come for all our skill and bravery to be tested. But our country lay bleeding before us, and we felt like offering our lives on its altar as a sacrifice if needs be."[1]

The Army of West Virginia was once more on the move, this time striking even deeper into Virginia, toward Lynchburg and some even thought toward Richmond itself. The army started for Lynchburg in the afternoon of June 2, advancing first toward Lewisburg.[2]

> The time came, struck tents, the bugle sounded, and off for Staunton, through Lewisburg, and across the Greenbrier river. The scouts to the advance to clear anything that might be in the way. Had but little trouble on the first day,

and went into camp near the White Sulphur Springs—a well known watering place, a beautiful situation, and one of the largest hotels, or boarding houses in Virginia, besides a hundred small houses for the use of visitors—all vacant at this time.

Next morning started early, and the whole army soon got in motion. Had not gone far before being fired into, being some distance ahead of the column. By mistake of some of Gen. Crook's orderlies coming back, we dismounted, and started ahead, but soon found, the rebs going at full speed, so ran back and remounted, then put the spurs to each side, and ran for about two miles. It seemed our horses were the best, for our boys picked up several wounded Johnnies, and got three or four good horses. By an accident one of our own good and brave fellows got shot. It proved fatal. All that day we had a hard time of it.[3]

The chaplain of the 13th West Virginia, in a letter to the *Point Pleasant Register*, places this action at Rocky Gap. He notes that Blazer's unit took about five prisoners.[4] Asbe Montgomery goes on to describe the Scouts' entry into the town of Covington, Virginia, to engage a force much larger than their own:

I'll here mention to the disgrace of Wm. Jackson and his brigade of cowardly rebs that our scouts left the command and drove our number or more over to Covington, on Jackson river. Dismounting, we left our horses, and seeing the Johnnies thick over in town, we deployed, waded the river, and charged into the town on double-quick, putting the rebels to flight, drove them out of town about a mile, till they drew up in line of battle. We had only about eighty men, but fought them two hours, in a very thin skirmish line, although they were said to be a brigade!

After using about fifty rounds of ammunition, and being out, we were bound to draw off, and passed through the town with some loss by capture. Citizens told us that Jackson reported as having a heavy fight with Gen. Crook, his own loss in killed and wounded being thirty. But if Jackson should happen to read this, I, as one of the party, can tell him it was only Crook's scouts. If his [Crook's] army had got hold of him not a grease spot would have been left of Jackson.

The men captured were Sam Harrop of the 91st Ohio and Sgt. Charles M. Schofield of the 12th Ohio. Harrop is actually reported captured near Callaghan's Station, a stage stop and tavern on the James and Kanawha Turnpike. Harrop and Schofield would now have to fight their own personal battles in the prison camps of the south.[5]

Sgt. Joseph Frith
Joseph Frith served with
the 34th Ohio Mounted
Infantry. He was killed
by friendly fire.
Courtesy Art Frith

The man shot was Joseph Frith of Company D, 34th Ohio Mounted Infantry. James J. Wood of the 34th Ohio wrote that Joseph was mistaken for a Confederate by a soldier of the 23rd Ohio Infantry. "Frith was shot by one 23rd, thought he was rebel as he was a piece off with big hat on & they were being fired on at the time Oh noble man thy fate was sudden and hard."[6]

However, another letter, possibly written by a Scout, tells a very different story. Excerpts of that letter were published in the *Norwalk Reflector* by Joe's father, George Frith, to dispel rumors that might be heard about the circumstances of his boy's death.

Joe, while in advance of Crook's division, with his company of scouts, ran upon a party of rebels; while skirmishing with them, one of Gen. Crook's headquarters clerks, of whom there were a number along with the advance, and where they had no business, was riding with revolver in hand, directly in the rear of Joe. His horse stumbled and fell, causing the discharge of his pistol. The ball entered poor Joe's back, coming out at the pit of his stomach. He was carried to the house of a Mrs. Dickinson, about three o'clock in the afternoon. He was in good spirits, and the surgeon who examined the wound

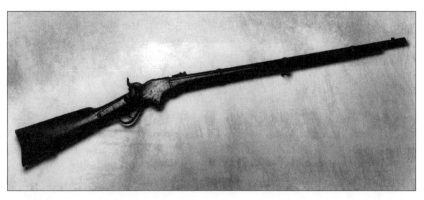

Spencer repeating rifle
This rifle, carried by Joseph Frith of the 34th Ohio Mounted Infantry, was not part of the issue to Blazer's Scouts in accordance with Gen. Philip Sheridan's orders in August 1864.
Courtesy Art Frith, photo by Stephen D. Wright

thought he would recover. But Joe would not believe it; he said he could not live. He did not fear to die, but regretted to be shot by one of his own men. He spoke of his mother frequently and wanted her to know he died like a soldier.

He seemed to suffer considerable pain during the night of the 3rd, and part of the day of the 4th; but towards noon he got easier, and seemed to rest some, but at intervals during the afternoon he seemed to suffer some pain; at seven o'clock he folded his arms across his breast, turning over on his side, and seemed to fall asleep—he was gone to his rest.

He was buried next morning on a rise of ground back of the house where he died, with the honors of a soldier. Poor Joe. His death has left a vacancy in his regt. that can never be filled. He was always ready for any thing, and always in good humor. I don't think there was a man in the regt. who had more friends, or whose loss could be more regretted. He had the best care and attendance while he lived, and when he died he was buried in as good form as the circumstances would allow.

George Frith took solace in the stoic bravery of his son and hoped it would be an example to the community in which Joe had been born and raised. "In his own pure and unselfish life, he taught you a lesson *how to live,* and in his calm composure in the hour of death, he has left you his example *how to die.*"[7]

Crook's columns now turned north, starting at half past four in the morning. The army crossed Jackson River at noon and after a seventeen-mile march camped nine miles from Warm Springs. During the day "bushwhackers showed themselves to stragglers." At four the next morning the march resumed with Hayes's brigade in the advance. At Warm Springs, Blazer's Scouts had a skirmish with the enemy. Private Frederick Spotts (Spatz) of the 34th Ohio "was shot and killed by rebels in ambush while he was in advance of the army with a squad." Companies A and F of the 23rd Ohio were ordered forward to support the Scouts and "skirmished over the mountain, when the rebels fell back." Crook's force started out the next morning at five o'clock, crossed the Cowpasture River, and went through Panther's Gap.[8]

Confederate Countermoves

During Crook's advance, Confederate forces attempted to ascertain his movements. Scouts were sent out to track the progress of Crook's column and report back to Confederate commanders. Among these was James Z. M'Chesney of the 14th Virginia Cavalry. On June 7, he and three other men were sent to scout Crook's army. They almost certainly ran into Captain Blazer and his Independent Scouts, some of whom were in Confederate uniforms.

One of the men with M'Chesney called his attention to a group of mounted men coming toward them up the mountain. M'Chesney drew his pistol and with William I. Kunkle advanced toward the group. M'Chesney and Kunkle halted about fifty or seventy-five yards from the men. The Confederate cavalryman noted that the horsemen were dressed in gray, returned his pistol to his holster, and told Kunkle to advance. He had decided they were also Confederates and M'Chesney's group would "find out where the Yankees were, which we surely did."[9] The two groups of riders rode up and greeted each other. M'Chesney asked the captain of the group if he had seen any Yankees that morning and the captain answered no. M'Chesney now notes that the whole party, some twenty in all, still had their pistols drawn, as if expecting an enemy from his direction. M'Chesney told the captain that they must have mistaken his men for enemies, to which the captain agreed. The two groups advanced, with the larger group approaching M'Chesney's group in a column of fours. They were now close enough to touch and the captain, according to M'Chesney, asked very brusquely where they had come from. M'Chesney replied, "From over the mountain." The captain repeated his question and M'Chesney gave the same evasive answer. M'Chesney was now thoroughly suspicious: "My eyes now quickly took in the situation, and I observed that, while they wore grey coats or jackets and slouch hats like our men, they all wore blue pants, their horses were branded 'U.S.' and their saddles, bridles, and all of their equipments were such as the Yankee cavalry used. I knew at once that I was in the midst of the Jessie Scouts, a body of men selected for courage and shrewdness, and felt that either Camp Chase or the grave had opened before me."[10]

M'Chesney now decided he had to act, but he must not give himself away to the "Jessie Scouts." He was also concerned that his companion, Kunkle, had come to the same realization about the true allegiance of this group of men. He was concerned Kunkle would do something before he could plan his actions. He loudly announced, and hoped Kunkle understood, that since the captain had not seen any Yankees, it would be useless for him to advance and that he would return. At the same time he began backing his mare away from the group to get room to wheel her. Just as he turned, the captain cried "Halt!" M'Chesney gave his horse the spur and in a shower of bullets escaped. His companion was not so lucky. Kunkle was wounded and captured.[11]

M'Chesney states that he was not followed very far because the pursuing Scouts saw his two other companions, McCutcheon and Fishburne, and feared additional Confederates were around who would ambush them. Fishburne was sent to Gen. John McCausland to report they had met the enemy's scouts, dressed in Confederate gray. M'Chesney and McCutcheon then hid their horses in a thicket and took a position where they could see General Crook's army passing by in the valley below. They counted "six thousand in all, as it marched by, led by the scouts, whom we had taken for comrades a short time before."[12]

Kunkle reports that he "never had the remotest idea that they were Yankees until you [M'Chesney] wheeled your horse and they commenced firing at you. How you escaped with your life is a wonder to me." Kunkle claims that these scouts fired fifteen or twenty shots at M'Chesney, including one man who fired his pistol from not ten feet away and missed. Kunkle asserts that twenty-five or thirty shots were fired in all. Just as Kunkle wheeled his horse to try to escape, a bullet struck him on the head. "Fortunately, it was a pointed ball, and striking obliquely the round surface of the skull, it did but little damage, only stunning me for a few seconds. I was determined to escape if possible. Unfortunately, three of them had gotten between you and me. I passed two

James Z. M'Chesney
James Z. M'Chesney of the 14th
Virginia Cavalry fell victim to
Blazer's "Jessie Scouts" during
the Lynchburg Campaign.
Confederate Veteran magazine

directly, both firing at me, one shot shattering my left arm and another passing through my right at the elbow." Kunkle was now helpless, with two useless arms and unable to guide his horse. Kunkle still had a third Scout to pass, one who had started off after M'Chesney. As Kunkle tried to get by the Scout, the man took "deliberate aim" but "missed me, just as I hoped he would." However, the smoke from the discharge of the pistol frightened Kunkle's horse and the animal took a path that led up a steep bank. The Scout saw his chance, dashed ahead of the fleeing Confederate, seized the reins of his horse, and "with his cocked pistol pointed at my heart ordered me to surrender. Not seeing my way clear to countermand his order, I quietly succumbed to the inevitable." Kunkle was mounted on one of the Scouts' horses and taken to General Crook, who was at the foot of the mountain with his staff.[13]

On the way the "captain of the Jessie Scouts" rode up beside Kunkle with his pistol in hand and "addressing me in a very savage tone," said, "Now, old fellow, we have you safe; and if you don't tell where [your] general is and the number of his forces, I'll d———n soon put you up the spout." Kunkle replied that he was a Confederate soldier who "had the pleasure of guarding some of your men, and I have never spoken an unkind word to one of them; and if you were a gentleman and a brave man, you would not do it either." Kunkle believed his words had their intended effect, for the "captain" turned his horse and dashed away, and "I have not seen him from that sad day to this, and I am not sorry." This man was probably not Richard Blazer himself, but perhaps one of his sergeants playing the role of a Confederate captain. The tone of voice, if related faithfully by Kunkle, does not seem to fit the soft-spoken Blazer. There is a similarity in tone and word choice that indicates the captain could have been Asbe Montgomery. However, there certainly is the possibility that Blazer was out of sorts because of the death of men such as Joe Frith, and the loss of Sam Harrop and Charles Schofield.[14]

Kunkle reports that the men who were guarding him were very uneasy as they rode down the mountain, probably expecting an ambush at every turn. The Scouts hurried the horse along by prodding the animal with two long sticks. Every time the horse was urged along, often lunging forward when beaten or prodded, Kunkle could feel the bones of his left arm grating together, which caused him excruciating pain. Eventually he was brought into the presence of George Crook, who asked him the name of his brigade, his regiment, and his colonels. Kunkle answered these questions and the interview was short. "He treated me kindly and courteously and did not try to obtain any information concerning the locations and movements of our army, for which I was truly thankful."[15] Kunkle was then taken to a spring a little further on where the soldiers lifted him from the saddle and laid him on the ground. A regiment of infantry was now passing by and Kunkle asked a soldier to call for a surgeon. "A large fine-looking man soon stepped out of the ranks to my side. I had been bleeding freely all the way down the mountain, and I told him I was about to faint." The surgeon called to a soldier who had just filled his canteen to bring the injured Confederate a drink, which revived Kunkle. The surgeon ripped Kunkle's shirtsleeves to the shoulders to examine his arms. "My boy, you will not lose your arms, but it is lucky you have fallen into my hands. Had you been taken off the battlefield to a hospital, they would have been amputated as an experiment, if for no other reason." The surgeon then pointed to a house, which just happened to be Kunkle's aunt's house, and reported that he would be left there as he was too badly wounded to be taken prisoner.

Kunkle was assisted to the house, where the surgeon dressed his arms. When approached by the "medical director," and asked if the Confederate could be put on an ambulance, the surgeon replied he could not. Kunkle was left at his aunt's house and would not have the honor of Yankee hospitality at Camp Chase, at least not at that point. Kunkle reports that he would never forget the surgeon as long as he lived. "Had he been a brother, he could not have been kinder to me. . . . He was a son of Dr. Warrick, who practiced medicine in Middlebrook, Va., years before the war and moved to Ohio." In fact the regiment of infantry was the 91st Ohio and the surgeon was Dr. John B. Warrick, a man of competence and compassion. Kunkle had indeed been lucky this day.[16]

Operations around Staunton and Lexington

Once again, the Scouts took the advance, moving on toward Staunton, "every day having some fun, and making it pay in getting horses and capturing Johnnies. At Cowpasture River had quite a little spot of fun; and on the other side the 91st Ohio had a heavy skirmish, as we did not then have the advance, after our fight at the river." Asbe reports the Rebels started to fall back after heavy skirmishing. When some cavalry delayed charging the Rebels as ordered, Captain Blazer shouted: "'Come on, boys!' No sooner said than done, started off at full speed, and soon dashed in among them—then for work. Some of them fall, and breaking like quarter horses the rest took to the brush, but not till several had been killed, and several more taken prisoners. I must mention that a Major stood to the last and fought—a fine looking man and appeared as if he ought to have been engaged in a better cause. The column came up, and all moved out tolerably quiet till nigh Staunton. Here had some skirmishing."[17]

Crook's force now joined Gen. David Hunter's, with Hunter now being in charge of the whole expedition. Hunter's command had just fought the Battle of Piedmont and had taken hundreds of prisoners. The command remained at Staunton for three days and then left for Lynchburg.

> We had the honor of advance as usual. Had not proceeded but a short distance till bang, bang rung out, and whiz came the balls, telling us they were going to dispute our advance to Lynchburg; but we thought to "try titles," so began to drive them, as usual, and to make them "git." Soon some shelter they had thrown up came in sight, telling that they would check our advance if they could. We dismounted and deployed, and had some heavy firing, and as usual left some of them to lay quiet. Finally they had to give back. The forces came up, and moved on Middlebrook. We had quite a skirmish here. I

had the best horse shot I ever rode. His loss to me was great, although he did not cost me anything. He was captured from the rebel 14th Va. cavalry.[18]

We marched on to Lexington and took possession after a day's contention. The forces lay here for a short rest, except that we did not lay any time, but did some of the boldest acts of the whole trip. We learned that some boats loaded with stores lay down the canal about two miles, and started in search of them. Found two of them lying near the reb forces. Had a few shots just above the boats, but found them unguarded. Looked them over and found a large number of small arms, six brass guns, a large lot of bacon, sugar, whisky, wines, and other property, worth $50,000 in all.[19]

Various newspaper correspondents picked up the story of the capture of the canal boats as one of the more audacious exploits of the raid. Correspondent "Cras" of the *Cincinnati Daily Gazette* reports the incident in its July 1st edition:

In the afternoon a contraband brought in word that seven Canal boats were hidden nine miles off, deeply laden with stores, &c. To secure them, Captain Blazer, with his scouts, was sent out, and skirmishing the whole route, he found the boats as reported. Burning five of them he dismounted his men and hauled the remaining two to Lexington. In them were six cannon; two six-pounders, one twelve pounder, and three mountain howitzers; nine thousand rounds of artillery ammunition, a ton and a half of powder, and Commissary stores in great abundance.[20]

The Scouts did take one casualty in this operation. While riding to get into position, William L. Harris of the 13th West Virginia Infantry, riding with his "rifle being strapped on my right side with muzzle to my foot, it prematurely discharged injuring my toes."[21] One reference to how successful the Scouts were at Lexington is in the report of the reunion of the 91st Ohio at Gallipolis, Ohio, in 1888. In an editorial statement aimed derisively at Grover Cleveland, who had apparently vetoed a special pension voted by Congress for Mrs. Dolly Blazer, the captain's widow, the *Ohio Soldier* states: "Capt. Blazer captured at one dash near Lexington, Va., more prisoners from the rebel army than the government can pay for at the rate of $30.00 in one hundred years, and this is only one of the hundreds of valuable services he performed."[22]

After capturing this lot, the Scouts took the goods safely to camp and then made a raid into the surrounding mountains, where other goods were hidden by the citizens, in hopes of keeping them from the enemy. The Scouts, Montgomery explains,

> Captured a lot of cattle which the citizens had driven out. I and two others went out perhaps twenty miles, till dark, and found seven wagons loaded with bacon, flour, etc. As we could do no more, we set them on fire and left, as it was not very healthy to remain there, as a darky had been left there to watch the wagons, and said the rebs were thick just over at Mr. Somebody's—I don't recollect the name. Started back to camp, and rode till a late hour, coming up to a house, in full trot, and seeing a light halted. The lady of the house came to the door, and passing ourselves as rebel soldiers, asked if any Yankees had passed there that day, and she replied none only a small company. She answered many questions promptly, adding that her husband had got his leg broken the day before. We then called for supper, as we had rode hard all day, telling her we would pay for it. She said, get off [dismount], which we did, and went in. Before eating, we informed them we were Yankees. At this the woman seemed scared, but the man lay contented, and told us about his broken leg. After a hearty supper, remounted, and struck a line for camp in haste. Found all right.[23]

Montgomery notes that after the affairs of Lexington, the columns marched on toward Lynchburg. They camped near Buchanan and found that General Averell's cavalry force had defeated a Rebel force and burned part of the town. The force crossed the mountains the next morning, passing by the Peaks of Otter, "considerable of a curiosity to travelers, several peaks towering to the clouds, looking very small at the top." In fact almost everyone in the Army of West Virginia who wrote a letter or made a diary entry wrote about passing the Peaks of Otter, the highest point in the state of Virginia. There was a profusion of rhododendron in full bloom on the southern slope of the mountains. As Rutherford B. Hayes's adjutant reached the base of the Peaks, he looked back at the army winding its way down through the rhododendron flowers, which they picked as they passed down the mountain. Now each man had a sprig of blossoms in the muzzle of his rifle, making the column look like "a moving bank of flowers."[24]

After passing the mountains, the force came to what Montgomery calls Farmer's Valley, "splendid looking country of well-cultivated land." Hunter's combined force rested here for two or three days, engaging in foraging. However, this rest did not set well with some of the troops, who were sure that they were "waiting for the rebs to reinforce so as to whip us when we got Lynchburg —for Hunter, who was in command, at that time, could march men well, and take good care of an army, if there were no enemy to contend with or meet."[25]

"But after his own time," General Hunter left their present camp and moved on down the valley toward Lynchburg, striking the railroad at Liberty. The army tore some of the railroad up while the Scouts went foraging "and gathering all the good horses we could find without much opposition, only once in a while a nice little chase, as we could route a small party, which would leave in the direction of Lynchburg, proving by the way they went that the rebs were collecting there for a fight. So they did for we had quite a battle."[26]

The army moved slowly forward, in Montgomery's opinion. "At 12 o'clock we halted to get a bite of something to eat, and rest a short time, giving all chances for preparation on the enemy's side." Finally, they moved again slowly and cautiously up the road. Around 3:30, while moving slowly, with a strong advance, the Scouts being in the rear of the advance regiment, "the first rest we had from Lewisburg, the first crash of a defending 12 pounder was heard." Asbe reports: "here comes the messenger of death, screaming and telling us if we came any closer there would be more trouble. But that one had scarcely started on its way, before boom, boom, went the heavy growl of the iron bull dogs."[27]

The Battle of Lynchburg

The army moved into position, with Crook forming his small "army" and engaging the Confederate forces about 4 P.M. The rattle of small arms fire and the crash of the big guns was soon heard widespread across the field, with the Union men cheering while "everything is in motion. Soon the dust took a rise." The Confederates had selected a good position, behind breastworks at the edge of a thick woods, "leaving to our brave-hearted boys a long range, in open land, and a hollow to pass." Crook's men knew only three choices awaited them. They would have to assault the position and

> put the rebels out of that place [or] suffer awful loss, or fall back and leave the field. To fall back was not their way of doing, and to stand there and let the enemy have all the advantage did not pay, so while everything was interesting, and men were falling, and the very earth seemed to shake, the order came to charge. With terrific yells and cheers, comrades encouraging, officers

waving swords and leading on to battle, like a whirlwind the lines swept across the fields, and, with strong arms and brave hearts, they soon gained cover of the woods. Then they cheered in token of victory, which made the blood thrill through every loyal man's heart. In a moment, seemingly, the battle was won. Dark had now covered the land, only the gentle moon was kindly aiding our comrades, the scouts and musicians, to carry off the wounded and take charge of the prisoners.[28]

General Hunter's leadership was harshly criticized by officers and men during this campaign. Save for the anger that flared in the enlisted men and lower-ranking officers at Petersburg when the initial successful assaults were not exploited, nowhere else do Union men rail so against slothful leadership. As one newspaper put it, "Gen. Hunter is responsible. But we didn't take Lynchburg, and why? Simply because Major General Hunter allowed a failure in the first most important element of a raid, *celerity of movement.*" The correspondent noted that a raid must be made quickly, taking advantage of surprise before the enemy can bring forces to bear. Clearly, Hunter's dawdling had deprived the Union of a major accomplishment.[29] Montgomery describes Hunter's inaction:

Now was the time to strike at Lynchburg. But no! Hunter was in command, and must hew his way, so the men lay in line all night, or rather skirmished, for there was a continual firing. In the morning, about seven o'clock, the work commenced again. By 10 o'clock the air was full of lead and shells flying, while orderlies and aids were loping in every direction, carrying orders. Every brave man was at his post, some dealing out death to the foe, while others were waiting with anxiety for orders. So desperate was the struggle that no man seemed to desire to speak. By this time the enemy had been reinforced to that number that we could easily see that the odds were against us; and constantly cheers were sent up from the rebel lines, telling us that they were gaining in number. Yet it did not seem to discourage our tired, but brave and unflinching comrades. One o'clock came, and still the battle raged desperately. About this time, I do not believe any one of our brave comrades will ever forget the trying moments. God bless them, poor fellows, some of them lost sight of the scene and their country forever. Just at the time when you would think no more could be done, the rebs were reinforced so strongly that they thought our artillery and trains and horses were all at their mercy. So they formed in mass, thickly as stubble on a newly harvested field—charged our little lines, and came driving our men back; with fiendish looks and savage screams—the air dark with lead, smoke and dust—and the ground strewn with the slain and stained with blood.

They forced our lines back by inches, till our main line formed strong and firm, when our artillery seemingly sprang from the ground, as though it saw the danger, and in its strength poured charges of grape into the rebel hordes, awfully scattering their fiendish forces. Our boys made a desperate effort, straightened their lines, and charged them close with the bayonet, and poured deadly volleys into their faces, with clenched teeth. Many of their gray covered frames now lay over the field. In turn, our men had started forward; their lines reeled and staggered; our men dashed into them and drove the whole force back and over their works. The reader may judge for himself the loss in such a struggle.

When this desperate effort was over, a kind of lull seemed to prevail. The firing was less, there being only occasionally a heavy boom of cannon at a distance, and a few shots nearby, and a heavy skirmish, till dark, when our trains being out of the way and everything ready our infantry drew off quietly and left the field. The scouts were then ordered to form a skirmish line and hold the rebs in check until the infantry could get ahead as far as possible. Our orders were to keep up a continual fire just as fast as we could, so as to deceive the enemy. This we did by dismounting and advancing in range, and there pouring a constant fire into the rebs, until by coming slowly toward us they found what our force was, when we had to mount and skedaddle to save ourselves. After riding a mile or so, I with the Ninth Virginia boys, and perhaps some others, took the rear and kept a sharp lookout for anything that might come up. So we traveled all night, with our scouts in the rear. Daylight found us some two miles behind the column, and all moving along, tired, sleepy, and hungry, and no time to sleep, rest or eat—only those who had a bit of cracker could eat it, and march. By this time rations had become scarce and likely to get scarcer; so marched on till about 9 o'clock, when in our rear we could discover, as we thought, Johnnies, and so they were, but not in much force. Had some skirmishing until the next morning, when the skirmishing became lively; and during that day had several hot skirmishes. Lost one of our scouts, but thinking ourselves the lucky men, had no complaints to make here.[30]

The casualty was Ephraim Helm of Company H of the 12th Ohio Infantry at Buford's Gap. The 5th West Virginia Infantry had been under fire when they were ordered to open ranks to let Blazer's men through. While the Scouts were passing through the ranks, "the rebel balls were whizzing about in a very lively manner." One of the balls struck Ephraim in the forehead, killing him instantly.

The dead Scout tumbled from his horse onto Private James Chambers of the 5th West Virginia, who describes "his crushed and mangled head striking my shoulder and smearing the blood and brains over my coat. I tell you that looked like war. . . . So soiled was my blouse and it being warm weather, so unpleasant was the odor, that I threw the blouse away, and went through the Lynchburg campaign in my shirtsleeves."[31]

Ephraim's mother, Keziah, was left to mourn her son. He was killed on June 19 as the Scouts acted as the rear guard. The Scouts would often act in concert with regiments of infantry, alternating as the rear guard. The heavier infantry regiments would probably be brought up if the scouts were pressed hard enough. The Scouts' being constantly "at the point," in modern military terminology, was one of the reasons only the best men were detached to the unit. It was dangerous work and even the best men took casualties.[32]

> At Liberty we halted and gave the Johnnies a dressing, then moved slowly on, leaving a regiment to give them a salute. On the Johnnies came, riding quietly along till in range, when a volley was poured into their ranks leaving a number in the road—the whole command about facing and off like so many wild cattle, our boys then quickly coming on. Rations being very scarce, and no prospect of being plentier, our men felt bound to make the best of it they could, and gain a point more desirable for sleep or rations. As there was a fine lot of darkies, and Gen. Hunter being a great friend to this class, many of the rations had to be divided out to them and empty wagons filled with his friends, while tired and worn out soldiers had to walk, or lay down and starve and die; so over the mountains we came, such as I never crossed before. Poor fellows, . . . dragging their weary legs along. No wonder many of them gave out, for it was enough to kill a mule, and did a great many, as well as horses. I cannot say how many, but a large amount in value, besides some artillery and many wagons.[33]

Famine on the March—The Aftermath of the Lynchburg Campaign

In fact the Lynchburg campaign may have been proportionately the hardest of the war on men and horses. Unlike the just-concluded Dublin Raid, where the main climatic enemy had been cold rain, hail, sleet, and snow, the men now faced steamy temperatures and hot, dusty roads. As always there were the mountains. For the men of the Army of West Virginia, there was never straight-line mileage; the route had to be measured in height climbed as well. Perhaps no command in the Civil War, including Jackson's vaunted "foot cavalry," marched as hard as these men on these two campaigns. Major T. W. Turner of the 36th Ohio, another veteran of the campaign, observed, "Men actually marched asleep. There were rumors that men starved to death, but I think this is an error. For my part I can truthfully assert that for the last four days I had only the crumbs that were left in my haversack, probably equal to one army cracker." Turner found a broken-down wagon that had three sacks of roasted coffee, which he threw into the headquarters tent. "The last of it was dealt out at Anderson [unlocated]. Gen. Crook sent over to ask for coffee. This may have kept up our strength, but I cannot now recall that I really suffered on account of hunger. There were thousands, however, who did not even have coffee, and I have no doubt suffered greatly. Clover heads were a luxury and were sought out earnestly."[34]

Food for both horses and men became a real problem. Cavalrymen slept in the saddle and were often surprised when they awoke to discover the nose bags of their horses had been taken while they passed an infantry regiment. Another officer reported that men took corn from the mules as they were fed and ate the grain raw. Some of the men may have gone even further. After the war, Pvt. Samuel Spencer of the 9th West Virginia related that a messmate had cooked up dog to eat. Samuel said to his comrade, "I know this is dog. It's tough and stringy and smells." While this incident's actual location is not known, the men were certainly famished enough at the end of the Lynchburg Raid to have devoured a pooch. Some men took an even more extreme measure. "It was credibly stated in the Twelfth Ohio that men were even known— so great was their suffering for food—to have gathered up the undigested kernels of corn left by the cavalry and train animals, and washed, cooked, and ate them."[35]

The men eventually reached New River and their accustomed camps. There they received rations that revived many. In fact, couriers had been sent out with orders for wagon trains to be sent to relieve the column. One such train was under escort of the Butler County (Ohio) National Guard. They were to meet and report with the first train to General Crook, at Big Sewell Mountain.

Pvt. William Doran
William Doran of Company G, 2nd West Virginia Cavalry, was detailed to Blazer's Scouts for duty as a blacksmith, April 5, 1864.
Courtesy Cumberland Gallery Collection

Nothing occurred on the march worthy of note until we were nearing Dogwood Gap, when we suddenly came upon a squad of about half a dozen mounted men in rebel uniform, with feathers stuck in their hats, and presenting altogether a gay and fanciful appearance. When questioned, their answers were no more satisfactory than their appearance; but by the time suspicion could take definite shape, the supposed rebs were gone. Several officers, acting on the military maxim, "leave no enemy in the rear," rode back to look after them, when they proved to be a detachment from the celebrated "Blazer's Scouts," who, as we afterward learned, had been into Lynchburg, and gone the whole round of their works.[36]

The fact that all these "Rebels" had feathers stuck in their hats may have been a recognition signal for other units in Crook's army. Earlier Jessie Scouts had used white scarves knotted in a special way around the neck to identify them to their own comrades. Also, special recognition greetings were used, with words that would only be known to the Jessies and those of their companions who might meet them on the road.[37]

Asbe Montgomery summed up the expedition with no blame placed against General Crook, but with convictions that Hunter would have to atone for his sluggishness before a higher command: "I have told of some of the hardships, but as I write my mind runs over the trip, and I find my pen has failed to portray our difficulties, and my language is far short of the trials and starvation our brave boys endured. There was not a murmur against Gen. Crook, but I don't say that some did not curse Hunter, and forever will as long as they can curse at all. I will leave Hunter alone, with him and his God, for his mishaps."[38]

Actually, Asbe's language quite eloquently describes the ordeals of the Lynchburg raid. The men were bitterly disappointed that Crook had not been in command of all the forces on the raid. He inspired confidence in the men and they loved him for his quiet, unassuming leadership. He would probably have pressed the men, as he did on the Dublin Raid, but victory would have been the result.

In fact, the Lynchburg Raid did have its accomplishments. Even the Southern press had to acknowledge the destruction of valuable property of the Confederacy. The *Lynchburg Virginian* is cited in the Yankee press by correspondents of the *Cincinnati Gazette:* "The damage done by the Yankees to the Virginia and Tennessee Railroad, while not fully ascertained, is reported to be very heavy. Besides burning the bridges across Big and Little Otter Rivers, and Elk Creek, the track is said to be torn up for several miles, all the depots between here and Big Lick are burned, and the water tanks destroyed. If these damages be correctly stated, it will take some time to put the road in running order again."[39]

Prelude to Shenandoah Valley Operations

The men had scant time to rest. They returned to the Kanawha Valley briefly, with most of the command stopping at Camp Piatt, while the Scouts returned to their old camp. The men were paid, and probably attempted to take care of their affairs as much as possible, writing letters home and to newspapers relating the events of the last few weeks.[40]

However, a crisis was brewing in the war. Despite Federal successes and constant pressure by Grant and Sherman, the Confederates now had an opportunity with Hunter's retreat into West Virginia. Jubal Early was now free to march down the Shenandoah Valley and threaten Washington itself. On July 9, just outside Frederick, Maryland, Early defeated a hastily organized force under Gen. Lew Wallace. Although a Union defeat, Wallace gained time for the defense of Washington. Early, slowed by battle, and slow to advance, eventually went all the way to Fort Stevens, just outside the city. However, faced with Union reinforcements and the realization that he probably could not prevail, Early started back to the Shenandoah.

On July 8, just one day before the Battle of Monocacy, the Army of West Virginia was on its way to the east to reinforce Federal forces against Early. Some of the Army marched by land to Parkersburg and others went by steamship. From Parkersburg, the entire force would be moved by train to Harpers Ferry, and into the Shenandoah Valley.

Montgomery, in his usual colorful language, reported that they "found the Valley infested with rebs, and blowing over what they would do. Gen. Crook took them in hand with Gen. Duvall, with other brave officers, and their gallant little army went to work. Soon there was business enough for our scouts in attending to Mosby and White, the greatest guerrillas perhaps in the war."[41]

After retreating from Washington, Early was pursued by the 6th Army Corps. After asking to be relieved of command when General Wright was placed in command of the forces concentrating on Early, Hunter remained in command of the Department of West Virginia, but Crook was now placed in command of the troops in the field. That was probably a cause for celebration in the Army of West Virginia for the men knew Crook would not let them down. Crook and Wright attempted to catch Early between them, but the Confederates were able to pass between the two forces and get through Snicker's Gap on July 17. Early's rear guard slowed up the Federals. Montgomery notes that the scouts "served as sharpshooters, and got highly complimented." The Scouts, along with the rest of the army, were now fully engaged in the Shenandoah campaign. "From that time we were constantly riding and catching up such men as were a terror to any army."[42]

The great Shenandoah Valley had seen much conflict in three years of war. The Valley had been a breadbasket for the Confederacy and a key strategic feature of the eastern theater of war. The Valley itself is mostly gently rolling and, at the time of the Civil War, "interspersed by oak forests without underbrush, vast cultivated fields, and innumerable springs of cool, hard or limestone water." The undersurface is limestone that crops out in every direction, making a convenient source of cheap building material for roads and fences. "Corn, wheat, oats, and rye are the principal crops raised in peacetime, and much attention is paid to the raising of cattle, horses, and sheep, also. The butter made here is equal in quality to any in the known world." This describes the Valley in peacetime, but it has now known three years of war and only about one-third of the Valley is under cultivation. "[F]ields for miles in extent on either hand, are one vast waste of wire grass. Literally this is now a land overflowing with milk and honey, and the soldiers of both armies have had a bountiful supply." Although it has been supposed that Early was in the Valley to secure crops, "he has not sent a single barrel of wheat out of the valley." He had his men thresh large quantities of grain, but it was for his own use. "The cornfields are more extended, but the yield of corn will not be one tithe of what it would have been had not two armies passed backward and forward through the fields just when the ears were in the most tempting state of roast or boil. Our men have been luxuriated on green corn for six weeks, and serious fears are entertained that so little food remains that there will be much actual suffering among the citizens compelled by circumstances to remain here during the coming Winter." For two seasons, the farmers had been trying to plant as much ground as possible but they noted that it did not pay. "The bulk of the crops were taken by the rebels, and paid for in worthless Confederate notes; nearly all the remainder would be taken by the Union troops, and paid for in worthless receipts, so that between the two they got their labor for their pains."[43]

Philip Sheridan Takes Command

The army pursued Early, but a critical mistake was made when the 6th Corps was ordered out of the Valley. Early then turned on Crook's command and attacked at Kernstown. Crook's infantry was defended on the flanks by the cavalry of Averell and Duffie. Unfortunately, when the Confederates attacked, Averell failed to support Crook and the army had to fall back. It was only through the skill of Crook and the tenacity of his infantrymen that a rout was avoided. Asbe reports that the Scouts also had to fall back, crossing the Potomac at Williamsport, and marched into Maryland. It was at this time that the town of Chambersburg, Pennsylvania, was burned. The army proceeded to Frederick and then to Harpers Ferry.

Now Asbe Montgomery relates the actions which would give Blazer's Scouts a place in Civil War history and especially in the lore of the Shenandoah Valley:

> Here [Harpers Ferry], received reinforcements, and Gen. Sheridan took command of the Army of the Shenandoah. Our scouts by this time had become greatly reduced in numbers, and Sheridan hearing of our untiring energies, issued an order to fill up our number to one hundred men, and that we should be armed with Spencer's Repeating Rifles. This was done while lying at Halltown. Each man of us had a revolver, the most two, and his seven-shot rifle. Although Mosby had some five men to our one, yet we felt like trying him on all occasions. Had several smart brushes with him, "flaxed him out," and took several of his men, while he had not got one of our scouts.[44]

Sheridan's order to Gen. Christopher C. Augur requested Spencer rifles for the Scouts. "I have 100 men who will take the contract to clean out Mosby's gang. I want 100 Spencer rifles for them. Send them to me if they can be found in Washington."[45]

Sheridan may not have had to equip all the men with Spencer rifles. The men of the 34th Ohio and the 2nd West Virginia Cavalry were probably already equipped with these weapons. In a telegram dated April 25th, 1864, from Charleston, West Virginia, to the chief of the Cavalry Department, General Duffie requested information about Spencer rifles ordered for the 34th Ohio. A previous telegram sent from Washington on April 16 by Brig. Gen. George D. Ramsey, chief of ordnance, states that mounted infantry could not be armed with cavalry arms. A Spencer rifle in the possession of the family of Joseph Allen Frith may be the only documentation that General Duffie eventually won the argument with the ordnance department.[46]

Asbe gives a vivid description of Mosby and White:

> Some of my readers may not know the character of Mosby and White. Mosby was said to have in the neighborhood of 1,000 men, himself being a shrewd fellow, formerly a lawyer. This body of men were bound by oaths never to yield to the Yankee forces, also sworn to spare no energies, going through all the hardships of guerrilla warfare, destroying even home friends to carry their point. They were well trained, daring imps. By the aid of their friends at Berryville, Charlestown [Charles Town], Halltown, Winchester, in Loudoun Valley, and in other parts, continually knew of the movement of our army and trains. With a picket looking from a high point, or a child sent to let them

know of a squad of men, or a dozen stragglers, or part or the whole of a train not safely guarded, they would, with good horses under them, pounce down on anything they could manage, then put off with their prisoners or plunder to the mountains in Loudoun county. Then they were safe, for few of our men know anything about the fords on the Shenandoah river. So Mosby and White's men became a source of terror, not only to small bodies of the army but to all travelers, and even to some of their own friends. Anything they wished from their Confederate brethren, they took, as a good horse, or feed, or clothes, or anything else.[47]

Asbe's evaluation of the environment in which Mosby operated shows the Scouts understood how Mosby could have acted with such seeming immunity for so long. Montgomery makes a good point when he notes that few of the men in the army knew anything about the fords of the Shenandoah. Most of the regular units of the army probably had only limited knowledge of these fords, perhaps only from studying maps. The fords across the Shenandoah became a major source of contention between Mosby's men and Blazer's Scouts. Asbe is very proud that Blazer's men soon became intimately acquainted with the country and were able to operate in it very well. In fact, the mountains of Loudoun County probably appeared quite hospitable compared to the extreme terrain of the Gauley, Kanawha, and New River country:

I must tell you how we managed to compete with Mosby and his desperate gang of cut-throats. In moving with the army from the 15th of August to the 23rd, we were constantly in motion, and fighting all the time from Winchester to Berryville; thence to Cedar Creek; capturing numbers of Johnnies— then falling back to Winchester, and to Halltown. In this time by watching all the movements of the gang, we had not only caught some of Mosby's men, and caused a number of them to come to trouble anybody; but also Mosby had learned that somebody else could hide, shoot, and dash, and swim rivers as well as his fellows. We had the liberty to take any good horse we could find; besides, by this time, we had taken fifteen or twenty of Col. Mosby's best stock of Virginia blood, and found ourselves as good on horseback as any in either army; and having the advantage of taking any good horse we could find, and each one wanting the best horse, oftentimes our small squads ventured farther than was prudent. This caused us to have to get up and "dust" sometimes, like a streak of lightning, for three or four miles. Go out and leave the company for four or five miles, and the first thing would be: "Halt, you d——d Yankees!" Then we knew what to do. It was "git." Very often, bang would be our first salutation, then a yell, so now for the fastest horses.[48]

Although Asbe's colorful language makes this activity appear to be organized horse thievery, the unit was undoubtedly under General Crook's strict orders to reimburse civilians for horses. Of course taking horses from combatants was a different story. It is also well to understand that Blazer's men were well mounted and could compete with Mosby's men in quality of horseflesh.

Crook's Army Victorious at Berryville

The Scouts operated in this manner until August 23, when they drew their Spencer rifles and their numbers grew to 100. Blazer and his officers now told the men that their mission was to drive Mosby out of the Shenandoah Valley. The attitude of the Scouts is related by Montgomery:

> That was just what we wanted, so left the command [main body of the army] entirely, and struck for tall timber, as we called—that is crossed the Shenandoah river and the mountain [Blue Ridge], and took our stand in Loudoun Valley—calling ourselves "boss." On Thursday, 25th [August] had quite a skirmish, took six of White's men, after a long chase, and five or six good horses. This gave a name to us in the Valley, and word was carried, far and near, that Blazer and his scouts were in Loudoun Valley. . . . Mosby and his men outnumbered us so materially that we had to look sharp, to save our necks, for it was no use to talk of being captured, unless we wanted our throats cut from ear to ear, or to be swung up by the neck. Every day brought fresh scenes. Almost every day we crossed the river and mountain, and had a race and sometimes quite a spat. The reb army lay in the Valley, and it being full of rebs, and nothing but the river and mountains to hinder the reb cavalry from cutting us off, and Mosby in the same valley and mountains that we were, made it pretty scaly times. But we rode all over the valley and any place we desired.
>
> In a week's time, White, who was a thief, had to leave Loudoun Valley, "broke," with one man left him. We all the time made inroads, clearing out all lawless parties, and gathering up good horses, making the rebs think we were in earnest, for we "used up" Mosby's men on every occasion.[49]

Asbe reported the unit crossed the Shenandoah at Snicker's Ford on August 31 with "a lot of horses" and made their way to the camp of the army,

which was located at Bolivar Heights, above Harpers Ferry. Montgomery now relates his part in one of the most important actions between Mosby and Blazer's Scouts. The Scouts rested until the September 3, 1864, when the army began moving again in the direction of Berryville.[50]

Berryville was described by one correspondent as a "dilapidated and unfortunate town," known to the local residents "by the unenviable *nom de plume* of 'Battle Town'—so named because of the pugilistic character of the country people, who used in former times, to meet here once a week to purchase their small supplies. On these occasions, an immense amount of poor whiskey would be consumed, and as a necessary consequence, there was always more or less fighting; and broken heads and bloody noses were the rule, not the exception." Berryville's alias would soon be appropriate for more than Saturday afternoon market brawls. A much deadlier brawl was in the making.[51]

The Scouts screened the force along the Shenandoah because they expected Mosby to try to pick up stragglers, ambulances, or supply trains. "We moved cautiously, watching every bird, almost, that flew across our path, finally gaining the gap or ferry, but found no signs. Turned our course and cautiously moved down the river. Learned of a large force of Mosby's scouts, from a colored man, he telling us they had gone in the direction of the ferry. From this we knew they would learn of our whereabouts." The hour was late and Blazer's men suspected Mosby's force would cross the river or join Early's army at Berryville. This was but a short distance from the Scouts, and since the Union army was proceeding on Berryville, they proceeded down the river about five miles and halted at dark.[52]

> We had scarcely dismounted when we saw the blaze of the guns, and soon heard the booming of the cannon, which told us plainly what was going on. So desperate was the engagement, and the firing so heavy, though we were three or four miles off, there was a constant blaze to be seen. We waited for the signal of victory some time, for sometimes the forces on both sides would cheer, and you could tell from the sound of the small arms when either side was falling back. . . . Finally, we heard the yells start at the head of the lines, and like a telegraphic dispatch, it flew from one to the other of the regiments.[53]

The Scouts realized the battle had been won. It was a major engagement at Berryville. It is also unusual that it took place when it was really quite dark; the Scouts could see the flash of battle at some distance. "All right, boys" said the captain, "you have had a hard time, but stood nobly." The Scouts were now permitted to rest, but for Asbe Montgomery, sleep was elusive; "there was no sleep for me," he observed, "for I had a son and many friends whom I well knew had been struggling on that battle field for their country's cause." Asbe's son James had come through this battle unharmed, but would be wounded later at Winchester on September 19. Asbe was not to know of the fate of his son or of his friends, for the Scouts were in the saddle the next morning to make sure that Mosby did not operate against the army, for this was "a good time for them to 'pitch in' and gather up some ambulances and wounded men." They started in the direction of Snicker's Ferry at daylight and after some time arrived at that point, but once again saw no sign.[54]

The Fight at Myer's Ford

They crossed the Shenandoah again and started up the mountain. "Over the mountain is a smart little village. Here by close examination, as rain had fallen the night before, we discovered a sign of horsemen, some hundreds, as we supposed, but turned out to be 150 of Mosby's picked men, as they told us that day about 1 o'clock." The Scouts followed the trail and discovered the force had once again taken to the mountain, "five or six miles below here [Snickersville or perhaps Purcellville] and wound their way to the top, as though they intended to cross the river and come below where we had been the day before, and get in rear of our army; and while we were hunting for them near Snicker's Gap or Berryville, they could pounce on some weak point, and gobble up some trains, or tired and wounded men, commit some cruelty, and then gallop off, pleasing their fancy at the Government's expense"[55]

The Scouts suspected that Mosby's force was trying to get further south and come through one of the other gaps across the Blue Ridge. "But the time was over for Mosby to have such fun without its costing him something, which had already been proven to him too clearly to be a disbeliever in matters of that kind, for we had been thrown in his way for some time."[56]

The Scouts finally gained the summit of the Blue Ridge, from which they could observe the broad expanse of the Valley and actually observe both armies. They could see parts of their own army and at a distance of seven or eight miles Confederate forces were moving.

Ford on the Shenandoah River

Fords such as this one on the Shenandoah, as well as the passes in the Blue Ridge Mountains, were key strategic positions in the campaign for the Shenandoah Valley in 1864.

Massachusetts Commandery, Military Order of the Loyal Legion

U.S. Army Military History Institute

But that was not our business. We knew our enemy was near, and in numbers
the odds in his favor, for they had halted on the mountain and fed, which
gave us some idea how far they were ahead and of their numbers. We turned
down the mountain, following them, and after riding some two miles slowly
and cautiously, came to the bottom of the hill, and halting, sat listening a
short time. Just below us we heard something like troops. The first division
dismounted, and we crept slowly up, thinking them halted and resting, and
expecting to pour a volley into them, then the rest of our company to charge,
hoping to use them up. But when we got to the spot found two fellows drinking at an applejack establishment. Taking them, we accused them of being
Mosby's men. They became alarmed and promised if we would not hurt them
that they would give us information and go with us to the place, so they got
their grant from the Captain and the men in general.

We mounted, riding slowly and carefully so as not to be led into a snare
by the young men. Soon we came near the river and large farms being cleared,
and the road we were on led square up to the field. As the advance came
within about one hundred yards of the field it was fired into from the edge of
the field. Soon several shots were fired, and the noise of horses told us plainly

that the rebs had been overhauled. The road was narrow, just so that two horses could handily run abreast. Being at the head of the company, riding by the Captain's side, I saw them forming four deep, and then commence firing very fast as they fell in. I said to the Captain, there they are as thick as fleas, he turning his horse around to see that the company was all right. They were overshooting us. I saw that we should soon be exposed to a more certain range of their shots, and not liking to give them the advantage in shots, as the Captain was turned around, I shouted, "Come on, boys," in order to charge them face to face. Putting spurs to my horse, he being large and active, and only about fifty yards from them, I was in a breath up to them, and yelling to them like a madman: "You scoundrels; we will give you something else to do besides taking ambulances and wagon trains."

Without knowing their number, we were all in a heap in a moment, shooting them off, and dashing around among them. They stood for a short time, but finding that we were shooting them off, none of our men having yet fallen, they began to fall back. Soon everything was on our side and crowding up, they began to run in the direction of the river, which they had to do to effect their escape, rushing along by the side of a stone fence, and our boys after them. My horse, by this time, was wounded; and some of our men were now wounded, and unfortunately some had been thrown off. But we charged down on them furiously. Here one of our men just by me received a shot in the left cheek, and soon, poor fellow, bid good bye to all that was dear in the world.[57]

The fatality was most likely William Sloan of Company C, 34th Ohio Volunteer Infantry. Among the other wounded were Jeremiah Wilson of Company K, 9th West Virginia, and Benjamin F. M. Fletcher of Company C, 14th West Virginia, who was wounded in the middle of the left thigh. Sgt. William Leaf of the 12th Ohio was wounded through the shoulder and left lung. Montgomery continues:

My horse was large and stout, so notwithstanding he was wounded, I rushed him on some of their horses; and the fellow who had just shot my poor comrade on my right, directing his revolver at my face, luckily I saw it just about two feet from me. Not having time to pull the hammer back I aimed a blow at his arm, and sent his revolver over his head. Then I said to him, "my time next," so just as soon as I could pull my hammer back and place my finger, I sent him whirling, not to shoot any Union man again.

Being in the thickest ranks of the rebs I had a chance to do all the work I wished for a short time. Having a seven-shooter and two navy [Colt] revolvers, you may guess how I used them, till a shot struck me in my left shoulder, and passing through my body, it lodged against my right shoulder blade, stopping me from fighting for that day. But it did not stop our men from the fun. Soon the rebs left for a land more healthy, leaving their dead and wounded in our hands, with some fourteen or fifteen of their horses killed and wounded. The rebs numbered 150 as we learned from one of their lieutenants who had his arm shot off. One of their lieutenants was also killed. They had about 20 men killed and wounded. Our loss was one killed and five wounded. Being in Mosby's range it became necessary for us to get over the river and take care of our wounded men and the prisoners. Some old wagons were prepared, and after attending to the wounded as well as could be done, they were put in the wagons, myself being among the number, and conveyed to Sandy Hook Hospital.[58]

Asbe notes, "My wound was bad, the ball being lodged under the shoulder blade so it could not be extracted. I lay for some time under the treatment of the best physicians." Indeed, Montgomery was very lucky, for the ball nearly hit his spinal column. He remained at the field hospital at Sandy Hook to allow him to strengthen and the wound to heal enough so he could be moved. On September 13 he was transferred to the general hospital in Frederick, Maryland. Asbe was then transferred to Mower General Hospital, Chestnut Hill, Pennsylvania (near Philadelphia), on September 20. Mower was a large hospital with probably some of the best facilities and doctors available to the Union. The principal part of his recovery would take place here. He left Mower on October 28, 1864, and arrived at the general hospital in Parkersburg on November 2, 1864, where he remained until he was returned to duty December 19.[59]

It is difficult to reconcile the Mosby accounts, Asbe Montgomery's account, and the newspaper stories of what happened on September 4. Blazer defeated Lt. Joseph N. Nelson and his men at Myer's Ford, but it also appears he was involved in an affair between one of Crook's ambulance trains and another ambulance train in the area. The distance between the two incidents is only a few miles, so it is possible.

Williamson reported that Mosby and part of his command were out in search of more pickings behind Union lines on the west side of the Shenandoah. Williamson asserts that Mosby, after dividing his command several times, was down to five or six men, including himself. Nevertheless, he captured a couple of ambulances and some prisoners, about fourteen in all, including a lady who supposedly was married to an officer in Gen. Nathaniel Banks's command. After capturing this group, Mosby was reported to have been surprised in turn by Captain Hull of the 2nd New York Cavalry, who rescued five ambulances. Mosby sent the prisoners off with Joseph W. Owen. Mosby is reported to have captured about thirteen horses in the affair.[60]

Various newspaper accounts put the size of the ambulance train that belonged to Crook's command at thirty-five wagons. Initially, it was reported to have been without an escort. Later reports indicate that the train was guarded but that the force was badly deployed for its defense. The *Philadelphia Inquirer* carried the story on the front page, dateline Harpers Ferry, September 5, 1864:

> The ubiquitous MOSBY is around again. An ambulance train of thirty-five wagons, which started from here yesterday, were all, except four, captured by that guerrilla. These wagons had delivered their wounded and were returning to the front, and it was known that it would have to pass through a country . . . all of which was infested by the enemy, yet, strange to say, no escort was offered or given them. This is not the first train that has been captured, and the enemy need feel no uneasiness about either stock, supplies, wagons or munitions of war, if this thing is to be permanent.
>
> This same train from the front, with its cargo of wounded, without any escort, deposited them, and returned without reporting to General STEVENSON. The latter, hearing of the guerrillas whereabouts, ordered Captain BLAZER, with one hundred picked men, to proceed in search [of] MOSBY, and endeavor to recapture our lost property. He met the enemy, two hundred strong, and after a gallant contest, succeeded in retaking forty horses and about five of Mosby's followers.[61]

This account is interesting in that it differs considerably from the accounts of Mosby's men. The taking of an ambulance train of thirty-five wagons would have been a considerable feather in Mosby's cap. However, he lost it almost immediately. Initially, the report of the wagon train taken without an escort was quite an embarrassment in the papers and people started asking why. Sheridan replied to chief of staff Gen. Henry Halleck on September 8, "There is no truth in the newspaper report of the loss of Crook's ambulance train. Only one ambulance was lost and some 12 or 13 horses. The train was *attacked and stampeded by 6 of Mosby's men.*" Could Mosby's chroniclers have picked up on Sheridan's report that only six men had stampeded the train to come up with their stories of the action and cover a rather embarrassing turn-around of events? Also, two officers were taken in this raid: Maj. Horace Kellogg, 123rd Ohio Infantry, and Surgeon J. Phillip Shelling, 34th Ohio Infantry. They were among those who were rescued, so Mosby missed a chance to get two prize officers. It is curious that this capture is not mentioned in the Mosby accounts. But the trophies had escaped, so could not be hung above the fireplace for the hunter to brag about in later years.[62]

Captain Blazer filed the following report of the engagement at Myer's Ford. He does not indicate he was involved in rescuing Crook's train, but it is possible since he would have been on the west side of the Shenandoah after driving Mosby's force across the ford.

> Myer's Ford, Va., September 4, 1864.
>
> SIR: I came upon Mosby's guerrillas, 200 strong, at this place, and after a sharp fight of thirty minutes we succeeded in routing him. . . . They fought with a will, but the seven shooters proved too much for them. My loss is 1 killed and 4 wounded, 1 severely; his is, 1 commissioned officer and 6 privates killed, and 1 commissioned officer and 4 privates wounded. I have 6 prisoners; the circumstances are such that I am compelled to send them in. I have my wounded and entire command over the river.[63]

Blazer's report closely agrees with Montgomery's account, although there are some differences. The total number of Mosby's men engaged is placed at 150 by Montgomery and 200 by Blazer. In any case, it is a lopsided fight that Blazer wins, although outnumbered. Blazer says he has only one man wounded severely, but both Asbe Montgomery's and Sergeant Leaf's wounds are severe. Sergeant Leaf will be able to return to the Independent Scouts and serve in future engagements, but Asbe Montgomery's "fun" with the Scouts is over. Blazer has also lost a key and aggressive sergeant. Men like Montgomery were the reason Blazer was able to "get the bulge" on their enemies so often. Attrition, such as the loss of Asbe Montgomery, will be a factor in the eventual demise of the Independent Scouts as a fighting unit.

6

Escape from Mosby

A Typical Mosby Operation—Fall 1864

Mosby's chroniclers make much of spectacular exploits such as the Berryville Wagon Train Raid or the Greenback Raid that occurred during the summer and fall of 1864. But newspaper accounts of this time indicate most of Mosby's operations were small affairs involving ten to twenty of his men capturing isolated soldiers on the roads over the Blue Ridge or in the Shenandoah Valley. In nearly all cases Mosby's men were dressed in full or partial Union uniform. The following account is indicative of the way these raids operated. It also shows the caliber of men in Blazer's Scouts and their cool thinking and action under duress.

In early November 1864, George W. "Mack" McCauley and several other members of Blazer's Scouts were captured by Mosby's men. Other Union men were also captured about the same time. Among them was Capt. Nicholas D'Evereaux Badger, acting assistant inspector of cavalry of the 2nd Cavalry Division in the Army of the Shenandoah, who was on Gen. William Powell's staff.[1]

Captain Badger was a veteran of the 8th Ohio Cavalry. Before the war he had been a student at little Antioch College in Yellow Springs, Ohio. He had

Capt. Nicholas D. Badger
Author's collection

two brothers in the service. Joseph was also a veteran of the 8th Cavalry and his brother William W. served in a New York infantry regiment. All three brothers were originally from Montgomery County, New York. Nicholas and Joseph had gone west to Ohio, where their father, Henry, was a professor at Antioch.[2]

Badger's account differs significantly from an account published in the *National Tribune* on October 31, 1889, as recounted by Pvt. Joseph Brown of Company G, 23rd Ohio Volunteer Infantry, and also of Blazer's Scouts. Badger's story appears embellished and self-serving in comparison to Private Brown's account. However, many aspects of both stories correspond.[3]

The Capture of Captain Badger

The morning Badger started his adventure was "cold and brilliant, and the first crisp of frost had just sufficiently stiffened the sod to make a brisk gallop agreeable to both rider and horse. The bold Shenandoah shook the icy wrinkles from its morning face, and rolled smoothly away before me into the gorgeous forest of crimson and gold below Front Royal." It was "the day of the regular train, and a thousand army wagons are already rolling away from Sheridan's headquarters down the famous Valley Pike." Badger had been ordered to accompany one of the trains and he was somewhat late. He was accompanied this morning by a single orderly and his black servant, George Washington, nicknamed Wash. In the company of these two, he "pass[ed] out into the guerrilla infested country."[4]

Badger was feeling rather cocky this fall morning and according to his account was rather defiant of any of the infamous guerrillas who preyed on the supply trains. He was mounted on Belle, a horse he had ridden for three years, and confident of his position. He gave Belle the rein and dashed on at a sweeping gallop till he came in sight of the train, a mile ahead, winding its way through the village of Newtown, nine miles south of Winchester.

"Mosby be hanged!" he said to himself as he slackened his speed and passed leisurely through the little town. He noticed an unusually large number of women of the town waving handkerchiefs at him from doors and windows. He saw that one or two were waving their handkerchiefs "in a significant manner," which, however, he failed to understand. Supposing himself to be an object of their affection, he failed to notice they were probably warning him of danger. "Who would suppose a pretty woman waving a handkerchief to be a sign of danger?" His answer to himself was, "no one but a cynic or a crusty old bachelor, and, as I am neither, I failed to interpret the well-meant warning."[5]

He had nearly passed the town when he overtook a small party of what he thought was the rear guard of the train, under command of a noncommissioned officer. They were lounging around a small grocery, lighting pipes, and buying cakes and apples.

"Good morning, Sergeant," Badger said, in answer to the sergeant's salute. "You had better close up at once. The train is getting well ahead, and this is the favorite beat of Mosby."

The sergeant replied, "All right, Sir." Badger noticed the sergeant had a "smile of peculiar intelligence" and he nodded to his men as they mounted at once and moved in behind the Union officer. At this time Badger suddenly noticed three more of this party, whom he had overlooked and who had moved in front of him.

Badger relates, "An instinct of danger at once possessed me." At present he had no reason for the feeling but "felt a presence of evil which I could not shake off." The dress and deportment of the group he was with gave no hint of trouble. They were dressed completely in Union blue with the Greek cross of the 6th Corps on their caps. "They were young, intelligent, cleanly, and good looking soldiers, armed with revolvers and Spencer's repeating carbines. I noticed the absence of sabers, but the presence of the Spencer, which is a comparatively new arm in our service, reassured me, as I thought it impossible for the enemy to be as yet, possessed of them."

They rode along for awhile until Wash, who had been riding behind Badger, and who had heard some of the comments of their fellow riders, brushed up alongside and whispered through his teeth, which were chattering with fear, "Massa, Secesh sure! Run like de debbel!"

The servant's movements had not been lost on the other riders, and as Badger turned in the saddle to look back, he saw six carbines leveled at him from only twenty paces. The sergeant came riding toward the Union officer, revolver drawn, and sharply ordered, "Halt—surrender!"

Badger was in no position to make an escape, although he states he gave it a thought. They were a mile from Newtown, with the train ahead but still out of sight. He was hemmed in by stone walls on both sides of the pike. A narrow bridge across the Epicene was ahead of him and was also occupied by three of the party with carbines leveled at him. The temptation to escape, however, was strong because this was in the period following the hanging of some of Mosby's men by Gen. George Custer and Union prisoners were in an even more precarious position than they normally would have been facing the prospect of a Rebel prison.

The sergeant repeated, "Surrender," and added "you damned Yankee son of a bitch," for emphasis. The presence of the sergeant's revolver immediately in the officer's face added the final note of discouragement to thoughts of escape at this point.

Badger claimed that his sword and revolver were taken by the "sergeant," who proved to be Lt. Carlisle F. Whiting of Clark County, Virginia, in disguise.[6] Whiting jokingly repeated Badger's command, "We closed up, Captain, as you directed; as this is a favorite beat of Mosby's, I hope our drill was satisfactory."

"All right, Sergeant," Badger replied. "Every dog has his day, and yours happens to come now . . . and possibly my turn will come tomorrow."

Whiting replied that it just might be "[y]our turn to be hung." Whiting then explained with great satisfaction how he and his men had lain in wait for stragglers from the train and had just reached the grocery store from the woods behind it. (The good captain indeed seems to have been a straggler and skirts this issue in his narrative.) Whiting now informed Badger that Mosby himself was just three miles behind them with a hundred men and that the Union officer would meet him in person.

Badger took some time to look at the men who had captured him as he had complacently ridden down the Valley Pike. "They were a jolly, good-natured set of fellows, who evidently thought they had done a big thing; and as I scanned them more closely, the only distinction in appearance between them and our equal soldiers which I could discover, was that the Greek Cross on their caps was embroidered in yellow worsted."[7]

Other men captured around this time by Mosby's men included Thomas (Tom) Green and Curtis (Curt) McIntosh of Company I, 23rd Ohio Volunteer Infantry; John W. (Bill) Tatman and Thomas (Tom) Wilson of the 2nd West Virginia Cavalry; and George Johnson of the 9th West Virginia Infantry, as well as George McCauley and Joseph Brown.

Joseph Brown Is Captured

It was on the morning of October 4th [sic] 1864 that I bridled and saddled my horse, which I called "Mosby" having captured him at Myer's Ford on the Shenandoah River, a short time before, in a fight with Mosby's command. I mounted him, and bidding my comrades good-bye started for Cedar Creek, distant 19 miles. I had ridden about four miles, . . . when I saw five soldiers about one-fourth of a mile ahead of me. Just then I passed a man with a cart-load of sugar cane, and asked him if the five soldiers were Yanks, and he said they were, being dressed in our overcoats. Fearing treachery, I pulled my revolvers around to the front and opened the holsters of the same. As they were coming toward me, we soon closed up, and as I passed them bidding them the time of day, their response was three cocked pistols at my head, with a demand for my surrender.

Mosby's soldiers relieved Brown of his revolvers and his Spencer repeating rifle. They removed the cartridges from the weapons and took Brown's cartridge box from the front of his saddle. The guerrillas led Brown to a stand of woods about a third of a mile from the pike. After riding about forty rods [about two hundred yards], they returned his rifle, saying it would be useless without ammunition.[8]

Pvt. Joseph A. Brown
Joseph A. Brown served
with the 23rd Ohio Volunteer
Infantry.
Courtesy L. M. Strayer Collection

After arriving at the woods, Brown was left with one man while the others returned to the pike, probably looking for more unsuspecting prey. The man who remained with Brown questioned him about his military affiliation, particularly if he belonged to the Scouts. Brown said he did not, "knowing the penalty for scouts and spies. But he thought I was too well armed for a common soldier, having two Navies [Colts] and a Spencer rifle." Brown made up a story that he was a safeguard at Winchester. Mosby's man then indicated that Brown would be taken to Gen. Thomas Rosser's headquarters at Brentsville [Bentonville], and questioned. He assured Brown, "I would be shot or hung if found to be a scout or spy."[9]

James Thompson, the commissary sergeant of the 23rd Ohio, had sent privates Green and McIntosh and some others to Winchester for supplies and then followed them. He met "General" Mosby's men on the way but got around them. When he reached Winchester he found that several men had been captured, including Green and Sergeant Brown of the 23rd Ohio.

Curt McIntosh, who was assigned to the commissary department, remembers his capture: "I was sent to Winchester on a pass by Quarter Master

Sergeant James Thompson latter part of October 1864 [we had just been paid off] for supplies for the noncommissioned officers mess. I also bought a pair of boots for myself. It was on my return from Winchester that Mosby's men captured myself and Thomas Green the butcher of the regiment who was with me."[10]

The last man who was "gobbled up" by Mosby's ersatz Yankees was Pvt. Stephen P. Drake of the 2nd West Virginia Cavalry. Like most of the men of the 2nd, he was from southeastern Ohio. Before his enlistment in the army he had been well known as a printer and newspaper publisher in Adams, Scioto, and Lawrence Counties. Older than most other soldiers, he was presently serving as the postmaster and mail courier for the 2nd Brigade, 2nd Division of the Army of West Virginia. This morning he had sallied out in front of the train and had been captured by probably the same group that had captured Captain Badger.[11]

With the Great Guerrilla Chief

For the present, Badger and the other mounted men were allowed to ride their own horses. Mosby informed Badger that he intended to hang the first officer they encountered in retribution for the execution of his men at Front Royal. Badger began to get the idea he just might be offered the honor. In this circumstance, he relates he was "ushered into the presence of the great highwayman, John S. Mosby, then Lieutenant-Colonel C.S.A."[12]

Badger's description of Mosby and his men is a classic firsthand account of the great guerrilla:

> He stood a little apart from his men, by the side of a splendid grey horse, with his right hand grasping the bridle rein, the forearm resting on the pommel of his saddle, his left arm akimbo, and his right foot thrown across the left ankle and resting on its toe. He is a slight, medium-sized man, sharp of feature, quick of sight, lithe of limb, with a bronzed face of the color and tension of whip-cord; his hair a yellow brown, with full but light beard, and mustache of the same. A straight Grecian nose, firm-set expressive mouth, large ears, deep-grey eyes, high forehead, large well-shaped head, and his whole expression denoting hard services, energy, and love of whiskey.
>
> He wore top-boots, and a civilian's overcoat—black, lined with red—and beneath it the complete grey uniform of a Confederate lieutenant-colonel,

with its two stars on the sides of the standing collar, and the whole surmounted by the inevitable slouch hat of the Southern race. His men were about half in blue and half in butternut.[13]

Mosby scarcely noticed the Union officer as he approached, but ordered a servant to take Belle. Badger was clearly distressed at this for he notes that he had ridden her "through many a bloody field and hair's-breadth escape, and who loved me with an almost human love." Badger had thought twice of entrusting his fate to the ability of the horse to outdistance his pursuers, but thoughts of home and loved ones tempered his thoughts of desperate escape. In the incomparable attachment of man and beast often present in war he "could not refrain from throwing [his] arms around Belle's neck, and tenderly caressing her for the last time before she was led away."[14]

A brief disagreement broke out as Whiting realized he would not be able to keep the Yankee officer's best horse. However, he quickly accepted the consolation prize of the two other horses captured. Mosby then examined the Union officer's papers and realized he had a fairly important individual. He notes that the only person he would rather have seen at this point was the Union cavalry's commander himself. He then asked Badger an unwelcome question, whether he was present at the hanging of Mosby's men at Front Royal. Badger, believing an audacious answer would be best accepted, answered, "I was present, Sir, and like you, have only to regret that it was not the commander, instead of his unfortunate men."

This answer proved satisfactory. Badger was searched and his personal valuables taken, including a "gold hunting watch and chain, several rings, a set of shirt studs and buttons, some coins, a Masonic pin, and about three hundred dollars in greenbacks, with some letters and pictures of the dear ones at home and a small pocket Bible." Their worth was judged by a board of Mosby's officers and then distributed among the captors, according to Badger's account.

The officer's valuables were converted by some formula to Confederate dollars for this distribution among the "gang," as Badger termed them. This included a valuation for his servant, Wash, who was not satisfied that they set his worth at only two thousand Confederate dollars. Mosby eventually took Badger aside and returned the letters, pictures, Bible, and Masonic pin: "You may as well keep this: it may be of use to you somewhere. Some of my men pay attention to this sort of thing."[15]

Mosby's men searched each captive for valuables, although sometimes their searches were not always diligent enough to find every treasure. Joseph Brown knew he would be searched and took efforts to hide his valuables: "I took the precaution to hide my money which amounted to $10 in greenbacks, eight silver 50-cent pieces, and 90 cents in scrip. It was a wet, drizzling day, and I had my oilcloth over me. I took my knife and cut a slit in the waistband of my pantaloons and slipped all the money in excepting the 90 cents in scrip." Brown's precautions averted the loss of most of his valuables, but Mosby's men "liberated" the Yanks of almost $700, several watches, and other valuables. Nothing was too small. Tom Wilson was cleaned out of the only money he had—ten cents in silver. Brown lost his ninety cents in scrip, nineteen postage stamps, a gold ring, gold penholder and pen, knife, boots, and overcoat. In return he was given a pair of shoes and a small gray hat minus its rim. After Mosby and his key officers made their choice of horses, the rest were divided by lot among the rest of the men.[16]

Brown also relates that in searching him, "Jim Crow," one of the Rebels, took two letters from him written by Miss Mary J. Smith, who would eventually marry Brown in 1867. The letters were addressed to Brown "in care of Capt. Blazer, commanding scouts." Brown remarked that this was a "dead giveaway," but he coolly told Jim Crow that the letters were from his girl, and the Rebel returned them. Brown concluded that Jim Crow probably could not read, otherwise his identity as a Scout would have been found out. Brown supplemented his diet by eating the envelopes from his girl's letters as the party began its journey.[17]

Mosby, meanwhile, explained his view of the current situation to Captain Badger and deplored the Union view that his men were mere guerrillas: "Every man of mine is a duly enlisted soldier, and detailed to my command from various Confederate regiments." Mosby then related how he had hung Union soldiers in retaliation for the execution of his own men and had written to Sheridan offering a cessation of this conduct.

Badger thanked Mosby for his kindness and, as they shook hands, realized that Mosby too was a member of the "brethren of the Mystic tie." He "began to think of Mosby almost as a gentlemen and a soldier, although he had just robbed me in the most approved manner of modern highwaymen."[18]

On the Way to Hell

The day was now getting late and arrangements were made for a trip south and imprisonment at Libby Prison for Badger and the others, and an unsure fate for his servant. A guard of fifteen men, in command of "Lieutenant" Whiting, was detailed as an escort and initially was accompanied by Mosby himself. The route led east, toward the Shenandoah and the Blue Ridge. Brown recounts that the party crossed the Shenandoah at Conrad's Ford, three miles above Ashby's Gap, in the Blue Ridge. This route was used by Mosby in 1864 to take advantage of the seam between the Army of the Shenandoah and the Army of the Potomac. Although they would have to cross Union picket posts on major lines of communications, it was a line they could use to transport prisoners to Richmond. Badger was now joined by Brown and the other prisoners of various Union organizations. Together with his "contraband" servant, the number of prisoners numbered ten or eleven, according to the various accounts of the incident.[19]

Badger's bad day was about to improve and his eventual escape would be enabled not by men who knew the Masonic handshake, but by men who knew the caress of a Spencer repeating rifle along the cheek. Badger got to know his fellow prisoners and attempted to gain their confidence through familiar banter. He soon was convinced that at least some of them could be counted on to acquit themselves in a desperate attempt to escape before reaching the forbidding walls of Libby Prison. Two of the men he met were George W. McCauley of western Virginia, nicknamed Mack, and a "Brown" of Blazer's Scouts. Brown is of course Joseph Brown of the 23rd Ohio and Blazer's Scouts. Badger says they afterward proved themselves "heroes of the truest metal."[20]

The trip south progressed swiftly, the men joking with each other and with the Rebel guard. They reached Howettsville, nine miles below Front Royal, where they bivouacked for the night in an old schoolhouse. In Badger's mind it was "the sole relic left by a former civilization. It is an old, unpainted two-story building, with wooden blinds nailed shut, and seems to have been fitted up by Mosby as a kind of way station, in which to camp with his stranger guests." Badger and his newfound friends had time to speculate on how many Union prisoners had inhabited this forsaken place before them. The guards confirmed the organization of Mosby's command and the execution of the

Union men the previous day (November 6) in retaliation for the hanging of Mosby's men by Custer.[21]

Badger describes the sleeping arrangements of both captive and captor:

> Our party of eleven were assigned to one side of the lower floor of the school house, where we lay down side by side, with our heads to the wall, and our feet nearly touching the feet of the guard, who lay in the same manner, opposite to us, with their heads to the other wall, except three who formed a relief guard for the sentry's post at the door. Above the heads of the guard, along the wall, ran a low school desk, on which each man of them stood his carbine and laid his revolver before disposing himself to sleep. A fire before the door dimly lighted the room, and the scene as they dropped gradually to sleep was warlike in the extreme, and made a Rembrandt picture on my memory which will never be effaced.[22]

Brown busied himself making a fire, using for kindling his letters and an old Testament he found in the building. The Rebels, meanwhile, continued their depredations by looting the mailbag captured from Private Drake. Mosby's men gained considerable additional loot from the money in letters sent from soldiers to their wives or mothers. They also enjoyed themselves with love letters written by soldiers to girlfriends or fiancées.[23]

Badger, having decided that McCauley and Brown would be worth being around in a pinch, positioned himself to bunk between them for the night. As the Rebels dropped off to sleep and the guard began to nod over his pipe, Badger began a furtive conversation with the two captive Scouts. It quickly became apparent who the real leader in this situation was to be: "*McCauley proposed to unite our party and make a simultaneous rush for the carbines.*" This private of scouts proposed to his fellow captive officer a brash plan. They would stampede the guards and make their escape. However, once the scheme was whispered among the men, only three were willing to take the risk. The plan was abandoned.[24]

McCauley then proposed to go by himself among the sleeping Rebels and bring over every carbine and revolver before an alarm could be given, if only the rest of the party would use the weapons when placed in their hands. Unfortunately, timidity once more prevailed and this plan was abandoned also. Badger refused McCauley's plan or talked him out of it, fearing for both McCauley's life and those of all others in the group.[25]

Badger could not approve of the brash attempt at escape, but he was stunned by McCauley's bravery. He clasped McCauley to him and kissed him as a brother. He described McCauley as "a fair boy of but eighteen summers, with soft black eyes, and a rosy, round face, as smooth and delicate as a girl's, with a noble forehead and an unusually intelligent countenance. I had picked him out at first sight as a hero, and every hour was increasing my admiration of him." The officer and private fell asleep, spooning to keep away the cold, and awakened to a dull and rainy morning "exhausted and thoroughly wretched and despondent."[26]

Joseph Brown tells a different tale of the plans for escape. During the "horse lottery," he informed George McCauley that he had cartridges for the Spencer rifles. McCauley had also kept his weapon. Brown and McCauley decided that when they reached the Luray Valley they would ride side by side and try to load their guns and make their escape. The horse lottery also provided the opportunity for Tom Wilson of the 2nd West Virginia Cavalry to slip down a lane and make his escape.[27]

In the morning the march began early and went straight south down the Blue Ridge. They had emerged from the forest and Badger could see the "full Shenandoah Valley below them showing plainly the lines of our army, its routes of supply, its foraging parties out, and my own camp at Front Royal as distinctly as if we stood in one of its streets." The unit now struck a wooded path running southward and parallel with the ridge of the mountain, which was traveled for hours, "with this wonderful panorama of forest and river, mountain and plain, before us in all the gorgeous beauty of autumn."[28] As a Federal patrol approached, Mosby talked about how he enjoyed taking this "promenade" and watching Federal raids coming toward him. He noted that one was coming now and that they would stop behind a point and watch it pass. "It may be the last sight you will have of your old friends for some time," he told his captives. Mosby's coolness enraged Badger, yet he also admired Mosby for his quiet audacity. Badger and the others watched as a squadron of cavalry, which Badger recognized as his own regiment, passed near them under the mountain. Mosby stood with folded arms on a rock above them, appearing defiant at the Federal forces below. "Like patience on a monument smiling at grief," Mack whispered to Badger.[29]

Mosby's Men Pay a Fearful Toll

The column moved on and as they reached the road running through Manassas Gap, they were signaled by a group of Mosby's men numbering approximately one hundred. At this point Mosby parted with the prisoners, bidding Badger a "kindly goodbye" and noting that they would now have no chance of rescue or escape.[30]

The prisoners were hurried through the gap and down the eastern side of the mountain. They then turned south and passed Chester's Gap, which was also held by Mosby's men. The column of prisoners and guards was able to pass only after exchanging the proper signals.[31]

Badger notes that holding the gaps was one of the keys to Mosby's success. Mosby was thus able to make forays into the Valley. He could concentrate these garrisons, communicating with them from the mountaintops to warn him of danger or where to strike. If pursued, he could retreat in the direction of his forces, often drawing the pursuers into a trap. They were attacked by men with fresh horses, just as they had exhausted theirs by pursuit of Mosby's men. These tactics had been successful in allowing Mosby to prey on Union forces for the past two years.[32]

After passing Chester's Gap, the column once more descended into the Valley, since they were now well behind Confederate lines. They could now take the direct road to Richmond and the chances for escape had closed behind the prisoners. Badger now reports that the guard was reduced to Whiting and three other men, plus the eleven prisoners. The guards were well mounted and "doubly armed." The prisoners had seven horses to share among them so that four were constantly dismounted. There was also a pack horse carrying forage, rations, and blankets. Two Spencer rifles were also strapped to the pack-horse, muzzle down, and were complete with accoutrements, including two full cartridge boxes.[33]

Badger reports that he called Mack's attention to the carbines at the first opportunity. This was probably not necessary, because Mack would have almost certainly have been aware of the presence of what were undoubtedly their own rifles. Soon after discovering the presence of the rifles on the pack horse, Mack dismounted. When it came time for him to mount again, he obtained the poorest, most broken down of all the horses in the group. Mack made the most of being unable to keep up with this animal and Badger indicates that Mack actually succeeded in laming the unfortunate beast.[34]

Once again, Joseph Brown gives a different account of the actual events, and probably a more plausible one. Brown had a number of Spencer cartridges in the saddle pockets of his horse, which the Rebels had not been diligent enough to search. After a stop, the men were again ordered to remount—at least those that could. Brown relates that they traveled several miles, leaving the road, arriving at Blacktown, on the Manassas Railroad, about seven miles from Front Royal. One of the guards had left his prize horse while passing through the mountains and the rider was a little lame. To accommodate this man, Mosby ordered Brown to dismount and take hold of the tail of his horse. While crossing the valley, Brown trotted along behind the great guerrilla's large, fine horse, "my heels keeping pace with the iron-grey's hind feet."[35]

After reclimbing the mountain a horse was somehow obtained for the lame rider and Brown was allowed to remount his own horse, whose name was Mosby. They then descended into the Luray Valley and, just as Badger recounts, Mosby informed the men they were behind Confederate lines and escape would be hopeless. At this point Brown notes Mosby's departure from the group, leaving "Lieutenant" Whiting, "Jim Crow," and a man named McKinsley as the guard.[36]

According to Badger's account, Mack then dropped back to ask the lieutenant in charge to exchange his lame horse for the pack horse. Mack made this request with complete boldness and the lieutenant agreed, apparently unaware of the sinister intent of the request and forgetful of the deadly cargo of the packhorse. Captain Badger also diverted the lieutenant's attention while the pack was being readjusted to allow McCauley to ride on the animal. Also, since "rain had begun to fall freely, no one of the guard was particularly alert."[37]

Mack McCauley was now riding ahead on the packhorse with the two rifles still strapped to it, but loosened and covered by Mack's heavy poncho, which was spread as protection from the rain. The seven-shot Spencer is loaded from the breech by drawing out a spiral spring from the hollow stock and dropping in the seven cartridges, then reinserting the spring behind them. The spring coils as it is pressed down and forces the cartridges forward, one at a time, into the barrel when the lever action is pumped.[38]

Badger could now see the movements of Mack's right arm by the shape into which it threw the poncho. Mack guided the horse with his left hand. He chatted glibly with the other boys while looking in the opposite direction. Mack carefully drew the springs from the rifles with his right hand and hooked them into the upper buttonhole of his coat to hold them, while he dropped in the cartridges, one after the other. The clicks of the cartridges as they were dropped in was masked by the trotting of the horse. Finally, Mack forced the springs back into place and looked around at Badger "with a look of the fiercest triumph and heroism I have ever beheld."[39]

The officer nodded his approval to the scout, at the same time fearing Mack might precipitate the action too soon. To forestall such an event, the captain rode carelessly over to Brown, who was dismounted. Badger dismounted and asked the enlisted man to tighten the girth on his saddle. During the operation, he quietly told Brown of the situation and asked him to gradually get up by the side of Mack, to communicate with him and at a signal from the captain to grab one of the carbines and do his duty if he valued his liberty.[40]

Badger judged Brown a plucky soldier, but not of the quality of Mack. Brown appeared frightened and "trembled like a leaf." However, he went to his post and Captain Badger did not doubt that he would do his duty well. Badger's disparagement of Brown in this story is undoubtedly what led to Brown's account in the *National Tribune*.[41]

Badger rode up again to Whiting, and "like an echo from the past came back to me my words of yesterday, 'Possibly my turn may come tomorrow.'" Badger engaged the Ranger in conversation and "among other things spoke of the prospect of sudden death as one always present in our army life, and the tendency it had to either harden or ameliorate the character according to the quality of the individual." The Mosby man expressed the view that brutal men are made more brutal by war, but that "a refined and cultivated man is softened and made more refined by it." Badger notes this view is held by many who observe the effects of war on men.[42]

Badger now scanned the country closely for the chance to escape if they should regain their liberty. Badger knew that to fail or be recaptured would lead to instant death. Badger undoubtedly reflected the view of many that Mosby's men would deal harshly with any who attempted such actions. As the ranking man, Badger also brooded over the responsibility of risking the lives of the whole party. He "had an instinctive horror of the shedding of blood, as it were, with my own hand, and the sweet faces of home were haunting me again."

This time however, he notes that they were, "strange to say, urging me on, and apparently crying aloud for vengeance."[43]

The party of prisoners and their guards were now on the immediate flank of Early's army. Confederate cavalry was all around. "The road was thickly inhabited" and it was almost night. The party had just passed a Rebel picket a mile back and Badger fretted about how soon they might strike another camp. The three Rebel guards were riding in front of them and on their left flank, the party of prisoners was in the center, and Badger was by the side of Whiting, who was acting as rear guard. The party now entered a small copse of willows which covered the road for a short time.[44]

"The hour was propitious; Mack looked around impatiently." Badger now wove the prearranged signal—"Now's the time boys"—into a story he was telling Whiting about the Union charge at Winchester, which he was using to distract the "lieutenant." As soon as he uttered the crucial words, he threw himself upon Whiting, grasping him around the arms and dragging him from his horse, in hopes of capturing him, and compelling him to guide his former prisoners outside Confederate lines.[45]

At the signal from Badger, Mack McCauley raised one of the loaded carbines and "in less time than I can write it, shot two of the guard in front of him, killing them instantly; and then coolly turning in his saddle and seeing me struggling in the road with the Lieutenant, and the chances of securing the revolver apparently against me, he raised the carbine the third time, and as I strained the now desperate rebel to my breast, with his livid face over my left shoulder, he shot him directly between the eyes as [easily as] he could have done if firing at a target at ten paces' distance." Badger notes that "the bullet went crashing through his skull, the hot blood spurted from his mouth and nostrils into my face, his hold relaxed, and his ghastly corpse fell from my arms." The scene left "an impression of horror and soul-sickness which can never be effaced."[46]

Badger then turned around in alarm at what was still a desperate situation. He saw Mack smiling at him. According to Badger, Mack remarked, "Golly, Cap! I could have killed five or six more of them as well as not. This is a bully carbine; I think I will take it home with me."[47]

According to Badger, Brown had not accomplished so much. He had seized the second rifle at the signal, and had fired at the third guard on the flank. However, at least compared to McCauley, his aim was "shaky" and he had only wounded the man in the side, allowing him to escape. The escaping Ranger was now a half mile in front of their position, riding at full speed and firing his pistols to further alert the country.[48]

Joseph Brown's account of the escape differs sharply from Badger's. According to his account, after Mosby separated from the group, Brown rode up beside McCauley on the "big road," a probable reference to a turnpike as opposed to one of the mountain trails. Brown passed his cartridges to McCauley and McCauley was successful in loading his weapon. Brown had some difficulty. The Rebels, probably unfamiliar with the Spencer, had failed to completely empty the chamber. Brown, not knowing this, proceeded to load seven more cartridges and jammed the weapon. Brown realized the predicament when he attempted to get the spring back. He became agitated, for his knife had been taken away and he could not turn the rifle up, to free the cartridge, for fear of being discovered. Finally, he used the stub of a lead pencil that had been split in two, to insert under the rim of the cartridge and extract it, which allowed the spring to go back in its place. Brown's heart was now "beating in my breast once more, and not in my mouth, as a few minutes before; for having seven loads and a good partner, I felt better."[49]

According to Brown, he managed to speak to Captain Badger and inform him of their plans; he asked the captain to take charge of the group and "pilot us back when we had done the shooting." He reports that the captain assented to this plan.[50]

Brown was riding on McCauley's left side and told him to fire when he touched his left foot. Brown placed Whiting in front of him, with "Jim Crow" in front of McCauley and McKinsley bringing up the rear. Brown now asked Whiting how far it was to General Rosser's camp at Brentsville (Bentonville). Whiting replied that it was about two and a half miles. Brown says they rode about two hundred yards further when Whiting said to "Jim Crow," "I would just as leave have a good navy revolver as a hundred dollar greenback." At this point Brown touched McCauley's left foot and both scouts fired together. Whiting fell dead from the saddle. "Jim Crow" (actually Marquis Calmes) dropped about ten feet from him, in a sitting position in the road. Brown then dropped from his horse and turned back to shoot McKinsley.[51]

When the fight had started, McKinsley had started to the front. Tom Green, however, grabbed him and attempted to hold him securely. However, as Brown approached to within about fifteen feet, McKinsley was able to draw his revolver and fire at Brown, grazing his shoulder. Brown reports that at the first shot, Captain Badger had disappeared and was not seen again until seven days later, when he appeared in camp. Brown reports that he raised his gun and fired, the ball taking McKinsley above the left eye, killing him instantly, with Tom Green being covered by the blood and brain matter from the wound. Green held to him as the two fell to the ground, McKinsley's revolver still at half cock for a second shot. Brown turned again, seeing Marquis Calmes still sitting in the road, probably still stunned, holding his horse by the bridle and with the cape from his overcoat turned over his head. Brown went up to him, put his gun to his head and fired through the cape, killing him. Brown took four revolvers from the dead man, jumped on his horse, and commenced to fasten the revolvers around him. However, one of the revolvers fell out of the holster and when Brown jumped down to get it, the horse became frightened and managed to get away.[52]

Brown notes that all this happened very quickly and by the time it was over, everyone had scattered. Captain Badger, according to Brown, had "vamosed with the first crack of the rifle." The only man still in sight was Tom Green, who was going up the mountain. Brown caught up with him and Bill Tatman. They ran about three miles bearing due west as well as they could and eventually were joined by Badger's orderly and Wash, the servant. Green had three revolvers from the unfortunate McKinsley and Brown had the four taken from Calmes.[53]

Making Their Way to Union Lines

The entire party was now in dire straits. Their group had been split up by the suddenness of the fight and were far behind Confederate lines. None had seen the country before, so they knew of it in only the most general way. Darkness was approaching and Rebel camps could not be far away. If the initial gunshots had not alarmed the country, the escaping Ranger would surely do so. Badger notes, "I doubted not that before sundown even bloodhounds would be on our track." Once again, Badger's account differs from Brown's. He reports that half the prisoners had already scattered, panic-stricken at the first sound of the fight. They had fled "every man for himself . . . scouring the country in every direction."[54]

According to Badger, five of the party of prisoners remained, including

Badger's servant, Wash. Wash had immediately begun searching the bodies of the slain and recovered Badger's gold hunting watch from the person of "Lieutenant" Whiting as well as over one thousand dollars in Union greenbacks, "the proceeds, doubtless of their various robberies of our men." Even Wash could now joke about their previous predicament. "Not quite 'nuff," he said, grinning from ear to ear. "Dey valley dis nigger at two tousand dollars —I think I ought ter git de money."[55]

They now selected the best horses, mounted, and, well armed with carbines and revolvers, struck directly toward the mountain on their right. However, they realized this would be the first place pursuers would look, so they headed south, riding as fast as they could directly into the enemy's country for four hours. While not stated, it is quite likely that the wily scout McCauley may have come up with this plan. It seems unlikely the staff officer would have thought of riding deeper into enemy country to escape pursuit. This is just the kind of independent thinking for which men were selected for Blazer's Scouts. Badger now claims they put thirty miles between themselves and the place of their escape before complete darkness, a statement that conflicts with the time of day previously given, just after the fight. No matter the timing, they certainly would have covered a lot of ground. They then turned "sharp up the mountain," pushing their exhausted horses as far as they could climb. They then abandoned the horses and continued on foot, all night to the "very summit of the Blue Ridge, whence we could see the rebel camp fires, and view their entire lines and positions just as daylight was breaking over the valley."[56]

They then bent down twigs from several trees in line to indicate the points of the compass and the direction of the Confederate camps and pickets after it became light. They crawled into a thicket to rest their exhausted bodies and await the return of friendly darkness before continuing their flight. Badger notes that "the length of this weary day, and the terrible pangs of hunger and thirst which we suffered on this barren mountain pertain to the more common experiences of soldier life" and he does not describe them in detail.[57]

Brown's narrative about the aftermath of the escape continues. He reports the group was fired on by two Rebels as the fugitives moved from one woods to another. At this point, Badger's orderly and "the darky" became separated from the group again. Brown and his group reported that they lay in the brush until about 8 or 9 P.M., listening to the sounds of Rebel horses on the stony road, patrolling and watching for them. Then, "with a revolver in each hand,"

Climbing the Blue Ridge

they started out, taking a step and then stopping to listen. When they came once again to the road, Brown crawled through the fence and lay down, looking up and down the road for a guard or patrol. Upon seeing none, he crawled back and led Green and Tatman across the road and up the mountain, where the group kept going all night, resting every few minutes.[58]

About eight in the morning, they came within hearing distance of the Shenandoah River. About the same time they heard the "baying of the terrible bloodhounds." The men knew that if the dogs were indeed after them, it would do no good to run. They backed up against a big oak tree, determined to make a stand and "sell our lives as dearly as possible." However, the dogs were on another trail and they ran past the group within sight. They crossed the trail of the dogs, going into a deep ravine, and took to water, keeping to it for a half mile or more. When they emerged, they were within sight of the river and a small log house, which stood about two hundred yards from the east bank.[59]

The men had been taken prisoner two days before and, with little remaining in their haversacks, they were desperately hungry. Brown put one revolver in his blouse and went up to the cabin and told the woman of the house he was a Reb and "that the yanks had starved me; that I had got away from them at Front Royal; and wanted to know how far I had traveled." The woman informed Brown that he was thirteen miles from Front Royal, which was exactly the information he needed. Brown then asked the woman for something to eat, and offered to pay her for what he received. At this point the woman said, "You are no rebel" and told a boy of about ten to go and tell [the Rebels]. In response Brown drew his revolver and threatened to shoot the boy if he moved and told the woman that if she had anything to eat he wanted it. The woman produced some corn pone and fat bacon from the house, which Brown asked her to sample to make sure it wasn't poisoned. Brown started off toward the Rebel lines, informing the woman that he belonged to General Rosser's command and if she still thought them Yankees, she could tell. As soon as he was out of her sight, Brown went back to where he had left Green and Tatman. He shared his food with them and the three got out of the area as soon as possible.[60]

They then came upon a couple of boys working in a cane patch and the Yankees "played rebels on them," asking if there were any Yankees around. The boys replied that the closest Yankees were at Front Royal, "but seven of your boys went along the road a few minutes ago." This provided the party with further incentive to depart from that area as soon as they could, going along the banks of the river, intending to cross at the first ford. The fugitives liberated some cabbages and turnips from fields they came across. The food was so welcome that Brown remarks they had "struck oil indeed" at the size of the turnips they found. They crossed the river where it was about 150 yards wide, wading in up to their arms. After crossing the river, they once again took to the woods, avoiding all roads and there "found black-haws, persimmons, and pawpaws in great abundance."[61]

At dark, the men struck the pickets of General Powell's division, feeling like new men and that a heavy load had been taken off their shoulders. The men were taken to General Powell's headquarters, in a large brick house in Front Royal. The general inquired about Captain Badger, wondering if he were with the crowd, as he had not arrived to inspect the troops. The general then ordered the cook to get the former prisoners some "'grub' which was furnished, and the way the potatoes, beefsteak, and biscuit were despatched was a caution to the natives." The escapees were assigned a room in the brick headquarters building, which must have been quite an honor. However, Brown reports they slept poorly, "feeling every minute as if the Johnnies were on us."[62]

Brown reports that Badger, McCauley, Johnson, and McIntosh were dodging the Rebels for seven days before they sighted the Federal pickets. "The mail carrier was never heard from again. They probably caught and made way with him." The next morning Brown and the others were furnished horses to ride to Cedar Creek, where General Sheridan had his headquarters. After arriving at Cedar Creek, the band was taken to General Custer's headquarters, where the cavalry commander informed them that they should go to General Crook's headquarters, and if anyone knew them, they could be sent to their own commands. After arriving at General Crook's headquarters, Brown was recognized by Capt. Homer Cherington of the general's staff. Brown was led in to see the commander of the Army of West Virginia. While relating his adventures, Tatman and Green were returned to Custer's camp, where they were placed under arrest and told that, as soon as convenient, they would be sent to their own commands.[63]

When Brown returned from General Crook's headquarters, he too was put under arrest—Custer's men were still suspicious that these men might be spies. Brown requested the sergeant of the guard to return him to General

Crook's headquarters to straighten out the situation. The guard refused, not willing to "get into trouble" on Brown's account. Finally, Brown convinced the sergeant to let him go under guard to the Sutler's to get tobacco for the boys. This the sergeant agreed to, putting Brown under a young guard whom the wily scout soon gave the slip. Brown returned to the 23rd Ohio, which was camped about a half mile away. Here he reported to Col. Rutherford B. Hayes, the future president and another commander well acquainted with Blazer's command.[64]

Hayes told Brown to report to him after dinner and everything would be all right. He sent Brown along with Capt. Albert (Al) Logan, a former member of Blazer's Scouts, back to General Crook. Crook, surprised at the men's being under arrest, sent a letter arranging for their release. Brown returned to Custer's headquarters, where after some good-natured kidding he convinced the sergeant of the guard, who was reluctant to "get into trouble" for him, to produce the release order, and the men finally returned to their own regiments.[65]

Brown and the others had probably become near celebrities, having made their way out of the clutches of the notorious guerrilla Mosby. The next morning Brown was sent for by Gen. Phil Sheridan himself. Brown made a report of the route over which the men had been taken. Based on this intelligence, Sheridan sent a regiment of cavalry into the mountains a few days after this, which succeeded in capturing a "fine lot of horses" that had been left in the mountains.

The Saga Ends

Badger and the others returned a few days after Brown. He reported that three men were recaptured by either Mosby's men or other Confederate units. However, the only man documented to be recaptured was the "feeble old man" mentioned by Badger, probably Stephen P. Drake, the mail courier. His service record carries him as a prisoner of war for the rest of the war. However, Maj. Jewitt Palmer of the 2nd West Virginia Cavalry, in a letter to the *Marietta Register*, reports Drake was killed after his recapture.[66] George McCauley would be remembered by Lt. Youthless Pullins of the 9th West Virginia Infantry as a soldier who "was among the brave and daring spirits detailed from the 9th Regiment, [West] Virginia Infantry Volunteers to form a company of scouts and placed under the command of Capt. Dick Blazer—for the purpose of watching movements and harassing Col. Mosby and his command."

Mack McCauley married Sarah McCauley, the widow of his brother, on December 10, 1869. They had two children: Samuel Martin McCauley, who lived only two years, and Ida May McCauley. George died at Point Pleasant, West Virginia, on February 18, 1880, his health having never recovered from his severe ordeal in the Blue Ridge Mountains during November 1864.[67]

Capt. Nicholas D'Evereaux Badger received a regular commission in the 10th U.S. Cavalry, one of the Buffalo Soldiers outfits, on July 28, 1867. He served in this unit, including a stint as regimental commissary of subsistence, until January 1, 1871, when he was transferred to the 22nd Infantry. He retired in 1871 and died July 19, 1882.[68]

7

Kabletown: The Final Conflict

Dogging Mosby

IN the opinion of Asbe Montgomery after the Myer's Ford fight, "This whipping . . . did Mosby a great deal of good. He was so shy it took hunting to find him, and his depredations were partially cured." A newspaper correspondent noted shortly after the Myer's Ford skirmish, "News this morning, as has been hinted, is a scarce article; even MOSBY'S gang have retired from active business for a time." Also, shortly after this encounter Mosby was wounded in the groin on September 14 and put out of action until he could once more take to the saddle. Captain Blazer even notes in one of his intelligence reports that Mosby was forced to ride in a carriage because of the wound.[1]

Asbe would be unable to continue his story of the Scouts' conflict with Mosby, so he depended on some accounts from others in the unit. He closed his personal narrative with his own assessment of Capt. Richard Blazer, an account that agrees with other descriptions of the scout commander. He describes a very ordinary man, not one of flamboyance or one prone to self-aggrandizement.

> "Old Dick" as we called Capt. Blazer, was not a man to rest when his country was bleeding, so he would ride, sick or well. Often I have felt truly sorry

for that man. I have known him to ride days and nights, and not eat one bite, and scarcely sleep, only when halted in the day time, lay down and sleep an hour, when he would up, mount, and off again. He would risk life, health and everything for his country. He was firm, slow to speak, a kind man to his men, always looking after their interests, and although he would fight the rebs, almost asleep or awake, yet he was kind to prisoners—to those who were entitled to be recognized as prisoners of war, and you could plainly see it pained him to do anything else.[2]

Asbe remarked that after the Myer's Ford fight the Scouts "continued to dog Mosby, and even crossed the Valley of the Shenandoah, and penetrated the North Mountain, in search of Mc[Neil] and caught several of his men, partially routing him. Back again, crossing the Shenandoah River time and time again, whipping Mosby's men, so that he was obliged to travel with large numbers, or leave the valley." In fact Mosby would lead his entire command if the object of a raid were large enough, such as a large wagon train.[3]

Previous chroniclers of Mosby and his encounters with Blazer have often dismissed Blazer's efforts because there were only a few major encounters between the two units, the final action being a Mosby victory. However, Asbe Montgomery correctly assesses Blazer's real effect on Mosby's operations. Blazer's Scouts disrupted Mosby's scouting parties that identified Federal units vulnerable for attack. Mosby's intent was to disrupt Sheridan's rear, but Blazer now turned the tables on him. A small, audacious Federal unit was now attacking Mosby's rear and outriders wherever it could. That was the real importance of Blazer's Scouts and their actions against Mosby.

So this scheme was adopted by the rogue, he feeling that if Blazer was not soon stopped, his day was over. If another company of scouts, with just such men, could have been raised, I have no doubt Mosby would have had to leave the Valley of the Shenandoah entirely. Every man of our army will say the same. I have often wondered why more men were not raised for the same purpose. Every general in the valley knew all about us, and so highly complimented us, that we were allowed to pass at any time and in any place. Even provost guards had their orders to let Blazer's Scouts pass in any town or place in which the army was encamped. In fact, no one seemed disposed to take any command over us, only to inquire to whom we belonged, when they would say, "all right!" and we went on our way rejoicing.

The scouts were always on the lookout for the interest of the army. When any word or report came from "Old Dick" it was always credited, as sent

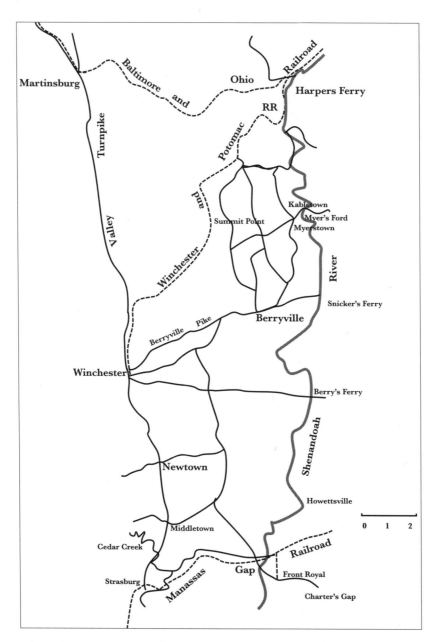

Shenandoah Valley

In this area of the Shenandoah Valley Blazer's Scouts fought Mosby's command and other Confederate guerrilla and cavalry units.

Adapted from *The Official Atlas of the Civil War*

with judgement and truth. When our brave army, large in spirit moved, the scouts were always on the alert. We would risk anything to save our comrades and our beloved country from drawbacks, and the boys, as well as the officers, had the confidence in us that when on the move, or in camp, and we passed by, they were careful to inquire, and if we told them the enemy was nigh, they would look out. After a scout, and "Old Dick," and his gallant little band would come in, the officers would collect and listen almost as carefully as if we had risen from the dead, and was delivering a message from the other world concerning the prospects and conduct of the war.[4]

Captain Blazer made a report of his operations on October 24, 1864, including the Myer's Ford fight.

Captain BIER,
Assistant Adjutant-General.

HEADQUARTERS INDEPENDENT SCOUTS,
Middletown, Va., October 24, 1864.

SIR: I have the honor of submitting the following report of the operations of my command since the 18th of August: On the 18th, learning that a party of Mosby's guerrillas were in the vicinity of Myerstown, I proceeded to that place and overtook them near the Shenandoah River, and after a chase of three miles I drove them across the river, capturing one prisoner. The army having fallen back to Halltown, on the 25th, according to your orders, I went into Loudoun County, and after operating for several days I killed five of Mosby's gang and captured three prisoners. The army having again advanced to Berryville, on the night of the 3d of September I learned that Mosby with a considerable force was at Snickersville. Early on the morning of the 4th I crossed the river at Backus' Ford and moved up the river to where I could get up the mountain through the woods. I struck the pike east of the top of the mountain and moved on their camp. Finding that he had left during the night in the direction of Charles Town, I determined to follow. I re-crossed the mountain through Lewis' Gap, and by a forced march I overtook them about 2 p.m. at Myer's Ford, and after a spirited fight of several minutes I completely routed them, with a loss on his part of 13 killed, 6 wounded, 5 prisoners, and 17 horses; my loss was 1 killed and 6 wounded. Since that I have had several small affairs with them, in which I have always defeated them, except twice. On the 20th Lieutenant Ewing with five men was attacked on the Berryville pike near the Opequon [Creek] by a superior force and was all captured except himself. On the 23d Sergeant Fuller, of the Fifth Virginia Infantry, with ten men was attacked near Summit Point by fifty or sixty guerrillas; he fought them until he was overpowered and four of his men were killed, one wounded, and the rest all captured but three, who made their escape.

Having learned that a man by the name of Marshall was recruiting a company in the vicinity of Ashby's Gap, and that they were to organize on the 25th, I proceeded to their reported rendezvous near White Post, and completely surprised them, getting Marshall and four of his men, and capturing all his papers. In another affair below Front Royal I left eight of his murderers to keep company with some that [were] left by General Custer; these, with a number of others that I have picked up through the country, make an aggregate in killed, 44; wounded, 12; and prisoners, including 2 captured in the advance to Cedar Creek the first time, 12. My entire loss is 5 men killed, 7 wounded, and 8 prisoners. I am, sir, very respectfully, your obedient servant,

R. BLAZER,
Captain, Commanding Independent Scouts [5]

Summit Point

Blazer's loss up till this time was slight in actual casualties. However, he would lose a few more to military operations in the coming month. At least two of the men were erroneously listed as killed in action. Barnett Locy (Losey) and John W. Leach of the 5th West Virginia Infantry were actually captured at the Summit Point fight, but this was not known until a few months later. Little is known about the fight at Summit Point. George Nottingham states in his pension that the Scouts were detailed to guard a supply train from Winchester to Harpers Ferry. However, this statement was made long after the war and may be in error. It may have been that they were scouting for Mosby's men along the probable line of travel for trains going to the front and ambulances leaving for hospitals from the battle at Winchester.[6]

Among those killed was James Webb, a former sergeant of the 9th West Virginia. Webb was stripped of all his effects after the fight. His pregnant wife, Malvina, would be left to care for five children. George S. Webb was born in February 1865 and would never see his father. Among the captured were Sgt. Richard Fuller, commanding the detail, and Robert F. Defoe, both of the 5th West Virginia; Ulysus Mason (probably) and George Nottingham, 14th West Virginia; Charles Shafer, William S. Smith (probably), and Charles Thompson, 34th Ohio. George Nottingham received two wounds, one ball hitting him in the right hip. The other shot struck him in the left shoulder, completely penetrating his body and exiting through his left chest. Barnett Locy also was wounded in the left shoulder, his horse also being shot and killed. As the animal fell, it caught Locy's right leg, fracturing the limb between the knee and ankle. Barnett Locy was a prisoner in very bad shape to head for Libby and perhaps other notorious Southern prison camps.[7]

Mosby's Men Masquerade as Federals

Besides traveling in large numbers, as Montgomery notes, Mosby and his men were forced to resort to other ruses to maintain their activities in the Shenandoah Valley. His scouting parties were at real risk if dressed in Confederate uniform, because they were totally outmatched by the combined Federal forces in the Valley. Disguised in captured Federal uniforms, they began to capture isolated soldiers, couriers, mail riders, stragglers, and the occasional ill-guarded train. The major supply trains, often stretching for miles, were generally guarded by several thousand soldiers and Mosby and his men usually left them alone, unless they could isolate a portion of the train that was less heavily guarded. In fact, most of the newspaper accounts of Mosby's actions from August to November 1864 are of small groups of his men, almost always dressed in Union uniform, capturing small numbers of isolated Union troops. Although Mosby was considered ubiquitous by such actions, they had very little impact on the strategic situation.[8]

In a sincere example of flattery, Mosby's men even began to impersonate Blazer's Scouts themselves. A foraging party of the 1st New York Dragoons was sent out in early November about four miles from Front Royal, taking their colonel's mess wagon with them to gather in the goods. They were assaulted by guerrillas and word was sent back to the regiment. A Major Smith was sent out with a squadron in pursuit of the raiders.

> The major encountered them at last; but as they were dressed in Union uniforms he was in some doubt whether they were rebels or not. He rode up within easy pistol range and inquired who they were of their commanding officer. He was informed it was an independent company, consisting of ninety men and commanded by Capt. Blaizer [*sic*]. The rascals succeeded in getting into timber hard by before Maj. Smith discovered who they actually were. However, he succeeded in retaking some seven or eight prisoners whom they had gobbled up, and in capturing two of the guerrillas.[9]

Williamson asserts that Mosby's men never masqueraded as Union soldiers, except "out of circumstances" wearing overcoats which they acquired. They also wore rubber blankets used by both armies, which would have hidden their uniforms. However, the above account and numerous others really make this a most amazing statement, from an individual who must have known it was false. Henry Pancake of the 5th West Virginia and Blazer's Scouts remarked about such operations: "[W]e were organized to fight Mosby's guerrillas, and we had to fight them as they fought us, and wearing each other's uniform was a part of the game."[10] Occasionally, Mosby's men were taken prisoner in actual operations dressed in civilian garb as well, another ruse to maintain his operations in the Valley. With the Shenandoah Valley fairly crawling with Yankees in the summer and fall of 1864, wearing the uniform of the Federal army or dressing as a civilian was probably a necessity at times, even if it wasn't up to the standards of Southern chivalry, which is probably the reason for Williamson's denial.[11]

The "Vineyard" Fight

By early November, the weather in the Shenandoah Valley starts to get very cold. The wind blows strongly across the flatter, open spaces of the Valley, such as around Berryville. One Scout, Sylvester Keith of the 13th West Virginia Infantry, writing to his mother on November 14, 1864, reports he is "well and weigh heverry than I ever did in my life. I persume that you think me dead but it is all a mustake for I am still here soldering like a dog." He complains about the lack of pay: "Mother, I am tired soldering without money for ever thing that I get I have to beg or steal and that is a verry hard way to serve the lorde." Sylvester was homesick and looking forward to coming home if military operations slowed during the winter: "I have once more thought of home mother the company that I am in is going to be disbanded for thirty days this winter and we are all coming home that is what our capt [Blazer] tells us and I dont think that he would tell us a lye I think that about the first of new month we will start home the wether will be to bad to scout then it is gitting cold wether out here it is so cold in this country that men dont have to youse razors for the wind blough so hard that beard wont grow."[12]

However, there was still scouting to be done and about this time the Scouts had another serious brush with Mosby's men. On November 16, 1864, Capt.

Richard Montjoy of Mosby's command, in charge of Company D, had split his force to allow men from Loudoun County to return home after an operation. The Loudoun County men crossed the Shenandoah at Castleman's Ferry, while Montjoy, proceeding with twenty-five to thirty men and seventeen prisoners and horses from an encounter with an unknown Federal cavalry unit the previous day, moved up the Shenandoah to cross at Berry's Ferry.[13]

About two miles west of the crossing, near Clay Hill, the home of Frank Whiting, Blazer or part of his unit attacked Montjoy's force. The Confederates were caught completely by surprise and broke and ran. Edward Bredell of Mosby's command was probably killed in the initial shower of bullets at Whiting's home. The stampeding Confederates crossed to Burwell's Island, where they ran headlong into a group of youngsters who were doing their duty for the rebellion by hiding a "valuable lot of horses." "L. M. L." recounted in 1894:

> Suddenly Mosby's battalion dashed into us, being hotly pursued by Captain Blazer. . . . I was in charge of a very fine blooded horse, on which steed I made a dive for the east side of the Shenandoah, jumping a stone fence and down a perpendicular bank some fifteen feet, with bullets flying as thick as gnats in August. I made for a lane on the opposite side which was inclosed by a very high fence. Being so closely pursued I became frightened and jumped from my steed and ran to the bushes; my horse wheeled and ran back to the enemy. After this excitement was over a deathlike silence seemed to prevail.[14]

Montjoy and Lt. Charles Grogan tried to rally the Rangers at the Vineyard, the home of John Esten Cooke, who was one of Jeb Stuart's staff officers.

> On the retreat from Whiting's house William Armstead Braxton, of King William County, Virginia, a gallant soldier who had recently joined the battalion received a mortal wound, but was able to reach the Vineyard, where he was tenderly nursed till he died. As he lay wounded on a sofa, Lieutenant Cole[s], of Blazer's command, entered the house, and, approaching the dying soldier, expressed commiseration for his condition, and offered such religious consolation as he could command.[15]

L. M. L. reported seeing Mosby's men who had escaped into the brush bring back the "lifeless body of a stately looking gentlemen, a stranger. He was laid out at uncle's house; the night I shall never forget; the sad expression of that face, and how I felt for his loved ones at home." L. M. L. saw the soldier buried the next day in a pine box on the bend of the river. He remembered seeing that the soldier had his name on his collar, Col. Edward Bredell, N.C. This is interesting because most accounts indicate Bredell served as a private in Mosby's command, but bore the rank of lieutenant due to a staff position he had formerly held.[16]

Blazer probably suffered very few casualties in this sharp little engagement. It may have been during the stand at the Vineyard that Sgt. William H. Leaf of the 23rd Ohio was wounded for the second time in the left shoulder. Sergeant Leaf received a thirty-day furlough for this wound and was gone from Captain Blazer's command.[17]

Attrition in Blazer's Command

At this point, let us look at Captain Blazer's little company of scouts. He had lost several key officers and sergeants and a good number of men. Those losses were not totally compensated by additional details. Sgt. Asbe Montgomery of the 9th West Virginia had been taken by wounds, as had Sgt. William Leaf. Sgt. Richard Fuller of the 5th West Virginia was a prisoner of war. Sgt. Jesse Middaugh did not reenlist when his time was up. As early as March 1864, he had advised his younger brother Frederick, who was in the 83rd Pennsylvania Infantry, not to do so either, but to come to see him down in southern Ohio or West Virginia. A very incomplete POW record for Jesse shows him at Camp Parole at Baltimore on September 7, 1864. A letter he wrote to his sister, probably dated September 8, is written on U.S. Sanitary Commission stationery. With his dry sense of humor, Jesse writes that he will be out of the service in a few days. "I suppose you want to know why I write from Camp Parole. it is this. I have been in service 3 years 5 months, never had a furlough nor bin in the Hospital and I thought that I would come here and rest up so that I can do something for myself." Jesse mustered out of the service and returned to Ceredo, West Virginia, just west of present-day Huntington, West Virginia, and just across the Big Sandy River from Kentucky. It was a place tormented by lawless bands who swore fealty to the Confederacy, but were more brigand than true guerrilla. They preyed on anyone they felt weak enough to give little resistance. Jesse's choice to remain in this tough country with his family would turn tragic several months later.[18]

Lt. James Ewing, who had been personally recommended for the Scouts by Asbe Montgomery, left the service on October 15, 1864. Besides his most experienced noncommissioned officers, Richard Blazer had now lost his most experienced second in command. Ewing's replacement was Lt. Thomas Kip Coles of Company A, 91st Ohio Infantry, assigned to the Scouts on October 25. His experience at scouting was not known, but he was well known by Capt. Blazer and had the reputation of a good officer.

Tom Coles was a handsome young officer, the eldest son of Capt. Samuel Coles of Hanging Rock, Ohio, close by the Ohio River. The family was influential in the community and very wealthy by the standards of the area. Tom was descended from Quaker ancestors—his grandparents were Benjamin and Hannah Coles. Samuel was a farmer who came to the Ohio country in its early years. He initially settled at Rising Sun, Indiana, and moved to Franklin, Ohio, about fifteen miles south of Dayton, where he was involved in building a part of the Ohio Canal. In 1830 he moved to Portsmouth, where along with his brother-in-law, Lemuel Moss, he superintended the construction of the terminus of the canal. In 1835 he commanded the steamboat *Fairy Queen*. Later he built the steamboat *Home*, which plied the Ohio and Mississippi Rivers. He eventually expanded into leather tanning and became involved with coal mining, iron foundry, and the railroad business, as president of the Big Sandy Railroad.[19]

With his Quaker forebears and his family's influence in the community, Tom was the epitome of a young Union officer. Despite the Copperhead sentiment in the area, his family was probably pro-abolition due to their religious heritage. Tom was a courteous, affectionate young man and "as brave and chivalrous a soldier who ever wore the blue." He had survived six or seven battles, including the severe fights at Cloyd's Mountain, Carter's Farm, and the retreat at Kernstown, without a scratch. Tom volunteered for a position in the Scouts after Lieutenant Ewing mustered out and was selected for the position for being among "the bravest of the brave."[20]

By this time in the war, attrition and the chaotic replacement system of the Union army were having an effect on Blazer's command. Many men, such as Sgt. Jesse Middaugh, left when their terms of service expired. The 12th and 23rd Ohio were consolidated on July 1, 1864, with the remaining men of the 12th transferred to the 23rd. The 5th and 9th West Virginia were consolidated into the 1st West Virginia Veteran Volunteers on November 9, 1864. The non-veterans of the 34th Ohio Infantry had departed on the day of the Berryville

Lt. Thomas K. Coles
Lieutenant Tom Coles came
from a Christian family and
was noted for his generosity
and bravery. It is unlikely he
tortured a prisoner in his
care.
History of Scioto County

fight. The soldiers returning home were still within sound of the guns as the
battle began.[21]

Some of Blazer's men were such good soldiers that they were promoted
out of the Scouts. Benjamin Killam of the 23rd Ohio served only a month in
the Scouts when he was promoted and assigned daily duty as acting commissary sergeant in April 1864. The next month he became the regimental quartermaster. In July he was discharged to accept promotion as a "commish"
—second lieutenant. Albert Logan of the same regiment served as a Scout
from April to June 1864, when he was assigned to regimental headquarters.
In August he became sergeant major and in October also became second
lieutenant. By the time of the Vineyard fight Blazer's unit was down to about
sixty-three men. Never really strong enough to take on Mosby's command
when concentrated, Blazer's little band was now especially vulnerable. However, it does not seem to have bothered Blazer much; if anything, he was
overconfident in his men.[22]

Lt. Albert B. Logan
Albert Logan of the 23rd Ohio Infantry received promotions that took
him out of Blazer's unit.

Courtesy Hayes Presidential Center

An Assessment of Blazer by Foe and Friend

Blazer was now "a thorn in Mosby's side."[23] His little command had done a great deal to break up Mosby's operations and as usual has provided good intelligence on enemy operations. Maj. John Scott was a Confederate officer well versed in guerrilla tactics and Mosby's first historian. Unfortunately he is also the source of some of the myth about Richard Blazer. He gives an account of Blazer's activities which is consistent with Asbe Montgomery's accounts and Blazer's earlier actions in the mountains of West Virginia:

> His movements were rapid and generally successful. His expeditions lasted about three days, during which time he rarely went into camp until late at night, and always moved before daybreak. He appeared to be ever in the saddle, and was constantly turning up where he was least expected and least desired. Such was his activity that scouts and furloughed soldiers never felt safe within the enemy's lines, or in that broad neutral border which separated the hostile forces.
>
> But these were not the only men who had reason to respect the valor of Captain Blazer. He often assailed the outposts of the Confederate Army, and not unfrequently participated in larger combats. Already he had surprised and routed the 1st Battalion and had won the respect, if he had not excited the apprehension of the rest of it. Scouts who had been sent to the Valley would, when they returned, often entertain their comrades with accounts of their escape from Blazer. His kindness to citizens was proverbial, and everywhere within the range of his activities the citizens were ready to bear honorable testimony to his character. His kindness sprang from the heart, but it might well have been the dictate of a refined policy, for it engendered for him a sympathy among the people which opened to him many a channel of information.[24]

James E. Taylor, the noted sketch artist, came across Captain Blazer's unit in the Shenandoah Valley on October 11, 1864. Taylor saw a chance to speed his travel to Harpers Ferry and take his chances with "Blazer's Invincibles," as he called them. Taylor had a pleasant trip with the Scouts. At noontime they stopped at Morrow's Spring to eat lunch. Taylor notes that "the repast could be enjoyed with small fear of interruption from an enemy as the prudent captain had his pickets well out in a strong cordon to guard the approaches from a surprise." Taylor, Captain Blazer, and Lieutenant Coles ate their lunch

Blazer's Scouts on the march

The Scouts are shown turning onto the Summit Point Road from the Martinsburg Pike.

Courtesy Western Reserve Historical Society, Cleveland, Ohio

Blazer's Scouts at rest

James E. Taylor sketched Blazer's men in October 1864 as he relaxed with them for lunch. His sketches represent the only known visual representation of Blazer's Scouts in the field.

Courtesy Western Reserve Historical Society, Cleveland, Ohio together in the shadow of Morrow's blacksmith shop (located northeast of Winchester).

Taylor noticed a striking similarity between Blazer and his commander, George Crook: "Blazer strongly resembled his chief Crook, in features, in high cheekbones, straight outshooting sandy hair, mustache and chinwhiskers, eyelids slanting downward to the nose in which set steel grey eyes of eagle sharpness, marred somewhat by a kink or cross in one, but to judge by their glitter, of vision evidently flawless. If he possessed the power of vision of his chief, he certainly had a great advantage in detecting from afar the stealthy approach of the meteoric Mosby and Gilmore."[25] Taylor also accurately describes the incredible woods sense of General Crook. He notes that Crook's vision was "phenomenal—he had a habit of closing his eyelashes so that he appeared to have a very small eye, whereas he could show a very large one, as also see as far with his naked eye as most of us could see with our double journelle glasses [binoculars]."[26]

Scott attributes Blazer's success, as does Asbe Montgomery from the other side, to the disruption of Mosby's scouting parties that enabled him to isolate vulnerable Union columns. This was the real value of Blazer's operations. Also, his observation that Blazer's actions toward the inhabitants of the Shenandoah Valley came from a "refined policy" is actually probably on the mark. Decades later, counterinsurgency warfare would institute the concept of winning the hearts and minds of the opposition, but Richard Blazer practiced it in the Shenandoah Valley campaign of 1864.[27]

Wearing Confederate Uniforms

One method by which Blazer may have disrupted Mosby's scouting operations was to dress his own men in Confederate uniform and penetrate Mosby's ranks. The very young Bill Wass of the 14th West Virginia Infantry "wore the butternut" and is even reported to have ridden with Mosby. Henry Pancake says, "Why, I've got in with the rebels and rode for miles without their suspecting I was a Union soldier. One time Mosby's men captured a mail wagon, and some of us wearing rebel uniforms caught up with them and helped guard the wagon until our pursuing force came in sight. That's the way we had to fight Mosby, and it was part of the regulations that some of us wore the gray."[28]

Maj. Adolphus Richards
Adolphus "Dolly" Richards
was sent out by Mosby to
even the score with Blazer's
Scouts.
Scott, *Partisan Life*

Hunter or Hunted?

As Blazer's and Mosby's men continued their dangerous game, the stage was set for a climactic showdown between the audacious little band of Union scouts and one of the most famous Confederate cavalry commanders of the war. John Scott writes, "Mosby and Blazer could not long inhabit opposite sides of the Blue Ridge Mountains and Mosby was resolved to bring the rivalry to a speedy and decisive issue." After the whipping at Myer's Ford, Mosby is reported to have mocked the 1st Squadron with the words, "You let the Yankees whip you? I'll get hoop skirts for you! I'll send you into the first Yankee regiment we come across!"[29]

According to the Mosby accounts, Companies A and B of the 1st Squadron, under command of Maj. Adolphus (Dolly) Richards, met at Bloomfield and were sent out to "hunt up Blazer." It is interesting that Companies A, B, and D comprised the 1st Squadron at Myer's Ford and there is no explanation why Company D was left out of accounts of the Kabletown fight. In fact, Mosby Ranger Richard E. Hopkins of Company D describes the fight in his own memoirs, indicating that Company D was at Kabletown.[30]

Scouts were sent out to gain intelligence about Blazer's movements. First Blazer was reported to be at Snickersville, but when the 1st Squadron reached that place "the birds had flown." The squadron then crossed the Shenandoah River below Castleman's Ferry and made camp in Castleman's Woods. Scouts reported that Blazer had been at Hillsborough in Loudoun County at 1:00 P.M., then had left and, crossing the river, reached Kabletown before daylight.[31]

Charley McDonough and John Puryear were scouting when they rode up a hill and discovered they were within a short distance of several other riders in Confederate uniform. The two men thought these were probably scouts from their own command. However, McDonough, who was outlawed by Federal authorities, was leery of approaching a group of riders they did not know by sight. McDonough's reluctance proved prudent, for Puryear, impatient with his partner's timidity, soon found himself captured by a group of Blazer's men dressed as Jessie Scouts.[32]

Puryear was taken to Lieutenant Coles, Blazer's second in command. According to the tales of Mosby's men, Coles attempted to wrest information from Puryear in a way that would probably not have been approved by Captain Blazer and seems unlike the courteous Coles, who had been so solicitous toward the dying William Braxton. John Scott recounts that Puryear, who Blazer's men were aware was "one of Mosby's men . . . was roughly treated by his captors, having been stripped of his hat, overcoat, and other articles of clothing, and in addition, *it is said, had been threatened by Lieutenant Cole with hanging*." This incident becomes even more embellished in later accounts by Mosby's men after the turn of the century. The hanging threat could in fact have been invented to explain away the actual hanging of an African American boy after the Kabletown fight (see appendix A).[33]

Richards learned that Blazer and his command were proceeding south from Charles Town. He positioned himself on good ground east of the little crossroads at Myer's Shop (Myers Town). There is little doubt that Mosby's command achieved a victory fought on ground of their own choosing. It is the nagging details of this fight that have been distorted over the years. Blazer, by now emboldened by his string of successes in the Valley, lost his usual caution, or perhaps he thought that "getting the bulge" on the enemy was the most important tactic. He had never in his career as a volunteer soldier been short of audacity.[34]

Most of the Mosby accounts put the engagement at Kabletown (sometimes

named for the closer town of Myers Town) about a half-mile east of the crossroads at Myers Town and two hundred yards south of the road to Kabletown.
Richards positioned his command south of the road, which was bordered by
trees about a hundred yards deep. His intention was to fight in open ground
south of the stand of trees. He also undoubtedly did not want to get in a slug-
ging match with long arms, for Blazer's repeating rifles would have had a decided superiority over the hodgepodge of long arms with which Mosby's men
were equipped. In the engagement that followed, contemporaneous Federal
accounts are very sketchy. The stories of Mosby's men are filled with discrep-
ancies and embellishments and do not match the lay of the land near Myers
Town, even considering the changes which have occurred over decades.[35]

According to legend, Blazer was lured into a trap set by Richards when
Richards's skirmishers feigned a retreat. Blazer, feeling he had the upper hand,
mounted his men—who had been fighting on foot with their Spencers—and
charged. Richards's Company A fell back in retreat, with Blazer's command
after them. After passing the top of the hill, Company B, which had been
concealed by the hill, charged in a surprise attack. At this point, Company A
halted its retreat, wheeled about, and struck Blazer's unit on its left flank.[36]

Accounts close to the actual battle, however, suggest that the encounter
may not have occurred according to fable. It is very likely that this was a "meeting engagement" that turned out disastrously for Blazer's little band of scouts.

Several contemporary accounts put the number of Mosby's men in this
engagement at more than 300. Joseph Brown put the number at 319 and several
of Blazer's men said they were "overwhelmed by numbers." Three hundred
may have been an exaggeration, but if the entire 1st Squadron of Mosby's command was involved, as well as possible reinforcements for Mosby's command
or stragglers from Early's command that may not have been incorporated in
Mosby's own organization, this could have been close to the mark. There is
no explanation in the Mosby accounts for why only Companies A and B were
involved. In fact, the account of Richard Hopkins of Company D indicates
this company was present. On November 20, 1864, Mosby reported to an inspector of the Confederate army that he had 500 men. Even if only Mosby's
men were involved and no men from other commands, this would place 1st
Squadron strength at around 250. Almost certainly men of other commands
were riding with the 1st Squadron, which would make the figure of 300 in the
Union accounts very plausible.[37]

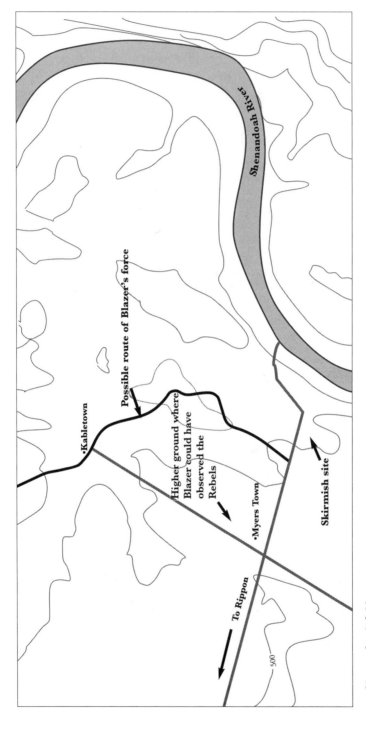

Kabletown battlefield

The gently rolling land south of the Myerstown road leading to the Shenandoah does not lend itself to the type of ambush described in the Mosby accounts. Blazer and his men probably came from Kabletown along the route shown by the old wagon track. From this higher ground, they would have had a good view of Richard's deployment, even through a screen of trees.

U.S. Geological Service

Kabletown battlefield

The Kabletown battle area, photographed from the Myer's Ford Road. It is unlikely this terrain could have concealed a large proportion of Mosby's force, especially since Blazer's men were approaching from higher ground to the north.
Author's photo

A contemporary account filed by a correspondent of the *Philadelphia Inquirer* is close to the Mosby accounts but supports the idea of a headlong meeting engagement by Blazer, who encountered an overwhelming force. This story is close enough to some of the Mosby narratives to have actually been the source of some of the stories about an ambush. Of course, the subsequent narratives would have been embellished to add additional detail and panache. Interestingly, Captain Blazer's name was distorted in the dispatch to Captain Brasher. At least one of Mosby's men believed that this was Blazer's true name and that Blazer was an alias. This misapprehension, however, does confirm the fact that Mosby's men were drawing at least some of their stories from Northern newspaper accounts.

The next morning, Capt Brasher [Blazer] captured two of Mosby's men and received information from them that a small party from the guerrilla chieftain's outlaws were about two miles from Cabletown. Captain Brasher started with two of his men on a reconnoitering expedition, and discovered a party of between 30 and 40 of the enemy. He quickly returned to his main body, consisting of 62 men, and proceeded at once to meet them. As soon as the enemy were in sight Captain Brasher drew up his men in line and charged them. The rebels fell back until the rear of Capt Brasher's command had passed a crossroad, when Moseby, with over two hundred men made a sudden dash on both sides of the road, and a sharp engagement ensued. The Union scouts were pinned at this time in a narrow lane without much chance to maneuver and were consequently surrounded and subjected to a deadly fire.[38]

Henry Pancake's Story

Henry Pancake recounts a different story some twenty years later. Despite the time lag, Henry's story has the ring of truth. He is being interviewed for his hometown newspaper and is not playing to a national audience. The illiterate grocer's story sounds as if he is totally unaware of published Mosby accounts of the battle because he makes no attempt to refute them. His story is straightforward and if there is any embellishment in the story it is probably in Henry's own role.

Henry recounts that the Scouts had been in the saddle two days and nights and were returning toward Winchester from the Luray Valley. They crossed the Shenandoah River at Jackson's Ford about daylight and rode into Kabletown, about a mile from the ford and back on the Harpers Ferry road, where they stopped to cook breakfast. Henry was within earshot of Captain Blazer and Lieutenant Coles when a "little colored boy" came up and reported that 300 of Mosby's men had crossed the ford and taken up a position about halfway between the ford and Kabletown and were watching the Scouts.[39]

The opposing forces were only about a half mile or so apart. The boy had been sent by a Union woman near the ford to let the Scouts know about their danger. Henry recalled that Captain Blazer sent Lieutenant Coles and himself forward to a little hill to ascertain the situation. This differs from accounts that it was Captain Blazer himself who made the scout and it may be Henry's exaggeration of his own part in the affair.

"We proceeded up the hill and got a good view of the rebs, and confirmed all the intelligence given by the colored boy," says Henry. In fact, the ground north of the Myer's Ford road is higher than the ground chosen by Richards, so Blazer's men would have had a good view of Mosby's men even with the screen of trees, which at that time of year would have lost most of their foliage. Ranger Richard Hopkins states that they were in "full view of Blazer's men," which adds credence to Pancake's account. Captain Blazer had mounted his command and proceeded some distance when Lieutenant Coles and Henry rejoined him. Pancake says, "We told him there were 300 of them, that they were in a good position and it wouldn't do to attack them with our little force, amounting to 65 men all told."[40]

Capt. Blazer's decision to force an engagement against an overwhelming force seems uncharacteristic. Could he just have been tired from two days in the saddle and constant action over several months or did he have the "Robert E. Lee disease"—overconfidence in his men? It may have been a simple matter of mistiming the engagement, not realizing his men would not have time to fire a few volleys from their Spencers to even the odds.

Captain Blazer, at any rate, told them to fall in "and the way we went." In order to attack Mosby's force, "who were across the road" (probably the Myer's Ford road), Henry reports that they had to let down two big rail fences. They then filed into the field, skirted by woods, where the Rebels were "in plain view of them." Henry remembers it as a "desperately daring thing to do." Blazer's men hurried as much as possible, "coming around into line like whip cracker." Blazer's men were barely in line when the Confederate force was upon them with a yell. Blazer's men got off one good volley at what must have been very close range "and then they were on us blazing away."[41]

"To get through the gap in the fence and out of that scrape, and into the road, was the aim of all," Henry remembers. However, the two sides were now completely intermingled, with "the rebs shooting our boys down and hacking our ranks to pieces. Every fellow was for himself, and when those got into the road who could get out, they flew in all directions." Some fled back toward Kabletown, some toward Rippon, and some toward the ford. "Oh, it was a nasty fight! We stood no show at all."[42]

Henry was among the last to get through the gap and into the road, with Rebels all around him and after him. He credits his escape to having on a Rebel uniform, "and that's what saved my head, just there." Henry took off down the road toward Kabletown, with Lieutenant Coles ahead of him and Captain Blazer ahead of the lieutenant. One of the Scouts following Henry was soon captured. "The balls whizzed all around me." Near the crossroads at Myers Town, Lieutenant Coles fell from his horse wounded, and he lay with his head resting on his arm as Henry passed by. "After I had passed him," says Henry, "I looked back and the foremost reb, whom I recognized as one of the prisoners we had when we made the attack, stopped right over him, aimed his carbine and shot Lieut. Coles dead." This account of the death of Coles differs markedly from the dramatized Mosby accounts, but still documents a wound received after the lieutenant had ceased being a combatant.[43]

The Capture of Captain Blazer

At this point Henry reports that only he and Captain Blazer were left on the road, with thirty to forty of Mosby's men in pursuit:

> I gained on Blazer and soon caught up with him. The Captain asked, "Where's the boys?" I replied, "All I know is one just behind and I guess they've got him by this time." "I am going to surrender," said he and I said "I'm going to get out of this." The Captain halted and gave himself up. The rebs were not over 30 yards from us and peppering away. The surrender of the Captain stopped them a moment and I gained a little, but on came the rebs mighty soon again and chased me for two miles further. The pursuing party was reduced to about ten, and those finally gave up the chase by sending a volley that whizzed all around me. When I looked back and saw they were not pursuing me, I never felt so happy in my life.[44]

Once again Henry's report of the capture of Captain Blazer is much more prosaic than the dramatized Mosby accounts that have Syd Ferguson of Mosby's Rangers riding Blazer down from behind and dropping him from the saddle with a pistol blow to the head. Blazer probably saved a few of his men by voluntarily surrendering, an action consistent with Blazer's personality and caring for his men.[45]

Richard Hopkins of Mosby's Rangers relates that Blazer threw his gun at Ferguson after it was emptied but missed. Then Ferguson, who had also emptied his pistol, struck Blazer over the head and "then they fought with fists." The truth of Captain Blazer's surrender is probably someplace between Henry's story and Hopkins's account. There may have been a struggle, but the dramatic chase is almost certainly another myth that developed over time.[46]

There is no record that Major Richards filed an after-action report; if he did it has been lost in history. Mosby simply reported to an inspector of the Confederate army that "in an action with a partisan command about 80 in number on the 18th of November he killed wounded and captured a greater

Captain Blazer's capture

Blazer's capture probably did not happen as usually depicted in the highly dramatized Mosby legends.

Harper's Weekly

part of the same." A contemporary account from the *Charlottesville Chronicle* (reprinted in the *Philadelphia Inquirer*) also supports a meeting engagement where the Confederates chose the ground. Even this "enemy" dispatch notes that Captain Blazer was "a man remarkable for skill and courage" who had been detailed with a lieutenant and eighty picked men armed with Spencer repeating rifles to hunt down guerrillas in northern Virginia, including men of Mosby's command. "In the course of several months, by indomitable scouting, he has managed to pick up a number of detached and individual members of Colonel Mosby's command, and has made for himself a creditable reputation for energy and vigilance, both in the Valley and Northern Virginia east of the Blue Ridge."[47]

The report inaccurately notes, however, that Blazer never took on a force equal to his own in number. Apparently the newspaper had never heard about the stampedes at Myer's Ford or the Vineyard. The report also clairvoyantly notes that Blazer had been "espousing himself, expecting to encounter some innumerable, unlimited numbers of guerrillas." The paper claims that Capt. A. [E.] Richards had been ordered into Clark County to do battle with "the doughty Blazer if he so wills it."[48]

The dispatch goes on to describe the encounter at Kabletown:

> On reaching the neighborhood of Cabletown, seven miles west of Snicker's Gap, scouts reported BLAZER and his force advancing from the direction of Winchester. Capt. RICHARDS drew up his men in line of battle and awaited his approach. BLAZER heralded his arrival with a shower of bullets from the Spencer carbines and then rushed down upon our troops. Capt. RICHARDS, instead of awaiting his onset, determined to meet him in full career; and when the enemy was fifty yards distant, gave the order for his men to charge. It has since been learned that BLAZER believed his men to be attacking a greatly inferior force, who would fly before his first onslaught. He discovered his error too late to save him from its consequences.
>
> The opposing squadrons rushed together with a crash. There was a momentary struggle, an uproar of shouts, and the report of fire-arms as BLAZER's men gave way before the valor of our troops, and attempted to save themselves by flight. On one side of the road was a wood; on the other a fence enclosing fields. The fugitives made for a gap in this fence; a number were shot down before reaching it; others succeeded in reaching the field, hotly pursued by our men.[49]

This account coincides in some details with Henry Pancake's story and the few other sparse accounts that have come down from the Federal side. The report notes that only one of Mosby's men was killed and five wounded, attributing most of the casualties to friendly fire. It gives the exaggerated figures of Blazer and thirty of his men captured and thirty killed outright, with the remnants scattered. Reportedly Blazer admitted to having been "beaten and broken up in a fair fight." The report notes correctly that Blazer and eighteen of his men had arrived in Charlottesville in charge of privates John A. Payne and Harry Shand of Company B of Mosby's command. That figure coincides with the testimony of Blazer's men about the number who were captured.[50]

Desperate Fighting of the Scouts

Physical evidence also supports the claims that Blazer was outnumbered by more than two to one. Several of his men where shot from multiple directions. Also, in order to ride many of Blazer's men down, Mosby's men would have needed to act much like a pack of dogs running down its prey. Blazer's men were well mounted, often on blooded horses taken from Mosby's men and other guerrilla bands. Mosby's men would have had to tire the horses out by riding in relays to wear them down over several miles.

Tobias Haught of the 13th West Virginia was surrounded on all sides by Mosby's men. He fought desperately until he was mortally wounded. Tobias died that same night of his wounds. He was remembered to have said often, "I never will surrender to them." The company's descriptive book states, "He was loved by all who knew him."[51]

Moses Swarner was also nearly surrounded and received multiple gunshot wounds to both groins, his right thigh, and back. Amazingly, Moses survived these wounds and after a long stay in hospitals was discharged for disability on May 20, 1865.[52]

Bill Wass of the 14th West Virginia tried to get away from the pursuing Rebels. His horse was running full speed when it was shot behind the shoulder and killed. When Bill saw his horse was shot, he tried to dismount but the horse fell, throwing him across a rail fence. Bill struck the fence with the small of his back and the horse catapulted on top of him. He was wearing his Spencer across his chest and the horse pinned the rifle against him. Bill was pinned in this position until the battle was over and the Rebels took the dead horse off him.[53]

Edwin R. Gibbs was a member of Bill's regiment who thought Wass had been killed. He settled Bill's accounts and wrote a letter to Bill's mother from Cedar Creek stating that Bill had been killed in a fight between Blazer and Mosby in the Valley on November 18, 1864. Gibbs did not know the particulars of the battle when he wrote the letter. The first definite information Gibbs had that Bill had not been killed was a letter from him stating that he was a prisoner in Richmond.[54]

The ferocious clash of the two sides and the close confinement of Blazer's men in the road caused horses to bolt and rear, as well as to be shot from under their riders. John G. Lyons of Company E of the 14th West Virginia also had his horse killed. The animal fell on his right lower leg, crushing his foot and ankle. John was another of Blazer's men headed for a Southern prison camp. John survived the ordeal, but he received no medical care in prison. As a result, the bones in his foot and ankle fused so that they could not be restored to their original positions.[55]

Three of Blazer's men received nearly identical wounds in their flight from the killing field. Charles Nowlin of the 36th Ohio was putting the spurs to his horse when he was hit in the back of the left elbow. Because of his position holding the reins while hunched over his horse's neck, the ball continued through his left arm and exited just above his wrist. John Parsons of Company E of the 23rd Ohio and David Price of the 2nd West Virginia Cavalry were wounded similarly in the back of the arm as they attempted to flee the disaster. Parsons had already been hit in the foot by a carbine ball that was probably fired in the initial encounter.[56]

"Captain" Hamner, a corporal in Company B of Mosby's Rangers, was pursuing an especially tall fellow. This was probably John Smith of Company H of the 91st Ohio, who was six feet two inches tall. John was also attempting to escape and was luckier than many in his unit. Williamson wrote, "Hamner fired at him repeatedly, especially each time that Smith would turn in his saddle and put up his carbine to get a shot at him." Smith may have been out of ammunition, because Williamson states that "In lieu of bullets, Smith sent back volleys of curses at each shot, but refused to surrender, until a pistol was snapped in his face and he found escape impossible."[57]

Mosby's men were in a killing frenzy during this fight. The long summer and fall rivalry between the two commands and the recent bad blood brought about by the Custer hangings and Mosby's retaliation probably had their effect. Charles McDonough, who had evaded capture earlier, is said by Williamson to have been in hand-to-hand combat with a member of Blazer's Scouts named Farrell. McDonough had fired his last shot and killed the Scout's horse. He shouted, "Farrell, you _____ _____, I am going to kill you." He called to another of Mosby's men, John Foster, to lend him a pistol. McDonough had sworn never to be captured or be taken prisoner and Foster knew this. He told McDonough, "Go on, and I'll take him." McDonough replied, "No, the _____ _____ has shot me." Williamson reports that McDonough was given the gun and "snapped it three times" at the man pinned beneath the horse. On the fourth try, the gun finally fired, striking the man in the top of the head and killing him. Unlike some of the other encounters in this fight, this incident cannot be matched to a known member of Blazer's command. No Farrell is known to have been detached to Blazer's Scouts.[58]

The Killing of Lieutenant Coles

John Alexander may have seen Lieutenant Coles killed but the accounts were probably exaggerated after the fact. Coles was indeed shot a second time by John Puryear, since this agrees with Henry Pancake's account. Puryear had escaped from his guard at the beginning of the fray and managed to obtain a weapon. "Lieutenant Cole [sic] became the single object of his pursuit, and, his eye once falling upon him, he had followed him like a Nemesis throughout the whole desperate race." After Coles was shot the second time Alexander dismounted and took his belt with two revolvers from around him, saying, "Let me pay this tribute to his memory—both pistols were empty."[59]

Alexander recounts that Coles was already bleeding profusely from a wound in the chest received during the fight. "As I moved away he rolled his dying eyes toward me with a look I shall never forget, and I would gladly have tarried to give him such comfort as I could. But this was no time for sympathy, and I hurried back to the road." Another member of Mosby's command, who looted Coles's body, told Alexander that the officer was dead when he found him. The wound received by Tom Coles in the fight was probably mortal by itself. The ball which caused him to "bleed profusely" had entered his left side and came out under his right shoulder. Puryear's shot was probably an unneeded and unchivalrous coup de grâce administered to a brave officer. Tom Coles's body was buried by some Union people who lived in the vicinity and were personally acquainted with him.[60]

The Murder of "the Little Colored Boy"

There was at least one other casualty that day who was not a member of Blazer's command. The boy who had given Blazer the report on Mosby's command was also killed. He had probably tagged after Blazer's men fully expecting the Scouts to be victorious. After the battle Captain Blazer learned the little boy had been hung by Mosby's men, undoubtedly in retaliation for Union sympathies in that area and for his providing information to Blazer's men. Not surprisingly, none of Mosby's men ever mentioned this killing in their narratives.[61]

Henry Pancake knew he had to get out of that fight and not be captured. He was one of sixteen Scouts wearing Confederate uniforms and it is likely most were killed—some possibly after having surrendered. "The chase after me was different from that after Capt. Blazer. He could surrender and live. I couldn't. I had to beat in that horse race or die and as there were 40 horses on the track after me it looked every minute like dying."[62]

After the pursuit stopped Henry rode on a little more leisurely and eventually came upon another member of the command who had been wounded but escaped. They rode on together until they reached the Union picket lines after dusk. Henry had not totally escaped his troubles for the day. "There I was captured sure enough, because I had on the rebel uniform, and put in prison. I could not make the pickets or officers believe that I was a Union soldier, and wore the rebel uniform because I was ordered to do so, but about 11 o'clock that night my story was found to be true and I was released."[63]

The other survivors of Blazer's command made it back to their units as best they could. Many ran into the camps of other commands and spread the news of disaster. Most of these men thought they were the only survivors and helped spread the myths of the encounter through Union camps and newspapers. A report from Brig. Gen. John Stevenson to Lt. Col. J. W. Forsyth, chief of staff of the Middle Military Division, on November 20 has been widely quoted:

COLONEL: Two of Captain Blazer's men came in this morning, Privates Harris and Johnson. They report that Mosby, with 300 men, attacked Blazer near Kabletown yesterday about 11 o'clock. They say that the entire command, with the exception of themselves, was either captured or killed.

I have ordered out Major Congdon, with 300 Twelfth Pennsylvania Cavalry, to Kabletown, to bury dead and take care of wounded, if any, and report all facts he can learn. Shall immediately furnish report as soon as received.[64]

The two privates who arrived at Stevenson's command were probably George Johnson of the 9th West Virginia and William Harris of the 13th West Virginia. Lt. Col. Casper Croninshield of the 2nd Massachusetts Cavalry also reported the outcome of the fight and that Blazer and most of his men had been captured: "Three of Blazer's men came into my camp. I sent them to Harper's Ferry. The fight took place near Kabletown. I suppose Mosby re-crossed the river at Smither's Ford. He is reported to have had about 300 men."[65]

Counting the Cost

It would be several days before the orderly sergeants of the various regiments could sort out the actual casualty reports. General Sheridan's report is fairly accurate, although the death toll would rise with the deaths of a couple of men who were mortally wounded but did not die on the field. Various newspaper accounts also verify most of the casualties. Appendix B gives the actual casualty figures from service records and official records of the units involved.

> *Major-General HALLECK,*
> *Chief of Staff:*
> Captain Blazer, with his company of scouts, had a fight with Mosby on the 18th instant; killed seven or eight of Mosby's men, and followed him across into Loudoun County. Blazer then returned and went to Kabletown. On the 19th Mosby recrossed the mountains and attacked Blazer; killed 16, wounded 6, and scattered the command. Twenty-nine have come in; eleven are still missing. Blazer had 62 and Mosby 115 men.
>
> *P. H. SHERIDAN,*
> *Major-General.*[66]

Sheridan's report adds up to only 52 men, so he does not have a full accounting of the casualties. From the actual records, Blazer lost 19 men killed and 16 captured. When those casualties are subtracted from the 63 men who went into the fight, Sheridan's report that 29 men had come in matches my research. Rutherford B. Hayes notes in his diary that 32 of Blazer's men had come in. Also, the number of wounded in Sheridan's report who were not captured matches the available records.[67]

Various accounts of this fight often misquote the official records to indicate that only two, three, or five of Blazer's men escaped. Some accounts assert the whole command was wiped out. In fact, Blazer suffered over 50 percent casualties, which is very high. Sheridan's count for the number of Mosby's command engaged does not make sense given the firsthand accounts of men like Henry Pancake and Joseph Brown, who put the number of Mosby's men at more than 300. Sheridan's figure may indicate that he already is contemplating a plan to elevate the scouts known as "Sheridan's Scouts" under Major Young by minimizing the number of Mosby's men Blazer encountered.

Henry Pancake reports that he went down the next day to the scene of the fight: "Twenty-two of our boys were buried near the road. The colored people had buried them. Lieut. Coles body was exhumed and sent home." The bodies of George M. Towslee of the 23rd Ohio and William E. Beatty of the 36th Ohio were also sent to their families in Ohio. Beatty's body was sent home at the request of his mother. It was sent to Jackson, Ohio, where the stationmaster did not know the whereabouts of the Rev. E. Beatty, to whom the body had been shipped. A letter addressed To Whom It May Concern, December 4, 1864, announced that a body had arrived at Jackson with a letter addressed to the Rev. E. Beatty, giving an account of the death of the soldier. The writer was distressed that no such person as the Rev E. Beatty lived in that part of the country. Notices were put in the local papers to find the family. Eventually, the family, which lived in the little town of Limerick, must have been notified, for William's body was eventually buried in the Limerick cemetery. The letter also noted that the body of Lieutenant Coles had been sent to Hanging Rock, Ohio, and would be interred there.[68]

John Opie, a Confederate cavalryman who was a short distance away, came upon the scene shortly afterward and reported "twenty-two dead men of Blazer's command in the village blacksmith's shop." Numerous after-action and casualty reports, newspaper articles, and diary records of Union men do not support as many as twenty-two dead, at least from Captain Blazer's command. At least one of the twenty-two was listed as "colored," probably the little colored boy who had given Blazer the information on Mosby's Rangers. Who were the other two? Were they hangers-on not officially in Blazer's

Pvt. John W. Robertson
John Robertson of
the 2nd West Virginia
Cavalry was among
those killed or mortally
wounded at Kabletown.
*Courtesy Dave Zullo
Collection, U.S. Army
Military History Institute*

Scouts, local Union people who may have also been working with Blazer (like the colored boy), or perhaps Confederates killed in the fight? The number of dead interred at Winchester and the men known to be in Blazer's unit whose bodies were sent back home also supports at least eighteen of Blazer's command killed plus the "colored." The two extra bodies or graves reported by Pancake and Opie are unexplained.[69]

Philip Noblit of the 23rd Ohio Infantry remembered that the Rebels "doubled our file [line] and whipped us!" Philip was shot in the back, the ball missing his spine and exiting above his groin. He was taken by Mosby's men to a house in Loudoun Valley, where he was held for several days. There he was treated by an old civilian doctor who poured cold water onto the wound and left instructions for this treatment to continue.[70]

Mosby's men probably considered the wound fatal and became careless with their attention to Philip. After three or four days, two of Mosby's men arrived at the house, leaving their pistols hanging on their horses, and left the house for some reason. Philip got up, took both pistols, climbed on one of the men's horses, shot the other horse, and made his escape back to Union forces. In the end the final encounter between Blazer's Scouts and Mosby's men was a Scout victory: one prisoner, two horses, and two revolvers lost. After arriving back at his regiment, Philip refused to go to the hospital. He continued treating the wound with cold water, thinking himself a "gritty" fellow, and did not want to be "butchered up" at the hospital. Philip survived the wound and lived for many more years.[71]

The fight at Kabletown was over. The Union mourned its dead. Archibald Waxler, the young veteran of the 36th Ohio who had survived Antietam, Chickamauga, and Missionary Ridge, was killed at Kabletown. On November 25, Capt. James Stanley of Archibald's company wrote to Archibald's father Michael: "Dear Sir It being my painful duty to inform you that your son Archibald V. Waxler, a Sergeant of my co. D on detached service as scout with Capt Blazer was killed in an engagement with the noted Rebel Guerilla Mosby near Snickers Gap on the 18th of this month. I can vouch for him, that he was in full discharge of his duty when he fell, as I know him to have been a brave and good soldier."[72]

Lt. William N. Hawkins of the 13th West Virginia wrote to his mother on December 3, 1864, about the killing of George Lamasters of Company C. He wrote that "his wife lives at point pleasant you will please go and see her and tell her of his fate and try and make up her claim and pension as she is very needy. Tell her to apply to provo marshal at Charleston and get rations. You can vouch for her being needy from this letter."[73]

Thomas Coles has been portrayed in the Mosby narratives as a heartless officer who cruelly tortured and threatened to hang a prisoner to gain information from him. Whatever the validity of those accounts, his fellow officers of the 91st Ohio remembered him as a noble soldier. Maj. Lemuel Z. Cadot of the 91st chaired a meeting of those officers on December 1, 1864, to draft a letter of condolence to the family of Thomas Coles:

> Whereas we have heard with pain and regret of the death of our worthy fellow soldier Lieutenant Thomas K. Coles while on detached duty as a member of Captain Blazers Scouts, in Jefferson Co. Virginia on the 18th ultimo:
>
> Therefore be it resolved that we bow in humble submission to the will of an all wise Providence. We cannot refrain from an expression of our sorrow

Killing of Lieutenant Coles

This dramatization was drawn by an artist not present at the scene; it was based on the Mosby accounts. The Scout officer is accurately portrayed as having been armed with two pistols but no sword or saber.

Courtesy Western Reserve Historical Society, Cleveland, Ohio

for the loss of this brave gallant and meritorious young officer who has thus fallen at the very beginning of manhood in the cause of his country.

Resolved that we tender to his parents, sisters and brother our heart felt condolence in this their sad bereavement.[74]

Tom Coles's body had been removed from the field through the aid of Rev. Joseph Little of the 5th West Virginia Infantry and Charles Kinsberry, assistant adjutant general under General Sheridan. Tom's funeral was held at Hanging Rock, Ohio, on November 30, 1864. Many friends attended the service, including several soldiers and officers. Brig. Gen. William Powell, commander of one of the divisions of cavalry under Sheridan, attended, probably indicating the importance of the death of this young officer: "Lieutenant Coles was borne to his grave by his companions in arms, with some of whom he had fought on many a bloody field, and under the starry flag which he so dearly loved, and which he laid down his young life to defend." He was remembered in a funeral announcement in the *Portsmouth Times*. Tom was "a young man of unblemished character, and had earned the reputation of a brave soldier and faithful officer."[75]

Blazer's Scouts were disbanded in January 1865 in accordance with special order no. 1, issued January 2, 1865, at Cumberland, Maryland: "The detachment of scouts formerly commanded by Capt Blazer, serving at these Headquarters, are relieved from duty and will join their respective commands without delay. The ordnance and quartermaster stores will be turned over to the ordnance officer and quartermaster at Cumberland, Md."[76]

Sheridan's Betrayal

It has been generally believed that Blazer's unit was destroyed at Kabletown. However, additional men could have been detailed from the 8th Corps and suitable officers could have been found with scouting experience to take Captain Blazer's place. However, there was a Union general named Phil Sheridan who was not above taking a good idea from a subordinate and making it his own. In the summer of 1864, Sheridan formed a unit of scouts under Major Henry Young of the 2nd Rhode Island Infantry. In organization, it was very similar to Blazer's Scouts, with men detailed from both cavalry and infantry units. However, most of the men were from cavalry units instead of infantry.[77]

Not much is known of Young's operations early in the unit's organization. However, by at least December 1864, Phil Sheridan was writing bank drafts to fund the operations of this unit. Young's Scouts became known as Sheridan's Scouts, as he put his imprimatur on the unit. Despite Captain Blazer's contribution to the protection of Sheridan's command, Sheridan does not mention Blazer in his autobiography. He does, however, mention Major Young's scouts and praises them highly. Young's unit is most famous for the capture of Confederate partisan Harry Gilmore in 1864. Sheridan loved to be associated with success, so it is likely that he would take note of Young's accomplishments but not mention Blazer because of the perceived failure of that unit at Kabletown.[78]

George Crook was bitter about Sheridan's egotism and failure to give due credit to Crook and other officers who had served Sheridan well: "General Sheridan organized a similar force for the whole army, after which *I was relieved* from any further service of that nature. These men of Gen. Sheridan were under a Major Young. Just what they accomplished I don't know, but they would dress at times in Confederate uniforms, and at times in our uniform."[79]

Crook's bitter distaste for Sheridan's self-aggrandizement is epitomized in his evaluation of Sheridan's taking credit for the outcome of the Battle of Cedar Creek. Crook is distressed that his little division (he asserts he did not really have a corps, his numbers being too small) was not given proper credit for its actions in that fight and received too much criticism for being surprised and overwhelmed on the morning of October 19, 1864. "The adulations heaped on him by a grateful nation for his supposed genius turned his head, which, added to his natural disposition, caused him to bloat his little carcass with debauchery and dissipation, which carried him off prematurely." Sheridan's possible betrayal of Blazer is unfortunately all too characteristic of the character flaws that afflicted Sheridan. These flaws unfortunately blemished his otherwise distinctive Civil War career.[80]

Capt. Richard Blazer's little command was gone, but it would leave a legacy in other wars. Lt. Harrison Gray Otis was not through with his military career. Thirty years later he would go to the Philippines and influence a soldier of fortune named Frederick Funston. George Crook, with his experience in fighting irregular forces in the American Civil War, would go west to fight Indians, arguably some of the best irregular fighters in history. He would take with him his experience in using scouts in the mountains of West Virginia and the great Shenandoah Valley.

Lieutenant Coles's grave
Author's photos

8

Until the Dawn of Peace

Return to the Infantry Line

THE 1863 Scouts from the 12th Ohio, 91st Ohio, and the 9th West Virginia who were not chosen for the mounted unit of 1864 returned to the infantry line, and most served honorably until their terms of service expired or the war ended. Many suffered greatly on grueling marches in all sorts of weather and not a few paid the ultimate sacrifice for their country. After returning from veterans' furloughs, former Scouts had a couple of months of relative inactivity before the coordinated spring campaign of Ulysses Grant began.

Many former Scouts fell at the Battle of Cloyd's Mountain on May 9, 1864. The 9th West Virginia was especially hard hit, suffering 150 casualties in their daring charge on the Confederate works. Their victory was costly. Sgt. William A. Edens of Company H was killed. Among the wounded were David M. Baker, Lawson Duffy, Hiram Lyons, Daniel V. Moore, John W. Teel, and Hiram Waugh. Martin Bruner was wounded and captured. Daniel Laughlin of Company B and Lorenzo D. Nicholas of Company F were captured. Both Daniel and Lorenzo died in Andersonville Prison.[1]

Stephen S. Glaze of the 9th West Virginia was listed as slightly wounded in the leg at Cloyd's Mountain. Stephen was fortunate this time, but he would not be so lucky at Fisher's Hill. He was wounded severely there through the left shoulder and left breast. Stephen wrote his mother and father from the hospital near Winchester on the October 4, 1864: "Dear Father and Mother, I avail myself this morning to address you a few lines which will inform you. I am in the hospital at Winchester. Wounded very bad through the left breast and shoulder but I am on the mend fine. I was wounded on the 22nd day of last month in the battle of fishers hill." Stephen did not dwell on his wound but proudly recounted the victory of the army at Fisher's Hill. "We destroyed Early's whole army nearly and took 25 pieces of artillery. Our army is follow-ing him closely."[2]

Stephen continues: "We fought a hard battle at this place [Winchester] on the 19th day of last month which lasted all day. We captured 8 pieces of artillery and three thousand prisoners and routed them completely." Stephen then writes about getting a furlough to come home, although "it will be a month before I am able. . . . you need not rite to me for I am expecting to be moved to some other hospital soon." Stephen was moved to the U.S. Army General Hospital at Broad and Cherry Streets, Philadelphia, where his wound was operated on October 17, 1864, by Assistant Surgeon T. C. Brainard. The stress of the operation was too much for Stephen; he died October 25, 1864, "of exhaustion." He was twenty-two years old.[3]

Stephen's father, Henry, wrote to the hospital about Stephen's last days and his personal effects. Both the chaplain of the hospital, William Phillips, and a member of the Sanitary Commission wrote condolence letters to Stephen's father. Chaplain Phillips sent Stephen's pocket book, containing $6.95 and some papers of value, home by express. He wrote, "I inclosed a letter with all the information I was able to collect in reference to your son. I am sorry I could not give you more satisfactory information in regard to his last moments. But he was out of his mind the last few days of his life."[4]

The 12th Ohio was more fortunate at Cloyd's Mountain. David Albaugh was struck by a minnie ball at the point of the breastbone. The ball passed through David's side, came out about eight inches from where it entered, then went through his left arm. After David fell, John Bell went to his side, loos-ened his knapsack straps and examined his wounds, which he assumed to be mortal. John returned to the line convinced he could do no more for his com-rade. Ambulances took David and other men to a barn some half a mile away where he lay overnight and the next day and night. On the morning of May 11 the Rebels captured them all, some fifteen or twenty men. One wounded man had died in the barn on the night of the 10th; there was no surgeon to treat the prisoners.

The men were put into wagons and transported to the railroad at New-burn and then on cars to Emory and Henry Hospital at Danville. Here David's wounds were dressed by a Rebel surgeon. After a week David was taken to Lynchburg, where he was put in a hospital located in a converted warehouse. Here his arm was amputated at the shoulder and two ribs removed where the ball had exited. He remained in the hospital for about three months and was then transferred to a prison at Richmond. The Confederates were probably convinced that David would never serve in the army again and he was paroled about two weeks after reaching Richmond. He was sent to Annapolis, Mary-land, where he was discharged.[5]

Patrick Collins of Company K was also wounded and captured. Samuel Irvine was captured at Cloyd's Mountain while remaining at the hospital with the wounded. He was sent to Andersonville and paroled November 20, 1864. Jonathan Miller was listed as wounded and missing in action. Jonathan died in prison at a place and date unknown.

Surprisingly, none of the former Scouts from the 91st Ohio were casualties at Cloyd's Mountain. However, many of them would become casualties at the many other battles faced by the Army of West Virginia.[6]

Colonel White Leaves the Army

After the Lynchburg Raid, the Army of West Virginia and the Scouts saw the loss of a brave and respected leader. Col. Carr B. White resigned from the army, apparently due to the effects of "a sure-destroying disease" that he had had for years. Although apparently suffering severely from his ailments, he had campaigned actively for three years with "acknowledged military skill" and "always with distinguished gallantry in action." Certainly his creation of the elite Independent Scouts demonstrated his military skill and vision in dealing with unusual military circumstances.[7]

In an unnumbered order dated July 2, 1864, Charleston, West Virginia, Carr B. White bade an emotional farewell to the men of the 2nd Brigade, which included many Scouts. He said that "with the exception of the separation of my family I am breaking up the tenderest and dearest ties I have on earth . . . and if I have one wish above another it is that every man who wears a 'White

Star' will resolve that no act of his will ever tarnish the fair name of the brigade. May god bless you and give you courage and the will to do your duty is the prayer of your grateful friend." Harrison Gray Otis remembered White as "the sweetest, gentlest, truest, bravest soul of all those gallant spirits within my personal memory that went up to God from the sacred fields of the War for Union and Liberty." Carr B. White died September 30, 1871, at Georgetown, Ohio.[8]

Harrison Gray Otis Wounded at Kernstown

The Battle of Kernstown, on July 24, 1864, was a particularly nasty affair for the former Scouts who were back in the infantry ranks. The brigades of Rutherford B. Hayes and J. A. Mulligan were ordered south from Winchester to Kernstown to oppose what was thought to be just a Confederate reconnaissance force. Instead, they found Jubal Early's entire army. Fire from the Confederates poured into the Union ranks. Harrison Gray Otis, the former commander of scouts in 1863 was in the infantry line that day. "Our First Brigade veterans returned the fire with their Saxony rifles and Enfields. . . . Men were falling by the scores on all sides. I saw Mulligan go down within a few rods of where I stood, pierced by five balls. Lieut. Col. [James M.] Comly fell by my side, stunned by a shot in the head; but giving him a helping hand he soon rose again." The Confederate force was now pushing farther and farther to the right and rear of the Union force and under the "terrible fire" of the overwhelming numbers in their front, "our little line was fast melting away." It was at this point that Otis received a severe flesh wound to the thigh: "Here I got a musket ball through the right leg. I continued, however, to take a lively interest in the 'subsequent proceedings' while getting off the field in an ambulance wagon."[9]

Harrison Gray Otis was out of action for several months with his leg wound. His wife, Eliza, came to nurse him in the military hospital and he went home on convalescent leave to Marietta, where his second child, Beulah Lillian Otis, was born in the same room with the disabled officer. Otis returned to duty on November 3, thus missing the Battle of Cedar Creek. He moved south with his regiment, riding on "the 'hurricane deck' of a mule." However, with active campaigning nearly over for the season, Otis performed duties such as courts-martial, allowing his wound to heal.[10]

Samuel Spencer's Wound

Samuel Spencer suffered an unusual wound at Third Winchester on September 19, 1864. In its charge against the Confederate flank, the Army of West Virginia had to cross the morass of swamp known as Red Bud Run. Samuel and other men decided that crossing on tree trunks would be better than trying to wade through the muck. Unfortunately, the tree trunks were also covered in moss and slime from the swamp. As more men attempted to cross on them they became even more slippery. While jumping from one log to another, Samuel fell, directly straddling the log. After the battle R. H. Barnes went to the hospital to see his brother I. A. Barnes. Here he encountered Samuel who threw off his covers, showing his privates, which Barnes could see had been wounded and were bloody. "It looked like both testicles were all gone, and like the place was swollen." Barnes was about ten feet from Spencer at the time and only got a glance. Samuel exclaimed to him, "Look what they have done for me, they have shot my ballocks off." Despite the fact that Samuel suffered from ruptures the rest of his life, it did not prevent him from having a large family, including children born in 1903 and 1911.[11]

Prison and Escape

Many Scouts who were captured ended up at some of the most notorious prisoner of war camps in the South. Several, such as Lorenzo Nichols and Daniel Laughlin, would not make it back from these hellholes. However, the temperament and intelligence that made these men Scouts served them well even in their confinement. They were resourceful fighters and their wits would see them through. Consequently, four former Scouts escaped from their captors and made it back to Union lines.

Sgt. Adam R. Head of the 12th Ohio had been sent to Andersonville after his capture. He was admitted to the prison hospital July 13, 1864, suffering from scurvy, and returned to the prison pen on August 3. Sometime after this he escaped and reported to the Union lines at Nashville, Tennessee, on August 27, 1864. Sergeant Head had weighed more than 200 pounds when he was captured, a man of "wonderful constitution and strength." T. C. Gaddis of Head's community recalled seeing Adam after he returned home: "I was unable to recognize him. He was surrounded by a party of citizens to whom he was restating his escape from prison and the incidents of his trip through the mountains of Tennessee and Kentucky. He was much reduced in flesh and otherwise physically changed. I did not recognize him, but it took only one conversation to assure one he was what was left of Sergeant Head. At the time of his capture, he was in good health, weighing over 200 pounds. . . . In my opinion he was a wreck of his former handsome self."[12]

R. E. Barrett noted that Head "was in a very bad condition, emaciated and his limbs swollen and ankles purple in color." Head's brother William stated that Adam "was nothing more than a walking skeleton. It was a marvel that he survived at all."[13]

After his horrible treatment, escape, and journey to return to the army, Adam Head was restored to his unit in good standing and honorably discharged. Some years later no less an authority than Probate Judge Jonathan Weaver knew Head as "a worthy and deserving gentleman and from the character and disposition of this man there is no doubt in my mind that he served his country nobly at the time when *she* was in need of brave and true defenders."[14]

Sgt. William May, of Company I, 91st Ohio, was captured near Liberty, Virginia, perhaps in the vicinity of the Peaks of Otter. May was also sent to Andersonville, but he escaped September 12, 1864. May reported within the Union lines at Knoxville, Tennessee, on November 8, 1864, after traveling over the mountains in the cool weather. When he came back to his unit he had a very bad cough. William May was never healthy again. He died June 23, 1891, of hemorrhaging of the lungs.[15]

Sgt. Richard Fuller and Pvt. Barnett Locy of the 5th West Virginia Infantry were sent to Salisbury Prison Camp in North Carolina after their capture at Summit Point. Union prisoners intent on escaping Salisbury had a couple of advantages they may not have had at other prison camps. Union prisoners were often helped out of Salisbury by Union loyalists, officers, and men who were in the Confederate army. "These men were forced by circumstances of having family and businesses in the South to serve the Confederate army, but secretly aided Union prisoners." Also, men who tried to tunnel out at Salisbury found it was not necessary to conceal the dirt from the tunneling because many of the prisoners lived in holes excavated in the ground and dirt from these was constantly being dumped on the grounds.[16]

Escape from Salisbury Prison

Sergeant Fuller escaped from Salisbury on October 27, 1864. He and other prisoners were probably aware of the well-traveled escape route from the prison.
Loyal officers and men would direct them to communities with known Union
sympathies. Prisoners only needed to make it to the first spurs of the Appalachians. In these hilly regions, unadapted to cotton culture, there were few
Negroes, "and where there was no slavery, there was no rebellion." This route
probably also duplicated the previously established way of the Underground
Railroad. Once it had served runaway slaves. Now it would serve their libera-
tors, who had become captives themselves. In the mountains, the number of
Union sympathizers multiplied. Wilkes County, North Carolina, among the
outlying spurs of the Alleghenies, was so strong in its Union sentiments that
it was known as the Old United States.[17]

Aid to escaping prisoners took several forms. Guides helped escapees find
their way north and elude home guards and cavalry patrols. Additionally, the
mountains were filled with "Union bushwhackers" who harried Confederate
units in the mountains. They would not leave their families to join the Union
army, fearing for their safety, and they adopted the philosophy of "When the
rebels let us alone, we let them alone; when they come out to hunt us, we hunt
them!"[18] Friendly Negroes also gladly aided the escaped prisoners and took
enormous risks to help them. Thus, Richard Fuller made his way through a
country more friendly than hostile. Despite having to march hard and ford
streams during the cold weather, he reported at the office of the provost marshal guard near Knoxville, on December 6, 1864.[19]

Barnett Locy was not well acquainted with the country when he escaped
about February 18 or 19, 1865. He ended up reaching the Union lines at Wilmington, North Carolina. Also at Wilmington was Robert F. Defoe of Company F, 5th West Virginia. After his capture, he was first confined at Richmond
about September 23 and then was sent to Danville on the 24th. It is uncertain
how Robert Defoe got away from prison. However, his name appears on a list
of prisoners of war who were confined at Salisbury and enlisted in the Confederate army. This list was an unofficial one prepared by Moses Palmer Jr. of
Lyon, Massachusetts, who had been a quartermaster sergeant in the 7th Maine
Infantry. This list was forwarded to the judge advocate at the military command of North Carolina. It was not used as the basis for any official report until

Union bushwhackers

Union bushwhackers were a scourge to Confederate cavalry that attempted to track down escaped Union prisoners in the mountains of North Carolina.

further investigation was made. If Robert Defoe had joined the Confederate army, it was probably a ruse to get outside of the camp where he took the first opportunity to make for the woods.[20]

The Burning of the General Lyon

In an incredible twist of fate, Barnett Locy and Robert Defoe were among 634 persons who boarded the contract steamer *General Lyon,* which sailed from Wilmington for Fortress Monroe on March 29, 1865. The *General Lyon* was a 1,026-ton screw steamer reported to have been a blockade runner. Her passengers included more than 200 discharged members of the 56th Illinois Infantry and at least 160 paroled or escaped prisoners of war. Besides the soldiers and crew, she also carried thirty to forty refugee families, including about thirty women and twenty-five small children. Two Negroes were also among the refugees. The weather was fair when the steamer left Wilmington, pro-

Union prisoners at Wilmington, North Carolina
Illustrations such as this one in *Harper's Weekly* inflamed public opinion in the North over the prisoner of war issue.
Harper's Weekly

ceeded down the Cape Fear River, and put into Smithfield (now Southport, North Carolina) on the Cape Fear that night.[21]

Soon after they left Smithfield the next morning, the wind, which had been blowing from the southwest, increased sharply. The *General Lyon* was a slow ship and made little progress. At ten o'clock the vessel was about sixty miles off Cape Hatteras, with the wind now nearly hurricane force and the seas running very high. About this time an alarm of fire was given and flames could be seen shooting out from behind the pilot house, located nearly in the center of the ship. Several of the ship's crew were in the rigging and very few persons were on deck. Many of the invalid passengers were confined to their berths and many of those who had started the voyage well had become violently seasick.[22]

First Mate James Gibbs and other officers immediately got the pumps working and tried to extinguish the flames with fire hoses. However, the flames gained steadily, and despite the heroic efforts of the crew and the passengers who were assisting them, the fire spread to the entire center portion of the ship, driving the firefighters to the bow and stern. The hatches had been closed because of the high seas and now those who were below rushed on deck as smoke spread through the cabins, but they were driven back by the flames. The shrieks of the women and children and their cries for help were drowned by the roar of the storm. Several of the sick, broken soldiers, who had just left the misery of the prison camps and expected to be returning home, managed to crawl on deck, only to be swept away by the waves.[23]

About half an hour after the fire broke out the engines partially shut down and the *General Lyon* swung broadside to the wind, with the flames sweeping the deck. It was now apparent that the ship could not be saved, despite the heroic efforts of the first officer, who abandoned ship only when all hope was gone. The pumps were kept going until the last minute and the fire was fought with determination. Many of the poor souls trapped below had already suffocated from the smoke. Those on deck could hear the screams and moans of the dying but could do nothing for them.[24]

At that time the steamer *General Sedgwick*, commanded by Captain Starkey, and a small schooner hove into sight, but these two ships could do nothing because of the violence of the storm and the drift of the *General Lyon* toward the breakers. The flames were now spreading violently and the boats were ordered put into the water, despite little hope that they could survive the hurricane raging around them. The first boat lowered contained ten men and the captain, who was crazed with fear and determined to save himself rather than look to his helpless passengers. His cowardice, however, was soon avenged. Barely had the lifeboat been cast loose when it drifted under the stern and was struck by the screw, going down almost instantly. One of two survivors of this boat saw the captain sink beneath the waves.[25]

Robert Defoe and Barnett Locy were among the passengers who managed to get on deck with some hope of escape. However, Robert knew that if his lifeboat foundered he would be lost anyway. He bade Barnett good-bye and asked him "to tell his wife that he would be lost as he could not swim and was therefore unable to save his life."[26]

Barnett and twenty-seven others boarded the lifeboat. It had about a mile and a half to go to reach the *General Sedgwick*. As it touched the *Sedgwick*'s side after about four hours at sea, a wave dashed it against the ship, filling it with water and sinking it. Barnett was among seven who survived, including First Mate Gibbs and Jasper Fitzgerald of the 56th Illinois. Many of those remaining on board now hurled themselves into the sea in desperate attempts to save themselves. Isaiah Colby of the 5th Ohio Cavalry, who had worked the pumps until nearly exhausted, seized a door from the galley and jumped overboard. He was in the water three hours before he was picked up. Only twenty-nine survivors were rescued.[27]

When the *General Sedgwick* left, the ill-fated *General Lyon* was burned to the waterline and drifting toward the breakers off Cape Hatteras, another victim of this terrible graveyard of ships. The fire was probably started by barrels of kerosene and oil which were kept in the engine room and overturned by the rolling ship. The contents ignited when they fell on the boiler, causing a blaze that was probably uncontrollable from the beginning. Barnett and the other survivors picked up by the *General Sedgwick* were taken to New York City, where they stayed in the soldiers home for about two weeks before being sent on to Annapolis. The largest maritime disaster, in terms of loss of life, along the North Carolina coast has been nearly forgotten.[28]

One other member of Blazer's Scouts suffered a nautical fate. After surviving prison, possibly Danville, Patrick Collins of the 12th Ohio was paroled at Vicksburg, Mississippi, on April 24, 1865. He was one of more than a thousand men to perish when the steamer *Sultana* blew up on April 27, 1865.[29]

Samuel Harrop at Andersonville

Samuel Harrop also was imprisoned at Andersonville from June 18 to the last of September 1864, when he was transferred to Savannah, Georgia. The prison must have traumatized Samuel. He was probably in a delirious state during his imprisonment and his condition may have been one reason why he was paroled.[30] Years later Sam remembered his experience through one of his poems, "Andersonville."

Long years ago—'twas on a summer night—
Between the fleecy clouds the stars were peeping
When dimly seen by their pale trembling light,
Stretched on the ground, a boy lay sleeping
Within a far-off Georgian prison pen;
And round about, there lay full twenty thousand men.

Beside him was the "dead line's" fatal bound,
Below the noisome swamp and putrid stream;
Above upon the stockade ranged around,
The sentries; you could see their rifles gleam
In the starlight as they paced to and fro,
Watching for a "shot" and thirty days' furlough.

The boy was dreaming; wild his fancy ranged;
On rapid wing to Northern climes it bore him,
And low he murmured: "I'm exchanged!" "I'm exchanged!"
His native valley sees extend before him,
Its village spire he in the distance sees,
And now his cottage home low nestling 'mong the trees.

With trembling haste its threshold he has crossed,
And father, mother, brother, sister come
To welcome him their soldier mourned as lost,
With smiles and tears back to his childhood's home,
Their words of fond endearment pleased he hears
Excess of grateful joy doth prompt the tears.

To soldier dreaming, from the church hard by
Comes floating the soft sweet sound of singing.
Hungry he wakes—'twas but the sentries cry,
From each to each repeated loud out-ringing,
Re-echoing through the night air, damp and cool,
Of twelve o'clock, all right, and here's your mule.[31]

"Here's your mule" was a common army expression that signified the
soldier's passive obedience to discipline or the submissive patience required by

army discipline. In Sam's poem, he probably refers to the submissive state of being a prisoner of war. Samuel was finally paroled at Savannah on November 24, 1864. He was admitted to Camp Parole USA General Hospital with chronic diarrhea. He was then sent to College Green Barracks at Baltimore on November 27, a common transfer point for prisoners exchanged on the East Coast. Because of his condition he was sent to Washington and admitted to the Government Hospital for the Insane for treatment on December 5. Dr. C. H. Nichols, the superintendent, reported that Harrop was suffering from diarrhea and in a condition of great emaciation and mental weakness when he was admitted.[32]

On December 31, Dr. Nichols noted that Samuel "has somewhat improved and it appears to me that the chances are about equal that he will so fully regain his health both body and mind, as to be able to return to duty. . . . He could in my opinion be removed to his friends in Ohio with safety to himself and he would probably do as well under good home nursing as at this institution." Samuel was discharged on a surgeon's certificate of disability on January 3, 1865, at Washington, D.C. Joseph Morrison, Samuel's brother-in-law, came to Washington to escort him home for he still was not able take care of himself.

Sam's mother, Mary, remembered the condition of her "Sammy" when he came home. He was "almost unable to talk to us; his flesh was blue and he had dropsy his feet being so terribly swollen that he was unable to wear his shoes. . . . His teeth became loose and one of them came out before he got well. He had a hole in his hip you could have put a silver dollar in. . . . He was not able to talk much to tell us what was the matter with him."

Sam was unable to walk much after he came home and was unable to go downtown. His first trip to downtown Gallipolis was just after the assassination of Lincoln in April 1865. By the time the 91st Ohio was mustered out Sam was well enough to rejoin the regiment at Gallia County, to go with it to Camp Dennison, near Cincinnati, as a "pleasure trip."

Silas S. Pritchit remembered that Sam seemed a little flighty at times. "One incident I particularly recollect, a squad of us went to a restaurant in the city (this was after the boys had been discharged and left Camp Dennison) and ordered dinner. Sam said to the waiter, 'You must have been expecting us.' The waiter asked why. 'Why,' said Sam, 'you've got so much prepared to eat.' . . . it was generally remarked among the boys that he was a little bit off." Sam

Cpl. Samuel Harrop
Samuel Harrop's intellectual nature is shown in this probable postwar photo of the
scout, poet, and champion of the common man.
Courtesy Nancy Morebeck Collection, U.S. Army Military History Institute

Harrop's life would never be the same after Andersonville. He would suffer
both physically and mentally the rest of his life, but the same courage that
served him as a scout would enable him to face his troubles and not become a
victim of them.[33]

Libby Prison

Captain Blazer and the men captured at Kabletown were almost exclusively
confined in Richmond-area prisons. Only one or two of the Scouts captured
at Kabletown were sent south to other prisons such as Danville. However,
while avoiding the South's more notorious prisons at Andersonville and Salisbury, Blazer and his men had to put up with the conditions of such prisons
around Richmond as Libby, Pemberton, and Belle Isle. Libby is often thought
to have been exclusively an officer's prison, but enlisted troops were kept here
as well. The third story and attic were used for the confinement of enlisted men;
officers were confined on the first and second floors.[34]

Libby Prison was a cold, dreary warehouse that had but little heat for the prisoners except that generated by their own bodies. Some of the cells were so dark that the men could only know by feel the numerous vermin crawling over them as they slept. The food was scarce and the quality of what little was provided was poor to the extreme.

> The fare for breakfast consisted of a piece of cornbread about two inches long and half an inch in breadth and thickness, with a pint of liquid called rice soup, containing about a teaspoonful of an inferior quality of rice. The dinner ration was a similar allowance of bread, with a section of boiled pork about two inches square and from one-quarter to one third of an inch in thickness. About once a fortnight a quantum of pea soup, or of water in which cabbage had been boiled, to the fulness of a pint, was doled out to each of the wretched captives, and occasionally, they were stimulated, to prevent starvation with a small portion of bacon cured in hickory ashes, oftentimes so tainted as to be not retainable by even the strongest stomachs. In both Libby and Castle Thunder, Negroes would catch rats, dress them out and sell [them] to prisoners who had the means to purchase the rats.[35]

William Lewellen arrived at Libby with a gunshot wound in his right shoulder. While in Libby, his left foot became frostbitten. He eventually lost part of the second toe due to frostbite, and an abscess on top of the instep had to be drained with an incision. David West was first sent to Belle Isle Prison, where the prisoners were camped out in rain and snow during the winter. When captured, David weighed 187 pounds and when exchanged he weighed only 129 pounds. Almost all the men imprisoned suffered to some degree from chronic diarrhea and rheumatism.[36]

John G. Lyons of the 14th West Virginia Infantry had his horse fall on him at Kabletown, breaking the bones of his right instep. Lyons was initially confined at Libby for a short time, but was then removed to the Pemberton warehouse, across the street from Libby. Pemberton was a three-story tobacco warehouse, ninety by one hundred feet, used exclusively for the confinement of enlisted men. The basement was used to receive taxes-in-kind; the remaining floors were for prisoners. In one of its rooms, twenty-five by ninety-eight feet, three hundred prisoners were confined at one time. John Lyons had to survive on the prison rations: "the same old story, vermin abounded and food was insufficient and almost poisonously bad." As with most of the other Southern prisons, medical treatment was scarce for prisoners. Lyons claimed he received no medical treatment for the injuries to his foot and ankle while in prison. By the time he was exchanged, the bones had fused and could not be reset, leaving the foot far out of shape.[37]

Captain Blazer and the men captured at Kabletown were exchanged from February 5 to 22, 1865. Blazer and his men were among those aided by the resumption of the exchange system, which General Grant agreed to on January 21, 1865. Unconfirmed stories were passed down in the families of some of Blazer's men that they had escaped from Libby Prison. Although undocumented, the stories are representative of the wit exhibited by the Scouts in other escapes. In any case, Blazer's men fared better than if they had been sent south to Andersonville or other prisons.[38]

Freedom!

The men who came back from the prison camps followed a well-established routine, depending on their health, when they arrived back North. For the most part, almost all needed some sort of medical attention. The trip home for those imprisoned in Richmond and sometimes other prisons such as Danville would begin with a journey down the James River to Aiken's Landing. Here, the men were exchanged and boarded steamers for the North. The officers and crews of these ships were solicitous if not overindulgent to the scarecrows coming onto their vessels. The men would be given a tin of coffee, a large piece of beef, and about eight ounces of bread. Such a meal, with variations such as pork instead of beef and sometimes soup, was given to the men three times a day until they reached Annapolis. Sometimes the captains would leave boxes of hardtack out between meals and invite the boys to help themselves. Unfortunately, because stomachs and constitutions had grown weak from poor food, men sometimes overate and died on board.[39]

After arriving at Annapolis, the men were marched off, although some were kept on board until decent clothing, especially shoes, could be delivered to those who lacked sufficient garb to make a winter trip through the city. They were taken to College Green Barracks, where they were given baths and a new Union uniform. The cook houses operated almost constantly from five o'clock in the morning till seven in the evening. The line would extend about a quarter of a mile and men would get back in line as soon as they ate their portion to get another.[40]

Many of the men had to be transported directly to hospitals for more treatment of their diseases or to nurse their famished bodies back to health. After spending approximately ten days at College Green Barracks the men would be transferred to Camp Parole in Annapolis and given their commutation money and two-month furloughs. The commutation money was about thirty cents for each day spent in prison, arguably the hardest money ever earned by many of these men.[41]

Although the army tried to do as much as it could for the men coming home from prison or hospitalized for wounds, the vagaries of life in the Army of 1861 often frustrated the men. Pay was a constant problem. Not always prompt during regular service, it became even more irregular for men separated from their units. One former Scout, impatient with the slowness of army pay, went all the way to the top to try to get the situation corrected. On January 24, 1865, William Emmons wrote directly to the secretary of war about the situation from Jarvis Hospital in Baltimore.

> Hon E. M. Stanton
>
> Secretary of War I seat myself to drop you a few lines to see if you cannot do something towards having us paid off at this Hospital I come into the service of my country in August 1862 and was to receive my pay every two months and I have not received any pay now for thirteen months and has a wife and children looking to me for Suport and I think it was time I was getting Some pay for I have Served my Country faithful until the 19 of October last when I received a wound and was Sent to the hospital and They are Several more here in the same fix and none has got pay for four months and Some a great deal longer and if you can do any thing towards having us paid it would be a great favor to us and Comfort to our wives and Children. . . . You will please try and have us paid Your most obedient Servant
>
> *William J. Emons [sic]*[42]

William's letter went all the way up through channels, and reports and investigations were made. The surgeon general referred the letter to Medical Director Simpson of the U.S. Army. The authorities at Jarvis Hospital indicated they had made numerous complaints about the men not being paid and confirmed that no pay had been received for four months. Indirectly, it was asserted by the army's paymaster that they were short of funds to pay the men. Whether or not the situation improved is not known, but given the woeful state of promptness of pay throughout the war, it is unlikely.[43]

Captain Blazer himself returned to duty in the Shenandoah after stays in various hospitals. He was appointed to act as the provost marshal at Winchester, Virginia. He carried out this important task with the same sense of diligence he showed in all his army duties. The duty of a provost marshal at the end of the war would have been exacting. There were still active guerrilla bands, disloyal citizens, deserters, and those who would take advantage of the chaos for their own lawless ways.[44]

Not all of Blazer's men served with distinction to the end of the war. Samuel Burdett of the 9th West Virginia, who had written a patriotic letter to the *Ironton Register* on September 26, 1863, was listed as a deserter at Cedar Creek on October 26, 1864. Samuel seems an unlikely deserter, having done secret service and appearing to be a man proud of his regiment and a staunch Republican. Samuel never applied for a pension after the war. Could he have decided after Cedar Creek that he had enough money from his secret service duties to flee the further hazards of conflict? Or perhaps he disappeared while on special duty and was erroneously listed as a deserter by an officer or orderly sergeant who did not know of his service? It is a mystery that may never have a good answer.[45]

Deadly Incident at Cherry Run

John Clute of Company E, 36th Ohio, was a hothead who had an exaggerated view of his rights as a citizen soldier. In November 1864 he was awaiting the sentence of a general court-martial for disobeying an order from a Sergeant Phillips of his regiment. With winter approaching, men were scrounging materials to make their tents more livable. Boards for flooring were a prized commodity. Boards from cracker boxes and other discarded packing boxes were available for the taking. But John Clute had his eyes on some higher-quality boards belonging to the government or an officer. As he attempted to procure them for his own comfort, he was accosted by Sergeant Phillips, who told him he could not use them. Clute snapped at Phillips that "he had as good a right to them as anyone else" and took the boards in complete disregard for the sergeant's order.[46]

Thus awaiting sentence, John was on a train from Winchester carrying soldiers of the 36th Ohio and 13th West Virginia on December 31, 1864. At Cherry Run, West Virginia, along the Potomac River, the train stopped for fuel or water and the soldiers of both regiments clambered off the cars. The night had been bitterly cold and the men had been in the unheated cars for several hours. They immediately sought ways to warm themselves, if only for a while. A large bonfire was burning along the tracks and many of the men gathered around it for warmth. Many officers of the regiments remained in their heated cars, a dereliction of duty that contributed to the tragedy that would follow.[47]

Across the tracks from the fire was a small general store owned by a Mr. Roach. He and his family lived upstairs from the store. The area around the station was under command of Capt. Daniel Link of the 1st Maryland Home Guard Cavalry. It was a veteran unit, but the battle-hardened men of the 36th Ohio probably were unaware of its service. There had been a problem with a train earlier in the day when troops had attempted to crowd into the little store to escape the cold, causing a great deal of disorder. Captain Link was determined to prevent a repetition of that scene and posted his cavalrymen at the store to strictly limit the number of men allowed into the store.[48]

The first group of nine or ten men allowed into the store stayed about ten minutes, behaved well, bought what they wanted, and left. The next group included John Clute. Several of the men were using "insulting language." Clute in particular used some very "blackguard language," in the words of one witness. There were ladies in the store and Captain Link asked Clute to show a little respect and to behave as a soldier and gentleman. Clute then asked Roach if he had "any razor straps, shoulder straps or any other kind of straps to sell," a remark intended to disparage Link's officer status by equating his officer's straps with common items. About this time there was a push at the door as more men attempted to get inside. The guard told the men to wait a while and they would be let in. Clute told the guard, "Damn you, they should have as much right in as you have."[49]

Captain Link admonished Clute for the second time to watch his language as there were ladies present. Clute's reply was, "I don't care a damn if there is." The captain then informed Clute that he would have to leave if he could not behave himself. "I can't see it," was the curt reply from Clute. At this point, Link had had enough of the brash Ohio soldier. He grabbed Clute by the collar and shoved him out the door.[50]

Clute now joined his comrades around the fire. Whether there was any alcohol involved on this New Year's Eve is not known, but the Ohio men were fired up nonetheless. The veterans of Second Bull Run, Antietam, Chickamauga, and the Valley of the Shenandoah were probably less than pleased to be ordered about by a group of soldiers they regarded as prima donna railroad guards. A few minutes after Clute joined the group around the campfire a rock crashed against the wall of the store just below a window. Witnesses testified that the men dared Captain Link to come out, calling him a "dammed shoulder strap son-of-a-bitch." A man in the crowd stooped to pick up another rock. Link said, "I will go out and try to quiet the boys," and stepped out onto the porch. He approached the group of men who were rubbing their hands and warming their backs at the fire.[51]

Link approached the man with the rock and said, "If the man that picked up that rock to throw at me, now let him throw it." Clute responded, "I did not pick up any rock to throw at you, but if you will lay off your straps I will give you a damn good whipping." The captain mildly replied, "I don't hold myself in that line of business." What happened next was seen in different ways by those who viewed the scene in the flickering firelight. Some thought Clute brought his arm back to strike at the captain. Others did not see the move. Link clearly felt threatened, drew a revolver, and, at point-blank range, cocked it. Clute saw the move and attempted to run, but the captain fired before he had taken a step. Clute ran about twenty-five yards and fell dead.[52]

Captain Link was brought up on court-martial charges on January 26, 1865, at Cumberland, Maryland. Col. W. S. Lincoln of the 34th Massachusetts served as president. The court was heavily stacked against Captain Link, for many of the officers of the court came from units that had served together and had also detailed men to Blazer's Scouts. Whether they knew Clute had been a member of the Scouts is unknown, but it is likely they did. Among the members of the court were Col. Benjamin. F. Coates of the 91st Ohio, Col. William H. Eunochs of the 1st West Virginia Veteran Infantry (originally colonel of the 5th West Virginia), and Capt. Harrison Gray Otis of the 23rd Ohio Volunteer Infantry. Otis almost certainly would have heard through the ranks that Clute had been a member of the fabled Scouts.[53]

It was charged that Link did "unlawfully and willfully shoot and kill, without just cause or provocation, one John Clute, private Co. E, 34th [sic] Regiment Ohio Volunteers." Link pleaded not guilty to the charge but was found guilty and sentenced to be dishonorably discharged from the service and to serve a term of hard labor for two years. Considering that he had killed a man, it was a light sentence. Upon review, Gen. Winfield Scott Hancock dismissed the sentence, believing that Link acted in the rightful discharge of his duties. "The interests of the service in enforcing good order and military discipline demand that Captain Link should be exonerated." Link was released from arrest and returned to his command. Despite the dismissal, Captain Link probably could have handled the situation better. He had armed guards whom he could have used rather than attempting to confront an unruly enlisted man himself. But the loudmouthed John Clute had brought the situation on himself. It may have been fated that Captain Link or some other officer or soldier would have eventually sealed Clute's fate. John Clute was initially interred near Cumberland, but his remains were later moved to Antietam National Cemetery.[54]

The Guerrilla Murder of Jesse Middaugh

Jesse Middaugh did not reenlist in the army. Jesse's service and close encounters had probably convinced him that he had done enough. On March 9, 1864, he wrote his sister that he had "just come from the railroad out in dixey and have had a vary hard and cold time of it. I have bin gone five weeks yesterday." He also advised his sister to tell his brother Frederick not to reenlist, but to "come down in this part of the world where he can see some of the Southern Ladys I have got one for him." Probably in jest, he tells his sister, "I think I shall marry out in dixey. I have become acquainted with some several young and handsome rich girls in my time A scouting service in the last 3 years." Jesse vows that he will "spend one month in old Erie" after he gets his discharge and visit his old friends "if eny such I can find."[55]

Jesse returned home to Ceredo, West Virginia, after his discharge. His wife had been struggling to survive in an area rife with guerrillas and pure brigands acting under the guise of guerrillas. Women who had been left alone made their home in Mary's eight-room house. She made suits and overcoats for Union men and taught the children who lived in the house. The women probably took solace that Mary Ann did not seem to be fearful of the many lawless bands in the area.

However, the guerrillas still were able to pillage her home. One group came to the house while Jesse was away. The captain of this group was either a friend or related to Mary and the men filled the house, helping themselves to what they wanted. Mary Ann had just had a hog butchered. She was forced to cook for the men and when they left there was not a scrap of meat left in the house.

Jesse was unfortunately home the next time a guerrilla band came calling. This time it was the gang of "cut-throats" under the command of the "notorious Bill Smith." They entered the town and went directly to Jesse's house. It is likely that they knew about Jesse's activities in the army and went intent on more than just pillage. Mary Ann called these men Jeff Davis Rebels. Jesse was shot through the heart before he could do anything. They drove Mary Ann and the children out of doors and set fire to the house. One of the "scoundrels" broke one of Mary Ann's legs with a blow from his gun. But the guerrillas were about to pay a price for their depredations. Mary chose the correct moment to draw a revolver she had hidden and shot one of the men— possibly Smith himself—stone-cold dead. She then turned her weapon on another man and seriously wounded him. The stouthearted Rebels now precipitously fled the area, leaving their dead companion unburied. The Middaugh family was left with nothing but the clothes on their backs. They were taken to Catlettsburg, Kentucky, on the Ohio River between Ashland and Huntington, West Virginia, where they were well cared for and where Jesse was buried.[56]

Jesse had been living under his old army alias, Jack Meadows, and that is how he was identified in a newspaper article published shortly after his killing. This name occurs in the order by General Crook that relieved Pvt. Jack Meadows of the 5th West Virginia from duty as a Scout. Curiously, Jack Meadows is not on the rolls of the 5th West Virginia, but Jesse Middaugh is. Both names begin with the same letters. Jesse probably chose a name which resembled his own to insure he could use it under duress. The clerk writing this order may have also used Jesse's alias rather than his real name. Jesse is listed as a scout in July 1864, almost certainly under Captain Blazer. This order could have been a temporary relief of duty or perhaps was never fulfilled.[57]

In April 1865, Lee surrendered to Grant, and Johnston to Sherman later in the month. Former members of the Scouts would celebrate the victories, but would also mourn the loss of Lincoln, their beloved commander-in-chief. By July 1865 all the regiments had been mustered out. Many Scouts from the 23rd Ohio posed with the regiment for their muster out photo in Cleveland, Ohio. In true Western fashion, these hardy Ohioans could not abide strict military regulations, even for such a formal setting. Officers and some enlisted men wore regulation headgear, but almost all the men wore the ubiquitous slouch hat of the Western soldier. A smattering of straw hats could be seen in the ranks, and a few—including even the color guard—wore light-toned bowlers. They were already on their way to being citizens again.[58]

9

The Untold Legacy of Blazer's Scouts

The Indian Wars and the Philippine Insurrection

The Death of Captain Blazer

THE great American tragedy was over. The great battlefields were silent, awaiting the time they would become shrines for the American people to remember momentous command decisions and the bravery of the soldiers of both sides. But no monuments would be raised in the mountains and valleys where Blazer's Scouts fought their desperate battles. The Scouts left little formal written record of their deeds. In 1865, Asbe Montgomery of company A of the 9th West Virginia wrote the little book that was the only attempt to present a complete record of their deeds. Most of the Scouts were content that they had helped win the great struggle, and they returned to their farms, their businesses, their families and friends.

Richard Blazer came home to Gallipolis and became a leading figure in the community. He and his wife, Dolly, had a large family, which Richard supported in a variety of occupations. He sold goods after the war and farmed and was elected sheriff of Gallia County for four years. His term as sheriff expired in 1872. After that, he became a coal operator, having learned the trade by working in coal mines sixteen miles above Gallipolis. Afterward, he became a contractor for building roads. Richard farmed the last year of his life.

In late October 1878, Richard and his son Jacob were doing farm chores—sowing wheat and hauling lumber—when a storm came up and they got wet. Richard took cold, which brought on kidney trouble, the same disease he contracted while a prisoner of war. After a few days his kidneys failed and he passed away on October 29, 1878.[1]

It has been alleged in many books and articles, and is an article of faith in the Blazer family, that the captain died of yellow fever brought up to Gallipolis on a ship from the plague-stricken city of New Orleans. However, there is much evidence from the captain's pension file, the weather reports of the day, and the way yellow fever is spread by mosquitoes that it would have been unlikely he was stricken by this disease. Although Captain Blazer's military career ended with the Civil War, the legacy of his unit would be passed on to other generations of warriors fighting wars against insurgents.[2]

Confederates Stir up the Western Tribes

During and after the American Civil War, the United States was faced with widespread Indian rebellions on the Great Plains. A good case can be made that the Indian tribes, particularly the Sioux, took advantage of the Civil War to try to roll back the tide of settlers that had descended on their homelands. The Confederate government, much like the French and British before, saw an opportunity to enlist Indian allies against its enemy.

Confederates in Missouri and Arkansas, such as Albert Pike, recruited Indian allies for the Confederacy. Cherokees were among the troops with the defeated Confederate forces at Pea Ridge, Arkansas. After the battle Union troops noted the large number of Indians dead on the field and captured eleven Indians among four hundred other Confederate prisoners. All these Indian prisoners were killed in escape attempts before they reached prison camps. The other Confederate prisoners noted the deaths of the Indians and word was spread back to the South. In the aftermath of what appeared to be premeditated killing, other Indians joined forces with the Confederacy and "great hostility spread through the entire Indian country as far north as the Canada line; all of which was fomented by the Confederacy." The regular army, almost to a man, had been withdrawn from the West to fight in the Civil War. Volunteer regiments of locals tried to fill their shoes to protect local settlements and guard the emigrant trains. By 1864 the bloodletting of the Civil War may have convinced some Indians that the whites would all kill each other. The Indians probably saw an opportunity and took it.[3]

Certainly the Confederacy continued to agitate the Indians wherever it could. In the area around Fort Riley, Kansas, it was reported that emissaries from the Confederate government were "making inflammatory speeches" and attempting to alienate the Southern Cheyennes and Oglala Sioux. Confederate efforts were not as successful north of the Platte River to stir up the Northern Sioux or Cheyennes "because such emissaries would be shot if they fell into our hands." However, there were even rumors that efforts were being made to incite insurrection in the villages north and northwest of Fort Riley.[4]

No matter how much influence the Confederacy had on the uprising, a full-scale Indian war was raging in 1864 that generated numerous newspaper stories about battles with the Indians and terrible massacres committed against the settlers. At the same time, Union authorities were dealing with irregular warfare waged by guerrillas in Arkansas, Missouri, Kentucky, West Virginia, Virginia, and elsewhere. As mentioned in chapter 1, the Union was already using organized groups of independent scouts in antiguerrilla activities and to guard regular forces by acting as front and rear guards or to undertake special missions. At least the activities of Captain Blazer's Independent Scouts against Confederate partisans had been made known to the War Department in 1863 and 1864. At the same time the War Department was receiving reports about the activities of such scouts, it was also responsible for planning actions against hostile Indian tribes. The influence of the actions and reports of counter-partisan units on the recruitment of Indian scouts to help with the Indian insurrection cannot be discounted.[5]

The First Recruitment of Organized Indian Scouts

In late 1864, Gen. Samuel R. Curtis recruited seventy-six Pawnees to help put down Cheyenne and Sioux turbulence on the Great Plains in what is now Kansas and Nebraska. This unit was organized as a typical company, which was supposed to be 100 men. At least one independent company of "Omaha Scouts" composed of whites was also organized to take the field against hostile Indians. Samuel Curtis had been a veteran of partisan warfare during the Mexican War when Mexican guerrilla bands threatened American supply lines and attacked vulnerable groups of soldiers. The scouting parties Curtis organized were ad hoc and usually small. His diary does not mention any use of organized groups of scouts to fight the guerrilla threat. It is interesting that he may have known Carr B. White, who went on to found the Independent Scouts in the Civil War. At the same time that Curtis was dealing with the Indian threat, he also had to deal with Confederate guerrillas. The experiment with the Pawnees was successful and two years later in 1866, the U.S. Congress passed "the act to increase and fix the Military Peace Establishment of the United States." Among its provisions, it authorized the president to "enlist and employ in the Territories and Indian country a force of Indians, not to exceed one thousand, to act as scouts."[6]

In an incredibly simplistic assessment, Time-Life's book *The Scouts* states that "neither the Civil War nor West Point trained officers to face the irregular warfare of the Indian Wars." This completely overlooks the activities of Crook in West Virginia and Virginia, Curtis in Kansas, and other officers in Arkansas, Missouri, and Kentucky, who faced constant combat with a wily and secretive foe in the form of partisan units. While not as woods wise as Indians, these men were nevertheless experienced woodsmen and deadly foes who knew when to fight and when to flee.[7]

When the Civil War was over, the march West commenced with even more vigor. Soldiers, many with pension money and bounty money saved from the war years, could take advantage of cheap or free land on the frontier. The Indians, facing the loss of still more tribal territory, resisted even more fiercely than before.

George Crook and His Indian Scouts

The Indian Wars against the Sioux and other Indian tribes are unfortunately identified in the popular culture with George Armstrong Custer and the various massacres perpetrated against the tribes by the United States Army. However, the greatest opponent, and at the same time friend, of the American Indian was George Crook. The unassuming Crook became the greatest "Indian fighter" in American history, but it was a role he did not relish. Writers have failed to take note of the connection between Crook's highly successful use of Captain Blazer's unit in the Civil War and Crook's later use of organized units of scouts during the Indian Wars. Almost as soon as Crook arrived in the West, he started organizing his units of scouts, which became one of his trademarks in warfare against the Indians. Although Crook had previous experience fighting Indians in the Rogue River War, he does not note any use of organized groups of Indian scouts. It is only after his association with Blazer's Scouts during the Civil War that he became absorbed in the formation and organization of groups of Indian scouts.

Organization and discipline were key items that Crook and other army officers gave the Indian scouts. They were organized along regular army lines, in companies, battalions, or even regiments. They were given army ranks. The Indians were valuable in themselves for their knowledge of Indian ways, but they became even more valuable if discipline limited some of their natural inclinations. Hence, Crook could use Indians from tribes normally hostile to each other in concert against the tribes warring against the army. Lack of discipline was what made many partisan ranger units ineffective during the American Civil War, and officers like Crook knew that no matter how good the fighter or his knowledge of terrain, discipline would make him even better.

In 1866 and 1867 George Crook was once again in the Pacific Northwest, dealing with a guerrilla war in the Oregon, Nevada, and Idaho region against the Paiutes, or "Snakes." Crook was put in charge of two companies of "Warm Spring scouts." Crook also raised a band of Snakes that were led by Crook's mixed-blood chief scout, Archie McIntosh. This was another example of Crook's preference for using scouts closely related to the language and culture of the people he was fighting. But of course Crook had already done this with his Southern Yankees of the Civil War era.[8]

Besides using Indian scouts against hostile tribes, Crook experimented with another method that attempted to use men who knew the ways of their enemies. When assigned to the Southwest about 1870, Crook organized a group of fifty Mexicans to use against the Indians. This was done at the recommendation of prominent men of the Southwest who believed the Mexicans could be highly successful since they knew the ways of the Indians. These worthy citizens influenced Crook, who took their advice that "they knew the country, the habits and mode of Indian warfare, that with a little pinole and dried beef they could travel all over the country without pack mules to carry their provisions, that with ten days' rations on their backs they could march over the roughest country at the rate of from thirty to fifty miles per day, that they could get inside an Apache and turn him wrong side out. In no time at all, I hired fifty of their people for scouts." Unfortunately, the Mexicans never lived up to their reputation and this experiment turned out to be a disappointment for Crook.[9]

Crook was a subtle warrior. He would often attempt to persuade the Indians to abandon hostile ways. In this he was often successful because he would gain the Indians' trust. "In dealing with the Indian you must first be *honest.*" At the beginning of his campaign against the hostile Apaches in 1871, he had a "long talk" with friendly Apaches and explained to them in simple terms the advantages of peace and how Crook would treat all Apaches. He never made promises he could not keep and proposed to be fair to all bands. Crook told the Apaches he was not interested in how the wars had started, but he only wanted peace as soon as possible. He explained to them that he hoped all the hostiles would come in without bloodshed, but if not he expected the "good men" to help him run down the bad ones. He told the Apaches that this was what the white men would do and sent word out to all the bands that this was how he would deal with the Apaches.[10]

Crook's own attitude toward the Indians is well stated in an address he made to the Society of the Army of West Virginia at its reunion in Cumberland, Maryland, September 2–4, 1884. Like most Americans of the time Crook believed in manifest destiny, but he did not believe in simply pushing the American Indians from their land. He believed that European expansion was inevitable and the army was its vanguard. However, he also believed that the tribes needed to understand that the only way they could survive was to adapt.

> The same lesson of magnanimity to a conquered foe which we learned together in Virginia and Georgia—the magnanimity which told the rebel that he was free, with no badge of tyranny or conquest to rest upon him, we wish to apply to the Cheyenne and Apache. After proving to him that our Government is strong enough to crush, we are trying to demonstrate that it is generous enough to save and instruct; that after having stricken the shackles from the limbs of millions of the black men, we do not intend to enslave the remnant of the red men.
>
> Our object is not to destroy, but to build up; to teach our weaker brother the dignity of labor and the wisdom of law and order; to instruct his children in rudiments of our knowledge, and prepare the race for the dignity of citizenship, and rescue it from the thraldom of vice and vagabondage.[11]

Crook would also use other Indians as intermediaries to convince hostiles that warfare was disastrous to the Indians. Some criticized Crook for avoiding

combat whenever he could, whether between Indians and whites or between the tribes: "Crook is forever trying to make peace." Scouts were a primary weapon in the general's methods of Indian pacification; for that is what Crook really desired. The idea was not just to use the Indians to find or fight other Indians, but to change the behavior of the scouts, influencing them to adopt the ways of the white man—and through them, the tribe. "In warfare with the Indian it has been Crook's policy—and the only effective one—to use them against each other. To polish a diamond there is nothing like its own dust. It is the same with these fellows. Nothing breaks them up like turning their own people against them."[12]

In 1875, Crook was assigned to the Department of the Platte. Here, Crook employed Shoshone and Crow scouts against the Sioux. A small party of eighty-six Shoshones joined Crook's column on June 14, 1876, and fought at the Battle of the Rosebud.

The Battle of the Rosebud, fought on the anniversary of the Battle of Bunker Hill, was the only engagement Crook ever lost in his campaigns against the Indians. Crook claimed: "The Rosebud was lost because of overwhelming superiority in numbers of Indians and their superior equipment, being armed with the latest repeating rifles. They outnumbered the soldiers three to one. The Indians used a system of tactics using their superior numbers to divide the soldiers and defeat them in sections." This same set of tactics would be used to devastating effect days later at the Battle of the Little Big Horn.[13]

At the conclusion of the Yellowstone campaign, Crook contemplated the superiority of Indian scouts: "I always try to get Indian scouts, because with them scouting is the business of their lives. They learn all the signs of a trail as a child learns the alphabet; it becomes an instinct. With a white man the knowledge is acquired in [the] after life." The Yellowstone campaign was followed by the Powder River campaign in late 1876 and the spring of 1877. On this campaign Crook was able to enlist Sioux as scouts and warriors, having broken through opposition by tribal chiefs and the Indian bureau.[14]

Crook and the Apaches

When Crook returned to Arizona in September 1882, reorganizing the scouts was one of his main occupations. In 1885, to handle the breakout of the Chiricahua Apaches in May 1885, Crook utilized large numbers of Indian scouts, well organized under his best officers, to chase the renegades. General Sheridan authorized Crook to enlist two hundred additional Indian scouts to be used against the hostile Chiricahuas. One group, under Lt. Charles B. Gatewood, numbered one hundred men.[15]

Crook's methods were very effective but even men such as General Sheridan often misunderstood or failed to appreciate Crook's ideas, especially his use of Indian scouts. Failure of the authorities in Washington, especially General Sheridan, prevented Crook from obtaining peace with honor with the Chiricahuas. Sheridan especially did not understand the scouts. In a telegram dated March 31, 1886, Sheridan disparaged Crook's scouts for allowing the Chiricahua leader, Geronimo, and his party to escape. This wounded Crook's pride, for the scouts and his use of pack trains were part of the system which he felt was "peculiarly his own." Crook believed that without his scouts the Apache campaign could not have been effectively pursued.[16]

Sheridan admonished Crook that with the amount of cavalry and infantry Crook had on hand he should be able to handle the situation. This of course revealed Sheridan's complete lack of understanding of Indian warfare in the Southwest. No amount of regular infantry or cavalry would be able to success-fully deal with the Apaches. Eventually, a complete break occurred between Sheridan and Crook, and Crook asked to be relieved if he could not follow his own methods. Crook's methods were eventually proved right. After Gen. Nelson Miles relieved Crook, he attempted to deal with the Chiricahuas ex-actly as Sheridan had ordered—with regular troops. He was unsuccessful and in the end had to deal with the Indians, eventually sending Lieutenant Gate-wood to set up a meeting with the hostiles and arrange their surrender.[17]

George Crook's use of organized scouts was very similar in both the Civil War and the Indian Wars. His ideas on scouts came out of a long tradition of scouting units, certainly going back to Rogers' Rangers. Crook's West Virginia scouts built on the ideas of Carr B. White, who organized the original Inde-pendent Scouts for the Kanawha Valley in 1863. Crook, however, really refined the operation. Whether it was to cut the diamond of a Confederate partisan ranger unit with the dust of West Virginia and Ohio woodsmen or to cut the diamond of hostile Indian tribes with the dust of other American Indians friendly to the whites, George Crook knew that knowledge of the enemy was all important. Sun Tzu, the great Chinese military strategist, knew this and perhaps this is where men such as Carr White and Crook ultimately took their example.

Harrison Gray Otis: Always a Warrior

Another scout who served in the Civil War also may have had an influence on future military operations. One of the former Scouts who returned to their West Virginia or Ohio homes after the Civil War was Bvt. Lt. Col. Harrison Gray Otis. Otis had already demonstrated that he was ambitious and the Civil War had given him a zest for army life that would last the rest of his life. Initially he returned to his home at Marietta, in the rolling hills of southeastern Ohio, along the Ohio River. For about eighteen months he was the publisher of a small local newspaper. In 1866 and 1867 he was official reporter for the Ohio House of Representatives.[18] However, after the excitement of the war, Marietta proved too confining for his abilities.

At this time, he began his attempts to obtain a commission in the regular army. He received endorsements from several prominent individuals who had held important positions during the war. These included Brig. Gen. J. D. Cox, who had held positions in West Virginia, and Brig. Gen. Isaac Duvall. Duvall had been the courageous commander of the 9th West Virginia Infantry and had gone on to division command. After the war he became adjutant general of West Virginia. Most important, his appointment was solicited by Rutherford B. Hayes, the colonel of the 23rd Ohio Infantry, to which Otis had been transferred in 1864. Hayes, at the time serving as a U.S. congressman from Ohio, had also gone on to command a division in the 8th Corps. In an endorsement for Otis's brevet promotions, Hayes had noted that he was distinguished for "intelligence, ability, good conduct, and gallantry."[19]

Otis received a provisional commission as a 2nd lieutenant in the 39th U.S. Infantry as a result of these endorsements. However, he had to pass an examination by a board composed of two regular officers who were West Point graduates: Maj. Gen. Samuel Heintzelman (Col.) of the 17th U.S. Infantry and Maj. Gen. (Lt. Col.) George Sykes of the 5th U.S. Infantry. Otis failed this examination. The board gave him good marks for his service as a volunteer, his record, writing and spelling, and physical condition. He received less sterling marks on other subjects, with mediocre or low marks for geography, the U.S. Constitution, grammar, tactics, and arithmetic. His low grades in some of these subjects probably reflected his less than formal civilian education, but may also have reflected his lack of a military education. However, there is also an element of suspicion in the final outcome of this test. The test results were handwritten on a printed scorecard. It is apparent that in two of the subject areas the original scores have been overwritten by lower scores. Could the two West Pointers have adjusted the grades to deny an army commission to a largely self-taught volunteer? It is not known whether these changed scores alone influenced the outcome of the exam, but the army's icy indifference to Otis's further efforts is also suspicious.[20]

Otis wrote to the War Department asking for a reexamination, stating that he was sure he could do better now that he knew the nature of the exam. However, his record does not reflect an answer from the War Department. He wrote frustrated letters, concerned that his request had been lost in the bureaucracy or even in the mail. Finally, in 1868 he asked the War Department to return the original papers and other documentation because he had made a decision to pursue other career options.[21] Had Harrison Gray Otis been given a regular commission in the U.S. Army, the history of newspaper publishing in the United States and southern California history might have been changed forever.

Otis moved to Washington, D.C., and became a foreman in the Government Printing Office in 1868 and 1869. During this time he also became the Washington correspondent for the *Ohio State Journal* and was in charge of the *Grand Army Journal*. Otis continued his interest in politics by becoming a member of the soldiers' and sailors' convention in Chicago that first nominated General Grant for the presidency. He closed out his Washington career as a chief of a division in the U.S. Patent Office from 1871 to 1875.[22]

In 1876, Otis moved to California, where he first settled in Santa Barbara and managed the *Santa Barbara Press*. He also served as a special agent of the U.S. Treasury to enforce the terms of the lease of the Alaska seal fisheries to the Alaska Commercial Company. In 1882 he moved to Los Angeles, where he purchased a substantial control in the *Times*, which had absorbed the *Weekly Mirror*. By 1886 he had acquired full control of the paper and served for the next thirty years as president and manager of the *Times Mirror*.[23]

Eventually the *Times Mirror* became the *Los Angeles Times* and Otis became wealthy and famous in southern California. Some might call him rich and infamous. Remaining the ardent Republican and a conservative, he detested the Progressive movement and had a continual war with unions. Harrison's attitude to his adversaries was to take no prisoners. Many probably do not realize that some of the forces that drove Harrison Gray Otis may have been formed in the Independent Scouts, fighting guerrillas in West Virginia. Here,

ROOMS OF EXAMINING BOARD, 125 BLEECKER STREET,

NEW YORK, October 14 1867.

The Board examined _Harrison S. Otis_ for
2d Lieut. 39th U.S. Infy may. 3.

Service as Volunteer:— 3

Record:— 3

Writing and Spelling:— 2½

Physical:— 3

General Aptitude:— 2¾

Geography:— 1

Regulations:— 1½

Constitution, U.S.:— 1½

Tactics:— ½

Grammar:— 1½

Arithmetic:— 1½

DECISION OF BOARD: Rejected —

President of Board.

The altered examination card of H. G. Otis

In the suspicious examination card of Harrison Gray Otis the grades for General Aptitude and Geography have been marked down from the grades originally given.
Courtesy National Archives

truly no quarter was given and none expected among the combatants. The Union man could expect a sudden bullet from the darkness of a thicket, and the bushwhacker, if caught, could expect an immediate firing squad or, more likely, death by hanging.

Harrison Gray Otis has been called an "angry, choleric man" who would

"punch out with either his fists or his newspaper at all who dared offend him."
It has been said, "He brooked no slights, however innocent, upon his person."
Chroniclers have made much of his feuds with his enemies in the unions or
his disagreements with other publishers and anyone who opposed his head-
strong beliefs. However, Otis was quite reasoned with his many friends from
the army, men he considered as honest and forthright as he. With these men
he remained lifelong friends and they showed their wholehearted support for
him. This was the case when he applied for an appointment as a brigadier general of volunteers in the Spanish American War.[24]

Brigadier General of Volunteers

In 1898 the nation was propelled into war against Spain by the sinking of the
battleship *Maine*. Otis, despite his position as a rich businessman, offered his
services to his country once again. He was still an imposing man even though
his hair was now white, and intellectually he was still very sharp. As with his
attempt to obtain a regular commission after the Civil War, many of his former colleagues now lobbied for his appointment as a brigadier general of volunteers to President William McKinley. McKinley, himself a former member
of the 23rd Ohio, received these endorsements favorably.[25]

However, his political enemies, primarily the trade unions, tried to sabo-
tage his appointment. They used one of his own editorials against him. The
government originally proposed using only the regular army and the National
Guard in the conflict against Spain. Otis, who had seen the tragic results of
green officers and men in the Civil War, proposed that veterans of that fight
be accepted as volunteers for the fight against Spain. The trade unions pounced
on the editorial to denounce Otis for "denigrating" the California National
Guard. Long telegrams were sent to President McKinley detailing Otis's trans-
gressions. However, despite their best efforts to railroad Otis's appointment,
the unions could not overcome the power of his army friends.[26]

Otis became commander of the 1st Brigade, 2nd Division of the 8th Army
Corps in the Philippines. He took part in the final campaigns against the Spanish and was present during the conventional part of the Philippine Insurrection.
His brigade played a significant part in the capture of Caloocan on February 10,
1899, and the seven days' "arduous and victorious" campaign against Majolos
at La Loma on March 25, 1899. Otis's service in this campaign is noted in his

*Brig. Gen. Harrison
Gray Otis*

Harrison Gray Otis was
a brigadier general of
volunteers in the Spanish-
American War.
Courtesy National Archives

citation to brevet major general: "he successfully executed the orders of his Corps and Division commanders to wit 'The first Brigade will pierce the enemy's center.' This part of the general movement having been impetuously carried out at the passages of the River Tuliahan, early in the forenoon of that day, in the face of a heavy fire from a numerous enemy intrenched along the northerly bank."[27]

As a result of these actions, the Philippine Insurrection was initially defeated. The Filipinos had made the mistake of trying to fight the Americans conventionally on fixed lines of defense. Inaction was never conducive to the temperament of Harrison Gray Otis and he resigned his commission on April 3, 1899. Otis had previously forwarded to the War Department a conditional resignation that was withdrawn at the request of his corps commander, Maj. Gen. Ewell S. Otis (no relation).[28]

Once again Otis's enemies tried their best to slander him. They started a rumor and then put it in print that he was going to be dismissed for cowardice and incompetence by Maj. Gen. Arthur MacArthur, his division commander, and had resigned rather than face dismissal. The story was made up out of whole cloth, for Arthur MacArthur was the officer who recommended Otis's brevet to major general. Also, his political enemies should have known that a man twice wounded in the Civil War and who had seen action at Antietam and many other heated engagements was no coward. It is no wonder Otis brooked no quarter for these enemies, considering their despicable attempts to slander his military career.[29]

Examples of Otis's personal courage were told by one of his staff officers. After Manila was taken from the Spanish, there was a short period of tension between the Americans and the natives before the Philippine Insurrection broke out. The brigade commanded by General Otis was stationed at a very dangerous point on the line. Units of rebels had entrenched themselves and were obviously looking for trouble. Orders had been received from American army headquarters that U.S. forces were not to engage in combat with the Filipinos.

One afternoon, the rebels in the trenches opposite the American position opened fire on Otis's brigade. "Bullets were popping all around." The general was aware of his orders not to engage in battle, but he was beside himself at the actions of the Filipinos. Ordering a staff officer to accompany him, "he started on foot, unarmed and alone, across the fire-swept zone and walked straight up to the rebel trench." The astonished Filipinos stopped firing. The general sternly ordered the rebel captain to come out and explain himself.

The rebel was startled and scared half to death even though the general was unarmed and alone except for the staff officer. He blurted out lame explanations. Otis then ordered him to form up his men, which he did. "Now," said the general, "I am an officer of the United States Army. I want you to present arms to me as evidence of your respect for my government." The Filipino officer meekly did as he was told. General Otis acknowledged the salute, turned on his heels, and walked coolly back to his own troops.[30]

On another occasion at the front, which just happened to fall on the general's sixty-second or sixty-third birthday, his unit was pinned down behind a mud wall by a Filipino detachment. "Bullets were pouring down like rain. The grass was cut down around them as though by a mowing machine." All the other officers were crouching down behind the wall, but General Otis was standing up. He was very indignant at getting hit in the face by the mud thrown up by the bullets hitting the wall. The other officers tried to get the general down by pulling on his coat, but he stood there all alone wiping the mud from his face and "calling down his wrath upon the concealed Filipino riflemen."

Finally one of the staff officers had a "happy thought." "Gen. Otis," he said. "This is your birthday. You wouldn't want to be killed on your birthday, would you?"

This seemed to have an effect. "Well," Otis said thoughtfully, "Now that would be a poor way to celebrate a birthday, wouldn't it?" So he finally sat down with the others.[31]

After his resignation from the army, Harrison Gray Otis returned to Los Angeles and his beloved *Times*, where he continued to work for many more years. He eventually turned over control of the operations of the paper to his son-in-law Harry Chandler. But Otis continued to take an active part in the operation until his death in 1917, and he influenced a man who would become legendary for his ability to conduct counterinsurgency warfare.

Frederick Funston and the Headquarter's Scouts

One of Otis's regimental commanders was Frederick Funston, the colonel in charge of the 20th Kansas Volunteer Infantry. Funston was an adventurer with no formal military training, a hero worshiper who admired the exploits of men such as Custer, Grant, and John Paul Jones. Funston was born in New Carlisle, Ohio, November 9, 1865, and was brought to Kansas when only two. He was the son of a Kansas farmer and politician. He had pursued a variety of careers, always seeking adventure. He pursued a career as a journalist and then embarked on government expeditions to Death Valley and Alaska as a botanist. After attending a rally in Manhattan in 1896 promoting the Cuban cause, he signed up with the rebels as an artillery officer. He saw much service, was twice wounded, and narrowly escaped execution after being captured by the Spanish. Quick-witted, he convinced the Spanish that he had deserted from the rebels and was spared. After the United States entered the war he convinced the governor of Kansas to appoint him a colonel of volunteers and thus found his way into the company of Harrison Gray Otis, former commander of scouts in the Civil War.[32]

It is not known how close Otis and Funston were as general and subordinate, but there must have been many long nights around campfires and in officers' quarters when Otis could have regaled the younger man with tales of

Brig. Gen. Frederick Funston
Frederick Funston was a
regimental commander under
Harrison Gray Otis during
the Spanish-American War.
His Headquarter's Scouts
were almost a direct copy of
Blazer's Scouts.
Courtesy Library of Congress

the Civil War, including the actions of a young scout officer in the mountains
of West Virginia. Funston's love of adventure and his varied experiences probably led him to be fascinated by tales of the great war and the men who had
endured that crucible of fire. After Harrison Gray Otis left the army, Funston
became commander of the 4th District during the Philippine Insurrection. Now
Funston was fighting a war much like that experienced by Otis and Richard
Blazer in the mountains of West Virginia. It pitted a stronger, better-equipped
army against a ragtag band of rebels who knew the country well and could take
advantage of that knowledge to engage their stronger foe on terms of their
own choosing.[33]

One of the first things Funston did was form a group of handpicked men
into a unit known as the Headquarter's Scouts. The men were chosen "by
their various commanders for their horsemanship, courage, and reliability" as
well as their ability with a rifle and knowledge of scouting techniques. Many
had been cowboys before the war and all shared Funston's love of adventure.

Funston, despite his rank, served as the de facto commander, going into the field to pursue guerrillas. Funston proudly noted, "They were in the field more than half of the time, and always on the go. . . . They could take care of themselves anywhere, and could whip ten times their number of Filipinos any day. I have often thought of the things that could be done with a regiment of cavalry made up entirely of such material. . . . They were a remarkable body of men. During the year and a half that they accompanied me on every trip or expedition of any kind, and including several 'hikes' that I was not on, the aggregate number of miles that they marched reached such a figure that I hesitate to give it."[34]

Local residents were initially suspicious of Funston, but he eventually won their trust and was able to gather valuable intelligence about guerrilla activities. Funston started to whittle down rebel capabilities. It was slow, desperate work in difficult terrain. There were mountains like Otis experienced in West Virginia, but the tropical vegetation provided even more cover for guerrillas than the tangled hills along the Kanawha, New, and Gauley Rivers or the shrouded, misty heights of the Blue Ridge. As in the mountains of West Virginia and the Blue Ridge, the peaceful farmer by day might be a desperate enemy at nightfall.[35]

Funston's accounts of his adventures with the Scouts indicates he reprised the role of Richard Blazer. It was something he probably relished doing, given his nature. As a brigadier general, he should not have been in the field, but this was the perfect opportunity to lead a band of men like the one Blazer had led during the Civil War. It is uncanny how many of Funston's comments mirror language used by Asbe Montgomery and how the methods of the two scout groups coincide. The similarity seems too close for mere coincidence. Besides using specially selected Anglos as scouts, Funston also used units of Filipinos, much as George Crook used Indian scouts. Here the direct connection to Blazer is murky, but certainly military officers and those who had studied military operations were probably well aware of Crook's use of Indian scouts. Many of the officers in the Philippines had served in the Indian Wars and they viewed the Filipinos much as they did Indians. In many respects, the Philippine Insurrection had many similarities to the Indian Wars and officers undoubtedly used the lessons learned from the American conflict in their prosecution of the insurgency in the Philippines.[36]

Conclusion

The accomplishments and legacy of Captain Blazer and his brave, resourceful men unfortunately have not been recognized by history until now. While suffering ultimate defeat at the hands of the enemy, the Scouts were also largely forgotten because Phil Sheridan never gave them the credit they deserved. Probably because of Kabletown, Blazer was never given any honorary brevet ranks, even though he greatly deserved these honors for his total service during the war. He was entrusted with responsibilities far greater than the rank he wore.

Blazer's men became mere props in the accounts of the war written by Mosby's men and later chroniclers of Mosby's command. Mosby's men certainly deserve credit for being a burr under the saddle of the Union army and, most visibly, almost at the doorstep of the Federal capital. However, Mosby never did affect the strategic situation, not even early in the summer of 1864, when some have given him credit for causing Sheridan to retreat from his planned advance up the Shenandoah. Captain Blazer's Scouts were an impediment to Mosby's operations throughout the critical summer and fall of 1864. By the time of the Scouts' defeat at Kabletown, the war would be all but lost for the Confederacy, even though the South would hold out through the spring of 1865. The defeat at Kabletown was also probably one of the reasons why Sheridan eventually sent his cavalry to clean out Loudoun County in December 1864. Sheridan could now devote more resources to halting Mosby's operations than when he was in direct conflict with Early.

The concepts of men such as Carr B. White and George Crook and the execution of those concepts under Captain Blazer eventually would become part of the strategies, doctrine, and tactics taught in American military schools for combating guerrillas in the modern world. Captain Blazer's unit was one of the first attempts to put together a truly elite unit to combat guerrillas on their own terms. They conducted deep raids and undertook special missions much as the modern Army Rangers or Green Berets would do.

Captain Blazer's ability to gather intelligence on enemy forces by methodically questioning local civilians and to gain the trust of local civilians by fair treatment would become part of the idea of winning the hearts and minds of populations in future conflicts. Despite the distortions and exaggerations, the respect shown Blazer's Scouts by Mosby's men also indicates that they were considered a much more formidable foe than the regular cavalry units.

Though not recognized, Blazer's unit also had an effect on future military operations through the operations of George Crook in the Indian Wars and Harrison Gray Otis's influence on Frederick Funston's use of scouts in the Philippine Insurrection. It is a legacy that deserves to be placed in the annals of American military history.

Appendix A

An Essay on Mosby's Command

In the 135 years since the end of the American Civil War, John Singleton Mosby and his Rangers have become legendary in the pantheon of Confederate heroes. First written about by Mosby's chosen chronicler, Major John Scott, and some of the Rangers themselves, the Gray Ghost and his men have been the subject of many books and articles. The problem with all of these accounts is that they have been decidedly one sided. This is especially evident in telling the tale of the encounters between Blazer's Scouts and Mosby's command.

With the exception of Robert E. Lee and Stonewall Jackson, more books and articles have probably been written about Mosby than any other Confederate leader even though his actual accomplishments fall far short of the exploits of Confederate cavalry leaders such as Nathan Bedford Forrest. It is as if Mosby's men and their admirers had made a conscious decision to publicize the Rangers. There seems to be an effort to justify themselves to the world and especially to the rest of the Confederate veterans who served in regular units. The latter endured the hard and bitter fighting in the trenches at Petersburg at the end of the war while Mosby and his men lived at home or in safe houses in their own region. With the exception of the occasional empty chair and men captured and sent off to prison, the life of the partisan ranger was glamorous and lucrative. They made the papers North and South; indeed they were often more noted in the Northern press than the Southern. They could also divide their spoils, with a portion going to the Confederate government and perhaps two portions to themselves—thus the need to show they did more and affected actual military operations rather than being a pesky annoyance.

John Scott and J. Marshall Crawford were the first chroniclers of Mosby's command, in 1867. Scott, who was not a member of Mosby's command, wrote his history at the request of Mosby himself. Mosby did not see the book until after it was in print and apparently did not criticize any of Scott's work. Scott's account became the bible for nearly all other Mosby accounts. Scott begins the distortions of the story of Blazer's Scouts by asserting that they were called the Legion of Honor, a term never used by any of Blazer's own men to describe themselves. He originates the dramatized accounts of the killing of Lieutenant Coles and the capture of Captain Blazer. He also exaggerates the number of casualties in the Kabletown fight.

Scott uses an interesting literary technique that gives his book an even greater aura of authenticity. All the accounts of incidents and engagements are written to an imaginary Percy, with dates concurrent with the actual happening. This gives the reader the impression that they are contemporaneous accounts. In fact, the stories were gathered by Scott two years after the war and blended into his narrative. Although the early publication of this book allows it to make use of material still fresh in the minds of many of the participants, it still is not the completely firsthand account he makes it seem.

The Kabletown fight is a classic case study of how the Mosby tales of their engagements with Union units are embellished and distorted to portray the Rangers as latter-day Robin Hoods who always best the clumsy and incompetent sheriff's men, as Brian Pohanka points out in his foreword. Very few authors have analyzed the engagements of Mosby's men and Union units in detail with full use of Union sources. Dennis Frye in his essay on Mosby as a factor in the Shenandoah Valley campaign of 1864 carefully examines two of Mosby's great exploits: the Berryville Wagon Train Raid and the Greenback Raid. Frye shows that the major importance of these two raids is the embarrassment they caused the Union government and army, brought to the citizens through the newspapers. Frye also makes the case that there were concrete things Mosby could have done but did not do to aid the Confederate cause, such as freeing Confederate prisoners on their way to prison camps. In fact, there is no evidence that Mosby ever freed a single Confederate prisoner. The prisoners waited in vain for Mosby to "make a dash" and free them.

Since Mosby fought against such a wide range of Union units, there has been little opportunity to analyze his myriad engagements in as great a depth as I have done here for a few actions. If such analyses were conducted, it is highly likely they would find the same exaggeration and distortion. Only by sifting through the various accounts from Mosby partisans, newspaper stories, and accounts from Union sources can the true story of Kabletown be established. Careful reading of the Mosby accounts reveals many inconsistencies. Most of the Union accounts about Kabletown are consistent and can be verified by a careful reading of the Confederate accounts.

The nearly contemporaneous account of Pvt. J. Marshall Crawford of the Kabletown fight also has many inaccuracies, but it does provide a few grains of truth from a member of Mosby's command who was there. Crawford asserts that Richards had "one third fewer men than he [Blazer] had." Crawford writes that Richards had only 75 men with him while Blazer had his whole command of 100. In fact my research indicates that Blazer had less than one-third the number that Richards did.

Crawford also never mentions Puryear's killing of Lieutenant Coles. He merely states that upon escaping from his captors, he had a club in one hand and a pistol in the other and "went in, knocking down on one side and shooting on the other." Crawford also says that Blazer had a "hand-to-hand fight" with Syd Ferguson, who knocked him off his horse, and that Blazer surrendered. This story matches very closely the Richard Hopkins account. It seems certain that some altercation occurred after Blazer told Henry Pancake he was going to surrender. The fabled horse chase probably did not happen.

One omission in all the Mosby accounts is the killing of the little African American boy who was sent to warn Blazer that he faced a large number of Mosby's men. The systematic omission of this incident indicates that all involved had agreed upon a code of silence. Scott, Williamson, Alexander, Munson, Crawford—none mention the affair. In the early accounts by Scott and Crawford, written during the first two years after the war, there may have been some fear that naming the perpetrators may have subjected them to criminal prosecution for war crimes. This is especially likely if additional retaliation was carried out on the family that sent the black child. One of the possible explanations for the additional graves witnessed at the blacksmith shop is that they were additional Union sympathizers who were killed but whose bodies were removed to local cemeteries. Unfortunately, death records for Jefferson County do not exist to confirm this. More likely, contemporary and later writers fail to mention the incident because it would have damaged the chivalrous image they wanted to project.

Besides the specifics of the Kabletown fight, other general distortions crop up in the Mosby accounts. The claim by Munson and Williamson that Mosby's men never wore complete Union uniforms is contradicted by numerous accounts. The Southerners looked with disdain on the so-called Jessie Scouts dressed in Confederate uniforms and so do not want to be tarred themselves by what they regard as unchivalrous methods. Mosby would have been able to acquire numerous Union uniforms from the dead and captured Yankees who were victims of his raids. In fact, one of the reasons most of Blazer's command lie in unknown graves is that the bodies were stripped of all clothing and equipment. Only those whose bodies the families specifically requested to have returned were identified, probably by someone in their unit who knew them well.

The Mosby chronicles make much of the superiority of the revolver and Mosby's preference for that weapon. The revolver was almost certainly the prime weapon in Mosby's arsenal, but there is evidence that Mosby's men carried carbines and probably shotguns as well. Mosby's men have been noted acting as sharpshooters in support of other Confederate units. In their pension affidavits, several of Blazer's men testified they were struck with carbine or shotgun pellets. In fact, the latter weapon is actually a very good close-in weapon. The assertions that the saber was a useless noisemaker are more well founded and Blazer's men also did not carry them. Sketches of Blazer's men show them armed only with pistols and their rifles.

Mosby's men often downplay the use of the revolver by Blazer's men. In fact, Blazer's men were generally as well armed as Mosby's with pistols, and Blazer believed in the same shock tactics as his foe. Blazer's men were also very good shots. Even in old age, Bill Wass was said to have been able to shoot the eye out of a squirrel when others could not even see the squirrel.

Modern writers have used the various Mosby accounts as the basis for their books and articles. While attempting a degree of objectivity, most have simply never plumbed the sources that would have presented a more balanced treatment of Mosby and his opponents. While many of the sources used for this book were quite scattered, Asbe Montgomery's little book has been listed in bibliographies such as Dornbusch's and also Shetler's *West Virginia Civil War Literature*, yet has not been used as a source in any of the modern accounts. Montgomery is not only ignored in the Mosby chronicles, but Jeffrey Weaver also leaves out any of Montgomery's account in his book on Thurmond's Partisan Rangers. This despite the fact that Shetler's bibliography is listed as a source for his book.

Another primary source that has not been used by most authors is the actual inspection report of Capt. R. K. Meade of General Early's staff, conducted on November 20, 1864. This report has some very interesting details that are in conflict with the secondary reporting of this inspection in the various Mosby accounts and books by modern authors. This report notes that all 500 of Mosby's command reported for the inspection. Although Meade reports that Mosby had turned in many deserters in his area of control, it is likely that he does not report men who had absented themselves from their own commands to ride with him. It is very likely that Mosby told any men who were not officially in his command to distance themselves from this inspection. The absence of descriptive books or morning reports of Mosby's command would have facilitated such a ruse. The men of the 6th Virginia Cavalry who were killed in the escape by George McCauley, Joseph Brown, and others are perfect examples of men riding with Mosby but not officially in his command.

The late Virgil Carrington Jones was really the first modern biographer of Mosby, but his writing is colored by his personal acquaintance with some of Mosby's Rangers, the Mosby family, and the family members and friends of Mosby's command who passed on stories. Jones added additional layers of myth to the Blazer versus Mosby legends by elevating Blazer to a "hardened Indian fighter." This was probably through a misreading of the autobiography of Gen. George Crook.

Jeffry Wert's book on Mosby's command is probably the best overall modern work with a more objective view of the Rangers. He uses more Union sources than most other accounts to give a more balanced account. However, even in Wert's account, additional layers of legend and myth are added. He repeats the story that Blazer's sword was found years later in the carriage house of Rose Hill, secreted away by Blazer's captor, Syd Ferguson. In fact, period drawings of Blazer and Lieutenant Coles show these two officers wore only pistols. An 1863 cavalry saber is in the possession of the Blazer family and is most likely the arm that Blazer possessed in 1864. Also, if Blazer had been armed with a saber on that fateful day, he almost surely would have used it to slash Ferguson from his horse. This is one additional detail which makes the fabled horse chase implausible.

Like the earlier book *Rebel: The Life and Times of John Singleton Mosby* by Kevin H. Siepel, the most recent biography of Mosby, *Gray Ghost*, by James A. Ramage, does justice to Mosby in its coverage of Mosby's distinguished postwar career, especially his role in reforming the foreign service. However, the book's coverage of the Mosby-Blazer fight at Kabletown repeats many of the errors of the past. In addition, Ramage considerably undercounts Mosby's command, making the exploits of the raider seem even more remarkable. Ramage places Mosby's strength at never more than 400 men, when almost all other writers place Mosby's total strength in late 1864 at over 800, counting his own men and all the hangers-on he had gathered from other Confederate commands who wanted a share of the loot. Like most writers before him, Ramage overstates the loss to Blazer's command at Kabletown and dismisses Sheridan's report of Blazer's strength, which in fact is right on the mark at sixty-two or sixty-three men. Most writers make the mistake of using the *Official Records* strength for Blazer's command as 100 men, as in Sheridan's famous message: "I have 100 men who will take the contract to clean out Mosby's gang." In fact Blazer's true strength in the field probably never exceeded eighty-some men. This was typical of nearly all companies in the mid-to-late war period. It would be a rarity for a unit to go into the field at full strength.

Ramage also recounts at face value the John Alexander story of the ambush at Kabletown. As I have discussed here, the lay of the land at Kabletown makes this ambush a near impossibility, especially if Blazer's Scouts came from Kabletown, where the land is higher in elevation, giving Blazer's men a clear view of the Rebels, as in Henry Pancake's account.

In his essay on Mosby's role in the 1864 Valley campaign in *Struggle for the Shenandoah*, Dennis Frye is one of the few writers to take a true, unprejudiced look at Mosby's effect on Sheridan's operations. He gives due credit to Blazer's Scouts as a factor in breaking up Mosby's scouting operations. Mosby's failure to significantly interdict Union supply efforts is carefully scrutinized. Perhaps Frye's most telling criticism of Mosby is his failure to free even one of the thousands of prisoners marched back to Harpers Ferry from the wreckage of Jubal Early's army.

A Note on Sources

To the greatest extent possible, I used primary sources for this book and secondary sources with a healthy dose of skepticism. Perhaps it is a combination of my training in a hard science and the natural suspicion from being a former intelligence officer that always leads me to question sources and then question them again. Obviously, I have been very hard on Confederate sources in this book and on later writers who have used them with too little caution. However, even Union sources need to be viewed in the context in which they were written. As an example, the article "The Legion of Honor: A History of That Invincible Band Know as the Blazer Scouts" in the *Ohio Soldier,* which I used for this book, is a very good source. The first part of the article was written or told by someone (possibly John Alexander) who knew firsthand Blazer's scouting techniques in 1863. The second part of the article, on the 1864 campaign, appears to use the Mosby accounts and repeats the myth of the Loyal Legion.

Many authors have used the wonderful sketches of the artist James E. Taylor but have not realized the timing sequence of these drawings—in particular as they relate to Blazer's Scouts. Taylor rode with Blazer in October 1864 and recounts his acquaintance with the officer. The drawings he made of Blazer's Scouts on the march and relaxing at a camp site are accurate and drawn from life. The drawings Taylor made of the killing of Lieutenant Coles and the capture of Captain Blazer were made long after the fact and based on the Mosby stories. Taylor obviously did not witness these events. What is accurate about the drawings is the appearance of the Union officers and how they were dressed and equipped. The drawing of Lieutenant Coles's pistol belt on the ground shows that Blazer's men did not carry swords or sabers.

The story of the conflict between Mosby's Rangers and Blazer's Scouts is a true classic. The efforts of men such as Carr B. White, George Crook, and Richard Blazer in creating such an elite unit would be emulated decades later with the creation of the Green Berets and Army Rangers. Blazer's Scouts were special forces in the truest sense and their story is a special one that can now be told. Defeat, myth, and intrigue cannot sully their record any longer.

Appendix B

Kabletown Casualties

Killed in Action at the Battle of Kabletown
(Myerstown) November 18, 1864

Thomas Coles, Lt. Co. C, 91st Ohio Vol. Inf. (Body removed to Ohio.)

Tolley, John W. Pvt. Co. F, 9th W.Va. Vol. Inf.

Hacker, John C. Pvt. Co. A, 13th W.Va. Vol. Inf.

Keith, Sylvester. Pvt. Co. F, 13th W.Va. Vol. Inf.

Lamasters, George. Pvt. Co. E, 13th W.Va. Vol. Inf.

Riley, John V. Pvt. Co. I, 13th W.Va. Vol. Inf.

Schmitter, Luke E. Pvt. Co. G, 13th W.Va. Vol. Inf.

Haught, Tobias. Pvt. Co. K, 14th W.Va. Vol. Inf.

Martin, Elias. Pvt. Co. I, 14th W.Va. Vol. Inf.

Rairdon, Daniel S. Pvt. Co. F, 14th W.Va. Vol. Inf.

Williams, Solomon. Pvt. Co. A, 14th W.Va. Vol. Inf.

Brown, John. Pvt. Co. F, 23rd Ohio Vol. Inf.

Towslee, George M. Sgt. Co. G, 23rd Ohio Vol. Inf. (MIA; body possibly removed to Ashland, Ohio.)

Heidschuck, Jacob. Pvt. Co. E, 34th Ohio Vol. Inf.

Beatty, William E. Pvt. Co. B, 36th Ohio Vol. Inf. (Body removed to Jackson Co., Ohio.)

Waxler, Archibald, Sgt. Co. D, 36th Ohio Vol. Inf.

Willington, Amos B. Pvt. Co. K, 36th Ohio Vol. Inf.

Barton, Thomas A. Pvt. Co. A, 91st Ohio Vol. Inf.

Robertson, John W. Pvt. Co. A, 2nd W.Va. Cavalry

Captured

Blazer, Richard. Capt., 91st Ohio Vol. Inf.

Lowe, Samuel F. Pvt. Co. B, 5th W.Va. Vol. Inf.

Drennen, Andrew. Pvt. Co. B, 9th W.Va. Vol. Inf.

McComas, George. Pvt. Co. D, 9th W.Va. Vol. Inf.

Haynes, John R. Pvt. Co. E, 13th W.Va. Vol. Inf.

Smith, Marshall. Co. D, 13th W.Va. Vol. Inf.

Lyons, John G. Pvt. Co. B, 14th W.Va. Vol. Inf.

Jones, Malon. Pvt. Co. C, 12th Ohio Vol. Inf. (consolidated with 23rd Ohio).

Parker, Andrew J. Pvt. Co. I, 12th Ohio Vol. Inf. (consolidated with 23rd Ohio).

Bentley, Albert. Pvt. Co. I, 23rd Ohio Vol. Inf.

Maynard, William. A. Pvt. Co. K, 23rd Ohio Vol. Inf.

Lewellen, William. Pvt. Co. C, 36th Ohio Vol. Inf.

West, David W. Pvt. Co. B, 36th Ohio Vol. Inf.

Schultz, Jacob. Pvt. Co. C, 91st Ohio Vol. Inf.

Smith, John. Pvt. Co. H, 91st Ohio Vol. Inf.

Thompson, John. Pvt. Co. D, 91st Ohio Vol. Inf.

Wounded

Giles, Sanda (Alexander B.). Pvt. Co. B, 23rd Ohio Vol. Inf.

Maynard, William A. Pvt. Co. K, 23rd Ohio Vol. Inf.

Noblit, Philip. Pvt. Co. I, 23rd Ohio Vol. Inf.

Parsons, John. A. Pvt. Co. E, 23rd Ohio Vol. Inf.

Price, David. Pvt. Co. B, 2nd W.Va. Cavalry

Swarner, Moses. Pvt. Co. K/G, 34th Ohio Vol. Inf. (mounted). (Severely wounded.)

Nowlin, Charles. Pvt. Co. I, 36th Ohio Vol. Inf.

Roster, Blazer's Independent Scouts

This is the most complete roster obtainable for the men who served in the unit officially known as the Independent Scouts. Unfortunately, it is undoubtedly incomplete and some of the brave men who served in this unit will never be known. Sources include unit morning reports; regimental muster rolls, returns, papers, and order books when available; compiled service records (CSRs); pension records; *The Roster of Ohio Soldiers; West Virginia Adjutant General's Reports* for 1864 and 1865; and other sources that mention men belonging to the Scouts. Based on a search of morning reports, muster rolls, and regimental returns, generally only men who are listed as detailed to the Independent Scouts, Division or Headquarters Scouts, or Blazer's Scouts are included in the roster unless additional evidence supports the individual's association with this unit. Also, the time frame in which men were detailed was used to separate the men of Blazer's Scouts from other scouting expeditions. The CSRs often did not have a full accounting of men detailed or detached. For these men the original returns of the units, on file at the National Archives, were particularly valuable.

Additional biographical information comes from county histories, family histories, cemetery records, obituaries, and local newspaper stories. The names used in the roster are the names borne on the rolls and used in the compiled service records. Additional names, nicknames, or actual aliases are given in parentheses. The term *alias* is used here in a broader sense than its usual definition. Hence mere misspellings of names or nicknames become aliases, as the term is used by the War Department in the CSR. In many cases the so-called alias is actually the correct family spelling of the name. Most common diminutives of names, such as Tom for Thomas, were in use during the Civil War. However, they are given only where they can be documented. The soldier's rank is that he held while a member of the Scouts. Additional ranks, whether higher or lower, are given in parentheses.

West Virginia place names are listed as Virginia if noted before the formation of the state in 1863 and thereafter as West Virginia. Jefferson County, the location of many of the encounters between Blazer's Scouts and Mosby's command, was incorporated into West Virginia in 1866. For locations in this county, Virginia is used. Virginia (Va) is also used if directly quoted, a practice that was very common at the time.

Abbreviations

Standard abbreviations are used for states and months. Additional abbreviations are as follows:

AAQM—Acting Assistant Quartermaster
abs—absent
AC—Army Corps
actg—acting
adm—admitted
AG—Adjutant General
AGO—Adjutant General's Office
aka—also known as
appt—appointed
assn—assigned
attch—attached
AWV—Army of West Virginia
b—born (date of birth)
batt'n—battalion
brig—brigade
brig gen—brigadier general
bur—buried
capt—captured
cav—cavalry
CCO—Camp Chase, Ohio
cem—cemetery
cert—certificate
CGB—College Green Barracks, Annapolis, Maryland
CH—Court House
CM—court-martial
CMO—chief muster officer
cmmdg, cmmdr—commanding, commander
co—county or company
commis—commissioned
comp—complexion
consol—consolidation
conval—convalescent
cpl—corporal
cpt—captain
CS—Confederate States
CSR—compiled service record
d—deceased

d—died (date of death)
dept—department
des—deserted
descr—descriptive
det—detached or detailed
ds—detached service
dis—disability
disch—discharged
dist—district
div—division
enl—enlistment
enr—enrolled
exch—exchanged
exp—expiration
febris intermitt.—intermittent fever
febris remitt.—remittent fever; a fever that drops but does not altogether disappear
furl—furlough or furloughed
gen—general
GO—General Order
GAR—Grand Army of the Republic
GCM—general court-martial
gen—general
gen hosp—General Hospital
govt—government
GSW—gunshot wound
hosp—hospital
HQ—headquarters
ind—independent
inf—infantry
IOOF—International Order of Odd Fellows
maj gen—major general
ME—Methodist Episcopal
MIA—missing in action
mid mil div—middle military division
mil—military
misc—miscellaneous

MO—muster officer

mus—mustered

mus and descr—muster and descriptive

nat—national

NCS—non-commissioned staff

NG—National Guard

no—number

obit—obituary

occ—occupation

ord—ordnance

OVI—Ohio Volunteer Infantry

OVMI—Ohio Volunteer Mounted Infantry

par—paroled

PC—Pike County

POW—prisoner of war

prom—promoted

pro mar—provost marshal

prov—provisional

pvt—private

QM—quartermaster

R&P—record and pension

readm—readmitted

rec—received

reenl—reenlisted

reg—regular

regt—regiment, regimental

rel—released

ret—returned

ROH—Roll of Honor

RQM—regimental quartermaster (dept)

sclop—sclopeticum. *See* vulnus Sclop

SD—staff duty

sgt—sergeant

SO—special order

trans—transferred

twp—township

USA—United States Army

vet—veteran

vol—volunteer

vulnus Sclop.—vulnus Sclopeticum; gunshot wound

Officers

BLAZER, RICHARD. CPT, 91ST OVI. Age 33. 5ft 10in. Gray eyes. Dark hair. Light comp. *b* 12 Apr 1829. Tradesman. Enr 22 July and mus with Cpt Niday's Co Sept 1862 as 1st Lt. Det on special duty 12 Sept 1863 by Col C. B. White, as 1 of 3 officers commanding the co of ind scouts. Ret to co 11 Nov 1863. GO 12, HQ 2nd brig, 3rd div Dept of WVa under command of Col White disbands the scouts and orders Lts Blazer and Otis to return to their regts. Co morning report dated 15 Feb 1864 again lists Lt Blazer on special duty. SO 210, dated 1 Nov 1864, Cpt Blazer is designated as commander of a co of ind scouts by order of Gen Crook to date back to 21 Nov 1864. Prom cpt 26 May 1864 vice Cpt James E. Niday, d; capt 18 Nov 1864, Kabletown. POW 23 Nov 1864-22 Feb 1865, Libby Prison. Sent 11 Dec 1864 to Danville, Va and ret to Richmond where he was confined until 21 Feb. Par 22 Feb 1865, Aiken's Landing/James River. Attch to hosp 23 Feb 1865 Officers USA Hosp (branch of Div 1 Gen Hosp, Annapolis, Md). Mus out 24 June 1865, Cumberland, Md. *d* 29 Oct 1878. Bur Mound Hill Cem, Gallipolis, Ohio.

SPENCER, JOHN W. CPT, CO B 9TH WVA INF. Age 44. *b* 11 Mar 1817, Boston, Mass. R&P Office, War Dept shows him as having been mus 14 Jan 1862, cpt, Co B, 9th WVa Inf to fill an original vacancy. Enr 16 Sept 1861, 3 years and mus 9 Dec 1861, Spencer, Va. Re-mus 8 July 1863 to date 20 Sept 1861, Loup Creek, WVa, first mus having being decided illegal by paymaster. Mar and Apr 1863: abs ds. This was probably scouting service. Jan and Feb 1864: abs in arrest, Charleston, WVa since 20 Jan 1864 by order of Gen Scammon. Honorably disch 5 Oct 1864, Harpers Ferry, WVa, by reason of exp of term of service. Bur with wife Permelia, Young Cem, Linden, WVa.

John and Permelia Spencer
Courtesy James M. Conley

COLES, THOMAS (TOM) K (KIP). LT, CO C 91ST OVI. *b* 25 Dec 1844, Portsmouth, Ohio. Joined service as recruit 22 Aug 1862, Camp Ponts. Mus 7 Sept 1862, sgt. Prom 2d lt 19 Feb 1863 and assn to duty by SO 38, Col James A. Turley dated Apr 1863 vice Rogers, resigned. Trans from Co H to Co G by GO 21, 6 July 1864. Prom lt. Assn to ind scouting co by order of Gen Crook, 28 Oct 1864. Killed 18 Nov 1864, Kabletown. Casualty sheet shows effects given to father. Initially bur Hanging Rock Cem, Scioto Co, Ohio. Subsequently disinterred and bur Greenlawn Cem, Portsmouth, Ohio.

OTIS, HARRISON G (GRAY). LT, CO B 12TH OVI. Age 24. 5ft 10in. Blue eyes. Light hair. Light comp. *b* 10 Feb 1837, Marietta, Washington Co, Ohio. Printer. Enr 25 June 1861, Lowell, Ohio. Mus 29 June 1861, Camp Dennison, Ohio, sgt, Co I, 12th OVI, 3 years. Prom 1st sgt 1 Mar 1862. Mus roll Mar and Apr 1862: slightly wounded 17 Sept 1862, Battle of Antietam. Prom 2d lt of the co and 1st lt, Co B of the 12th regt. Recognized by the War Dept as having been in the mil service of the US in those grades from 9 Nov 1862 and 21 Mar 1863, respectively. On special duty in command of Co G since 12 July 1863. Sept and Oct 1863: on det duty by order of Col C. B. White. Trans 1 July 1864, Co H, 23rd OVI. Commis cpt of Co H effective 1 July 1864. Rec GSW to the right thigh 24 July 1864, Kernstown. Abs wounded Aug 1864, Winchester, Va and was on furl sick Sept and Oct, Marietta, Ohio. Mus out 25 July 1865, Cumberland, Md. Appt brig gen, US Vols, war with Spain, 27 May 1898; accepted the appt 11 June 1896, and was honorably disch to date 2 July 1899 at the close of the war. Assn to 3rd Brig 2nd. Div 8th Corps, Philippines Expeditionary Forces 12 June 1898 and was in command of that brig until 20 July 1898. Arrived in Philippine Islands 24 Aug 1898 and was in command of a brig of 8th Corps until 2 Apr 1899 when he was relieved upon his request.

He rec the brevets of maj and lt col, US Vols, both commissions to rank from 13 March 1865 for gallant and meritorious services during the Civil War. He was breveted maj gen of vols, with rank from 25 March 1899, for meritorious conduct at the Battle of Caloocan, Philippine Islands, 25 March 1899. In 1867 he rec an interim appt as 2d lt in the 39th US Inf. *d* 30 July 1917, Los Angeles. Bur Hollywood Cem.

EWING, JAMES. 2D LT, CO A 9TH WVA INF. Age 32. Enr 12 Dec 1862, Mason City, Va, 3 years. Mus 9 Nov 1862, Mason City, Va. Re-mus 6 July 1863, Loop Creek, WVa to date 15 Oct 1861, original mus having been found illegal by paymaster. Commis 4 Jan 1862. Taken POW 25 July 1862, Summersville. Rel 13 Aug 1862, Richmond, Va. Mar-Aug 1864: shown on ds. Abs special duty at div HQ GO 58 by order of Gen Crook. Aug-Sept 1864: abs ds in scouting co as scout. Mus out at exp of term of service 15 Oct 1864, Harper's Ferry, Va. *d* 21 May 1879.

WILLIAMS, JOHN L. LT, CO A 91ST OVI. Age 23. 5ft 10in. Hazel eyes. Dark hair. Light comp. *b* Columbiana Co, Ohio. Grocer. Enr 29 July 1862, Columbus, Ohio, 3 years. Mus 4 Sept 1862, Ironton, Ohio. Appt 2d lt 29 July 1862. Prom 1st lt 25 June 1863 by SO 67 of Col Turley. May 1863: abs sick—sent to gen hosp by order of assistant surgeon Warwick 30 May 1863. Jan-Feb 1864: special duty in Co F by order of Col Turley. Sept 1864: abs det ind scouting co by SO 61 Gen Crook 2 Sept 1864. Prom cpt vice Levi M. Stephenson, resigned. Trans 25 Nov 1864, Co K. Morning report for 3 Sept 1864 shows him det scouting co. Apr 1865: on special duty as member of GCM by SO 10, 4 prov div, Army of Shenandoah 20 Apr 1865. Mus out 24 June 1865, Cumberland, Md. Occ: farmer. Adm Athens Asylum for the Insane, 23 May 1884. *d* 20 Sept 1892, asylum, Mount Pleasant, Iowa.

CHERINGTON, HOMER C. FIELD & STAff, CO G AND I 23RD OVI. Age 26. Enr 13 Aug 1861, Chambersburg, 3 years. Mus 27 Aug 1861, Marietta, Ohio, 2d lt. C. I. Joseph Brown recalls Cpt Cherrington as a member of Blazer's Scouts. No official record exists detailing him as a scout. However, in his capacity as Provost Marshal, he may have ridden with Blazer on occasion.

KEY NONCOMMISSIONED OFFICERS

MONTGOMERY, ASBE (ASBURY, ASHBEL). SGT, CO A 9TH WVA INF. Age 43. 6ft 2in. Dark eyes. Gray hair. Dark comp. *b* 3 Jan 1820, Preston Co, Va (Tyler Co in obit). Farmer. Resident of Wood Co, Va. Previous service as 2d lt, 10th regt Va Militia (aka Limestone Hill Co). Listed as POW Sept-Oct 1862. Par 13 Sept 1862, Aiken's Landing, Va. Prom 5th duty sgt 14 Mar 1863. CSR does not show him det Blazer, fall of 1863. Reenl vet 1 Jan 1864. Det Cpt Blazer by GO 2 to date from 16 Feb 1864. Wounded in shoulder 3 (4) Sept 1864, Berryville (Myer's Ford). Sent to hosp, Sandy Hook, Md approx 7 days. Sent to hosp, Frederick, Md, 10 days. Sent to Field Hosp Tent, Baltimore, Ohio, 1 day. Then sent to Chestnut Hill Hosp, Philadelphia, Pa, about 2 months. Then sent to hosp, Harper's Ferry. Trans 1 Nov 1864, 1st WVa Vet Inf. Feb 1865: abs det div HQ, Cumberland, Md. Mus out 11 July 1865, Cumberland, Md. Son James was also in 9th WVa Inf. *d* 21 Mar 1907, Rossville, Kans. Bur Rossville City Cem.

FULLER, RICHARD A. SGT, CO H 5TH WVA INF. Age 26. 6ft 2in. Blue eyes. Sandy hair. Dark comp. *b* 11 Mar 1835, Pike Co, Ky. Farmer. Enr 16 Nov 1861, 3 years. Mus 30 Apr 1862, Ceredo, Va. Prom sgt June 1863. July 1863: abs scouting. Det Cpt Blazer's Scouts May 1864. Capt by the enemy 23 Sept 1864 near Berryville (Summit Point), Va. Confined 27 Sept 1864, Richmond, Va and sent 9 Oct 1864, Salisbury, NC. Escaped at Salisbury 27 Oct 1864. Reported 14 Dec 1864, office of Pro Mar Guard near Knoxville, Tenn and ret to the regt. Trans 13 Nov 1864, Co A, 1st WVa Vet Inf, pvt. Reduced in rank due to consol of unit 14 Sept 1865. Mus out 10 Jan 1865, Cumberland, Md, exp of term of service. Complained he contracted rheumatism from hard marching and fording streams, and injured his left foot on way to prison. *d* 10 Mar 1912, Lawrence Co, Ky.

HEAD, ADAM R. SGT (PVT), CO H 12TH OVI. Age 23. 5ft 11in. Blue eyes. Light hair. Light comp. *b* Ripley (Brown Co), Ohio. Farmer. Enr 19 June 1861, Camp Dennison, Ohio, 3 years. Mus 21 June 1861, Camp Dennison to date 21 June 1861. Prior service in 12th OVI (3 months). Appt sgt 4 June 1861. Casualty sheet shows him wounded 20 Sept 1862 near Sharpsburg, Md. Shown on co morning report for 14 Sept 1863 on daily duty as scout. 15 Sept shows him det ind scout by order of Col C. B. White along with Pvts Peter S. Havens and William Hall. Ret to co from ds on 27 Oct 1863. Taken prisoner while out on a pass. Nov 1863: abs supposed to have been taken prisoner. Morning report for 26 Oct: reported AWOL Dec 1863-Mar 1864: AWOL Apr 1864 (pvt). 25 Nov 1863: Fayette CH Des said to have been capt by the enemy 15 miles beyond the lines at the time. Abs without leave. Reduced to the ranks 1 Dec 1863. Mus out at Columbus, Ohio 11 July 1864 by reason of exp of term of service. War Dept notation dated 9 June 1868 at Washington "The charge of desertion and the remark 'capt. by the enemy while out of the lines without permission Nov. 25, 1863,' will be removed." Note on rolls capt by the enemy 23 Nov 1863. POW record shows him capt at Fayetteville, Va 23 Nov 1863 and confined at Richmond 29 Nov (or 4 Dec). Sent to Andersonville, Ga 17 Mar 1864. Confined at Andersonville (no date). Adm to hosp at Andersonville 13 July 1864 for scurvy. Ret to prison 3 Aug 1864. Escaped Andersonville, crossed out date 12 July 1864. Reported within the Union lines 27 Aug 1864. Murdered in Saline Co, Kans, 3 Nov 1886.

LEAF, WILLIAM H. SGT, 12TH OVI. Age 22. 5ft 6in. Dark eyes. Dark hair. Dark comp. *b* 20 Dec 1840, Green Co, Ohio. Laborer. Mus 20 June 1861, Camp Dennison, 3 years. Appt cpl Jan or Feb 1863, Co B. Appears as sgt on special mus roll 10 Apr 1863. Prom sgt 1 Mar 1863. Sept and Oct 1863: abs det ind scouting co. Det ind scouts July-Dec 1864. Claimed to have been wounded through right shoulder and lung by Mosby's Guerrillas near Myerstown, Va 3 (4) Sept. Sent 5 Sept, field hosp, Sandy Hook, Harper's Ferry and then 14 Sept, Frederick City Hosp. From there he was sent 22 Sept, Jarvis Hosp, Baltimore where he remained about a month before rejoining unit 8 Oct 1864. Also claims to have been wounded 15 Nov 1864 near Myerstown through left shoulder. After this wound he was given a 30 day furl. (This wound is also noted on casualty list of Cpt Blazer's Scouts dated 18 Nov 1864.) Mus out 8 Jan 1864, to reenl as vet vol. Reenl 9 Jan 1864, vet vol, Charleston, WVa. Trans 1 July 1864, Co K, 23rd OVI by order of Gen Crook, SO 13. Mus out 26 July 1865. *d* 2 Mar 1926, Los Angeles.

WRIGHT, CHARLES. SGT (1ST SGT), CO D 91ST OVI. Age 19. 5ft 10⅜in. Black eyes. Black hair. Dark comp. *b* Gallia Co, Ohio. Farmer. Enr 6 Aug 1862, Symms, Ohio, 3 years. Mus 7 Sept 1862, Camp Ironton, Ohio. Feb 1863 (cpl): abs sick 13 Feb 1863 with regt, Fayetteville, Va. May-June 1863: appt sgt vice William A. Reed (prom), and has performed duty as such since 1 May 1863. July-Aug 1863: appt sgt 1 May 1863 and has only drawn cpl's wage. Mar-Apr 1864: scouting co. Mar-24 Dec 1864 (sgt): abs on ds ind scouting co since 11 Feb 1864 by order of Gen Crook. Det scouting co 5 Mar 1864. John Harvey and Henry Pancake attest he was orderly sgt for Cpt Blazer's Co. Prom cpl 1 Sept 1862. Prom 1st sgt 1 Jan 1865. *d* 20 July 1908.

5th West Virginia Volunteer Infantry

Organized summer 1861, Ceredo, Va and mus 18 Oct 1861. Unless otherwise noted, men enlisting as vet vols were disch 31 Dec 1863 to date 24 Dec 1863, Charleston, WVa by virtue of reenl as vet vol under the provs of GO 191, Series 1863, War Dept. Vets were mus in as vet vols 31 Dec 1863 to date 25 Dec 1863. All men reenlisting as vets rec a bounty. The regt was consol with the 9th WVa Inf as the 1st Regt WVa Vet Vols, 9 Nov 1864. Unless otherwise noted all men were mus out with the regt 21 July 1865, Cumberland, Md.

BLANKENSHIP, WILLIAM R. CPL, CO C. Age 20. 5ft 8in. Blue eyes. Light hair. Light comp. *b* 4 April 1842, Lawrence Co, Ohio. Farmer. Enr 2 Sept 1861, Camp Pierpont, Va, 3 years. Mus 2 Sept 1861, Ceredo, Va. Mus roll dated 28 Feb 1862: ds. Mus out 24 Mar 1864, Charleston, Va. Appears on mus and descr roll of vet vols dated 24 March 1864. Mus 25 Feb 1864. Shown det scout July and Aug 1864. Mus out 21 Sept 1864, Wheeling, WVa, exp of term of service. *d* 29 Jan 1915, Erie, WVa.

CHARLTON, THOMAS (TOM). PVT, CO H. This man's association with the scouts is only from the *Ironton Register*. It is unlikely that he would have made his claims about his experiences with Blazer's Scouts in an area where many former scouts lived if he had not been det. Regt returns show no man det from Co H except for Sgt Fuller. This would have been unlikely. Age 19. 5ft 7in. Hazel eyes. Brown hair. Fair comp. *b* 7 Feb 1845, Durham, England. Miner. Enr 15 Sept 1861, Ceredo, WVa. Mus 10 Sept 1861, Gauley Bridge, WVa on roll dated 30 Sept. Mus roll dated 31 Dec 1861: trans 29 Nov 1861 from Co K to Co H. Mus roll dated 28 Feb 1862: ds. July-Aug 1862: missing since Battle of Bulltown 30 Aug 1862. 1 Sept-30 Dec 1862: abs par prisoner. POW record shows him par 13 Sept 1862, Aiken's Landing. Mus out 8 Oct 1864, Wheeling, WVa. Trans 1 Jan 1862, Co H by order of Col John Zeigler. *d* 25 May 1913.

DEFOE, ROBERT F. PVT, CO F. Age 19. 5ft 10in. Blue eyes. Light hair. Fair comp. *b* Wayne Co, Va. Farmer. Enr 23 Sept 1861, Ceredo, Va, 3 years. Mus same time and place. Oct 1863: (5th WVa Inf) abs scout. Nov 1863: abs Camp Reynolds, WVa. Disch 31 Dec 1863, Charleston, WVa by virtue of reenl as vet vol under provs of GO 191, Series 1863, War Dept. Charged with loss of one Enfield Rifle ($18). Mus out 31 Dec to date 24 Dec. Mus vet 31 Dec 1863 to date 25 Dec. 31 Dec 1863: abs vet furl. June-July 1864: abs scout. Sept-Oct 1864: det Blazer's Scouts. Nov 1864-Jan 1865: abs det Blazer's Scouts. War Dept notation AGO, Washington, DC date 7 Jan 1880. Capt 20 Sept 1864, Winchester (supposed to be capt while in hosp at that place), confined 23 Sept 1864, Richmond, Va and sent 24 Sept, Danville, Va. *d* on or about 30 Mar 1865 on board steamer *General Lyon* which sailed from Wilmington, NC for New York 28 Mar 1865 and was burned at sea. Appears on an unsigned and unofficial list without caption, date, or cert. Caution: This card must not be used as the basis for an official report until after special investigation of the facts. "Letter of transmittal shows this record to be a list of prisoners of war who were taken from the United States Army, confined in the Rebel Prison at Salisbury, N.C. and enlisted in the rebel service. This list was copied from the original by Moses Palmer, Jr. of Lyon, Mass., late a Q.M. Sgt. in the 7th Regt. Maine Inf., while a POW at Salisbury, N.C. and it was forwarded, 22 June 1866 by Maj. Francis E. Walcott, Judge Advocate, Mil Comd of N.C. through military channels to the office of the adj. gen. of the Army where it was rec. 27 June 1866. A.G. 2175571. POW record shows Pvt. Defoe joined the rebel army while a POW at Salisbury, N.C. date not given."

(REV) DILLON, JOSHUA (JOSHUWAY) C (CLAY). PVT, CO D/E. Age 17. 5ft 10. Black eyes. Dark hair. Dark comp. *b* Oct 1844, Lawrence Co, Ohio. Farmer. Enr 2 Sept 1861, Camp Pierpont, Va, 3 years. Mus 2 Sept 1861, Ceredo, Va. Sept 1861: on duty cook. Feb 1862: on duty co cook. Mar-Apr 1863: AWOL. Nov-Dec 1863: disch 20 Dec 1863 by reason of reenl as vet vol under prov of GO 191, Series 1863, War Dept. Mus roll dated 23 Dec 1863 to date 21 Dec 1863, re-mus as vet vol. Mar-Apr 1864: abs det HQ scout. July-Aug 1864: abs sick. Mus out 20

Joshua C. Dillon
Courtesy Carl Sites and Michelle Dillon

Sept 1864, Wheeling, WVa. Feb 1865: abs furl. War Dept notation 25 Jan 1893: "It is determined from evidence before the Department that the charge of absence without leave on muster rolls for Mar. and Apr. 1863 is erroneous." Resident Coal Grove, Lawrence Co, Ohio. *d* 17 Apr 1908, Coal Grove, Ohio. Minister of the Zoar Missionary Baptist Church. Bur Zoar Missionary Baptist Church, Coal Grove.

GARRETT, JOHN. PVT, CO A. Age 28. 6ft 1¾in. Blue eyes. Light hair. Fair comp. *b* Lawrence Co, Ohio. Laborer. Worked on the furnaces near Ironton until he enl. Enr 2 Sept 1861, Ceredo, Va, 3 years. "Capt. by the enemy at Bull Run, Aug. 29/62." Listed in CSR as 1 Sept 1862. Struck by shell on left knee while on retreat from Second Bull Run battle. Confined Richmond. Par 3 Sept 1862, Centreville. Sept. 3, 1862. Reported 23 Oct 1862, Camp Parole, Md. Sent Nov 1862, Alexandria, Va and then 26 Nov 1862, Wheeling, Va. Jan and Feb 1862: sick hosp. Mar–June 1862: ds hosp, Parkersburg, Va. Mar and Apr 1864: det scout. May 1865: abs QM Corps. *d* 3 June 1899, Pell City, Ala.

HENRY, LEVI M. PVT, CO A. Age 20. 5ft 4in. Blue eyes. Brown hair. Fair comp. *b* 4 Mar 1841, Lawrence Co, Ohio. Carpenter. Enl 6 Aug 1861, Ironton, Ohio. Mus and enr 2 Sept 1861, Camp Pierpont, Ceredo, Va. Jan and Feb 1862: ds Newburn Station. Aug 1862: Adm 13 Aug 1862, Judiciary Square USA Gen Hosp. On hosp mus roll for Judiciary Square USA Gen Hosp, Washington, DC since 8 Aug 1862 suffering from debilitas. Adm 19 Sept 1862, USA Gen Hosp, West Building, Baltimore, Md. Adm 1 Sept 1862, Newton University Hosp, Baltimore, Md. Oct 1862: on mus roll for West Building, Gen Hosp, Baltimore, Md. Sick and AWOL. Shown des hosp 1 Nov 1862. Returns show him abs HQ scout Mar 1864. July 1864: abs sick Gallipolis hosp since 19 July with nephritis. Mus out 3 Oct 1864, Wheeling, WVa. *d* 13 Mar 1922, Ironton, Ohio. Bur Woodland Cem, Ironton.

HINES, JAMES R. PVT, CO B. Enr 20 July 1861, Ceredo, Va, 3 years. Mus roll dated 31 Oct 1861. 28 Feb–31 Aug 1862: mus 10 Aug 1861, Ceredo, Va. Regt returns show him det scout Mar

John W. Leach
Courtesy Scott Haggard

1864. Rec GSW of right foot summer 1864, Peter's Mt, WVa and also slight wound of right knee. Mus out 23 Sept 1864, Wheeling, WVa. Postwar occ: farmer. *d* 17 Mar 1909, Hennepin, near Knoxville, Tenn.

JEWELL, DANIEL G. PVT, CO E. Age 18. 5ft 8in. Dark eyes. Dark hair. Dark comp. *b* Hamilton, NY. Farmer. Enr and mus 2 Sept 1861, Ceredo, Va. Jan-Feb 1862: ds. Mus out 25 Dec 1863, reenl as vet vol to date 18 Dec. Reenl 19 Dec, Charleston under prov of GO 191, Series 1863, War Dept. Nov-Dec 1863: abs reenl as vet vol 19 Dec 1863. Mar-Apr 1864: det scout. Nov-Dec 1864: abs Cpt Blazer's Scouting Co. Feb-June 1865: abs div wagoner, QM Dept. *d* 18 Sept 1873, Guyandotte, WVa.

LEACH, JOHN W. PVT, CO C/G. Age 19. 5ft 11in. Blue eyes. Dark hair. Fair comp. *b* Fayette Co, Pa. Farmer. Enr 2 Sept 1861, Ceredo, Va, 3 years. Mus 2 Sept 1861, Camp Pierpont to date 2 Sept 1861. Enr 11th dist Ohio. Erroneously shown on co mus out roll 21 Sept 1864, Wheeling, WVa. Leach probably replaced William Blankenship who mus out 21 Sept 1864. He is not carried on regimental returns as det Blazer's Scouts, probably an oversight of the orderly sgt. Erroneously shown killed 22 Sept 1864. POW record shows him capt 23 Sept 1864, Winchester (Summit Point). Sent 27 Sept, Richmond. Sent 9 Oct 1864, Salisbury, NC. Trans 9 Nov 1864, 1st WVa Vet Inf. Par 2 Mar 1865, NE Ferry, NC. Sent 10 Mar 1865, CGB, Annapolis. Sent 11 Mar 1865, CCO. Reported 15 Mar 1865, CCO. Furl 15 Mar 1865, 30 days. No date of return. No surgeon cert on file. No further record. Notation 9870-B-79. Shown on rolls of 1st WVa Vet Inf. *d* 14 Apr 1901. Bur Leach graveyard, Jeffersonville, Ky.

LOCY (LOSEY), BARNETT. PVT, CO G. Age 20. 5ft ?in. Blue eyes. Dark hair. Dark comp. Enr 1 Oct 1861, Ceredo, Va, 3 years. Mus Gauley Bridge, WVa, 30 Sept 1863 to date 1 Oct 1861. Roll dated 28 Feb 1862: abs ds. Roll dated 30 June 1862: at Cumberland, Md sick in hosp. July 1864: Regt returns show him det as scout. Sept-Oct 1864: listed as killed 22 Sept 1864. Mus out roll dated 21 July 1865 at Cumberland, Md shows him POW since 31 Oct 1864. (He was capt at Summit Point, 23 Sept 1864) POW record shows him capt at Winchester 21 Sept 1864. Confined at Richmond, 27 Sept 1864. Sent to Salisbury, NC, 4 Oct 1864, where he joined the rebel army while a POW, date not given. Escaped from Salisbury about 18 or 19 Feb 1865. Reported at Wilmington, NC, 28 Mar 1865. (Was on board steamer *General Lyon* which caught fire and sank off the Carolina coast. Was one of 29 soldiers, refugees, and crew rescued.) Reported at CGB, Md, 5 Apr 1865. Sent to CCO 6 Apr 1865 where he arrived 10 Apr 1865. War Dept AGO notation dated 20 Mar 1886 notes, "The remarks on roll of co. for Sept. & Oct. 64 are cancelled and the charge of having joined the rebel army is removed." *d* 14 Jan 1889.

LOWE, SAMUEL F. PVT, CO B. Age 21. 5ft 6in. Blue eyes. Light hair. Light comp. *b* 20 May 1840, Logan Co, Va. Enr 2 Sept 1861, Camp Pierpont, 3 years. Mus 2 Sept 1861, Ceredo, Va. Mar and Apr 1863: abs scout. Mus out 22 Dec on roll dated 31 Dec 1863, Charleston, WVa to reenl as vet vol under provs of GO 191, Series 1863, War Dept. Mus 23 Dec 1864, vet vol. Trans 9 Nov 1864, Co A 1st WVa Vet Inf. Pension file of John Thompson, 91st Ohio, claimed to be member of Blazer's Scouts. Claimed to have been capt at same time as John Thomspon and also sent to Libby Prison and Pemberton Prison. Rolls for Nov-Dec 1864: abs capt by the enemy. Rolls for Jan-Apr 1865: abs POW due govt for one bayonet. May and June 1865: par. POW record shows him capt Myerstown and confined 22 Nov, Richmond brought from Gordonsville. Par 5 Feb 1865, Cox's Wharf, Va. Reported 24 Nov 1864, CCO. Mus out 30 June 1865, CCO. Shown capt by the enemy 18 Nov 1864, Myerstown. Reported 20 Feb 1865, CCO. Disch in obedience to GO 77 dated 28 Apr 1865. Mus out 11 July 1865, Cumberland, Md while in par camp. Three months extra pay due in obedience to orders from War Dept dated 31 May 1865. *d* 5 Mar 1920, Lavalette, WVa.

MIDDAUGH, JESSE C (CRAIG). PVT, CO B. Age 37. *b* about 1828, Pa. Enr and mus 2 Sept 1862, Camp Pierpont, Ceredo, Va, sgt. 4th sgt on mus rolls dated 31 Oct 1862. Mar-Apr 1863: abs scout. May-June 1863: ds. Prom 2d sgt 1 July 1863. Mar-July 1864: abs scout. Shown mus out 27 Sept 1864, Wheeling, WVa, pvt. Memo from POW records shows him ret 7 Sept 1864, Camp Parole, Md Trans 7 Sept, Ft Federal Hill, Baltimore, Md. In Gen Hosp, Patterson Park, Baltimore, Md. Alleged to have *d* 14 Feb 1865, Ceredo WVa. Bur Catlettsburg, Ky.

PANCAKE, HENRY. PVT (CPL), CO C/K. Age 20. 5ft 10¾in. Hazel eyes. Light hair. Fair comp. *b* Lawrence Co, Ohio. Farmer. Enr 15 Sept 1861, Ceredo, Va, 3 years. Mus 24 Apr 1863, Gauley Bridge, Va to date 15 Sept 1861. Mus roll dated 31 Dec 1861. Trans about 13 Oct 1861, Co K. Feb 1862: on duty cook. May 1863: on duty taking care of govt horses. Nov 1863: on duty cook. Disch 24 Dec 1863, reenl as vet vol. Reenl 26 Dec under prov of GO 191, Series 1863, War Dept. Enr 9th Dist Ky. Mar-Aug 1864: abs div scouts. Mus out 3 Oct 1864, Wheeling, WVa. Trans 9 Nov 1864, 1st WVa Vet Inf. Shown det Blazer's Scouts since 21 Nov 1864. Prom cpl 15 Mar 1865. Postwar occ: grocer. Resident of Ironton. James B. Bazell, late lt Co K, 5th WVa Inf attested "He is honorable as a citizen, was brave as a soldier." Col W. A. Eunochs, regt commander noted "He was a splendid soldier." *d* 9 Apr 1912, Burlington, Ohio (home).

PIKE, LEVI. PVT, CO A. Age 20. 5ft 9½in. Blue eyes. Sandy hair. Fair comp. *b* 28 Oct 1841, Tagwell, Va. Farmer. Enr 2 Sept 1861, Camp Pierpont. Mus 2 Sept 1861, Ceredo, Va. Jan-Feb 1862: ds New Creek Station. May-June 1862: abs sick. July-Aug 1862: abs since 3 July 1862 Frederick City Hosp, Md. 31 Aug-31 Dec 1862: prom from pvt 21 Sept 1862. Jan-Feb 1862: shown pvt. May-Aug 1864: ds scout. Mus out 3 Oct 1864, Wheeling, WVa. *d* 25 Apr 1916, Chesapeake, Ohio.

PRESTON, MORGAN. PVT, CO I/K. Age 19. 5ft 7½in. Blue eyes. Light hair. Light comp. *b* Johnson Co, Ky. Farmer. Enr 1 Oct 1861, Ceredo, Va. Mus 31 Oct. July-Aug 1862: AWOL. 31

Robert Sick (Zeek)

Courtesy Gerry E. Hartlage

Aug-31 Dec 1862: exch prisoner ret to duty. POW record shows him capt 1 Sept, Bull Run. Par 3 Sept, Centreville Sept. 3 and sent 23 Oct 1862, Camp Parole. Sent Nov 1862, Alexandria, Va and sent 26 Nov, Wheeling, WVa. Mar-Apr 1863: sent on a scout and has not ret. Nov-Dec 1863: vet vol. Apr-Aug 1864: ds Blazer's Scouts by order of Gen Crook. Nov-Dec 1864: abs det Cpt Blazer's Scouting Co. Feb-June 1865: on duty regt bugler. Mus out 6 Oct 1864, Wheeling, WVa. Trans 1 Nov 1864, Co K, 1st WVa Vet Inf. Nov-Dec 1864: vet vol ds Blazer's Scouts since 30 Apr 1864. *d* 7 Feb 1885, Catlettsburg, Ky.

SICK, ROBERT (FRANCIS MARION) (BOB) ALIAS (ROBERT ZEEK). PVT, CO I. Age 21. *b* 22 May 1842, Pikeville, Pike Co, Ky. Enr 14 Sept 1861, Ceredo, Va, 3 years. Mus same place and time. Moved from Pike Co, Ky to Ohio before outbreak of the war. The family was pro-Union in a hostile area. Supposed to have left Pike Co on a flat boat at night. Mus roll dated 28 Feb 1862: det. Prom cpl 25 Apr 1862. Affidavits in pension file attest he was on det duty with picked men from different commands known as Milroy's Sharp Shooters. Nov-Dec 1863: abs scout. Appears on rolls as pvt July-Aug 1863. Mar 1864: abs HQ Scout. June 1864: AWOL. Mus out 4 Oct 1864, Wheeling WVa. D. J. Hughes, 1899: "As to the man he is a stalwart Republican and a good citizen. He is a member of the GAR Dick Lambert Post No. 165, Ironton, Ohio." *d* 7 July 1911. Bur with wife Woodlawn Cem, Ironton, Ohio.

SMITH, WILLIAM J. PVT, CO B. (SEE ALSO ENTRY UNDER 13TH WVA INF.) Age 25. Enr 28 July 1861, Ceredo, Va, 3 years. Shown on mus roll dated 31 Oct 1861. Mus roll dated 31 Dec 1861 abs with leave. 28 Feb-31 Aug 1862: abs. Wounded accidentally. Abs with leave. Mus 10 Aug 1861, Ceredo, Va. Mar-Apr 1864: under arrest Charleston, WVa. Rolls continue same to Jan-Feb 1864: under arrest CCO. Continues under arrest until mus out 23 Sept 1864, Wheeling, WVa. "Sentenced by GCM to work out his term of service with ball and chain attch. to his leg & forfeit all pay & allowances & then to be drummed out of the service."

STREET, JONAS. PVT, CO D. Age 22. 5ft 5 ¾in. Blue eyes. Dark hair. Dark comp. *b* Perry Co, Ohio. Farmer. Enr and mus 2 Sept 1861, Camp Pierpont, Ceredo, Va. Mus out 23 Dec 1863, Charleston to reenl as vet vol. Mus 23 Dec 1863, Charleston. Jan-Feb 1864: abs with leave. July-Aug 1864: det scout. Killed by Mosby some time in 1864. Officer Alfred O. Enoch, (1st lt, Co E, 1st Regt WVa Vet Inf) states he was killed in skirmish with rebels near Summit Point, Va 14 Oct 1864. Scouts Henry Pancake and John W. Leach also attested to circumstances of death at Summit Point, Va. *d* 12 Oct or Nov 1864.

WILLIAMSON, AMOS. PVT, CO F. Age 22. *b* Ky. Enr and mus Camp Pierpont, Ceredo, Va, 2 Sept 1861, 3 years. Sept-Oct 1863: AWOL. Mar-Apr 1864: ds scouting. Mus out 23 Sept 1864, Wheeling, WVa. *d* 8 Apr 1904, Guilford, Wilson Co, Kans. "Bur. in a country cem. about two miles north of Middletown, a village in the north part of Wilson Co."

9th West Virginia Infantry

Organized Dec 1861. Consol 9 Nov 1864 with 5th WVa Inf as 1st Regt WVa Vol Inf. Unless noted otherwise all men mus out 21 July 1865, Cumberland, Md and arrived 23 July 1865, state general rendezvous, Wheeling, WVa.

ARGOBRITE (ARGABRITE), JACOB H. PVT, CO G. Age 18. 5ft 6in. Blue eyes. Light hair. Fair comp. *b* Monroe Co, Va. Farmer. Enr Spencer Va. Mus 1 Mar 1862, Spencer, Va. Det teamster Sept 1862. Ret to co 19 Dec 1862. Returns of regt show him det scout along with William R. Wilson and John McMullen, scouts by order of C. B. White since 12 Sept 1863. On det duty "brigade scout" Mar-Oct 1864. Nov 1864: abs det scout under Cpt Blazer. Trans Co I, 1st Regt WVa Vet Vol Inf. Mus out 19 Feb 1865, Cumberland, Md. Recruit, joined for service after original organization of regt which was mus out 1 Nov 1864, Cedar Creek by reason of consol. Mus out by reason of exp of term of service to date 19 Feb 1865. *d* 13 July 1909.

BAKER, DAVID M. PVT (CPL), CO E. Age 22. 5ft 9½in. Dark hair. Hazel eyes. Dark comp. *b* Monroe Co, Va. Loafer. Enr 15 Mar 1862, Mason City, Va. Shown on mus roll 30 Apr 1863, Winchester, Va mus to date from 15 Mar 1862. Mus Mason City, Va. Recruit. Vet. Sept-Oct 1863: det scouting co. Mar-Apr 1864: disch under provs of GO 359, Series 1863, War Dept. Disch to reenl as vet vol under provs of GO 191, Series 1863, War Dept. Jan-Feb 1864: reenl 29 Feb 1864, not mus. May-June 1864: abs wounded. Wounded 9 May 1864, Cloyd's Mt, GSW of left hand, caused by minnie ball. Thumb amputated. Index finger crippled by same wound. July-Aug 1864: abs wounded hosp, Gallipolis, Ohio since 9 May 1864. Trans 1 Nov 1865, Co F 1st WVa Vet Inf. *d* 17 Apr 1881, Bethal Township, Anoka Co, Minn.

BERRY, JOHN W. PVT, CO H. Age 23. Blue eyes. Light hair. Light comp. *b* Va. Farmer. Recruit. Enr Camp Carey, Va, 3 years. Mus 3 Aug 1863, Camp Carey. Sept 1863: regt returns show him det scout since 12 Sept 1863 by order of Col C. B. White along with H. Waugh, J. Darling and Joseph Redden. Des 28 May 1864, Meadow Bluff. Also shown des 29 July 1864. Notation removed by order of the President, GO 582 AGO 21 Nov 1866. Shown mus out 21 July 1865, Cumberland, Md with notation "des. July 12, 1864." Shown on misc abstracts of records des 1 June 1864, Meadow Bluff.

BOOTH, WILLIAM A. PVT, CO D. Age 32. 5ft 11½in. Blue eyes. Black hair. Light comp. *b* Fayette, Va. Farmer. Oct 1862: des 27 Oct, Buchannon, Va. 1 Nov 1862: gain from des, New

Creek, Va. Dec 1862-May 1863: abs sick hosp, Cumberland, Md. June 1863: 19 June 1863, Coalsmouth, WVa from des. Shown on hosp roll, USA Gen Hosp, Cumberland, Md Nov and Dec 1862. Sept 1863: abs scout brig by order of Col C. B. White 12 Sept 1863. Oct 1863: abs ind scout. Jan 1865: 7 Jan 1865, Camp Hastings, Md. Disch exp of service. War Dept notation 28 Oct 1886: "The charge of desertion of October 27, 1862 against this man is removed under the provision of the Act of Congress approved July 5, 1884. He was absent without proper authority from October 27, 1862 to November 18, 1862." *d* 4 Mar 1905.

BOSO (BOSSO), KINSMAN. PVT, CO A. Age 27. 5ft 5in. Gray eyes. Brown hair. Dark comp. *b* Wood Co, Va. Farmer. Enr 20 Oct 1861, Mason City, Va, 3 years. Mus 28 Nov 1861, Mason City. Cpt Davis, Co A reported that Kinsman Boso was capt with co 25 July 1862, Summersville, but escaped after capt. Nov-Dec 1862: hosp, Gallipolis, Ohio for general debility. Oct 1863: regt returns show him det scouts since 12 Sept 1863 by order of Col C. B. White along with John Lyons, Samuel Spencer, and Asbe Montgomery. Disch 28 Jan 1864 to date 31 Dec 1863 by virtue of reenl as vet vol under GO 191, Series 1863, War Dept. Mus 13 Jan 1864 to date 1 Jan 1864, Fayetteville, WVa. July-Aug 1864: MIA 24 July 1864, Winchester (Kernstown). Sept-Oct 1864: gain from MIA 9 Sept 1864. Bed card from gen hosp shows him adm 1 Aug 1864 with gun shot. Married. Gen Hosp, Grafton, WVa shows him adm 3 Aug 1864 from furl as "Malingerer." Ret to duty 22 Aug. Turned over to Court Post 23 Aug 1864. Adm USA Gen Hosp, Grafton, WVa with "debility." Mus out 17 Oct 1864, Harpers Ferry. Trans 1 Nov 1864, Co B 1st WVa Vet Inf by consol of 5th and 9th WVa Infs. Apr-June 1865: on duty regt pioneer. Postwar occ: farmer. *d* 14 Mar 1914, Belleville, WVa.

BRUNER, MARTIN (VAN BUREN). PVT, CO I. Age 29. 5ft 9in. Gray eyes. Light hair. Fair comp. *b* 1 Oct 1834, Hawkins Co, Tenn. Farmer. Enr 1 Mar 1862, Guyandotte, Va. Mus Camp Paxton 30 Apr 1862. Oct-Dec 1862: abs sick hosp, Gallipolis, Ohio. Noted on scout 9 Dec 1863. Also shown as 29 Dec on CSR. Appears on a list of men gained from desertion dated Fayette CH, WVa 5 Jan 1864. Des 4 Oct 1863 and ret 24 Oct 1863. Sept-Oct 1863: in arrest for desertion. Mus out 14 Mar 1864 to date 28 Feb 1864. Disch by reason of reenl as vet vol under SO 191, Series 1863, War Dept. Re-mus 29 Feb, vet. May-June 1864: listed KIA 9 May 1864, Cloyd's Mt. Subsequently carried as wounded and capt 9 May 1864, Cloyd's Mt. Jan 1865: gain 19 Jan 1865, Camp Hastings, Md from MIA. Abs POW. Feb 1865: abs POW. Mar-Apr 1865: abs sick hosp. May-June 1865: abs sick hosp, Gallipolis, Ohio. Shown on detachment mus out roll 29 June 1865, CCO. POW capt 9 May 1864, Cloyd's Mt, Va and reported at this post 10 Mar 1865, par prisoner. No descr list can be obtained. This man was sworn as to the place of his enr. Three months extra pay due soldier in pursuance of orders from Secretary of War dated Washington, DC 31 May 1865. Disch in pursuance of GO 77, AGO dated 28 Apr 1865. POW record does not show place of confinement. Pension record states he was imprisoned at Andersonville and Florence, SC, 10 months. Par 1 Mar 1865, NE Bridge, NC and reported 9 Mar 1865, CGB. Sent 10 Mar 1865, CCO where he reported 16 Mar 1865. *d* 13 Mar 1918, Paxton, Tex.

BURDETT, SAMUEL. PVT, CO I. Age 18. Enr 10 Oct 1862, Pt Pleasant, 3 years. Mus 9 Feb 1863, Winchester, Va to date 10 Oct 1862. Mar-Apr 1863: det 27 Mar 1863, gen scout. Shown on misc abstracts of records as "Milroy's Scout." May 1863: det scout along with James Webb and William Toppin, Winchester, Va by order of Gen Milroy. Shown det through July 1863. Noted abs scout Mar-Aug 1864. Det scout 15 Mar 1864. AWOL Sept-Oct 1864. Noted des 26 Oct 1864, Cedar Creek.

CHESSMAN (CHEESEMAN), ALEXANDER (ALMANDER). PVT, CO C/H. Age 19. 5ft 10in. Blue eyes. Red hair. Light comp. *b* Gallia Co, Ohio. Farmer. Enr 18 Sept 1861, Ceredo, Va. Mus 30 Apr 1862, Guyandotte, Va. Trans 1 July 1862, Co H. Mar 1863: abs scout. Sept 1863: regt returns show him abs scout for 1st brig by order of Col C. B. White. Mus out to reenl as vet 31 Dec 1863, Charleston, WVa. Reenl 1 Jan 1864, vet vol, Fayetteville, WVa under GO 191, Series 1863, War Dept. Trans to Co C, 1st WVa Vet Inf. *d* 27 Apr 1864, Fayetteville, WVa of disease.

COBB, WILLIAM W. PVT, CO A. Age 18. Recruit. Enr 21 Sept 1862, Pt Pleasant, Va, 3 years. Mus 9 Feb 1863, Pt Pleasant, WVa to date 21 Sept 1862. Sept 1863: scout per order of Col C. B. White. May-June 1864: hosp, Charleston, WVa. Jul-Aug 1864: des 13 July 1864. Sept-Oct 1864: gained from desertion. Mus out 15 Oct 1864, Harpers Ferry, WVa. Trans 1 Nov 1864, Co F 1st WVa Vet Inf by reason of consol of 5th and 9th WVa Infs. June 1865: Cumberland, disch by GO 53. *d* 16 Aug 1923, Charleston, WVa.

COTTRELL, SILAS. PVT, CO B. Age 42. *b* Monroe Co, Va. Farmer. Recruit. Enr 1 Mar 1862, Spencer, Va, 3 years. Mus 9 Feb 1863, Spencer, Va to date 1 Mar 1862. Sept 1862-Feb 1863: abs sick. Special mus roll dated 10 Apr 1863: abs sick, sent 15 Oct 1862, hosp, Gallipolis. May-June 1863: present for duty. Sept 1863: scout by order of Col C. B. White. Jan-Feb 1864: abs with leave Vinton Co, Ohio. Mus out 5 Oct 1864, Harpers Ferry, WVa. Trans 1 Nov 1864, Co I, 1st WVa Vet Inf by reason of consol of 5th and 9th WVa Infs. Mus out 28 Feb 1865 by reason of exp of term of service.

COTTRELL, WILLIAM P. PVT, CO B. Age 25. 5ft 6in. Black eyes. Black hair. Dark comp. *b* 1 Mar 1836, Kanawha Co, Va. Farmer. Enr 1 Mar 1862, Spencer, Va, 3 years. Mus 9 Feb 1863, Spencer, Va. Sept 1863: det scout by order of Col C. B. White. Mus out 2 May 1864 to date 30 Mar 1864 by virtue of reenl as vet vol under prov of GO 191, Series 1863, War Dept. Mus and descr roll dated 1 May 1864 shows him mus 31 Mar 1864. Wounded in arm 26 Aug 1864, Halltown, Va. Mus out 15 Oct 1864, Harpers Ferry, WVa. Trans 9 Nov 1864, Co I, 1st WVa Vet Inf by reason of consol of 5th and 9th WVa Infs. *d* 25 Nov 1919, Uler, WVa.

CREMEENS (CREMEANS), JAMES D. PVT (WAGONER), CO D. Age 18. 5ft 11in. Hazel eyes. Brown hair. Dark comp. *b* Mason Co, Va. Farmer. Enr Guyandotte, 3 years. Mus Feb 1862, Guyandotte. Shown det scout by order of Maj Gen Milroy, Mar and Apr 1863. Regt returns show him det scout by order of Col C. B. White, commanding 2d Brig, 3d Div, 8th Army Corps. Mus out 14 Mar 1864 to date 28 Feb 1864 by virtue of reenl as vet vol under GO 191, Series 1863, War Dept. Mus 14 Mar 1864, Fayetteville, WVa to date 29 Feb. Trans to 1st WVa Vet Inf. On mus rolls of Co B, 5th Regt US Artillery for month of Sept. Oct 1865: des 18 Sept 1865, Cumberland, Md. Not shown on subsequent rolls. Formerly belonged to Co D, 1st Va Inf. 13 Aug 1887 notation states "There is no law under which the charge of desertion can be removed or expunged."

CUNNINGHAM, JESSE C. SGT (PVT), CO C. Age 29. Enr 7 Nov 1861, Guyandotte, Va, 3 years. Mus Guyandotte 30 Apr 1862. Made 4th sgt 9 March 1862. Oct 1862: abs with leave. Sept-Oct 1862: det duty hunting deserters. Nov-Dec 1862: shown as 3d sgt. Oct 1863: regt returns show him det scout by order of Col C. B. White. Nov-Dec 1864: abs brigade teamster. Feb-Apr 1865: abs div ambulance driver. May-June 1865: abs det duty teamster. Mus out on roll dated 12 Jan 1864 to date 31 Dec 1863 disch by virtue of reenl as vet vol GO 191, Series 1863, War Dept. Mus as vet on roll dated 12 Jan 1864 to date 1 Jan. Reduced to ranks 30 June 1864. Trans 1 Nov 1864, Co D 1st WVa Vet Inf by consol of 5th and 9th WVa Infs.

DARLING, JAMES C. PVT (CPL), CO H. Age 18. 6ft ¼in. Blue eyes. Dark hair. Dark comp. *b* Lawrence Co, Ohio. Farmer. Enr 18 Sept 1861, Ceredo, Va, 3 years. Taken POW 10 Nov 1861, Guyandotte, Va. Sent to Libby Prison and then Salisbury, NC. Appears on mus roll of Co A, 1st Regt Par Prisoners, USA 1 Mar-31 Aug 1862, CCO. At Camp Wallace Nov and Dec as par POW. Shown on mus roll dated 9 Feb 1863, Winchester, Va. Sept and Oct 1863: abs det scout. 15 Nov 1863: ret from scout. Mus out 31 Dec, Charleston, WVa by reason of reenl as vet vol. Mus 13 Jan 1864, Charleston, WVa to date 1 Jan 1864. Prom 6th cpl in May or June 1864. Wounded 26 Aug 1864, Halltown in right side by minnie ball. Flesh wound. Abs sick Harper's Ferry (probably Sandy Hook Hosp). Trans 1 Sept 1864, Frederick, Md. Adm 8 Sept 1864, USA Gen Hosp, Patterson Park, Baltimore, Md. Shown on mus roll of Mower Gen Hosp, Chestnut Hill, Pa Sept and Oct 1864. Adm 21 Sept 1864. Shown at USA Gen Hosp, Gallipolis, Ohio Nov 1864-Feb 1865. Mar-Apr 1865: US Hosp, Gallipolis. Trans 1 Nov 1864, Co H 1st WVa Vet Inf. Disch for dis 25 Jan 1865 due to GSW of right side rec at Halltown; ball passed through abdominal cavity. *d* 9 May 1908.

DRENNEN, ANDREW C. PVT, CO B. Age 20. 5ft 5in. Gray eyes. Brown hair. Fair comp. *b* 1 Oct 1843, Roane Co, Va. Farmer. Enr and mus 29 Feb 1861, Fayetteville, Va, 3 years. Sept 1864: abs scout since 17 Aug 1864. Shown det through Nov 1864 under Cpt Blazer. Dec 1864: abs wounded Annapolis, Md. Jan 1865: abs sick. Feb 1865: abs det duty div HQ Cumberland, Md. Mar 1865: abs det div HQ. Apr-June 1865: abs det duty. Mus out of 9th WVa Inf 5 Oct 1864. Trans 1 Nov 1864, Co I, 1st WVa Vet Vols. POW record shows him capt 18 Nov, Myerstown (Kabletown), confined 22 Nov, Richmond, brought from Gordonsville. Par 5 Feb 1865. Furl 10 Mar 1865, 30 days. Ret from furl 7 May 1865. Name appears on mus out roll 10 June 1865, CCO. Entitled to 3 months extra pay in accordance with orders from Sec of War dated 31 May 1865. Honorably disch with GO 77 dated War Dept 28 Apr 1865. *d* 12 Apr 1915, Rosedale, Braxton Co, WVa.

DUFFY, LAWSON. PVT, CO E. Age 17. 5ft 4in. Gray eyes. Brown hair. Dark comp. *b* Moundsville, Ohio. Laborer. Enr and mus 28 Feb 1862, Mason City, Va, 3 years. Sept-Oct 1863: det scouting co. Mus out 14 Feb 1864 on exp of term of service. Mus 29 Feb 1864, Fayetteville, WVa, vet vol. Jul and Aug 1864: AWOL since 1 Jul 1864. Notation of R and P Office dated 6 Aug 1880 shows him wounded in the neck in action 9 May 1864, Cloyd's Mt. Adm 22 May, USA Gen Hosp, Gallipolis, Ohio. Ret to duty 28 June 1864. Killed 6 May 1882, industrial accident, Hartford City, Mason Co, WVa.

EDENS, WILLIAM A. SGT, CO H. Age 21. 5ft 6in. Blue eyes. Auburn hair. Dark comp. *b* Rockbridge Co, Va. Enr 9 Mar 1862, Guyandotte, Va, 3 years. Mus 30 Apr 1862, Guyandotte. Shown as sgt Mar-June 1862. Mus roll for 30 Apr-31 Aug 1862 shows him as cpl. Sept-Oct 1862: sick hosp as pvt. Disch by virtue of reenl as vet vol under prov of GO 191, Series 1863, War Dept. On roll dated Fayetteville, WVa 1 May 1864 to date 30 Mar 1864. Re-mus as vet vol on roll dated 1 May 1864, Fayette, WVa. Enl 31 Mar 1864 to have a furl of at least 30 days in his state before exp of original term. Feb 1864: regt returns show him det scout since 20 Feb 1864. May-June 1864: Listed killed 9 May 1864, battle of Cloyd's Mt. Shown on roll as cpl. Descr book lists him as 4th sgt. Mar-Apr 1865: abs POW since 9 May 1864. May-June 1865: abs par prisoner, 20 May 1864.

EPLING, JAMES. PVT, CO B. Age 22. 5ft 8½in. Black eyes. Black hair. Dark comp. *b* Giles Co, Va. Farmer. Enr 7 Oct 1861, Spencer, Va, 3 years. Mus 9 Dec 1861, Spencer, Va to date 7 Oct. Sept-Oct 1862: MIA 13 Sept 1862, Charleston, Va. Mar-Apr 1863: gain from MIA. Sept 1863: det scout by order of Col C. B. White 12 Sept 1863. Aug 1864: MIA 20 Aug, Berryville. Gain from

MIA 31 Aug. Sept 1864: loss 19 Sept 1864, Winchester. Sept-Oct 1864: des with gun and equipment complete. Sept-Oct 1864: shown on hosp mus roll at McClellan USA Gen Hosp, Philadelphia, Pa. Present. POW record shows no record subsequent to 12 Sept 1862. Trans to Co I, 1st WVa Vet Inf by reason of consol of 5th and 9th WVa Infs. Dishonorable disch 24 Feb 1865, Cumberland, Md. Sentence GCM. *d* 1878, Roane Co, WVa.

GANDEE, FREDERICK (C). PVT, CO B. Age 18. *b* 31 Jul 1842, Jackson Co, Va. Farmer. Enr 15 Oct 1861, Spencer, Va, 3 years. Previous service for 3 months in state militia. Mus 9 Dec 1861, Spencer, Va to date 9 Oct. Sept 1863: regt returns show him det scout since 12 Sep by order of Col C. B. White. Mus out 14 Oct 1864, Strausburg, Va at exp of term of service. Subsequently served with Cpt William Gandee's co of state troops 20 Oct 1864 and was disch in 1865. Postwar occ: farmer. Served variously as Justice of the Peace, secretary of the Board of Education, co treasurer and supervisor. *d* 29 Nov 1893, Newton, Roane Co, WVa.

GLAZE, STEPHEN S. PVT (SGT), CO B. Age 21. 6ft. Black eyes. Brown hair. Dark comp. *b* Lewis Co, Va. Farmer. Resident Rome, Va. Enr 28 Sept 1861, Spencer, Va, 3 years. Mus 9 Dec 1861, Spencer, Va to date 28 Sep. Appt cpl 15 Dec 1861. Prom 5th sgt 1 Jan 1862. Sept 1863: regt returns show him det scout by order of Col C. B. White. Mus out roll dated 18 Jan 1864 to date 31 Dec 1863 disch by virtue of reenl as vet vol under GO 191, Series 1863, War Dept. Re-mus as vet on roll dated 13 Jan 1864 to date 1 Jan 1864. Mar 1864: abs recruiting service since 17 Mar 1864. Slightly wounded in leg 9 May 1864, Cloyd's Mt. Sept-Oct 1864: abs wounded Fisher's Hill, Va. *d* 25 Oct 1864, hosp, Broad St, Philadelphia, Pa of GSW rec in action at Fisher's Hill, Va. Interred Mt Mortah Cem, no 276, *ROH* #12, p 22 lists him as grave no 695, Nat Cem, Philadelphia.

HATTEN, FRANCIS M. PVT, CO D Age 24. 5ft 10in. Gray eyes. Light hair. Dark comp. *b* Cabell Co, Va. Farmer. Enr 3 Feb 1862, Guyan, 3 years. Mus 30 Apr 1862, Camp Paxton, Guyandotte, Va. Dec 1862-Apr 1863: abs brig pioneer. Sept 1863: abs scout by order of Col C. B. White 12 Sept 1863. Mar 1864: disch by virtue of reenl as vet vol under prov of GO 191, Series 1863, War Dept. Co mus roll Jan-Feb 1864 shows him reenl, not mus. Mus and descr roll of vet vols Fayette CH, 14 Mar 1864. Mar-Apr 1864: disch per GO 359, Series 1863, War Dept. July 1864: des 24 July 1864, Winchester. Feb 1865: on duty working for chaplain, 10 days. Mar 1865: abs sick hosp. War Dept notation dated 14 Jan 1889: "The charge of desertion of July 24, 1864 against this man is removed under the provision of the Act of Congress approved July 5, 1884. He was absent without proper authority from July 24, 1864 to July 27, 1864 when he was adm. to Post Hosp. Chambersburg, Pa. diagnosis not stated and trans. July 29, 1864." Entered Post Hosp, Camp Curtin, near Harrisburg, Pa 30 July 1864 with pleurisy and was ret to duty 2 Aug 1864. Adm 5 Sept 1864, last named hosp, diagnosis not stated and trans 6 Sept 1864. Adm 7 Sept 1864, Gen Hosp, York, Pa with chills and fever. Furl 22 Sept 1864. Re-adm 10 Oct 1864 and ret to duty 29 Oct 1864.

HAUGHT, JOHN H. PVT, CO K. Age 20. 5ft 7in. Dark eyes. Dark hair. Dark comp. *b* 12 Aug 1841, Monongalia Co, Va. Farmer. Single. Recruit. Enr 4 Apr 1862, Marion Co, Va, 3 years. Mus 30 Apr 1862, Camp Paxton, Guyandotte, Va. May 1863: adm USA Gen Hosp, Clarksburg, WVa with febris remittus. Sept 1863: det scout by order of Col C. B. White. Sept-Oct 1864: abs wounded 19 Sept 1864, Winchester, Va. Adm 25 Sept 1864, Satterlee USA Gen Hosp, West Philadelphia, Pa. Adm USA Gen Hosp, Grafton, WVa for GSW of upper extremity (left forearm). Disch 23 Nov 1864, wound healed, slight contraction of muscles. Furl 5 Nov 1864, 15 days. Trans 1 Nov 1864, Co F 1st WVa Vet Inf by consol of 5th and 9th WVa Infs. Apr 1865: disch by exp of term of service 25 Apr Winchester. *d* 1 July 1922, Morgansville, WVa.

JOHNSON, GEORGE W. PVT, CO H. Age 18. 5ft 3in. Blue eyes. Light hair. Light comp. *b* 8 Mar 1845, Lawrence Co, Ohio. Farmer. Enr 3 Oct 1861, Ceredo, Va, 3 years. Mus 9 Feb 1863, Winchester, Va to date 3 Oct 1861. Capt 19 Nov 1861, Guyandotte raid. Sent 24 Dec, Salisbury Prison. Par 28 May 1862, Salisbury NC. List of absentees on special mus dated 18 Aug 1862 shows him "par. prisoner ordered to CCO by Secretary of War." Sept-Oct 1862: par prisoner, CCO. Nov-Dec 1862: par prisoner, Camp Lew Wallace. Jan-Feb 1864: Mus out 14 Jan 1864, Charleston, WVa to date 31 Dec 1863. Disch by virtue of reenl as vet vol under prov of GO 191, Series 1863, War Dept. Re-mus 18 Jan 1864, Charleston, WVa to date Jan 1864. Mar-Apr 1864: det duty. May-June 1864: det duty scout. Trans 1 Nov 1864, 1st WVa Vet Inf. *d* 8 Jan 1911.

KENNEDY, JASPER N. PVT, CO K. Age 18. 5ft 9in. Blue eyes. Dark hair. Light comp. *b* 28 Apr 1844, Monongalia Co, Va. Farmer. Enr 13 Mar 1862, Marion Co, Va, 3 years. Mus 30 Apr 1862, Camp Paxton, Guyandotte, Va. Sept 1863: regt returns show him det scout by order of Col C. B. White. Mus out 1 May 1864, Fayetteville, WVa to date 30 Mar 1865. Disch by virtue of reenl as vet vol under GO 191, Series 1863, War Dept. Re-mus 31 Mar 1864, vet vol, Fayette, WVa to have furl of at least 30 days. Trans 1 Nov 1864, Co H 1st WVa Vet Inf by consol of 5th and 9th WVa Infs. *d* 7 Feb 1919, N Deer Township, Alleghany Co, Pa.

KERNS, THOMAS. PVT, CO E. Age 22. 5ft 7in. Dark eyes. Brown hair. Light comp. *b* and resident Mason City, Va. Laborer. Enr 11 Dec 1861, Mason City, Va, 3 years. Mus 28 Feb 1862, Mason City, Va. Sept-Oct 1863: det scouting co. Shown on mus out roll dated 13 Jan 1864 to date 31 Dec 1863. Shown on mus roll dated 13 Jan 1864 to date 1 Jan. Re-mus 1 Jan 1864, vet vol, Fayetteville, WVa. Trans 2 Nov 1864, Co D 1st WVa Vet Inf by consol of 5th and 9th WVa Infs. *d* 7 Aug 1919, Anderson, Ind.

KNIGHT, LEONARD. PVT, CO I. Age 18. 6ft 1in. Blue eyes. Light hair. Light comp. Farmer. *b* 12 Apr 1843, Cabell Co, Va. Enr 12 Aug 1862, Guyandotte, Va. Mus 1 Sept 1863, Camp Carey, WVa to date 12 Aug 1862. Sept-Oct 1862: des 24 Sept 1862. Shown on list of deserters in mil prison, Wheeling, Va, aka Atheneum Prison, dated 10 May 1863. "Gave up 5th Va. Inf. at Barboursville, Charges, 'Deserter.' Sent to Grafton, May 11/63." May-June 1863: joined from desertion. Ret to duty with loss of pay to 30 May 1863. Sept-Oct 1863: bounty due for enl. Jan-Feb 1864: abs with leave on furl since 24 Jan 1864. Dec 1863: noted abs scout. May 1864: wounded left leg slightly 9 May 1864, Cloyd's Mt. Sept-Oct 1864: shown on roll as 4th cpl. Wounded 3 Sept 1864, Berryville, GSW of right leg. Adm 4 Sept 1864, USA Field Hosp, Sandy Hook, Md. Trans 5 Sept, USA Gen Hosp, Frederick, Md and adm 6 Sept. Adm 21 Sept 1864, Mower, USA Gen Hosp, Chestnut Hill, near Philadelphia, Pa. Trans 28 Oct 1864, Gen Hosp, Wheeling, WVa. Adm 2 Nov 1864, USA Gen Hosp, Gallipolis, Ohio. Furl 3 Nov and ret to duty 11 Dec 1864. Sept 1863: abs wounded Frederick, Md. Trans to Co D 1st WVa Vet Inf. Mus out 28 Jun 1865, Cumberland, Md. *d* 15 Aug 1917.

LAUGHLIN, DANIEL (DAN). PVT, CO B. Age 22. 5ft 7½in. Black eyes. Dark hair. Fair comp. *b* Crawford Co, Va. Farmer. Enr 16 Sept 1861, Spencer, Va, 3 years. Mus 2 Dec 1861, Spencer, Va to date 16 Sept. Prom cpl 1 Mar 1862 vice Uriah Dobbins. Shown det brig scout Sept 1863. Prom 1st sgt. Mus out 13 Jan 1864 to date 31 Dec 1863. Disch under provs of GO 368, Series 1863, War Dept. Disch by virtue of reenl as vet vol under GO 191, Series 1863, War Dept. Mus 13 Jan 1864, vet to date 1 Jan 1864. July-Aug 1864: shown as 4th sgt. Capt 9 May 1864, Cloyd's Mt. Confined at Andersonville (no date given). Adm 25 July 1864, hosp, Andersonville. *d* 28 Oct 1864, Andersonville, Ga of vulnus scIopeticum. Grave no 6155.

LYONS, HIRAM. PVT, CO K. Age 19. 5ft 11in. Blue eyes. Dark hair. Dark comp. *b* 15 Nov 1842, Braxton Co, Va. Farmer. Enr 9 Mar 1862, Jackson Co, Va, 3 years. Mus 30 Apr 1862, Camp Paxton, Guyandotte, Va. Oct 1863: regt returns show him det scout. Mus out on roll dated 1 May 1864 to date 30 Mar 1864. Disch by virtue of reenl as vet vol under prov of GO 191, Series 1863, War Dept. Mus as vet on roll dated 1 May 1864 to date 30 Mar 1864. May 1864: wounded slightly in neck 9 May 1864, Cloyd's Mt. Trans 1 Nov 1864, 1st WVa Vet Inf. *d* 15 June 1919.

LYONS, JOHN W. PVT, CO A. Age 18. 5ft 5½in. Black eyes. Black hair. Dark comp. *b* Wood Co, Va. Farmer. Enr 25 Oct 1861, Mason City, Va, 3 years. Mus 28 Mar 1861, Mason City, Va. Sept 1863: noted abs scout 12 Sept 1863 by order of Col C. B. White. Oct 1863: abs ind scout. Mus out 13 Jan 1864, Charleston, WVa to date 31 Dec 1863. Disch by virtue of reenl as vet vol under prov of GO 191, Series 1863, War Dept. Re-mus 13 Jan 1864, vet vol to date 1 Jan 1864. Mar-Sept 1864: on duty co clerk. Trans 1 Nov 1864, Co B 1st WVa Vet Inf by reason of consol of 5th and 9th WVa Infs. Mus out 26 July 1865. *d* 28 Nov 1911, Parkersburg, WVa.

MARKIN, EBENEZER W. PVT, CO H. Age 18. 5ft 8½in. Hazel eyes. Light hair. Light comp. *b* 16 Feb 1847, Lawrence Co, Ohio. Farmer. Enr 23 Sept 1861, Ceredo, Va, 3 years. Mus 30 Apr 1863, Winchester, Va to date 23 Sept 1861. Nov 1861: capt Guyandotte. POW records show him confined 22 Nov 1861, Richmond, Va. Sent 24 Dec 1861, Salisbury, NC. Par 28 May 1862, Washington, NC and reported 22 July 1862, CCO. Reported at Cincinnati, Ohio (date not given). Appears on mus roll dated 31 Oct 1862. Oct 1863: regt returns show him det scout. Ret from scout 15 Nov 1863. Mus out 13 Jan 1864, Charleston, WVa to date 31 Dec 1863. Disch by virtue of reenl as vet vol under GO 191, Series 1863, War Dept. Re-mus 13 Jan 1864, Charleston, WVa to date 1 Jan, vet. Trans 1 Nov 1864, Co E 1st WVa Vet Inf by consol of 5th and 9th WVa Infs. Jan 1865: AWOL since 1 Jan 1865. Postwar occ: laborer. *d* 1 Nov 1925, Wrightsville, near Atlanta, Ga.

MCCAULEY, GEORGE W (MACK). PVT, CO E. 5ft 7in. Hazel eyes. Brown hair. Light comp. Farmer. *b* Athens, Ohio. Enr 8 Dec 1861, Mason City, Va. Mus 28 Feb 1862, Mason City, Va, 3 years. Det 1 Dec 1862, Brig Pioneer Corps. Det scouting co for Sept-Oct 1863. Sept-Oct 1864: noted abs Blazer's scouting co since 12 Mar 1864. Trans to Co B 1st WVa Vet Vol Inf. Enl 1 Jan 1864, vet vol. Mus out 21 July 1865, Cumberland, Md, pvt. *d* 18 Feb 1880, Columbus, Ohio. Bur Pt Pleasant, WVa.

MCCOMAS, GEORGE K. PVT, CO D. Age 25. 6ft. Blue eyes. Black hair. Dark comp. *b* 15 Aug 1838, Lawrence Co, Ohio. Cooper. Enr 15 Dec 1862, Guyandotte, Va, 3 years. Mus 26 Feb 1862, Camp Paxton, Guyandotte, Va. Sept 1862-Mar 1863: on duty teamster. Apr 1863: on duty teamster. June-Aug 1863: abs sick hosp, Gallipolis, Ohio, June 1863. Mus out 31 Dec 1863 on roll dated 1 Jan 1864. Disch under prov of GO 359, Series 1863, War Dept. Mus 1 Jan 1864, vet on roll dated 13 Jan 1864. May and June 1864: wounded and in hosp, Gallipolis, Ohio, adm 22 May. Wounded slightly in right knee, flesh wound caused by conical bullet. Ret to duty 9 Sept 1864. Trans 14 Nov 1864, Co D, 1st WVa Vet Vols. Regt returns of 1st WVa Vet Inf show him det Cpt Blazer's Scouts. Shown on rolls for Nov and Dec as capt by Mosby's Guerrillas, Nov 1864. POW record shows him capt 18 Nov 1864, Myerstown and confined 22 Nov 1864, Richmond brought from Gordonsville. Par 5 Feb 1865, Cox's Wharf, Md and reported 7 Feb 1865, CGB. Adm 15 Feb 1865, hosp div 25, Annapolis. Furl 28 Feb, 30 days. *d* 14 Apr 1919, West Hamlin, WVa

MCCOMAS, JOHN. PVT, CO D. Age 26. 5ft 9in. Blue eyes. Brown hair. Light comp. Farmer. *b* Cabell Co, Va. Enr 19 Feb 1862, Guyan, 3 years. Mus 30 Apr 1862, Camp Paxton, Guyandotte, Va. Sept 1862: on duty teamster. Oct 1862: AWOL. Nov 1862: loss 3 Nov 1862,

Beverly, Va, des from hosp. Feb 1863: gain ret from desertion. Feb-Mar 1863: co teamster det 25 Feb 1863. Mar-June 1863: on duty teamster. Sept 1863: abs scout by order of Col C. B. White 2d Brig 3d Div 8AC 12 Sept 1863. Shown on mus out roll dated 14 Mar 1864 to date 25 Feb 1864; disch by virtue of reenl as vet vol under GO 191, Series 1863, War Dept. June 1864: loss 18 June 1864, Lynchburg, MIA. POW record shows him capt 19 June 1864, Lynchburg. Place of confinement not stated, but probably Salisbury Prison Camp. Par 26 Feb 1865, NE Ferry, NC. Notation for CCO 20 Mar 1865, no additional info on card. Jan 1865: gain 19 Jan 1865, Camp Hastings, Md from MIA. Abs POW. Feb-June 1865: abs POW. Mus out 20 July 1865.

MCGRAW, JOHN A. PVT, CO B. Age 42. 6ft. Blue eyes. Black hair. Dark comp. *b* Russell Co, Va. Farmer. Enr 15 Sept 1861, Spencer, Va, 3 years. Mus 9 Dec 1861, Spencer, Roane Co, Va to date 16 Sept 1861. May-June 1862: abs sick. Special mus dated 18 Aug 1862, (GO 92 AGO 1862) shows him AWOL. July-Aug 1862: AWOL. Shown on descr list of deserters dated 31 Aug 1863, Fayette CH, WVa. Shown des 1 Aug 1862, Pt Pleasant, Va. Sept-Oct 1862: abs sick. Jan-June 1863: abs sick. Appears on special mus roll dated 10 Apr 1863 abs sick hosp, Charleston. Sept-Oct 1863: dropped from roll as des 1 Sept 1863. Jan-Feb 1864: gain from des. Ret from des 8 Jan 1864 and ordered to duty by Brig Gen Scammon. Mar-Aug 1864: CSR shows him ds. Apr 1864: abs div scout 24 Mar. Regt returns show him det mounted scout 7 Apr 1864. Co mus out roll dated 15 Oct 1864 shows him des 10 July 1864. Shown on list of prisoners confined in miliary prison at Wheeling, WVa (aka Atheneum Prison) arrested by Cpt Spencer 10 Oct 1864, Wheeling, WVa. Sent 11 Oct 1864, Cumberland. Trans 1 Nov 1864, Co I 1st WVa Vet Inf by consol of 5th and 9th WVa Infs. June 1865: loss 10 June 1865, Cumberland, Md. Disch by exp of term of service.

MCMULLEN, JOHN. CPL, CO G. Age 18. 5ft 10½in. Blue eyes. Light hair. Fair comp. *b* 11 June 1845, Jackson Co, Va. Farmer. Enr 1 Mar 1862, Spencer, Va, 3 years. Mus 29 Feb, Spencer, Va on roll dated 30 Apr 1862. May-June 1862: roll dated 30 June, sick hosp. Sept 1863: regt returns show him det scout Sept 1863 by order of Col C. B. White. Descr book lists him as 7th cpl. KIA 13 Sept 1863, Roane Co, Va. "Was a meritorious soldier."

MCVICKERS, HILROY (HILLERY) A. PVT, CO H. Age 28. 6ft. Blue eyes. Light hair. Light comp. *b* Wayne Co, Va. Farmer. Enr 24 Oct 1861, Barboursville, Va, 3 years. Mus 30 Apr 1863, Winchester, Va to date 27 Oct 1861. Capt 10 Nov 1861, Guyandotte, Va. Confined 22 Nov 1861, Richmond, Va. Sent 24 Dec 1861, Salisbury, NC. Par 28 May 1862, Salisbury, NC. Shown on list of deserters at Camp Lew Wallace without date. Shown des 23 Sept 1862, Camp Lew Wallace. May-June 1862: furl from War Dept. Special mus dated 18 Aug 1862: "Par. prisoner ordered to CCO by Secretary of War." Nov-Dec 1862: par prisoner, Camp Lew Wallace. Oct 1863: abs det scout. Nov 1863: 15 Nov 1863 scout ret. Mus out 13 Jan 1864 to date 31 Dec 1863 to reenl as vet vol. Re-mus 13 Jan to date 1 Jan 1864. May-June 1864: abs brig pioneer. Aug 1864: abs sick hosp, Sandy Hook, Md. Mar 1865: abs div teamster 24 Jan 1865. Loss 5 Mar 1865, Beverly, WVa, exp of term of service. Also served Co C 18th Ohio Inf.

MILLER, ISAAC. PVT, CO I. Age 22. 6ft. Green eyes. Auburn hair. Fair comp. *b* Wayne Co, Va. Farmer. Recruit. Enr 16 Apr 1862, Guyandotte, Va, 3 years. Mus 30 Apr 1862, Camp Paxton, Guyandotte, Va. Oct 1863: regt returns show him det scout by order of Col C. B. White. MIA 18 June 1864, Lynchburg, Va. Trans 1 Nov 1864, Co D, 1st WVa Vet Inf by consol of 5th and 9th WVa Infs. Jan 1865: gain 19 Jan 1865, Camp Hastings, Md from MIA. POW. Feb-June 1865: abs POW.

MOORE, DANIEL V (VARNER). PVT, CO K. Age 18. 5ft 8in. Blue eyes. Light hair. Light comp. *b* 9 Sept 1844, Monongalia Co, Va. Farmer. Enr 19 Mar 1862, Marion Co, Va, 3 years. Mus

30 Apr 1862, Camp Paxton, Guyandotte, Va. Sept 1863: regt returns show him det scout by order Col C. B. White. Reenl 31 Mar 1864, vet vol under GO 191, Series 1863, War Dept. July-Aug 1864: wounded slightly in left hand while charging the enemy's breastworks under a severe fire at Cloyd's Mt and sent to Gallipolis Hosp. Trans 1 Nov 1864, Co H 1st WVa Vet Inf by consol of 5th and 9th WVa Infs.

MORTON, CHARLES. PVT, CO C. Age 19. 5ft 10in. Dark eyes. Black hair. Dark comp. *b* 9 Dec 1843, Nicholas Co, Va. Farmer. Recruit. Enr 31 Aug 1862, Gauley Bridge, 3 years. Mus 9 Feb 1863, Winchester, Va to date 31 Aug 1862. Sept-Oct 1862: hosp, Gallipolis. Oct 1863: regt returns show him det scout since 12 Sept 1863 by order of Col C. B. White. Mar-Apr 1864: det duty div scout co. June 1864: regt returns show him as brig scout. Sept 1864: Wounded in action 4 Sept 1864, Myer's Ford by a minnie ball in left shoulder (erroneous). Adm 5 Sept, USA Field Hosp, Sandy Hook. Trans 8 Sept, gen hosp. Adm 8 Sept, USA Gen Hosp, Camden Street, Baltimore, Md. Hosp cards now show GSW in 2 places: right leg and hip. Trans and adm 27 Sept 1864, USA Gen Hosp, West Philadelphia, Pa. Trans to Co C 1st WVa Vet Inf by consol of 5th and 9th WVa Infs. Postwar occ: farmer. *d* 25 Apr 1925, Lizemores, WVa.

NICHOLAS, LORENZO D. PVT, CO F. Age 18. Enr Summersville, Va. Mus 1 July 1862, Summersville. Recruit. Sept 1863: scout by order of Col White. Capt 9 May 1864, Cloyd's Mt. *d* 22 Aug 1864, Andersonville, Ga while a POW. Grave no 6442.

PAINTER, CHARLES G. SGT, CO F. Age 30. 6ft. Blue eyes. Dark hair. Fair comp. *b* Greenbrier Co, Va. Farmer. Enr 15 Feb 1862, Ripley, Va, 3 years. Mus 28 Feb 1862, Mouth of Mill Creek, Jackson Co, Va. Mar-Apr 1862: shown on rolls as cpl. Sept-Oct 1862: prom from 2d cpl to 4th duty sgt. Sept 1862: det ind scouting co 12 Sept 1863 by order of Col C. B. White. Mus rolls for July-Aug 1864 note him "capt. by bushwhackers." POW record shows him capt 29 Oct 1863, Boyce's (Bowyer's) Ferry, Va. Shown abs POW from this date. Confined 14 Nov 1863, Richmond. Sent 14 Mar 1864, Americus, Ga or Andersonville. Money taken $5.00. Adm hosp (no date). *d* 1 July 1864, Andersonville, Ga of acute diarrhea while POW. Grave no 2737.

PARSONS, GEORGE W. PVT, CO G. Age 20. 5ft 7in. Black eyes. Black hair. Dark comp. *b* Calhoun Co, Va. Farmer. Enr 5 Nov 1861, Spencer, Va, 3 years. Oct 1862: abs sick hosp, Parkersburg. Sept 1864: abs scout det since 17 Aug 1864. Nov 1864: abs det scout under Cpt Blazer. *d* 11 Nov 1909.

PARSONS, JAMES. PVT, CO D. Age 22. 6ft 1in. Gray eyes. Light hair. Dark comp. *b* Cabell Co, Va. Enr 26 Feb 1862, Guyandotte, Va, 3 years. Mus 26 Feb 1862, Camp Paxton, Guyandotte, Va. Jan-Mar 1863: on duty at work on fortifications. Nov-Dec 1863: sick, Guyandotte, Va, GSW in thigh caused accidentally while cleaning a revolver. Mar 1864: abs brig prov guard 3 Mar 1864. Det scout Mar and Apr 1864. Det scout to 30 Apr 1864. June-Aug 1864: abs div scout. Trans 1 Nov 1864, 1st WVa Vet Inf. Not shown on mus out roll. Honorably disch 28 Sept 1865. Also served with Co E 189th Ohio Inf. *d* 15 Apr 1885, possible suicide.

PRUDENCE, G (GEORGE) W. Filed affidavit in George McCauley's pension record as also being a scout. Not noted in military or pension record. *d* 10 Feb 1923, E Liverpool, Ohio.

PORTER, LEWIS. PVT, CO I. Age 26. 5ft 5in. Black hair. Gray eyes. Dark comp. Farmer. *b* Cabell Co, Va. Pension record shows *b* 28 Feb, Buffalo Shoals, Wayne Co, Va. Mus 30 Apr 1862 and enr 2 Nov 1861, Guyandotte. Capt 10 Nov 1861, Guyandotte, Va and confined 22 Nov, Richmond, Va and sent 24 Dec, Salisbury, NC. Par May 1862, Salisbury, NC and delivered on par 2

June 1862, Washington, NC. Reported 1 Aug 1862, Cincinnati, Ohio and then CCO. Reported there 2 Aug 1862, present 27 Aug 1862. Declared exch 19 Nov 1862. War Dept notations dated 30 Mar 1888 shows "The charge of desertion of Dec. 15, 1862 against this man is removed under the provision of the Act of Congress approved July 5, 1884. He was absent without proper authority from about Nov. 19, 1862-ca Feb 19, 1863 when he rejoined his co." Veteran. Det scout 16 Mar 1864. Rolls show him det scout through Aug 1864. Sept 1864: 28 Sept 1864 Harrisonburg, detachment. June 1865: loss 6 June, Staunton, Va. Des. *d* 19 Feb 1915, Salt Rock, WVa.

REDDEN, JOSEPH H. PVT, CO H. Age 41. 5ft 9in. Hazel eyes. Dark hair. Dark comp. *b* Fayette Co, Va. Farmer. Enr 24 Apr 1863, Winchester, Va, 3 years. Mus 30 Apr 1863, Winchester, Va to date 24 Apr. Recruit vet vol by reason of prior service in 27th OVI. Det scouts Sept 1863 by order of C. B. White. Capt 1 Nov 1863, Boyce's (Bowyer's) Ferry, Va. POW record shows him confined 14 Nov 1863, Richmond. Sent 12 Feb 1864, Americus, Ga or Andersonville. Adm 13 July 1864, hosp, Andersonville. *d* 20 July 1864, hosp, pluritis. Grave no 3641.

ROGERS, ELI. PVT (CPL), CO B. Age 18. 5ft 7½in. Gray eyes. Light hair. Light comp. Farmer. *b* 30 Apr 1845, Burnersville, Barbour Co, Va. Enr 20 Nov 1861, Spencer, Va, 3 years. Mus 9 Dec 1861, Spencer, Roane Co, Va. Mar-Apr 1862: abs sick (measles and mumps) when co was paid. Det scouts Sept 1863 by order of C. B. White. July-Aug 1864: abs wounded 20 July 1864, Winchester (Carter's Farm) by musket ball, flesh wound of right abdomen. Bed slip shows him adm 27 Sept 1864, hosp from Clarysville Gen Hosp with GSW to right side. Adm 23 July, USA Gen Hosp, Cumberland, Md from the field. Trans 27 Sept, Parkersburg Gen Hosp. Ret to duty 21 Oct 1864. Shown on mus roll as 7th cpl. Mus out 5 Oct 1864, Harper's Ferry, Va by reason of exp of term of service. Also shown on co mus out roll dated 21 Nov 1864, Camp Russell, Va mus out 21 Nov. Trans from Co B 9th WVa Inf 1 Nov 1864, Co I 1st WVa Vet Inf. Mus out 21 Nov 1864, Camp Russell. Shown on mus out sheet as 5th cpl. Postwar occ: farmer in Roane Co. *d* 11 Sept 1931. Bur Slate Church Memorial Cem, Roane Co, WVa.

SIMS, NEWTON G. PVT, CO G. Age 20. 5ft 11in. Black eyes. Light hair. Fair comp. *b* Harrison Co, Va. Farmer. Enr 5 Nov 1861, Spencer, Va, 3 years. Shown on mus roll dated 9 Dec 1861 to date 5 Nov 1861, Spencer, Va. May-June 1862: abs det duty and accidentally wounded where co was placed. May 1863: abs left sick at mouth of Sandy Elk River. Sept-Oct 1862: MIA 13 Sept 1862, Charleston. Carried MIA through Apr 1863. Shown on mus out roll dated 13 Jan to date 31 Dec 1863, disch by virtue of reenl as vet vol under prov of GO 191, Series 1863, War Dept. Remus 1 Jan 1864, vet vol on roll dated 13 Jan 1864. Sept 1864: abs scout since 17 Aug 1864. Nov 1864: abs det scout under Cpt Blazer. Shown on co mus out roll dated 5 Oct 1864. Trans to 1st WVa Vet Inf. Jan-Apr 1865: det color bearer (Corp). May 1865: abs furl. June 1865: color bearer. Mus out 26 July 1865, Wheeling, WVa. Postwar occ: carpenter. Committed 1866, Moundsville Penitentiary to serve 18 years for the murder of Alexander White. Pardoned 16 Feb 1881.

SPENCER, SAMUEL H. (HUNTER). PVT, CO A. Age 23. 5ft 6in. Hazel eyes. Dark hair. Dark comp. Farmer. Recruit. *b* 8 Dec 1840. Enr 1 May 1862, Summersville, 3 years. Mus 9 Feb 1863, Winchester, Va to date 1 May 1862. Jan 1863: on duty on fortifications. Feb 1863: on extra or daily duty. Mar 1863: on duty at work on fortifications. Sept-Oct 1863: abs ind scouts 12 Sept 1863 by order of Col C. B. White, commanding 2d Brig. Jan 1864: on duty Hosp Corps. Feb 1864: on duty hosp nurse. Mar-Apr 1864: abs provost guard 4 Mar 1864. June 1864: on duty provost guard. Aug 1864: abs sick hosp, Frederick, Md, 3d Div 8AC. Trans 1 Nov 1864, Co B 1st WVa Vet Inf by reason of consol. of 5th and 9th WVa Infs. Mus out 1 May 1865. *d* 1 June 1932, Hookersville, WVa.

Samuel Spencer
Courtesy Jack Spencer

STOUT, VINCENT A. PVT, CO F. Age 20. 5ft 7½in. Hazel eyes. Dark hair. Fair comp. *b* Gilmore Co, Va. Farmer. Recruit. Enr Ripley, Va, 3 years. Mus 28 _ 1862, Mouth of Mill Creek, Jackson Co, Va. Aug 1862: abs arrest. Jan 1863: gain from MIA 26 Jan 1863, Winchester, Va. Mar1864: regt returns show him as div scout since 3 Mar 1864. Sept 1864: GSW of right leg in knee joint 3 Sept 1864, Berryville,Va. Trans to Co F 1st WVa Vet Inf by consol of 5th and 9th WVa Infs. Feb 1865: loss 15 Feb, Camp Hastings, disch by exp of term of service. *d* 21 Jan 1890, Richland Co, Wis.

TEEL, JOHN W. PVT, CO H. Age 21. 5ft 8in. Black eyes. Black hair. Dark comp. *b* Rockbridge City, Va. Farmer. Enl 24 Oct 1861, 3 years. Capt 10 Nov 1861, Guyandotte. Confined 22 Nov, Richmond then sent 24 Dec, Salisbury NC. "Teel was in the hospital with measles. Instead of leaving him in the hospital, he was forced to march with the rest of us in the rain and mud wading streams of water all the way to Dublin Depot, Va. and from there in box cars to Richmond, Va." Testimony of Henry Stephenson, late cpt Co G 9th WVa Inf. Par 2 Jan 1862, Washington, NC. Oct 1863: noted abs det scout. 15 Nov: noted ret from scout. 1 Dec: also noted abs scout. Wounded in right thigh slightly at battle of Cloyd's Mt. Disch 1 Nov 1864, exp of term of service, Cedar Creek, Va. Postwar occ: farmer. *d* 14 Feb 1912, Waubansee, Kans.

TOLLEY, JOHN W. PVT, CO F. Age 19. 5ft 9in. Gray eyes. Dark hair. Dark comp. *b* Jackson Co, Va. Farmer. Enr 21 Nov 1861, Ripley, Va, 3 years. Mus 28 Feb 1862, Mouth of Mill Creek. Reenl 1 Jan 1864, Charleston, WVa, vet. Mar 1864: abs recruiting service in Roane Co, WVa. June-Aug 1864: det Blazer's Scouts since May 1864. Trans 1 Nov 1864, Co F 1st WVa Vet Inf. Killed 18 Nov 1864, Kabletown. Cpl Newton Sims of Co I testified that in a fight with Mosby on or about 21 Nov 1864 Pvt John W. Tolley of Co F was killed.

TOPPIN (TOPIN), WILLIAM. PVT (FIFER), CO I. Age 14. 5ft 5in. Gray eyes. Auburn hair. Fair comp. *b* Richmond, Va. Farmer. Enl 30 Apr 1862, Guyandotte, Va, fifer. Mus same date and place. Det scout 16 Mar 1863, Winchester by order of Maj Gen Milroy. Regt returns show

Samuel Burdett and William Toppin scouts since 23 Mar 1863. May 1863: James Webb, Samuel Burdett, William Toppin det scouts by Gen Milroy, Winchester, Va. July 1863: William Toppin, Samuel Burdett, and James Webb continue as scouts in 2d brig 3d div 8 AC by Gen Milroy. 26 Feb 1863. 27 Mar 1863: noted scout. Noted scout on rolls for Sept-Oct 1864, det since 16 Mar 1864. Also shown det gen scout. Trans 1 Nov 1864, Co I 1st WVa Vet Inf by consol of 5th and 9th WVa Infs. Mus out 1 May 1865, Wheeling, WVa.

WASHBURN, ELIAS H. PVT, CO C. Age 41. 5ft 11in. Blue eyes. Sandy hair. Light comp. *b* Harrison Co, Va. Farmer. Enr 30 Oct 1861, Ravenswood, Va, 3 years. Mus 27 Nov 1861, Mason City, Va. Sept 1862-Feb 1863: extra duty man, teamster. Oct 1863: regt returns show him det scout since 12 Sept 1863 by order Col C. B. White. Disch by virtue of reenl as vet vol on roll dated 13 Jan 1864 to date 31 Dec 1863. Re-mus 13 Jan 1864, vet vol to date 1 Jan 1864. Jan-Feb 1864: abs with leave on furl. Nov 1864-Mar 1865: brig and div pioneer. Trans 1 Nov 1864, 1st WVa Vet Inf. Postwar occ: farmer. *d* 1 Dec 1898, Lawrence Co Infirmary.

WAUGH, HIRAM. PVT, CO H. Age 26. 5ft 10in. Hazel eyes. Dark hair. Dark comp. *b* 5 July 1836, Gallipolis, Gallia Co, Ohio. Farmer. Enr 18 Sept 1861, Ceredo, Va, 3 years. Mus 28 Feb 1862, Ceredo, Va. Capt 10 Nov 1861, Guyandotte, Va. Confined 22 Nov 861, Richmond, Va and sent to Salisbury, NC 24 Dec. Par 2 June 1862, Washington, NC. No further record of first capture. Sept 1863: regt returns show him det scout by order of Col C. B. White. Nov 1863: 15 Nov, scout returns. Dec 1863: abs scout. Reenl 1 Jan 1864, vet vol, Fayetteville, WVa under GO 191, Series 1863, War Dept. Wounded 9 May 1864, Cloyd's Mt and a POW. (POW record shows place of confinement not given. Not borne at Andersonville.) Par 19 Nov 1864, Savannah, Ga. Adm on board USA Hosp Steamer *Atlantic* 20 Nov 1864. Reported 25 Nov 1864, CGB and adm hosp div no 1 same date with chronic diarrhea. Sent 27 Nov 1864, Baltimore, Md. Trans 1 Nov 1864, Co H 1st WVa Vet Inf by consol of 5th and 9th WVa Infs. *d* 13 Feb 1921, Nat Soldier's Home, Kans.

WAYNE, LEROY. PVT, CO F. Age 27. 6ft 5in. Black eyes. Black hair. Dark comp. *b* Calhoun Co, Va. Farmer. Enr 8 Feb 1862, Ripley, Va, 3 years. Mus 28 Feb 1862, Mouth of Mill Creek, Jackson Co, Va. Des 16 Oct 1862. Nov-Dec 1862: AWOL 15 Oct-17 Dec 1862. Nov-Dec 1863: AWOL 1 Nov-8 Dec 1863. On descr list of deserters dated 30 Nov 1863. Went home on furl and failed to return on time. Sept 1863: regt returns show him det scout by order of Col C. B. White. Appears on list of men gained from desertion dated Fayette CH 5 Jan 1864. Feb 1864: on roll dated 14 Mar 1864 to date 28 Feb 1864 disch to reenl as vet vol under prov of GO 191, Series 1863, War Dept. Re-mus 14 Mar 1864, vet to date 29 Feb 1864. Mar-Apr 1864: in arrest awaiting sentence of CM. July-Aug 1864: 1 month's pay stopped by order of GCM. Trans 1 Nov 1864, Co F 1st WVa Vet Inf by reason of consol of 5th and 9th WVa Infs. War Dept notation dated 28 Aug 1889: "The charge of desertion in 1862 and 1863 against this man is removed. He was AWOL from Oct. 15, 1862 to Dec. 10, 1862 and Nov. 1, 1863 to Dec. 8, 1863. If regimental records are correct, this man may have been ret. to his co. from scout duty." Claimed to have frozen feet while on picket in the winter of 1863 and 1864. Treated by regt surgeon. May 1865: abs brig teamster. Postwar occ: farmer. Lived near Letart, Meigs Co, Ohio and then at Ripley Landing, Jackson Co, WVa. "A temperate and industrious man." *d* 1 Jan 1900.

WEBB, JAMES. PVT (SGT), CO I. Age 22. 5ft 11 in. Dark comp. Hazel eyes. Dark hair. *b* Va. Farmer. Enr 28 Oct 1861, Guyandotte, 3 years and mus 30 Apr 1862, Guyandotte, sgt. Des 30 Oct 1862. Ret 18 Dec 1862. Prom 3d sgt 20 Jan 1862. Shown det scout since 26 Feb 1863, Winchester, Va. Mar-Apr 1863: det gen scout 26 Feb 1863. May-June 1863: Same. July-Aug 1863:

"det. as scout since Feb. 26/63." Jan and Feb 1863: shown as 2d sgt. Shown reduced to rank of pvt in rolls of July and Aug 1863. Mar-Apr 1864: det scout 3 Mar 1864. KIA 23 Sept 1864, Charles Town, WVa. (Final statement and casualty sheet show Summit Point.) Also shown on rolls for Mar and Apr 1864 as scout since 3 Mar 1864. *d* of wounds rec. in action near Summit Point, Va.

WILSON, JEREMIAH. PVT, CO K. Age 19. 6 ft. Black eyes. Dark hair. Light comp. *b* 2 Jan 1841, Marion Co, Va. Farmer. Enr 29 Apr 1862, Marion Co, Va, 3 years. Mus 30 Apr 1862, Guyandotte, Va. 18 Mar: on duty scout. Det teamster 1 May 1862. 1 Jan 1864: on duty ambulance driver. Entered post hosp, Gauley Bridge, Va 15 July 1862 with "febris remittus." Disch 26 Aug 1862. May 1863: sick hosp, Weston, Va. 1 April 1864: granted 30 days leave by order of Gen Crook. June-Aug1864: abs scout. Sept-Oct 1864: shown abs wounded. Wounded in right foot Sept 1864 in skirmish near Harper's Ferry (Myer's Ford). Record shows him wounded 3 Sept 1864, Berryville, and entered field hosp, Sandy Hook, Md. Record also shows treated for GSW of left foot 1-5 Nov. Trans 1 Nov 1864, Co C 1st WVa Vet Inf. Nov-Dec 1864: abs det Cpt Blazer's Ind Scouts. Disch 1 May (30 Apr) 1865. Mus out by exp of term of service to take effect 30 April 1865. Occ: miller for at least 30 years. *d* 24 Jan 1921. Bur Rymer Cem, Mannington District, Marion Co, WVa.

WILSON, EDGAR C. PVT, CO K. Age 23. 5ft 9in. Blue eyes. Dark hair. Light comp. *b* Monongalia Co, Va. Farmer. Enr 31 Mar 1862, Mason Co, Va for 3 years. Mus 30 Apr 1862, Camp Paxton, Guyandotte, Va. May-June 1862: prom cpl 8 June 1862. Special mus roll dated 10 Apr 1863: prom sgt 1 Apr 1863. July-Aug 1863: 5th sgt. Sept 1863: regt returns show him det scout by order of Col C. B. White along with J. N. Kennedy, John Haught, and Daniel Moore. May-June 1864: 4th sgt. Trans 1 Nov 1864, Co H 1st WVa Vet Inf by consol of 5th and 9th WVa Infs. Apr 1865: loss 24 Apr 1865, Winchester, Va. Disch exp of term of service.

WILSON, WILLIAM R (BILLY). PVT, CO G. Vet. Age 21. 5ft 11in. Blue eyes. Light hair. Fair comp. *b* 11 Apr 1842, Jackson Co, WVa. Laborer (also farmer). Enl 2 Feb 1862, Spencer, Va. July-Aug 1862: USA Post Hosp, Gauley Bridge, Va, typhoid fever, adm 10 July and ret to duty 4 Aug. MIA 13 Sept 1862, Charleston. Went to his home in Roane Co sick and listed as a deserter on 20 Nov. Sept 1863: abs scout by order of Col C. B. White 12 Sept 1863. Mar and Apr 1864: granted 30 days leave by order of Gen Crook. 24 July 1864. Abs sick hosp, Cumberland, Md, with GSW of right hand, an injury of right thumb incurred at Battle of Winchester. Trans 28 July 1864, Wheeling, WVa. Aug-Oct 1864: AWOL. Nov-Dec 1864: loss in the field, des. Trans to Co I, 1st WVa Vet Vols. AWOL until 5 Dec 1864. Ret to Camp Russell. Stopped for 1 month's pay by order of GCM. Feb-June 1865: abs sick Gen Hosp, Grafton, WVa, diarrhea. Reported for mus out 24 July 1865. Mus out to take effect from 21 July 1865 by reason of telegram dated War Dept AGO Washington, DC 23 June 1865. Occ: farmer postwar. *d* 24 Feb 1926, Frame, WVa.

Company G, 11th West Virginia Infantry (Attch to 13th WVA Inf)

MAY, JACOB C. CPL, CO G. Age 26. *b* 3 April 1841, Cabell Co, Va. Enr 26 Mar 1862, Coalsmouth, 3 years. Mus 23 May 1862, Coalsmouth. April 1862: Co G is attch. to 13th WVa Inf. Shown on mus roll as 7th cpl 30 Apr-30 Oct 1862. Nov-Dec 1863: shown as pvt. 10 Mar 1864: regt papers of 13th WVa Inf show him det mounted scout. Sept-Oct 1864: prom cpl. Mus out 15 May 1865, Richmond, Va. Retired farmer. He obtained his education in subscription schools in Lincoln Co. Mus out Richmond, Va and was cpl of his co. Wounded twice, once in right hand [not war related, accidental in 1868] and once in his foot. *d* 25 Oct 1912, St Albans, WVa.

13th West Virginia Infantry

Organized Oct 1862, Pt Pleasant and Barboursville. Unless noted all men mus out with regt 22 June 1865, Wheeling, WVa.

BRADLEY, WILLIAM L. SGT, CO F. Age 27. 5ft 6in. Gray eyes. Black hair. Dark comp. *b* Botetourt Co, Va. Farmer and cooper. Enr 9 Sept 1862, Pt Pleasant, Va, 3 years. Mus 9 Oct 1862, Pt Pleasant, as 5th cpl to date 9 Sept. May-June 1864: prom sgt 1 May 1864 by order of Col Brown vice P. W. Nicholson, reduced by order of Gen Crook. Det Blazer's Scouts 1 May 1864. Aug 1864: reported by Cpt Blazer as sick in hosp 2 Aug 1864. Left 8 Aug 1864, Harpers Ferry, with abscess of leg. Occ: postwar farmer, cooper, teacher, merchant, and hotel keeper.

CHERRY, HENRY A. PVT, CO D. Age 24. 5ft 9in. Blue eyes. Light hair. Light comp. Farmer (also boatman). *b* 14 June 1838, Trumbull Co, Ohio. Enr 18 Aug 1862, Hartford City, 3 years. Mus 8 Oct 1862, Pt Pleasant, Va. Sick in hosp for mus roll to 31 Oct 1862. Mus 26 Feb 1864. Det Blazer's Scouts since Aug 1864. Wounded in right breast near Cabletown, Va (WVa), Nov 1864. Nov and Dec in hosp at Annapolis, Md, wounded. *d* 21 July 1909, Chillicothe, Mo.

COBBS, WILLIAM R. PVT, CO E. Age 21. 5ft 9in. Gray eyes. Light hair. Fair Comp. *b* Kanawha Co, Va. Farmer. Enr 18 Aug 1863, Coalsmouth, WVa, 3 years. Mus 6 Oct 1863, Barboursville, WVa to date 18 Aug. Det mounted scout 20 Mar 1864. July-Aug 1864: abs hosp, Harper's Ferry since 10 May 1864. War Dept notation 31 Dec 1898 shows "this man was enr. Aug. 13, 1863." Postwar occ: carpenter. *d* 16 Aug 1928, Spring Hill, WVa.

ENGLAND. WILLIAM P. PVT, CO I. Age 30. 5ft 5in. Black eyes. Black hair. Dark comp. *b* 14 Sept 1834, Kanawha Co, Va. Farmer. Enr 23 Dec 1862, Charleston, Va, 3 years. Mus 26 July 1863, Charleston, WVa to date 23 Dec 1862. Det scout 20 Mar 1864. Apr 1864: ret to co along with James Ratliff as being unfit for scouting service by request of Lt Blazer 4 Apr 1864. *d* 11 March 1915, Grand Detour, Ill.

FURGUSON, ANDREW W. PVT, CO B. Age 37. 5ft 10in. Brown eyes. Dark hair. Dark comp. *b* Kanawha Co, Va. Carpenter. Enr 2 Aug 1862, Pt Pleasant, 3 years. Mus 8 Oct 1862, Pt Pleasant, Va. Aug 1864: regt returns show him det Blazer's Scouts.

HACKER, JOHN C. PVT, CO A. Age 18. 5ft 6in. Blue eyes. Brown hair. Fair comp. *b* Kanawha Co, Va. Farmer. Enr 20 Oct 1863, Barboursville, WVa. Mus 25 Nov 1863 to date 20 Oct 1863. On det duty with Cpt Blazer's Scouts since 9 Aug 1864. Killed 21 Nov 1864, Kabletown. Probably bur unknown grave at Winchester Nat Cem.

HARPER, ANDREW (JACKSON). PVT, CO K. Age 25. 5ft 8in. Gray eyes. Light hair. Fair comp. *b* Kanawha Co, Va. Farmer. Married. Enr 25 July 1863, Walton, Roane Co, WVa, 3 years and mus 3 Oct 1863, Charleston, WVa. Mar 1864: morning report shows him abs on ds scouting under GO No 2. Apr 1864: relieved from scouting duty 21 Apr 1864. May-June 1864: MIA 18 June 1864, Lynchburg, Va. POW record shows him confined at Richmond date not given. Par 14 Nov 1864, Charleston, reported Hosp Div 1, 17 Dec 1864. *d* 21 Dec 1864, US Hosp, Annapolis, Md, of chronic diarrhea. Bur at Ash Grove US Cem (grave number 1245). *ROH*, #VII, p29 lists him bur in US Gen Hosp Div #1 Cem, No 649.

HARRIS, WILLIAM L. PVT, CO B. Age 24. 5ft 6¾in. Gray eyes. Brown hair. Fair comp. *b* Mason Co, Va. Farmer. Enl 11 Dec 1863, Barboursville, WVa. Mus 26 Feb 1864, Barboursville, WVa, 3 years. Det in Blazer's Scouts Nov 1864. On det duty at Brig HQ since Mar 1864. 19 Mar

1864. Det for scouting according to GO No 2. May and June 1864: wounded accidentally near the village of Newport on the Staunton-Lexington Road. July and Aug 1864: abs sick at home in Mason Co, WVa. Det ind scout since 20 Sept 1864. Wounded in calf of right leg 18 Nov 1864, Kabletown. Jan and Feb 1865: sick in hosp, Clarrysville, Md since 15 Feb 1865. Mar and Apr 1865: sick in hosp, Clarrysville, Md. *d* 8 June 1924, Ambrosia, WVa.

HAYNES, JOHN R. PVT, CO E. Age 18. 5ft 6in. Gray eyes. Fair hair. Fair comp. *b* 15 Dec 1844, Kanawha Co, Va. Farmer. Enl 16 Aug 1862, Tupper's Creek, 3 years. Mus 9 Oct 1862, Pt Pleasant, Va. Aug-Nov 1864: abs ds in Cpt Blazer's Scouts. 25 May 1864: capt 18 Nov 1864, Cabletown. Jan 1865: confined since 22 Nov 1864, Richmond, Va. Par 5 Feb 1865, Cox's Wharf. Reported 7 Feb 1865, Camp Parole, Md. Sent 16 Feb 1865, CCO, where he reported 17 Feb 1865. Feb 1865: abs sick at Parole Camp since 18 Nov 1864. Mar 1865: still sick at Parole Camp. Dec 1864: abs POW. *d* 21 Mar 1929, Guthrie, WVa. Bur Guthrie, WVa.

HOGG, TAYLOR N. PVT, CO B. Age 20. 6ft. Blue eyes. Dark hair. Dark comp. *b* 3 Oct 1842, Mason Co, Va. Farmer. Service in 1861 in Va Militia. Enr 18 Aug 1862, Pt Pleasant, Va, 3 years. Mus 8 Oct 1862, Pt Pleasant. Jan-Feb 1862: sick in Mason Co, Va. Noted on special mus roll Apr 1863: sick at home in Mason Co, Va. Jul-Aug 1863: on daily duty teamster since 6 Aug 1863. Sept-Oct 1863: sick at home in Mason Co, WVa. Abs since 1 Sept 1863. Nov-Dec 1863: sick in post hosp, Pt Pleasant 1 Sept 1863. Det scout 30 May 1864. May-June 1864: wounded in action 10 June 1864. Report of operations of the 13th WVa Vols from 30 May to 1 July 1864 signed Col William R. Brown, 13th Regt WVa Vols. In post hosp, Gallipolis, Ohio since 30 June 1864. July-Oct 1864: in hosp, Gallispolis, wounded in action. Mar-Apr 1865: sick since 10 Mar 1865, Clarysville, Md. Mus out 31 1865, Cumberland, Md under GO 77, AGO CS. *d* 3 Oct 1923, Kokomo, Ind.

KEITH, SYLVESTER. PVT, CO F. Age 18. 5ft 6¾in. Black eyes. Black hair. Dark comp. *b* Washington Co, Ohio. Farmer. Enr 9 Sept 1862, Pt Pleasant, Va, 3 years. Mus 9 Oct 1863, Pt Pleasant. Nov-Dec 1863: abs sick regt hosp. Det scout in Cpt Blazer's co since 30 Aug 1864. (Also listed Aug 2.) *d* of wounds rec 26 Nov 1864, Kabletown. Probably bur in unknown grave, Winchester Nat Cem.

LAMASTERS, GEORGE. PVT, CO E. Age 28. 5ft 9in. Dark eyes. Dark hair. Dark comp. *b* Wayne Co, Va. Farmer. Enr 9 Aug 1862, Ceredo, Va, 3 years. Mus 9 Oct 1862, Pt Pleasant. May and June 1864: attch div scouts. *d* of wound rec 18 Nov 1864, Kabletown. Probably bur in unknown grave at Winchester Nat Cem.

LONG, ANDREW J (JACKSON). PVT, CO C. Age 19. 5ft 7½in. Dark eyes. Dark hair. Dark comp. *b* Gallia Co, Ohio. Farmer. Enr 23 Mar 1863, Pt Pleasant, WVa, 3 years. Mus 3 Aug 1863, Charleston, WVa to date 23 Mar 1863. Mar-Apr 1864: det scout since 22 Mar by order of Gen Crook. July-Aug 1864: shown capt by the enemy 7 May 1864. Jan and Feb 1865: ret from POW, 7 Jan 1865 and sick at home in Mason Co, WVa. Mar-Apr 1865: *d* 10 Mar 1865, home in Mason Co, WVa of effects of disease contracted while a POW. POW record shows him capt 5 May 1864, Sewell Mt, Va. Present 20 Nov 1864, Camp Lawton, Ga. Par 21 Nov 1864, Savannah, Ga and reported 1 Dec 1864, CGB, Md. Sent 2 Dec 1864, Camp Parole, Md. George Mayes testified to Andrew's condition when he came home: "I helped bring him to his home after he left the service and he was in very bad conditions. His hands and feet were badly swollen and he had chronic diarrhea of which he afterward died. He was in a perfect helpless condition at the time I assisted in bringing him home. He was also out of his mind and when we arrived at his home he didn't even recognize his own father." *d* 10 Mar 1865, home in Mason Co, WVa of scurvy.

MEANS, WILLIAM A. PVT, CO A. Age 19. Enr 22 Aug 1862, Charleston, Va, 3 years. Mus 6 Oct 1862, Pt Pleasant, Va. Apr 1864: relieved as scout per SO 80, 21 Apr 1864.

GEORGE MILLER. PVT (CPL), CO D. Age 34. 5ft 11½in. Hazel eyes. Dark hair. Dark comp. *b* Kanawha Co, Va. Coppersmith. Enr 19 Aug 1862, Hartford City, 3 years. Mus 8 Oct 1862, Pt Pleasant, Va. Mus roll to 31 Oct 1862 shows him sick in hosp. Morning report for 21 Mar 1864 shows him on ds by order of Gen Crook. Apr 1864: SO 80 relieves him from duty in the ind scouts. Mus reports for Jul-Aug 1864 shows him killed 24 July 1864, Winchester (Kernstown), left on the battlefield. Shown as cpl through Feb 1864 then as pvt.

NICHOLSON, PHILIP W. SGT, CO F. Age 23. 5ft 9¼in. Blue eyes. Light hair. Fair comp. *b* Guernsey Co, Ohio. Carpenter. Enr 9 Sept 1862, Pt Pleasant, Va, 3 years. Mus 9 Oct 1862, Pt Pleasant. Nov 1863: ds since 25 Nov 1863. March 1864: abs scout 10 Mar 1864. Apr 1864: relieved as scout 21 Apr and reduced to ranks 1 May 1864 by SO No 80 of Gen Crook, for allowing a prisoner to escape. Replaced by Sgt William L. Bradley. Shown on mus out roll as sgt. Resided at Rutland, Meigs Co, Ohio. *d* 19 Sept 1909.

ORTH, JOHN. PVT, CO A. Age 20. 5ft 3in. Black eyes. Brown hair. Dark comp. *b* Prussia. Farmer. Mus 6 Oct 1862, Pt Pleasant. Enr 15 Aug 1862, 3 years. Co mus roll dated 31 Dec 1862: "On extra duty 36 days from Aug. 25 to Oct. 8, assisting _____ at Pt. Pleasant." Co morning report shows him detailed for scout by order of Gen Crook. May-June 1864: abs sick since 22 May 1864, Charleston, Va. Mus out 22 June 1865, Wheeling, WVa. *d* 11 May 1909, Charleston, WVa.

PERDUE, LEVETT. PVT, CO H. Age 18. 5ft 6in. Gray eyes. Dark hair. Fair comp. *b* Wayne Co, WVa. Farmer. Enr 14 Aug 1862, Ceredo, Va, 3 years. Mus 9 Oct 1862, Pt Pleasant, Va. Morning report for 23 Mar 1864 shows him det reg scout in compliance with GO No 2. Apr 1864: relieved as scout 21 Apr 1864 by SO No 80. *d* 19 Sept 1964, Winchester, Va, GSW.

PUTNEY, ROBERT (W). PVT, CO K. Age 22. 5ft 10in. Blue eyes. Light hair. Fair comp. *b* 14 June 1840, Buckingham, Cumberland Co, Va. Mill wright. Enr 23 Oct 1863, Leon, WVa, 3 years. Mus 26 Nov 1863, Barboursville, WVa to date 23 Oct. Det scout 30 May 1864. Ret to his regt by order of Lt Blazer for getting drunk 7 June 1864. Nov-Dec 1864: on det duty carpenter 1st Div Ambulance Corps 22 Oct 1864. William McGuire remembered him as a good soldier. Postwar occ: carpenter. *d* 24 Aug 1908, Springfield, Mo.

RATLIFF, JAMES. PVT, CO G. Age 19. 5ft 9in. Black eyes. Dark hair. Dark comp. *b* Lawrence Co, Ohio. Residence: Guyandotte, Cabell Co, WVa. Farmer. Enl 20 Jan 1864, Guyandotte, WVa, 3 years. Mus 28 Feb 1864, Guyandotte. Mar 1864: "Det. for scout to take the place of William J. Smith, in arrest and confinement." Sept-Oct 1864: stopped for a Springfield rifle complete $19.25 and one cartridge box complete $3.25. Mar-Apr 1865: in US Gen Hosp, Clarysville, Md since 13 Apr 1865. Mus out 29 May 1865, US Gen Hosp, Cumberland, Md, in accordance with telegraphic instructions from AGO, War Dept, Washington, DC dated 3 May 1865.

RILEY, JOHN V. PVT, CO I. Age 18. 5ft 10in. Dark eyes. Dark hair. Dark comp. *b* Kanawha Co. Farmer. Enr 13 Dec 1862, Charleston, Va, 3 years. Mus 26 July 1863, Charleston, WVa, cpl to date 13 Dec 1862. Reduced to ranks 9 June 1864. July-Aug 1864: det. Nov-Dec 1864: KIA with rebel Mosby under command of Cpt Blazer near Kabletown 18 Nov 1864. Probably bur unknown grave Winchester Nat Cem.

SCHMITTER, LUKE E. PVT, CO G. Age 18. 5ft 8in. Blue eyes. Dark hair. Light comp. *b* Switzerland. Farmer. Resident of Buffalo, Putnam Co, WVa. Enr 28 Dec 1863, Buffalo, WVa.

Mus 28 Dec 1863, place not stated. Det ind scout since 30 May 1864. KIA 18 Nov 1864 near Kabletown. Probably bur unknown grave Winchester Nat Cem.

SMITH, GEORGE W. PVT, CO K. Age 24. 5ft 5in. Black eyes. Black hair. Dark Comp. *b* 30 Nov 1837, Kanawha Co, Va. Farmer. Enr 1 Jan 1864, Leon, WVa, 3 years. Mus 1 Jan 1864, Charleston, WVa. July-Aug 1864: Blazer's Scouts by order of Gen Crook since 24 Aug 1864. *d* 17 Apr 1932, Nitro, WVa.

SMITH, MARSHALL. PVT, CO D. Age 24. 5ft 10½in. Blue eyes. Sandy hair. Light comp. *b* Rappahannock Co, Va. Farmer. Enr 22 Aug 1862, Hartford City, Va, 3 years. Mus 8 Oct 1862, Pt Pleasant, Va. Mar and Apr 1863: sick since 20 Apr 1863, hosp, Hurricane Bridge. May-June 1863: sick since 11 May 1863, hosp, Pt Pleasant. July-Aug 1863: sick since 11 May 1863, hosp. Morning report for 30 Apr 1864 shows him det for an ind scout (CSR shows 29 Apr). Det scout since 1 May 1864. Det in Blazer's Scouts since 24 July 1864. Wounded and taken prisoner Nov 1864 in an engagement near Kabletown, Va. POW record shows him capt 18 Nov, Myerstown, Va, confined 22 Nov, Richmond, sent from Gordonsville. *d* as POW on or about 22 Jan 1865, CS Mil Prison hosp, Richmond, pneumonia. Blazer remembered him as "a good soldier and a man of good habits."

SMITH, WILLIAM J. PVT, CO G. Age 38. 5ft 6½in. Blue eyes. Fair hair. Fair comp. *b* England. Cooper. Residence: Guyandotte, Cabell Co, Va. Enr and mus 5 Dec 1863, 3 years. Det scouts. Relieved from duty scout; in arrest and confinement. Mar-Apr 1864: under arrest at Charleston, WVa by order of Col Tomlinson, 5th Va Vols. July-Aug 1864: no pay or bounty rec. in arrest by order of Col Tomlinson, 5th Va since 17 Apr 1864. Carried the same on the rolls to Mar-Apr 1865: illegally enl 5 Dec 1863 Cpt W. E. Teazel. "This man after his enl. was reported as a member of the 5th W.Va. Inf. was arrested and turned over to the HQ of the Regt."

STEEL, MANASSAS G. PVT, CO I. Age 29. 5ft 3in. Hazel eyes. Black hair. Dark comp. *b* Monroe Co, Va. Farmer. Enr 1 June 1863, Charleston, WVa, 3 years. Mus 26 July 1863, Charleston, WVa to date 1 June 1863. Jan-Feb 1864: under arrest for desertion. CSR does not show any entry for ds. May and June 1864: shown des 27 May 1864, Gauley Bridge. Casualty sheet shows des as 6 May. Listed in casualty list compiled by Cpt Blazer as des from arrest 6 May 1864. Book mark shows charge of des removed by order of the president SO 582. AGO 21 Nov 1866.

STOVER, GEORGE W. PVT, CO K. Age 19. 5ft 8in. Blue eyes. Dark hair. Fair comp. *b* Princeton, Va. Farmer. Enr 26 Dec 1863, Barboursville, 3 years. Mus 20 Jan 1864, Charleston, WVa. May-June 1864: abs on ds scout. July-Aug 1864: with Blazer's Scouts by order of Gen Crook since 7 July 1864. Sept-Oct 1864: in US Hosp, Winchester since 19 Oct 1864. Regt casualty lists report him "injured in action at Cedar Creek, Va. Oct.19, 1864" caused by "contusion by horse falling on him." Nov-Dec 1864: abs since 19 Oct 1864, hosp l. Mus roll dated 30 Apr 1865. In US Hosp, Clarysville. Mus out 8 June 1865, Wheeling, WVa. Reported form USA Gen Hosp, Cumberland, Md 7 June 1865 for mus out. Mus out to take effect from 8 June 1865 by reason of telegram dated 20 May 1865, War Dept, AGO, Washington DC. *d* 23 Dec 1872 of complications from being trampled by the horse.

THOMPSON, WILLIAM H. SGT, CO C. Age 22. 5ft 6½in. Blue eyes. Light hair. Light comp. *b* 1 Sept 1839, Cabell Co, Va. Shoemaker (pension lists steamboat pilot). Enr 1 Sept 1862, Pt Pleasant, Va, 3 years. Mus cpl 9 Oct 1862, Pt. Pleasant. Sept-Oct 1863: 2d cpl William H. Thompson prom 5th sgt. Mar-Apr 1864: on recruiting service since 24 Feb 1864 by order of Gen Duffie. July-Aug 1864: regt returns show him det scout Aug 1864. Det for ind scout by order Gen

Crook. Sept-Oct 1864: det for Blazer's Scouts by order of Brevet Maj Gen Crook. Nov-Dec 1864: det for scout by order of Maj Gen Crook. A. G. Mason, late cpt, Co G, 13th WVa Regt testified, "was a good soldier and brave to a fault, and never to my knowledge missing duty when able to perform it." *d* 1 July 1926, Charleston, WVa. Bur Columbus, Ohio.

WOLLWINE, HENRY. PVT, CO H. Age 19. 6ft 5in. Blue eyes. Dark hair. Fair comp. *b* Monroe Co, Va. Wagon maker. Enr 13 Aug 1862, Camp Piatt, 3 years. Mus 10 Oct 1862, Pt Pleasant, Va to date 15 Aug 1862. Mus roll to 31 Oct 1862 shows him on extra duty as a teamster. Nov 1862 to Feb 1863: on extra duty as a teamster. May and June 1863: wagoning for RQM since 1 June 1863 by order of Col Brown. July-Aug 1863: ret to duty with co 20 Aug 1863. Mar-Apr 1864: abs on ds in compliance with GO No 2 since 29 Apr 1864. Morning report for 30 Apr shows him det reg scout per GO No 2. Shown det scout through Dec 1864. Postwar occ: farmer. *d* 5 Sept 1883. Also listed 15 Jan 1893.

WOODYARD, MATHEW (MAT) E. PVT, CO G. Age 20. 5ft 8in. Hazel eyes. Dark hair. Fair comp. *b* Giles Co, Va. Residence: Guyandotte, Cabell Co, Va. Farmer. Enl 5 Jan 1864, Guyandotte, WVa, 3 years. Mus 28 Feb 1864, Guyandotte. May 1864: regt returns show him det scout since 12 Apr 1864. Aug 1864. Bed card shows him in gen hosp, Patterson Park, Baltimore, Md. Adm 12 Aug 1864 diagnosis, peritonitis. Married. Listed next of kin as James S. Woodyard, Procktersville, Oh. James served with Co C, 13th WVa Inf. Mar-Apr 1865: abs with leave. Postwar occ: teamster in Mo and Colo. *d* 8 Mar 1905.

14th West Virginia Infantry

Organized 25 Aug 1862, Wheeling, WVa. Unless otherwise noted all men mus out with regt 27 June 1865, Cumberland, Md. Dyers lists this regt mus out 28 June but all records show 27 June.

FLETCHER, BENJAMIN F. M. PVT, CO C. Age 18. 5ft 8½in. Hazel eyes. Black hair. Dark comp. *b* 4 Sept 1844 near Farmington, Marion Co, Va. Farmer. Enl and mus 10 Mar 1864, Grafton, WVa Sick hosp with measles; ret to duty 29 May 1864. July and Aug 1864: mus show him det Cpt Blazer since 23 Aug, Harper's Ferry, Va. GSW rec 4 Sept 1864, Myer's Ford. Adm 5 Sept, field hosp, Sandy Hook, Md, GSW middle of left thigh, wounded at Berryville; ball lodged severely. Trans 5 Sept. Adm 6 Sept, Gen Hosp, Frederick, Md, GSW left thigh, flesh and trans 8 Sept. Adm 9 Sept, Newton University Gen Hosp, Baltimore, Md, GSW left thight upper third, ball remaining, wounded 4 Sept, Myer's Ford, Va and trans 21 Sept 1864. Adm 21 Sept, Mower (Chestnut Hill) Gen Hosp, Philadelphia, Pa and trans 28 Oct. Adm 1 Nov 1864, Gen Hosp, Grafton, WVa, GSW middle left thigh ball lodged, severe, wounded 4 Sept 1864 in skirmish at Myer's Ford, Va, pistol ball. Furl 13 Dec 1864, 30 days. Wounds improving on crutches. Restored for duty 6 Mar 1865. Ret to hosp 3 Jan 1865 and ret to duty 6 Mar 1865. *d* 19 June 1921, Halleck (Independence), WVa.

HAUGHT, TOBIAS. PVT, CO K. Age 20. 5ft 10in. Hazel eyes. Light hair. Fair comp. *b* Monongalia Co, Va. Farmer. Enr 19 Aug 1862, Burton, 3 years. Mus 16 Sept 1862. Abs on ds in Cpt Blazer's Ind Scouts since July 1864. List of casualties with case of Charles Nowlin Co I, 36 Oh wounded shows Tobias Haught KIA 19 Nov, Myerstown, Va. *d* 25 Nov 1864 of wounds rec at Kabletown. Descr book of co describes his loss: "Was wounded in action at Cable Town (Kabletown) Nov. 25th [*sic*] dead from the wound the same evening. His remains were interred at or near Cable Town, Va. Pvt. Haught was a good and deserving soldier. When surrounded on all

William Heldreth and Mariah Roberts

William R. Heldreth and Mariah B. Roberts in a wedding tintype about 1870.
Courtesy Janet Benavente

sides by the enemy, he fought until he was mortally wounded. He has often been heard to say. 'I never will surrender to them.' He was loved by all who new him." Probably bur unknown grave, Winchester Nat Cem.

HELDRETH, WILLIAM R (RILEY). PVT, CO H. Age 18. 6ft 1in. Blue eyes. Light hair. Fair comp. *b* 27 June 1845, Hessville, Marion Co, Va. Farmer. Enr 30 Nov 1862, New Creek, Va, 3 years. Mus 1 Feb 1863, New Creek, Va. Noted on mus rolls for Nov and Dec 1864 attch with Blazer's Scouts. *d* 24 Jan 1916, Kingfisher, Okla. Bur Kingfisher Cem.

LYONS, JOHN G. PVT, CO E. Age 30. 6ft. Black eyes. Black hair. Dark comp. *b* 26 Oct 1831, Washington Co, Pa. Mill wright. Enr 14 Aug 1862, Middlebourne. Mus 29 Aug 1862, Wheeling, WVa. Capt by the enemy on or about 14 June 1863, Casuptown [as copied], Md. Confined 23-24 June 1863, Richmond, Va. Par 22 July, City Point, Va and reported 24 July 1863, Camp Parole. Sent 12 Oct 1863, Harper's Ferry. Ret to the rolls Sept and Oct 1863. Shown capt by the enemy 18 Nov 1864 (also shown 21 Nov, Myerstown, Va). Confined 22 Nov 1864, Richmond and par 5 Feb 1864, Cox's Wharf. Reported 7 Feb, Camp Parole and sent 16 Feb 1865, CCO, where he reported 20 Feb 1865 and was furl 20 Feb 1865 for 30 days. Det at brig HQ since 15 Feb 1864. *d* 12 June 1907, Cosmopolis, Wash.

MARTIN, ELIAS. PVT, CO I. Age 20. 5ft 10½in. Blue eyes. Light hair. Fair comp. *b* Monongalia Co, Va. Shoemaker. Enr 22 Aug 1862, Morgantown, Va, 3 years. Mus 11 Sept 1862, Wheeling, Va. On ds since 6 Nov 1863, Burlington, Va. Stoppage of pay of $10 by sentence of GCM 14 June 1863. Shown on ds in Blazer's Scouts since 28 Aug 1864. KIA 19 Nov 1864, Kabletown. Probably bur unknown grave, Winchester Nat Cem.

MASON, ULYSUS. PVT, CO H. Age 19. 5ft 11in. Blue eyes. Dark hair. Dark comp. *b* Monongalia Co, Va. Farmer. Descr book lists him as capt 18 Nov 1864 (probably an error). Enr

15 Aug 1862, Mannington, Va, 3 years. Mus 1 Sept 1862, Wheeling Va. CSR shows him POW Sept-Oct 1864. Wounded 26 Oct 1864 at or near Kernstown. Attested to by Isaac Martin, late lt Co H. Jan-Feb 1865: capt with Blazer's scouts. Mus out roll shows him "D. in rebel prison Richmond, date not known." Pension notation shows him d. of wounds 27 Oct 1864, Richmond.

NOTTINGHAM, GEORGE W. PVT, CO D. Age 20. 6ft 5½in. Blue eyes. Brown hair. Fair comp. *b* 15 June 1843, Pocahontas Co, Va. Farmer. Enl 15 Aug 1862, Parkersburg, Va, 3 years. Mus 25 Aug 1862, Wheeling, Va. Feb 1863: abs Provost Guard. June 1863: on det duty chopping timber. Oct 1863: abs on furl. 25 Aug-Nov 1864: abs det in Cpt Blazer's Scouts. Wounded 22 Sept 1864 near Winchester, Va (Summit Pt fight) by minnie ball by Mosby's men in the left chest. Adm 16 Oct 1864, USA Gen Hosp from Field Hosp. Dec 1864: abs wounded at hosp, Cumberland, Md. Jan 1864: abs on leave with surgeon's certificate. Ret to duty 7 Jan 1865. *d* 24 Feb 1923, Perkins, Okla.

PARNELL, JOHN (ANDREW JACKSON) (JACK) A. PVT, CO B. Age 32. 6ft 2in. Blue eyes. Dark hair. Dark comp. *b* 22 Feb 1829, Fayette Co, Pa. Farmer. Enr 14 Aug 1862, Brandonville, Va, 3 years. Mus 25 Aug 1862, Wheeling, Va. Mar-June 1864: in US Hosp, Clarksburg, WVa. July-Oct 1864: det in scouting party. Adm 20 Sept 1864, gen hosp, Patterson Park, for chronic diarrhea. Nov 1864-Feb 1865: in US Hosp, Washington, DC. Mus out 27 Jan 1865, Cumberland, Md. *d* 29 Mar 1897. Bur Johnson Chapel Cem, Rt 281, Confluence, Pa.

RAIRDON, DANIEL T. PVT, CO F. Age 25. 5ft 8in. Blue eyes. Dark hair. Fair comp. *b* Washington Co, Ohio. Farmer. Enr 11 Aug 1862, St Mary's, 3 years. Mus 30 Aug 1862, Wheeling, Va. Shown on ds since July 1864 scouting. Various dates listed for death. Apparently *d* 1 Dec 1864 of wounds rec 18 Nov 1864, Kabletown. Probably bur unknown grave, Winchester Nat Cem.

THOMAS, ELIAS. CPL, CO G. Age 27. 5ft 6in. Blue eyes. Dark hair. Fair comp. *b* Deep Valley, Doddridge Co, Va. Farmer. Enr 10 Sept 1862, Ellenboro, Va, 3 years. Mus 13 Sept 1862, Wheeling, Va. Appt cpl 15 June 1863. Wounded in action 15 Aug 1864, Massanutten Mt, Va. Det scout with Cpt Blazer 24 Aug 1864. Det to 31 Dec 1864. Due US for ordnance destroyed $21.18 at muster out. Postwar occ: farmer. *d* 7 Dec 1915, Central Station, WVa.

UNDERWOOD, NUTLEY W. PVT, CO E. Age 35. 5ft 9in. Blue eyes. Light hair. Fair comp. *b* Tyler, Va. Farmer. Enr 8 Aug 1862, Middleborn, 3 years. Mus 24 Aug 1862, Wheeling, Va. On det duty scout from 24 Aug 1864 to Nov/Dec 1864. *d* 25 Jan 1906.

WASS, WILLIAM. PVT, CO G. Age 18. 5ft 4½in. Hazel eyes. Dark hair. Fair comp. *b* 5 Sept 1844, Ritchie Co, Va. Farmer. Enr 9 Aug 1862, Ellenboro, Va, 3 years. Mus 13 Sept 1862, Wheeling, Va. Det scout with Cpt Blazer since 24 Aug 1864. Capt 18 Nov 1864, Kabletown. Jan-Feb 1865: abs POW. POW record reports him capt 18 Nov 1864, Myerstown. Confined 22 Nov 1864, Richmond, Va brought from Gordonsville. Par 5 Feb 1865, Cox's Wharf and reported 7 Feb 1865, CGB. Sent 16 Feb 1865, CCO where he reported 20 Feb 1865. Furl 23 Feb 1865, 30 days. Ret 3 Apr 1865. Reported des 31 Mar 1865. No surgeon's cert on file. Ret 11 Apr 1865 to the co. Adj gen's Office, War Dept. notation dated 19 Dec 1885: "Charge of desertion on POW records is removed under 2nd seal Act July 5, 1884." *d* 9 Dec 1937, Harrisville, WVa. Bur Harrisville, WVa.

WILLIAMS, SOLOMON. PVT, CO A. Age 18. 5ft 6in. Blue eyes. Light hair. Fair comp. *b* Woodridge Co, Va. Farmer. Enr West Union, Va, 3 years. Mus 23 Aug 1862, Wheeling, WVa. On ds with Blazer's Scouts since 26 Aug 1864. KIA 19 Nov 1864, Kabletown. Probably bur unknown grave Winchester Nat Cem.

12th OVI

Organized 28 June 1861, Camp Dennison, Ohio. Mus out 11 July, CCO. Vets and recruits trans 2 July to 23rd Ohio Inf.

ALBAUGH, DAVID. CPL, CO I. Age 18. 5ft 10in. Hazel eyes. Brown hair. Light comp. *b* 15 Oct 1842, Licking Co, Ohio. Farmer. Enr 2 July 1861, Utica, Ohio, 3 years. Mus 26 June 1863, Fayette CH to date 2 July 1861. Mus roll dated 31 Oct 1861: left sick at Cross Lanes, Va. Jan-Feb 1862: on 30 days leave of abs sick at Utica, Ohio commencing 2 Feb 1862. Prom cpl 1 Nov 1862. Sept-Oct 1863: abs in ind scouting co. Mus out 11 Nov 1864 by reason of exp of term of service. Severely wounded and capt by the enemy 9 May 1864, Cloyd's Mt. Medical records show GSW of left arm lower ⅓ fracturing humerus. Also listed as wounded in abdomen. POW record shows him confined 22 Sept, Richmond, Va and adm 23 Sept 1864, Gen Hosp 21 (CS Military Prison Hosp), Richmond, Va. Par 24 Sept 1864, Varina, Va. Adm 26 Sept, hosp Div 2, Annapolis, Md. Trans 6 Oct, Camp Parole Hosp, where he is shown on the rolls Sept-Oct 1864. *d* 16 Nov 1897.

ATKINSON, JOHN. PVT, CO B. Age 19. 5ft 9in. Gray eyes. Auburn hair. Light comp. *b* Green Co, Ohio. Farmer. Enr 20 June 1861, Camp Dennison, 3 years. Mus 20 June 1861, Camp Dennison. Aug 1862: abs det in McMullen's Battery. Sept 1862: abs det with 1st Ohio Battery. Sept-Oct 1863: abs det in ind scouting co. Shown det 13 Sept 1863 scouting co per GO No (no order no given). Shown ret to co 13 Nov 1863. Reenl 5 Jan 1864, vet vol. Jan-Feb 1864: abs on vet furl. Trans 1 July 1864, Co K 23rd, OVI by order of Gen Crook SO No 13. *d* 1 May 1884, prison in Joliet, Ill serving sentence for horse theft.

BARKER, ARMSTRONG. PVT (SGT), CO K. Age 38. 6ft. Hazel eyes. Dark hair. Dark comp. Two crooked fingers. Dark whiskers. *b* 9 May 1823, Perry Co, Ohio. Residence: Hillsborough, Ohio. Reenl and enr 19 June 1861, Camp Dennison, 1st cpl, 3 years. Mus same place and date. Prom sgt 9 Jan 1862. Nov-Dec 1862: abs on recruiting service. Mar-Sept 1863: abs det on recruiting service in Ohio since 25 Mar 1863. 1 June 1864: reduced to the ranks by his own request to give place to J. B. Gustin, a vet vol. Mar-Apr 1864: abs det in ind scouting co. June 1864: abs in div scouting co. Morning report shows him det scout 1 Mar 1864. Also served as pvt in Co A 2nd Batt'n Ohio Cav (NG). Enr 16 Aug 1864.

BAUSSMAN (BOUSEMAN), ABRAHAM. PVT, CO G. Age 28. 5ft 10in. Gray eyes. Sandy hair. Sandy comp. *b* Pa. Farmer. Enr and mus 21 June 1861, Camp Dennison, 3 years. Aug 1862: abs det with McMullen's Battery. Sept 1862: abs det with 1st Ohio Battery. Dec 1863: abs gone to Charleston, Va. to be mus as vet vol. June 1864: on furl. Mar-June 1864: det in ind scouts. Shown on morning report for Feb 1864 det with scouting party. Trans 1 July 1864, Co K, 23rd OVI. Also shown det in scouting co. Mar 1864. Mus out 26 July 1865. Vet. *d* 30 Sept 1897.

BLAIR, JOSEPH T. CPL, CO F. Age 19. 6ft 2in. Black eyes. Dark hair. Dark comp. *b* 6 May 1842, Adams Co, Ohio. No occ given. Enr 19 June 1861, Camp Dennison, 3 years. Mus 24 June 1861, Camp Dennison to date 19 June. Prior service with 12th OVI (3 months). Appt cpl 2 June 1862. Sept-Oct 1863: abs in ind scouting co. Nov 1863: wounded by guerrillas 31 Oct or 1 Nov 1863, Boyer's Ferry, WVa. *d* of wounds 10 Nov 1863.

BOWMAN, JAMES. PVT, CO A. Age 19. 5ft 7in. Gray eyes. Dark hair. Light comp. *b* Warren Co, Ohio. Laborer. Entered 15 Aug 1861, 3 years. Oct 1861: abs hosp, Gauley. Reenl 1 Jan 1864, vet vol, Fayette CH, Va, 3 years. Mus 1 Jan 1864, Charleston, Va. Shown det in ind scouting co on morning report for 8 Mar 1864, Fayette CH. Det scout through June 1864. Trans 1 July 1864, Co C, 23rd OVI. Det in Cpt Blazer's scouts July and Aug 1864. Loss, des 11 Sept, Summit

Jeremiah Cohen
Courtesy Roger D. Plummer

Point. Gain reported dropped as deserter. Ret to co 19 Oct 1864 (Corp). KIA, Cedar Creek. Bur Winchester Nat Cem, no 171.

BRODERICK, RICHARD. PVT, CO F. Age 25. 5ft 7in. Blue eyes. Brown hair. Light comp. *b* Ireland. No occ stated. Enr 19 June 1861, Camp Dennison, 3 years. Mus 24 June 1861, Camp Dennison to date 19 June. Sept 1863: abs in ind scouting co. Nov 1863: sick in regt hosp. June 1864: abs in hosp, Charleston, WVa. Shown adm USA Gen Hosp, Gallipolis, Ohio from Post Hosp, Charleston, 8 June 1864 and ret to duty 13 June. Sent to Columbus for mus out. Mus out 20 June 1864, Columbus, Ohio.

BUCKLEY, JOHN P. PVT, CO B. Age 18. 5ft 7in. Blue eyes. Auburn hair. Fair comp. *b* Green Co, Ohio. Farmer. Enr and mus 18 June 1861, Camp Dennison, 3 years. Shown det scouting co per GO No (no order no given) 13 Sept 1863. Shown ret to co 13 Nov 1863. Sept-Oct 1863: CSR shows him abs det in ind scouting co. Name appears on mus roll of Co D, 1st Regt Par Forces dated 30 Apr 1863, CCO. (No POW record available.)

BUTLER, RUEBEN J. PVT, CO A. Age 30. 5ft 7in. Brown eyes. Dair hair. Light comp. *b* 27 Mar 1831, Belmont Co, Ohio. Cooper. Enr 15 Aug1861, 3 years. Aug 1862: abs det in McMullen's Battery 14 Aug 1862. Sept 1862: abs det with the 1st Ohio Battery. Det scouts by order of Col C. B. White, Fayetteville, Va 14 Sept 1863. Ret from scout on 6 Oct. Reenl 1 Jan 1864, vet vol, Fayette CH, Va. Mus same day at Charleston, WVa. Trans 1 July 1864, Co C, 23rd OVI. Loss, 24 July 1864 MIA, Winchester, Va (Kernstown). Oct 1864: reported and dropped as MIA. Taken up as POW. Oct-Dec 1864: abs POW. POW rolls show him capt 21 July 1864, Fairview Mt, Va and confined 28 Aug 1864, Richmond, Va. Par 1 Sept 1864, Varina, Va and reported 3 Sept 1864, CGB. Reported 6 Sept 1864, Camp Parole, Md with remark. Retained at CGB. Present 31 Oct-31 Dec 1864, CGB. No further record. Vet mus out 26 July 1865, Cumberland, Md. *d* 25 Aug 1920, Indianapolis, Ind.

COHEN, JEREMIAH. PVT, CO I. Age 28. 5ft 10in. Hazel eyes. Sandy hair. Fair comp. *b* 30 June 1846, Waynesville, Ohio. Farmer. Recruit. Enl 4 Feb 1862, Lebanon, Ohio, 3 years. Mus 26 Apr 1862, Cincinnati, Ohio. Reported for duty in co 30 Apr 1862. Sept-Oct 1863: abs in scouting party. Dec 1863-Mar 1864: on duty in provost guard. Apr-June 1864: abs in provost guard. Trans

1 July 1864, 23rd OVI by SO No 13 HQ, Army of the Kanawha. Mus out 4 Feb 1865, Cumberland, Md. Postwar occ: farmer and bricklayer. *d* 11 Aug 1909, Cincinnati Hosp, Cincinnati, Ohio. Bur Hill Dale Cem, Morgan Co, Ind.

COLLINS, PATRICK. CPL, CO K. Age 19 (64) 5ft 7in. Hazel eyes. Brown hair. Dark comp. *b* Highland Co, Ohio. Blacksmith. Shown on morning report for 13 Sept 1863 det scout. Prom cpl 27 Oct 1863. Ret to co Nov 1863. Reenl 1 Jan 1864, vet vol, Fayette CH, Va, 3 years and mus same date at Charleston, WVa. Wounded and POW 9 May 1864, Cloyd's Mt. Reduced to the ranks by reason of consol 1 July 1864. Erroneously shown as "D. in Danville prison in the month of Mar., 1865." War Dept notation dated 13 May 1874 shows he was par 24 Apr 1865, Vicksburg, Miss and perished on board the steamer *Sultana* 27 Apr 1865.

COTTRELL, CORNELIUS. CPL, CO B. Age 20. 5ft 10½in. Black eyes. Black hair. Dark comp. *b* Clinton Co, Ohio. Cooper. Enr 20 June 1861, Camp Dennison, 3 years. (Previously served in Co E, 12th Ohio, 3 months, 1861.) Mus same place and date. Aug 1862: abs det in McMullen's battery. Sept 1862: abs det in 1st Ohio Battery. Shown det scouting co per GO No (no order no given) 13 Sept 1863. Sept-Oct 1863: det in ind scouting co. MIA 4 Nov 1863 near Blue Sulphur Springs, WVa. Capt 23 Oct 1863, battle of Lewisburg. Subsequently shown in morning report as des to the enemy 4 Nov 1863. This entry is an error and should have been MIA. CSR also shows him erroneously deserting. POW record shows him capt 23 Oct 1863, Green Brier Co, Va and confined at Richmond. Par 26-28 Feb 1865, NE Ferry, NC. Reported 10 Mar, CGB and sent 11 Mar, CCO. Reported 7 Apr 1865, CCO. Sent to Chief MO 7 Apr, Columbus, Ohio. Mus out as cpl 8 Apr 1865, Columbus, Ohio by reason of exp of term of service on certificate from mus out rolls of co furnished by adj gen of Ohio. *d* 6 Jan 1877, Danville, Ill. Bur Soldier's Circle, Springhill Cem, Danville, Ill.

FENNER, JOHN W. PVT, CO I/B. Age 22. 5ft 10½in. Gray eyes. Dark hair. Dark comp. *b* Adams Co, Ohio. Carpenter. Enr 25 June 1861, Xenia, Ohio, 3 years. Mus 29 June 1861, Camp Dennison. Prior service with 12th OVI (3 months). Trans 29 June 1861, Co B by order of Col J. W. Lowe. Sept 1863: abs in ind scouting co. Disch 4 Jan 1864 under provision of GO 359, Series 1863, War Dept. Mus out 19 Jan to date 4 Jan, Charleston, WVa. Re-mus 5 Jan 1864. Jan-Feb 1864: abs on vet furl. Trans 1 July 1864, 23rd OVI by order of Gen Crook.

FISHER, HENRY. PVT, CO H. Age 20. 5ft 6in. Dark eyes. Dark hair. Dark comp. *b* Highland Co, Ohio. Cooper. Shown det in ind scouting co by order of Col C. B. White on morning report for 10 Oct 1863. Ret to co 16 Nov 1863. Dec 1863: 11 Dec, Meadow Bluff, Va: capt by enemy while on picket duty. Also shown as missing in skirmish 12 Dec 1863, Sewell Mt, Va. POW record shows him confined Dec 1863, Richmond, Va. Sent 12 Feb 1864, Andersonville, Ga. Adm 6 Aug, hosp at Andersonville with scorbutus [scurvy]. Testimony of James W. Burnett, late Co H, 12th OVI. "He was capt. and while in reble Prison was vaxinated with impure vaxeean matter, (or said to be impure), by order of the commander of the Reble Prison. While there I seen him and gangrene had eaten all the flesh of the musles of his arms." Ret to prison 3 Sept 1864. Par 16 Dec 1864, Charleston, SC and reported 24 Dec 1864, Camp Parole, Md. Furl 25 Dec 1864, 30 days. Reported 24 Jan 1865, CCO and sent 24 Jan 1865, Chief MO, Columbus, Ohio. Postwar occ: cooper and painter. *d* 13 Feb 1914, Dayton, Ohio.

HALL, WILLIAM. PVT, CO H. Age 22. 5ft 7½in. Blue eyes. Dark hair. Fair comp. *b* 19 May 1840, Brown Co, Ohio. Enr 15 Jan 1862, Charleston, Va, 3 years. Mus 26 Jan 1863, Fayette CH, WVa to date 15 Jan. Aug 1862: abs det in McMullen's Battery. Sept 1862: regt teamster. Oct-Dec

1862: abs sick in hosp, Clarksburg, Va. Adm 10 Oct 1862, USA Gen Hosp, Cumberland, Md (Clarysville branch). Ret to duty 12 Oct 1862. Adm 25 Oct 1862, USA Gen Hosp, Parkersburg, Va with debility. Ret to duty 1 Jan 1863. Jan 1863: abs sick in hosp, Charleston, Va. Shown on morning report for 15 Sept 1863 det ind scout by order of Col C. B. White. Ret to co 6 Oct. Dec 1863: abs at Charleston to be mus as vet vol. Jan-Mar 1864: abs vet vol on furl. Trans 1 July 1864, 23rd OVI, SO 13 HQ of the Kanawha. *d* 8 Dec 1922, Hamilton, Ohio.

HAVENS, PETER S (SWIVER). PVT, CO I/H. Age 27. 5ft 11½in. Gray eyes. Dark hair. Fair comp. *b* 1 Oct 1834, Rushville or Millville, Ind. Farmer. Enr 25 June 1861, Ripley, Ohio, 3 years. Mus 29 June 1861, Camp Dennison. Prior service in 12th OVI (3 months). Trans July 1861, Co H. Shown det in ind scouting co by order of Col C. B. White on morning report for 15 Sept 1863 along with Sgt Adam R. Head and Pvt William Hall. Ret to co from det duty, 16 Nov 1863. Also served Co F, 18th Ohio Inf. *d* 8 May 1909, Kansas City, Mo. Bur Urick (Orrick), Mo.

HELM, EPHRAIM M. PVT, CO H. Age 18. 5ft 7in. Gray eyes. Light hair. Fair comp. *b* Brown Co, Ohio. Farmer. Enr 19 June 1861, Camp Dennison, 3 years. Mus 21 June 1861 to date 19 June. Wounded 27 Aug 1862, Bull Run and left at Alexandria. Adm King St USA Gen Hosp (conval branch of gen hosp, Alexandria, 27 Aug 1862). Trans 31 Aug 1862, Newport, RI. Adm Episcopal USA Gen Hosp, Philadelphia, Pa with flesh wound of left arm. Ret to duty 15 Oct 1862. (POW record shows him "sent from Provost Bks, Phila. Pa. to Washington, D.C. Oct. 15, 1862.") Conval. Aug-Sept 1862: abs sick in hosp, Alexandria, Va (Carver USA Gen Hosp with vulnus. Sclop). Mar 1864: abs det in mounted scouts. Apr 1864: abs in ind scouting co. June 1864: KIA 19 June, Buford's Gap, acting as a rear guard.

HESTER, JACOB. PVT, CO A. Age 29. 5ft 9in. Gray eyes. Dark hair. Light comp. *b* Warren Co, Ohio. Laborer. Enr 30 May 1861, 3 years. Shown on co morning reports on a scout with 3 days' rations 10 July 1863. Morning reports also show him det scouts 14 Sept 1863 by order of Col C. B. White, Fayetteville, VA. Ret to co 7 Oct 1863. Shown rel from arrest 15 Nov 1863 by Lt Col Hines. Reenl 1 Jan 1864, vet vol. Trans 1 July 1864, Co C, 23rd OVI. Aug 1864-June 1865: det in div ambulance train. Mus out 26 July 1865, Cumberland, Md.

HOLLISTER, DAVID H. CPL (PVT), CO E. Age 18. 5ft 7in. Blue eyes. Brown hair. Fair comp. *b* 17 Oct 1842, Naubot, Ill (one entry in pension record Newark, Hanover TWP, Ohio). Farmer. Enr 22 June 1861, Newark, Ohio, 3 years. Shown on mus roll dated 31 Oct 1861 abs nurse in hosp, Charleston. Aug 1862: abs det with McMullen's Battery. Sept 1862: abs det with 1st Ohio Battery. Apr 1862: abs in arrest at Charleston by GCM. May-June 1863: abs in Military Prison, Charleston, Va. Sept 1863 (corp): abs in ind scouting co. Shown as cpl for Sept-Oct 1863, then as pvt. May 1864 (pvt): abs sick in hosp, Charleston, WVa. War Dept notation dated 21 Feb 1878. "Was tried before a General CM on the following charges, viz: 'sleeping on post while on duty': 2. 'Disobedience to orders'. Found guilty and sentenced to be reduced to the ranks and perform six months of hard labor on some public works, at such place as the commanding general may direct and forfeit all pay and allowances for such period. Findings and sentence confirmed under date of April 1st 63 and the sentence ordered to be carried into effect as may hereafter be directed by proper authority." Postwar occ: brakeman. *d* 18 Apr 1923, Newark, Ohio. Bur Cedar Cem, Newark, Ohio.

HOWARD, CLARKSON. PVT, CO A. Age 18. 5ft 10in. Blue eyes. Dark hair. Light comp. *b* 6 Mar 1846 near Warren, Warren Co, Ohio. Farmer/laborer. Enr 30 May 1861, 3 years. Reenl 1 Jan 1964, vet vol, Fayette CH, Va. Mus same day, Charleston, Va. Det scouts 14 Sept 1863 by order of Col C. B. White, Fayetteville, Va. Also shown det scout 3 Dec 1863 with 3 days' rations.

Trans 1 July 1864, Co C, 23rd OVI. Aug 1864: abs in Battery B, 5th Artillery. Prom 2 Nov 1864, cpl. Prom 16 May 1865, sgt. *d* 24 Feb 1914, Hillsboro, Ill. Bur Van Voorhis Cem, Hillsboro, Ill.

HUGHES, JOSHUA. PVT, CO H. Age 18. 5ft 9in. Blue eyes. Sandy hair. Fair comp. *b* Wales. Farmer. Enr 22 June 1861, Newark, Ohio, 3 years. Mus 26 June, Camp Dennison, Ohio. Oct 1861: abs sick in hosp. Left at hosp, Clarksburg, Va 25 Aug 1861. Mar-Apr 1862: sent home on furl sick. Feb-Apr 1863: at work on govt sawmill. Sept-Oct 1863: abs ind scouting co. Dec1863: 11 Dec, Sewell Mt, capt by the enemy while on picket duty. POW record shows him confined 19 (30) Dec 1863, Richmond, Va. Sent 10 Feb 1864, Andersonville, Ga. Adm 6 Aug, hosp, Andersonville where he *d* 5 Sept 1864 of acute diarrhea. Grave number 7946.

HURT, PERRY. PVT, CO F. Age 21. 5ft 10in. Blue eyes. Brown hair. Light comp. *b* Warren Co, Ohio. No occ stated. Enr 19 June 1861, Camp Dennison 3 years. Mus 24 June 1861, Camp Dennison to date 19 June. Mus roll for 25 Apr to 31 Oct 1861: sick in hosp, Charleston, Va. July 1863: 7 July 1863, Gauley Road, supposed to have been capt by the enemy. Nov 1863: 20 Nov 1863, Fayette CH, exch and ret to duty. POW record shows him capt 7 July 1863, Cotton Mt, Va. Confined 15 July 1863, Richmond, Va. Par 19 July, City Point, Va. Reported 20 July 1863, Camp Parole, Md. Sent 5 Aug 1863, CCO. Shown on mus roll of Co I, 1 Regt, Par Inf Forces at CCO dated 1 Sept 1863. Dec 1863-Jan 1864: abs on vet furl. Mus out 3 Jan to date 31 Dec, disch by virtue of reenl as vet vol provision of GO 191, Series 1863, War Dept. Mus 3 Jan 1864, Charleston, WVa to date 1 Jan. Mar-Apr 1864: abs det in ind scouting co. Ret to regt by order of Lt Blazer for getting drunk 7 June 1864. Mus out 11 July 1864, trans 1 July 1864, 23rd OVI, SO 13—HQ, Army of Kanawha. Mus out roll of Co H, 23rd OVI (to which trans) shows him a pvt des from ds with Battery B, 5th US Artillery, Cumberland, Md. Reenl 1 Jan 1864, vet vol. Letter to Commissioner of Pensions War Dept AG 201, Hurt, Perry, 3 Apr 1924: "By direction of the Sec. of War, I have the honor to inform you that the charge of desertion of June 16, 1865 heretofore standing against Perry Hurt as a Pvt. of Co. H. 23rd, Ohio has been removed from his record in this department. Notation inside jacket AG 201 Apr 1, 1924." Postwar residence: Waynesville, Ohio.

IRWINE (IRVINE), SAMUEL (SAM) W. PVT, CO G/D. Age 21. 5ft 8in. Gray eyes. Light hair. Fair comp. *b* Rockbridge Co, Va. Blacksmith. Enr 21 June 1861, Camp Dennison, 3 years. Mus 26 June 1861, Camp Dennison to date 21 June. Previous service with 12th OVI (3 months). Trans 25 June, Co D, Camp Dennison. Oct 1861: co cook. Sept-Oct 1863: abs det in ind scouting co. Capt 9 May 1864, Cloyd's Mt, believed to have remained at hosp on the battlefield, reported by Lt Col J. D. Hines, commanding 12th Ohio Inf. POW record shows him confined at Andersonville, Ga. Par 1 Apr 1865, Vicksburg, Miss. Sent 6 Apr, Parole Camp USA Gen Hosp (Camp Fisk near Vicksburg, Miss). Ret to duty 8 Apr 1865. 12 Apr 1865, Gen Hosp. Adm 13 Apr, McPherson USA Gen Hosp, Vicksburg, Miss from parole camp with chronic diarrhea. Trans 16 Apr, USA Hosp steamer *Baltic* (Miss River steamer). Adm 23 Apr 1865, Jefferson Barracks USA Gen Hosp as a conval. Sent hosp, Benton Barracks, Mo. Reported 27 Apr 1865, Benton Barracks, Mo and sent 6 May 1865, CCO where he reported 5 June 1865. Mus out 7 June 1865, Columbus, Ohio. Mus out by reason of exp of term of service on cert form AG of Ohio Three months extra pay due under provisions of telegram from War Dept, 30 May 1865. Member of Currie Post No 94 of the GAR. *d* 18 June 1889, Cedarville, Ohio.

JONES, MALON B (BROADWELL). PVT, CO C. Age 21. 5ft 8in. Gray eyes. Dark hair. Fair comp. *b* Clermont Co, Ohio. Carpenter. Enr 19 June 1861, Camp Dennison, 3 years. Mus 22 June 1861, Camp Dennison to date 19 June. Shown on mus roll of 1st Div USA Gen Hosp, Alexandria, Va (Mansion House branch). Sept-Oct 1862: not stated but probably wounded at

South Mountain or Antietam. Disch 31 Dec 1863 to reenl as vet vol, GO 191. Re-mus 2 Jan 1864 to date 31 Dec. Oct 1863: abs in ind scouting co. Mar-Apr: abs det in ind scouting co. June 1864: abs in div scouting co. POW records show him capt Nov 1864, Myerstown, Va, brought from Gordonsville. Confined 22 Nov 1864, Richmond, Va, par 15 Feb 1865. Reported 17 Feb 1865, CGB, Md. Sent 19 Feb 1865, CCO. Reported there 24 Feb 1865. Furl 1 Mar 1865, 30 days. Trans 1 July 1864, 23rd Ohio. Samuel V. Wiseman testified that "comrade Jones was a good soldier and afterwards a good citizen." Postwar occ: machinist or stationary engineer. *d* 15 Nov 1898 and interred 18 Nov 1898, Evergreen Cem, Cincinnati, Ohio.

LAZURE, JASPER (JAS) N. PVT, CO G. Age 21. 6ft ½in. Blue eyes. Brown hair. Light comp. *b* Wirt Co, WVa (military record erroneously lists Clinton Co, Ohio). Farmer. Enr 18 June 1861, Camp Dennison, Ohio, 3 years. Mus 30 Aug 1863, Fayette CH, Va to date 18 June 1861. Wounded at Scary Creek suffering considerable pain "but did not leave the ranks." Sept 1862: abs in hosp wounded in right thigh at South Mountain, 14 Sept 1862. Oct 1862: abs in hosp, NYC. Nov 1862: abs wounded David's Island. Dec 1862: abs in hosp, Ft Schuyler, NY. On mus roll for Ft Schuyler for Nov and Dec. Trans 1 Dec 1862, Ft Hamilton. Ret to unit 31 Dec. Of his wound he said it became dreadfully swollen and filled with maggots after he lay in the hot sun for 48 hours. The five physicians who attended wanted to remove the leg at the socket but he said, "he would lose his life rather than the limb." He thought it a miracle he survived. Apr 1863: abs teamster. May and June 1863: regt teamster. John E. Spicer filed affidavit for James Turner that Lazure was in the scouts. Lazure also filed pension affidavit for James Turner as a member of the scouts. Also served with Co F, 5th US Vet Inf. Postwar occs: include butcher and sawyer.

LISTON, JOSEPH. PVT, CO G. Age 18. 6ft 1¼in. Blue eyes. Light hair. Fair comp. *b* 7 June 1843, Clinton Co, Ohio. Farmer. Enr 21 June 1861, Camp Dennison, 3 years. Mus 21 June 1861, Camp Dennison. Wounded in action in thigh 27 Aug 1861, Bull Run Bridge. In USA Hosp, (Wolfe Street branch) Alexandria. Listed adm with vulnus sclop. Sept-Oct 1862: abs in hosp, David's Island, RI. Name appears on a mus roll dated 30 Oct 1862, Ft Hamilton, NY of detachment of vols forwarded to Washington, DC en route to their respective regts. July 1862-Aug 1863: AWOL from 20-27 July. Shown on morning report for 13 Sept det in scouting party by order of Col C. B. White. Ret to co 15 Nov 1863. *d* 14 Mar 1913, Bristow, Okla.

LOYD, AUGUSTUS T. PVT, CO D. Age 22 5ft 7in. Blue eyes. Brown hair. *b* Monroe Co, Ohio. Marble engraver. Enr 25 June 1861, Camp Dennison, 3 years. Mus 26 June 1861, Fayette CH to date 25 June 1861. Nov-Dec 1861: home on furl sick. 27 Aug 1862: Bull Run Bridge, MIA. Dec 1862: gain Dec from MIA. Abs par prisoner. POW record shows him capt 28 Aug 1862, Manassas, Va and par 3 Sept 1862, Manassas. Sept-Oct 1862: abs in Camp Parole, Annapolis, Md. Nov-Dec 1862: par prisoner, Annapolis, Md. Sept-Oct 1863: abs det in ind scouting co. June 1864: abs in hosp, Gallipolis. Wounded in action 17 June 1864, Lynchburg, Va, suffered GSW of right arm middle 3rd. Fracture and severe laceration of muscle caused by conical ball. *d* 4 Mar 1876, Sardis, Ohio of complications from wartime wounds.

MEARS, NEWTON. PVT, CO G. Age 21. 5ft 8½in. Gray eyes. Black hair. Dark comp. *b* 5 Feb 1840, Butler Co, Ohio. Farmer. Enr 21 June 1861, Camp Dennison, 3 years. Mus 26 June 1861, Camp Dennison to date 21 June. Previous service in 12th Ohio (3 months). Morning report for 13 Sept 1863 shows him det in scouting party by order of Col C. B. White. Ret to co 15 Nov. Feb 1864: regt teamster. Member of GAR and IOOF. Member of Grace ME Church. *d* 12 July 1924, Piqua, Ohio. Bur Forest Hill Cem.

MCKNIGHT, ROBERT. PVT, CO B. Age 19. 5ft 11 ½in. Blue eyes. Light hair. Fair comp. *b* Ohio. Farmer. Enr 20 June 1861, Camp Dennison, 3 years. Mus same day and place. Morning report for 5 Mar 1864 lists him on daily duty mounted scouts. Report for 27 Mar 1864 lists him on ds instead of daily duty. Mar-Apr: det in ind scouting co. Edward Burnett, Co B, 12th Ohio: "was a good and faithful soldier always ready for duty." Postwar occ: farmer and laborer near Xenia, Ohio.

MIERS, JOHN A. PVT, CO F. Age 19. 5ft 10in. Hazel eyes. Brown hair. Fair comp. *b* Franklin Co, Ohio. Miller. Enr 19 June, Camp Dennison, Ohio, 3 years. Mus 24 June 1861, Camp Dennison to date 19 June. Previous service 12th OVI (3 months). Sept-Oct 1863: abs in ind scouting co. Mus out 19 Jan 1864, Charleston, WVa to date 4 Jan. Disch by reason of reenl as vet vol under provision of GO 191, Series 1863, War Dept. Also, GO 359, Series 1863. Re-mus 5 Jan 1864, Charleston. Jan-Feb 1864: abs on vct furl. Mar 1864: AWOL. Trans 1 July 1864, 23rd OVI, GO 13, Army of Kanawha.

MILLER, JONATHAN. PVT, CO A. Age 20. 5ft 5in. Gray eyes. Dark hair. Light comp. *b* Indiana. Laborer. Enr 19 June 1861, Camp Dennison, Ohio, 3 years. Mus 24 June 1861, Camp Dennison to date 19 June. Previous service with 12th Ohio (3 months). Oct 1861: abs hosp, Gauley. Aug-Sept 1862: abs det in McMullen's 1st Ohio Battery since 14 Aug 1862. Shown on co morning report for 29 Aug 1863 on a scout with 3 days' rations along with Pvt David McHugh. Oct 1863: abs in ind scouting co. Shown det in ind scouting co on 9 Oct 1863. Ret to co 15 Nov. Mus out 12 Mar 1864, Fayette CH, WVa to date 20 Feb 1864. Disch by virtue of reenl as vet vol under provisions of GO 191, Series 1863, War Dept. Mus 21 Feb 1864, Fayetteville, WVa. Jan-Apr 1864: abs on vet furl. July 1864: wounded and MIA 9 May 1864, Cloyd's Mt. Wounded left arm severe reported by Lt Col J. D. Hines, commanding 12th Ohio Inf. Aug 1864: gain, taken up from MIA. Aug-Jan 1865: abs POW. Feb 1865: loss, date not known while POW. *d* 9 May 1864 of wounds rec at Cloyd's Mt. Trans 1 July 1864, Co C, 23rd OVI.

MINSHALL, STEPHEN K. PVT (COLOR SGT, SGT), CO C. Age 20. Blue eyes. Brown hair. Light comp. *b* Clermont Co, Ohio. Blacksmith. Pvt to 6 June, appt color sgt 7 June 1861 (service with 12th OVI, 3 months). Enr 19 June 1861, Camp Dennison, 3 years. Mus 22 June 1861, Camp Dennison to date 19 June. Roster dated 31 Dec 1861 det regt color sgt and home on furl sick. Reduced from sgt 25 July 1863 by order of Col J. D. Hines, SO No 17. Sept 1863: det in scouting party by order of Col White commanding brig. Disch 31 Dec 1863 under provision of GO 359, Series 1863, War Dept. Mus out 2 Jan 1864 to date 31 Dec, by virtue of reenl as vet vol under provision of GO 191, Series 1863, War Dept. Mus 2 Jan 1864, vet to date 1 Jan, Charleston, WVa. Trans 1 July 1864, 23rd Ohio. Wounded 24 July 1864, Kernstown. Mus out 6 Aug 1865, Cleveland, Ohio. Postwar occ: blacksmith. Postwar residence: Cincinnati, Ohio (1869). Resident of Nat Military Home, Kans, 1890. *d* 20 Mar 1902.

NEADER, EDWARD. PVT, CO A. Age 19. 5ft 9in. Brown eyes. Sandy hair. Light comp. *b* Germany. Laborer. Enr 19 June 1861, Camp Dennison, 3 years. Mus 24 June 1861, Camp Dennison to date 19 June. Prior service in 12th OVI (3 months). Shown on co morning report for 4 Apr 1863 on scout with 3 days' rations. Also Pvts J. V. Homan and F. M. Osborne. Scouts ret 6 Apr. Sept-Oct 1863: abs det in ind scouting co. Mar-Apr 1864: ten days pay docked by order of GCM for failure to obey order to do police duty.

PARKER, ANDREW J. PVT, CO I. Age 25. 5ft 9½in. Gray eyes. Sandy hair. Light comp. *b* 23 Sept 1837, Morgan, Marion Co, Va. Farmer. Enr 2 July 1861, Newark, Ohio, 3 years. Mus 26

June 1863, Fayette CH, W Va to date 2 July 1861. Sept 1862: MIA 14 Sept, South Mountain. POW record shows him capt 14 Sept 1862, South Mt. Confined 28 Sept 1862, Richmond, Va. Par 6 Oct, Aiken's Landing, Va. Reported 23 Oct 1862, Camp Parole, Md. Sent 22 Dec 1862 from Camp Banks, Va to Kanawha Div. Reenl 1 Jan 1864, Fayetteville, Va as vet vol. Mus same date, Charleston, Va. Trans 1 July 1864, Co K, 23rd OVI. Shown det mounted scout on morning report for Feb 1864. Shown det June-July 1864 in Blazer's Scouts. Aug 1864: shown det in QM dept. Sept 1864-Jan 1865: shown det in ind scouting co. Feb-Mar 1865: abs POW. POW record shows him capt 18 Nov, Kabletown, confined 22 Nov 1865, Richmond, Va, brought from Gordonsville. Par 15 Feb 1865, Richmond, Va. Reported 15 Feb 1865, Camp Parole, Md. Sent 19 Feb 1865, CCO where he arrived 27 Mar 1865 from Annapolis. Mus out 26 July 1865. Vet. *d* 23 July 1926, Soldiers and Sailors Home, Homelake, Monte Vista, Colo.

PENWELL, ISAAC G. PVT, CO K. Age 33. 6ft. Blue eyes. Light hair. Fair comp. *b* Ross Co, Ohio. Farmer. Enr 19 June 1861, 5th pl, Camp Dennison, 3 years. Mus same date and place. Reduced from cpl to pvt 3 Oct 1861. April 1863: des Fayette CH, Va. June 1863: gain from desertion 29 June 1863, Charleston. Abs Charleston in confinement. Sept-Oct 1863: abs in ind scouting co. Nov and Dec 1863: in arrest Charleston, Va. Morning report shows him det scout 13 Sept 1863 along with Pvt Patrick Collins. Mus out 3 Jan 1864 to date 31 Dec 1863 to reenl as vet vol. Mus 3 Jan 1864 to date 1 Jan, Charleston, Va. Jan 1864: abs on vet furl. Cooking for cpt since 1 Mar 1864. Trans 1 July 1864, 23rd OVI by SO No 13 by order of Gen Crook. Missing and supposed to have been capt 1 Oct 1864 by Mosby's Cav.

REDD, ALEXANDER W. PVT, CO F. Age 19. 5ft 5in. Blue eyes. Auburn hair. Light comp. *b* 1 June 1842, Switzerland Co, Ind. Farmer. Enr 19 June 1861, Camp Dennison, Ohio, 3 years. Mus 24 June 1861, Camp Dennison to date 19 June. Sept-Oct 1863: abs in ind scouting co. Mus out 3 Jan 1864 to date 31 Dec 1863 to reenl as vet vol. Re-mus 3 Jan 1864 to date 1 Jan. Prom to cpl 24 Apr 1864. June 1864: abs in div scouting co. Shown det to 31 Dec as Blazer Scout. Trans 1 July 1864, Co H (new), 23rd OVI. Mus out 23 May 1865, Staunton, Va. Disch per GO 86 as supernumerary non-commissioned officer. *d* 17 Feb 1918, Monte Vista, Colo.

RIFFLE (RUEFLY, REUFLEY), GODFRIED D. PVT, CO I. Age 23. 5ft 5in. Gray eyes. Light hair. Light comp. *b* Rand, Switzerland. Watchmaker. Enr 25 June 1861, Lockport (near Columbus, Ohio), 3 years. Mus 29 June 1861, Camp Dennison, Ohio. Oct 1861: abs hosp, Gauley. Jan-Feb 1862: present due the US for Ordnance. One (1) brown musket stock and one (1) lock destroyed. Sept and Oct 1862: wounded in action at South Mountain, 14 Sept 1862: abs sick in hosp, Washington, DC. Nov 1862: abs wounded in hosp, Washington. Casualty sheet shows him wounded 20 Sept 1862, near Sharpsburg, Md. Regt returns show him det scout Sept 1863. Mus out 11 July 1864, Columbus, Ohio.

SCHOFIELD, CHARLES M. SGT, CO I/D. Age 22. Gray eyes. Dark hair. Dark comp. *b* Washington Co, Ohio. Engineer. Enr 25 June 1861, Marietta, Ohio. Mus 29 June 1861, Camp Dennison, Ohio. Trans 29 June 1861, Co D. Mus out 3 Jan 1864 to date 31 Dec to reenl as vet. Mus 3 Jan 1864 to date 1 Jan. Dec 1863: abs gone to Charleston to be mus as vet vol. Jan 1864: abs home on vet furl. Feb-May 1864: abs in ind scouts. June 1864: capt 2 June 1864, Covington, Va. Present 20 Nov 1864, Camp Lawton, Ga. Par at Savannah, Ga. 21 Nov 1864: reported at CGB, Md. 25 Nov 1864: sent Camp Parole, Md. 27 Nov 1864: adm Camp Parole USA Hosp near Annapolis, Md from Ga with scurvy. Mus rolls for Camp Parole Hosp for Nov-Dec 1864 reports him on furl date and term not stated. Furl 20 Dec 1864 in medical cards. Appt sgt 2 Feb 1863. Trans 1 July 1864, 23rd OVI.

SHIELDS, WILLIAM C. PVT, CO A. Age 21. 5ft 6in. Gray eyes. Dark hair. Light comp. *b* Warren Co, Ohio. Cooper. Enr 19 June 1861, Camp Dennison, 3 years. Mus 24 June 1861, Camp Dennison to date 19 June. Previous service with 12th OVI (3 months). Oct 1861: det cook. Oct 1863: abs in ind scouting co. Mus out 3 Jan 1864 to date 31 Dec 1863 to reenl as vet vol. Re-mus 3 Jan 1864 to date 1 Jan, Charleston, Va. Jan 1864: abs on vet furl. June 1864: *d* 17 June 1864, Lynchburg of wound rec in action (cpl).

SIMS, ANDREW J. CPL, CO G. Age 24. 5ft 7½in. Hazel eyes. Brown hair. Dark comp. *b* Gallia Co, Ohio. Farmer. Enr 21 June 1861, Camp Dennison. Mus 26 June 1861, Camp Dennison to date 21 June. Appt cpl 21 June 1861. Prior service 12th OVI (3 months). Morning report for 13 Sept 1863 shows him det in scouting party by order of Col C. B. White. Ret to co 15 Nov. *d* 26 Mar 1914, Central Branch, Nat Home for Disabled Vol Soldiers, Dayton, Ohio.

SLADE, GEORGE W. PVT, CO C. Age 20. 5ft 10in. Blue eyes. Sandy hair. Fair comp. *b* Clermont Co, Ohio. Farmer. Enr 19 June 1861, Camp Dennison, 3 years. Mus 22 June 1861, Camp Dennison to date 19 June. Aug 1862: abs teamster. Jan 1863: abs sawmill on Gauley Rd. Feb-Apr 1863: working at sawmill at Laurel Creek, Va. Sept-Oct 1863: abs det in ind scouting co by order of Col C. B. White, commanding brig. Feb-Apr 1864: abs det in Div Ord Dept, Charleston, Va by order of Brig Gen A. N. Duffie. June 1864: abs in Div Ord office. *d* 6 Feb 1832, Williamsburg, Ohio.

TERWILLIGER, MILTON. PVT, (CPL, ORDERLY SGT). CO C. Age 22. 6ft. Blue eyes. Dark hair. Sandy comp. *b* Clermont Co, Ohio. Farmer. Enr 19 June 1861, Camp Dennison, 3 years. Mus 22 June 1861, Camp Dennison to date 19 June. Cpl on rolls dated 31 Dec 1861. 1 Nov 1862: prom from cpl to orderly sgt. July-Aug 1863: reduced from 1st sgt by order of Lt Col J. D. Hines SO 22. Sept-Oct 1863: det in scouting party by order of Col White, commanding brig. Nov 1863: MIA 2 Nov 1863, Boyers Ferry, WVa. POW record shows him confined 14 Nov 1863, Richmond, Va. Sent 21 Mar 1864, Andersonville, Ga. Adm 6 Aug 1864, hosp, Andersonville, Ga where he *d* 14 Aug 1864 of scorbutus [scurvy]. Grave 5668.

TURNER, JAMES. PVT, CO F. Age 24. 5ft 8in. Gray eyes. Brown hair. Light comp. *b* Lebanon, Ohio. Tallow chandler. Enr 19 June 1861, Camp Dennison, 3 years. Mus 24 June 1861, Camp Dennison to date 19 June 1861. Prior service with 12th OVI (3 months). July 1862: on duty teamster in regt train. Aug-Oct 1862: on duty regt teamster. Oct 1863: abs in ind scouting co. Shown det scouting co per GO (no number given) 13 Sept 1863. Ret to duty in co 27 Oct. Sept-Oct 1863: one month's pay stopped by order of CM. Mus out 19 Jan 1864 to date 4 Jan 1864 to reenl as vet vol. Re-mus 19 Jan, Charleston, WVa. Trans to 23rd OVI. Statements of comrades, "They all say he was a most excellent soldier, fond of whiskey but always ready for duty."

TIMBERLAKE, WARREN THOMAS. PVT (SGT), CO D. Age 22. 6ft. Hazel eyes. Dark hair. Dark comp. *b* 30 Apr 1841, Green Co, Ohio. (Pension record states Sharon, Noble Co.) Farmer. Enr 20 June 1861, Camp Dennison, 3 years. Mus 20 June 1861. Previous service 12th OVI (3 months). Appt 1st sgt 20 June 1861. Shown on roll as 1st sgt but probably first duty sgt as the roll shows another man was "orderly sgt." Reduced from sgt to the ranks 14 Nov 1862. Apr-May 1863: co wood chopper. Sept-Oct 1863: abs in ind scouting co. 1 Nov 1863: MIA, Boyers Ferry, WVa. POW record shows him capt 30 Oct 1863, Boyce Ferry, Va and confined 14 Nov 1863, Richmond. Sent 21 Mar 1864, Andersonville, Ga. Adm 6 Aug 1864, hosp, Andersonville, Ga with scorbutus [scurvy]. Par 8 Apr 1865, Vicksburg, Miss. Reported 15 Apr 1865, Benton Barracks, Mo. Furl by instructions of Com Gen of Prisoners to report at CCO at exp. Reported 26

Apr 1865, CCO and was furl 18 Apr 1865, 30 days then to report to Columbus, Ohio. Mus out by Chief MO, 26 Apr 1865, Columbus. *d* 5 May 1924, Oak Hill, WVa.

WADKINS (WATKINS), JAMES. CPL, CO A. Age 20. 6ft. Gray eyes. Light hair. Light comp. *b* Clayborn Co, Ind. Laborer. Enr 15 Aug 1861, Morrow, Ohio, 3 years. Mus 26 June 1863, Fayette CH, WVa to date 15 Aug 1861. Appt cpl 1 June 1863. Sgt 23 Feb 1864. Det scouts by order of Col C. B. White, Fayetteville, Va 14 Sept 1863. Reenl 21 Feb 1864, vet vol, Fayette CH, Va and mus same date, Charleston, Va. Prom 15 July 1864, cpl, whence prom sgt. Trans 1 July 1864, Co C, 23rd OVI. KIA 19 Sept 1864, Winchester.

WEAVER, DAVID. PVT, CO E. Age 20. 5ft 7½in. Blue eyes. Light hair. Bronze comp. *b* 8 Aug 1842, Utica, Ohio. Farmer. Enr 25 June 1861, Newark, Ohio, 3 years. Mus 25 June 1861, Camp Dennison. Aug 1862: det with McMullen's Battery. Sept 1862: det with 1st Ohio Battery. Dec 1863: abs at Charleston, WVa to be mus as vet vol. Disch under GO No 359, Series 1863, War Dept. Mus out 2 Jan 1864 to date 31 Dec. Re-mus 2 Jan, Charleston, WVa. Jan 1864: on vet furl. Feb 1864: det scout. Apr 1864: abs in mounted scouts. May 1864: abs in div mounted scouts. Trans 1 July 1864, Co H, 23rd OVI. det scout. Mus out 26 July 1865. Postwar occ: blacksmith. *d* 13 Jan 1915, Homer, Ohio.

23rd OVI

Organized at Camp Chase, Columbus, Ohio, and mus 11 June 1851. Unless otherwise noted all men mus out with regt 26 July 1865, Cumberland, Md.

BARRETT, JAMES EDGAR. PVT (CPL), CO K. Age 23. 6ft. Blue eyes. Light hair. Fair comp. *b* Green Co, Ohio. Cooper. Enl 1 Jan 1864, vet vol, Fayetteville, WVa, 3 years. Mus 1 Jan 1864, Charleston, WVa. Mar 1864: on daily duty scout. Nov 1864 (cpl): loss 13 Oct 1864, Martinsburg, WVa. Des. Reduced from cpl to pvt 16 Nov 1864. AWOL since 16 Nov 1864. Jan 1865: gain, 14 Jan 1865, Grafton, WVa ret from desertion. Pay stopped 16 Nov 1864-12 Jan 1865 sentence of GCM. Trans from Co B. *d* 23 May 1900.

BARRETT, LEWIS. PVT, CO G/K. Age 24. 5ft 6in. Gray eyes. Brown hair. Light comp. *b* 22 June 1838, Avon, Lorain Co, Ohio. Wagon maker. Enr and mus 18 Aug 1862, Chardon, Ohio, 3 years. Sept 1862: Co K gain Antietam, recruit from depot. Oct 1863: on daily police duty. 25 May 1864: treated small pox. Ret to duty. Feb-Apr 1864: on daily duty scout. May 1864: abs sick. June 1864: abs sick, Charleston, WVa. July 1864 (Co E): gain 1 July, Charleston, Va trans from Co K by order of Lt Col Comly. Loss, 9 July, Charleston, WVa trans to Co F by order of Col J. M. Comly. Sept 1864-Feb 1865: on daily duty regt hosp (Co G). Apr-May 1865: on daily duty RQM. Mus out in compliance with GO No 53 to date 30 June 1865. Also served in Co F, 19th Regt Ohio Militia. *d* 31 Aug 1917, Milwaukee, Wis.

BENTLEY, ALBERT. PVT, CO I. Age 21. 5ft 7½in. Hazel eyes. Brown hair. Light comp. *b* Berne, Germany (Switzerland?). Enr 22 May 1861, Cleveland, Ohio, 3 years. Mus 11 June 1861, Camp Jackson, near Columbus, Ohio. Sept 1863: on daily duty patrol guard, Pt Pleasant, WVa. Jan-Feb 1864: abs on leave. Reenl 1 Jan 1864, vet vol, Camp White. Mus 11 Jan 1864, vet vol. Apr-Nov 1864: abs in ds with Blazer's Ind Scouts. Dec 1864-Mar 1865: abs POW, capt by the enemy near Kabletown 22 Nov 1864 while acting as a scout. POW record shows him confined 22 Nov 1864, Richmond brought from Gordonsville. Par 5 Feb 1865, Cox's Wharf, Va, reported 21 Feb 1865, CCO. Furl 28 Mar 1865, 30 days and ret 18 Apr 1865 and reported to regt 25 Apr 1865.

Mus roll of par prisoner at CCO for 31 Dec 1864-28 Feb 1865 shows him capt 18 Nov 1864, Myerstown, Va and rel 5 Feb 1865. Mus out 26 July 1865, Cumberland, Md. Enl 1 Jan 1872 and served on USS *California* to 5 Dec 1872 and then on USS *Independence* to 19 Dec 1872 when disch.

BROWN, JOHN. PVT, CO F. Age 19. 5ft 6in. Blue eyes. Light hair. Light comp. *b* Mooreland, Ohio. Farmer. Enr 15 Dec 1861, Nashville, Ohio, 3 years. Mus 10 Sept 1863, Charleston, WVa. Jan 1862: gain, recruit from depot Jan 1862 (Co H). Sept 1862: MIA, Antietam. Confined 28 Sept 1862, Richmond. Par 6 Oct 1862, Aiken's Landing, Va. Sent Nov 1862, Camp Wallace Depot. Sent Nov 1862, Alexandria, Va. On morning report 31 Oct 1862 gain from MIA. Abs par prisoner at Camp Parole, Annapolis, Md. Nov-Dec 1862: abs par prisoner. Mar and Apr 1864: abs on ds scout. May 1864: abs on ds since 1 May 1864. July 1864: trans to Co F. July-Oct 1864: on ds scout. Vet, trans from Co H 1 July 1864. Killed 19 Nov 1864, Kabletown. Bur Winchester Nat Cem, section 12, grave 741

BROWN, JOSEPH A. PVT, CO G. Age 18. 6ft. Gray eyes. Brown hair. Fair comp. *b* Ashland, Ohio. No occ stated. (Pension record attests he was a student.) Enr and mus 7 June 1861, near Columbus, Ohio, 3 years. Wounded 17 Sept 1862, Antietam slightly. Adm 22 Sept 1862, Emory USA Gen Hosp, Washington, DC. Sick 26 Sept 1861, hosp, Camp Lookout. Oct-Dec: abs wounded in action at Washington, DC. Aug 1863: furl at Ashland, Ohio. Oct 1863: abs ds guarding prisoners, Wheeling, WVa. Nov 1863: on furl, 30 days. Apparently having trouble with wound. Dec 1863: abs wounded, Antietam. Feb-Mar 1864: abs on ds with Col R. B. Hayes in Ohio. Apr-Oct 1864: abs det scout by order of Gen Crook. Det scout 14 Apr 1864. Nov and Dec (cpl): abs ds since 29 Apr 1864. Shown det through 31 Dec 1864. Feb 1865: on furl. Mar1865: sgt 23 Mar 1865 loss at Camp Carroll, Md. Des. Regt return of deserters for Apr 1865 reports him "des. Mar. 23, 1865 at Ashland, Ohio." War Dept notation AGO, 21 Apr 1887 shows "charge of desertion removed. Was on return furl. to Apr.13, 1865 and sick at home, unable to return, from Apr. 13, 1865 to May 21, 1865. Physician's affidavit sent as evidence." May 1865: Staunton, Va joined from desertion (pvt). Appt cpl 16 Nov 1864. Appt sgt 9 Mar 1865. Reduced to ranks 13 Apr 1865. Mus out 26 July 1865. Vet. *d* 1 Jan 1916.

BRYAN, THOMAS J. SGT, (NEW) CO C. Age 20. 5ft 8in. Hazel eyes. Dark hair. Dark comp. *b* Highland Co, Ohio. Farmer. Reenl 1 Jan 1864, vet vol, Fayette CH, 3 years. Mus 1 Jan, Charleston, WVa. Reduced to the ranks in consequence of consol. July-Dec 1864: vet vol det in Cpt Blazer's Scouting Co. Apr 1865: adm Island (Field) USA Hosp, Harper's Ferry, WVa. for contusion of face caused by a fall rec 5 Apr 1865. Ret to duty 10 Apr. 27 Apr 1865: loss, Winchester, Va. Disch by SO 95 HQ Mid Mil Div. Also, disch by order of Brevet Maj Gen Torbert coming within GO 86, Series 1863, War Dept.

BYERS, JAMES M.G. PVT, CO E. Age 40. 5ft 5in. Blue eyes. Black hair. Dark comp. *b* Mercer, Pa. Laborer. Entered service 8 June 1861, Poland, Ohio. Mus 12 June 1861, Camp Jackson. Feb 1862: det on guard duty on Gauley road. Mar 1863: abs on ds guarding prisoners. May 1863: on daily duty on fortifications. Dec 1863: abs ds guarding prisoners to Wheeling. Feb 1864: on daily duty scout. June 1864: abs sick. July-Aug 1864: abs sick in hosp. Reenl 1 Oct 1863, vet vol. Sept and Oct 1864: abs since 19 Oct, wounded (Cedar Creek) GSW of right thigh. Adm Jarvis USA Gen Hosp. 20 Nov 1864: trans from Martinsburg, Va. Trans 10 Dec 1864, Philadelphia. Nov and Dec: abs sick in hosp, Mower Gen Hosp, Chestnut Hill, Philadelphia, Pa. Mus out 26 July 1865, Cumberland, Md. Lived Cleveland, Mahoning Co, Ohio.

GILES, SANDA (ALIAS) ALEXANDER B. PVT, CO B. Age 33. 5ft 11in. Blue eyes.

Sandy hair. Sandy comp. *b* upper Canada. Farmer. Enr 2 June 1861 near Columbus. Mus 11 June 1861 near Columbus. Jan 1862: abs sick left at Fayette on march to Raleigh, 26 Jan 1862. Mus roll of US troops forwarded from Columbus, Ohio to Cincinnati, Ohio dated 18 Aug 1863 shows remarks as "straggler." Disch 29 Nov 1863 by reason of reenl. Reenl 30 Nov 1863, vet vol, Jefferson, Ashtabula Co, 3 years. Mus 30 Nov 1863, Charleston, WVa. Feb-Oct 1864: abs ds with ind scouts at Div HQ. Nov 1864: wounded in skirmish with Mosby, 18 Nov 1864. Medical records show him capt 21 Nov 1864, Cabletown, Va. Treated 3-4 May 1865 for abscess and ret to duty. Mus out 26 July 1865, Cumberland, Md. *d* 28 Nov 1895, Toronto, Canada.

HARPER, LEVI S. PVT, CO A. Age 18. 5ft 9½in. Dark eyes. Brown hair. Dark comp. *b* Bangor, Maine. Farmer. Enr 30 Nov 1863, Charleston, WVa, 3 years. Sept 1861: loss. 16 Sept Cross Lanes. Disch on surgeon's certificate of dis June 1863 gain 18 June 1863, Camp White. Irregularly disch. Disch not signed by Dept Commander. Ret to duty. Oct 1863: on daily duty at Brig HQ. Disch on account of reenl 29 Nov 1863. Reenl 30 Nov 1863, vet vol, Charleston, WVa. Feb 1864: on duty scout. Apr-June: abs on ds scout. Mus roll for May and June shows him as vet vol on ds with Blazer's Scouts. July 1864: abs sick in hosp, Cumberland, Md, adm 27 July, sunstroke. Aug-Oct: abs sick in hosp. Ret to duty 25 Oct 1864. Mus out with co 26 July 1865, Cumberland, Md. *d* 11 Mar 1920, Nat Soldier's Home, Tenn.

HOLEBAUGH, JOHN M. PVT, CO E. Age 19. 5ft 10½in. Brown eyes. Light hair. Light comp. *b* Mercer, Pa. Wagon maker. Enr 8 June 1861 near Columbus, Ohio. Mus 12 June 1861, Camp Jackson. Nov 1861: abs sick at Wheeling since 20 Oct. Dec 1862: abs sick, hosp, Cincinnati, Ohio from 3 Nov. Dec 1862: on daily duty ditching. May 1863: on daily duty fortification. Oct 1863: on daily duty building stables. Nov 1863: on daily duty sawing lumber. Reenl 30 Nov 1863, vet vol. Mar and Apr 1864: abs on ds ind scouts. May 1864: loss 9 May 1864, Meadow Bluff, MIA. Sept 1864: gain from MIA. Sept-Nov 1864: abs POW. *d* 11 Aug 1864, rebel prison. POW record shows him confined at Andersonville, date not given. Adm 4 Aug, hosp, where he *d* 11 Aug 1864, acute diarrhea. Grave no 5298. Erroneously listed as A. J. Holebaugh in *ROH* grave no 5293.

KILLAM, BENJAMIN. SGT (1ST LT), CO A. Age 25. 5ft 7½in. Gray eyes. Dark brown hair. Dark comp. *b* 21 Apr 1836, Yarmouth, Nova Scotia. Clerk. Enr 18 May 1861, Cleveland, Ohio. Mus 11 June 1861, cpl, Camp Jackson, Columbus, Ohio to date 18 May. Jan-Feb 1862: prom 1 Jan 1862 from cpl. On furl, 16 days, 13 Feb-1 Mar 1862. June 1862-Sept 1863: on extra duty actg ord sgt, 23 Regt OVI. Sept 1862: granted 10 days furl, 1st Brig, Kanawha Div near Sharpsburg, 20 Sept 1862. Nov 1863: appt sgt 30 Nov 1863. Dec 1863: Charleston, mus out on roll dated 9 Dec 1863 to date 29 Nov 1863 by reason of reenl as vet vol under GO 191, Series 1863 Re-mus as vet on roll dated 9 Dec 1863 to date 30 Nov 1863. Jan-Feb 1864: abs on furl in Ohio since 23 Jan 1864. Mar 1864: abs ds scout. Apr 1864: on daily duty actg commissary sgt. May and June 1864: on daily duty RQM. July 1864: Charleston, disch to accept prom. July 1864: (RQM) present. Commissioned 2d lt from sgt maj 2 July 1864; assn to Co B. Prom vice George Seaman, KIA. Commissioned 1st lt 15 July 1864 vice John S. Ellen, prom. Appt RQM to date 2 July 1864 order Lt Col Comly. Feb 1865: abs ds AAQM 1st Brig 1st Inf Div Dept, WVa since 20 Feb 1865 order Col Duval. Mar 1865: present rejoined from ds as AAQM. Apr 1865: present in arrest by order Cpt H. G. Otis commanding regt since 19 Mar 1865. May 1865 (1st lt, Co A): present in arrest. Assn from regt staff vice Hubbard trans to the regt staff as RQM trans from regt staff. June 1865: present awaiting sentence of GCM. Prom 14 June 1864, 2d lt; 1st lt 1 July 1864. Appt adjutant 1 July 1864. Trans from field and staff 1 May 1865. Mus out with co 26 July 1865. Postwar occ: grocer in Cleveland, Ohio. *d* 6 Feb 1928, Marion, Ohio.

Benjamin Killam

Benjamin Killam at a reunion of the 23rd Ohio Infantry.

Killam is centered in this enlargement of the reunion photo

LOGAN, ALBERT B. ORDERLY SGT (1ST LT), CO E. Age 19. 6 ft. Gray eyes. Brown hair. Light comp. *b* 29 Mar 1842, Mahoning, Ohio. Carpenter. Also read law. Enl 8 June 1861, Poland, Ohio, 3 years. Mus 12 June 1861, Camp Jackson. Oct 1861: on duty det pioneer. Prom cpl 24 Dec 1861. Reduced to the ranks by SO 24 Apr 1861. Prom cpl 20 Sept 1862 for gallant conduct in action. On duty Dec 1863 actg orderly sgt. Reenl 29 Dec 1863, vet vol. Apr-June 1864: on ds sgt in ind scouts. July 1864: on daily duty at regt HQ. Aug 1864: appt sgt maj and trans to (NCS). Recognized in orders dated Harrisonburg, 30 Sept 1864 "for gallant & meritorious conduct in capturing a piece of artillery in the fortifications at Winchester Sept. 19, 1864, he being the first to reach the gun." Oct 1864: 2d lt Co B from sgt maj to date 9 Oct 1864. Assn 11 Oct 1864, Co B on SD actg adjt order of Col Comly. Nov 1864: ret to co for special duty by order of Col Comly. Jan 1865: 1st lt Co F. Mar and Apr 1865: present commanding Co H. May 1865: trans back to Co F. Mus out 20 July 1865, Cumberland, Md. Read law after the war. Adm to the bar at Canfield, Ohio, 1866. *d* 25 Dec 1907

MASON, THOMAS L (LEROY) (LEROY THOMAS). PVT, CO C. Age 21. 5ft 9½in. Blue eyes. Brown hair. Dark comp. *b* Palermo, NY. Engineer. Enr 20 May 1861, Cleveland, Ohio. Mus 14 June 1861 near Columbus, Ohio. 20 May-31 Aug 1861: abs on ds, Weston, Va. Feb 1862: on daily duty building fortifications. June 1862: abs on furl, sick from wounds rec in action 1 May 1862, Clark's Hollow or Clark's Farm, Va. July 1862: abs on sick leave. Letter appears in this soldier's record that states the following: "HQ 3rd Div 8th AC Charleston, Sept 12, 1863. In consideration of the good soldiership of Pvt. Thomas Mason 23 OVI. as certified by his Brigade commander, so much of the sentence of general CM as requires wearing ball & chain is hereby remitted." Signed E. P. Scammon, Brig Gen. Sept and Oct 1862: abs on daily duty pioneer. Feb 1864: on daily duty scout. Mar 1864: on scout per GO from div HQ. May 1864: abs in hosp, Charles Town. 30 June 1864: disch by reason of exp of service, Staunton, Va. Shown det scout per GO No 2. Postwar occ: miner. Resident of Soldiers Home, Santa Monica, Calif. *d* 1903.

MAYNARD, WILLIAM A. PVT, CO K. Age 31. 5ft 7½in. Blue eyes. Brown hair. Light comp. *b* Newstead, NY, 19 Jan 1830. Farmer. Enl 22 June 1861, Elyria, Ohio. Mus 27 June 1861 near Columbus, Ohio. July 1861: abs left at hosp, CCO. Aug 1861: abs sick in hosp, Weston. Reenl 30 Nov 1864, vet vol. May 1864: abs det scout by order of Gen Crook. Mar 1865 (Co E): gain 4 Mar 1865, Camp Hastings by trans from Co K, 23rd OVI. Abs POW. POW record shows him capt 18 Nov 1864, Myerstown, Va. Confined 22 Nov, Richmond, brought from Gordonsville. Par 5 Feb 1865, Cox's Wharf, Va. Reported 7 Feb 1865, hosp l div 2. Reported 7 Feb 1865, Camp Parole, Md and sent 16 Feb 1865, CCO where he reported 20 Feb 1865. Furl 23 Feb, 30 days. He was erroneously carried as having died of chronic diarrhea on board the steamer *New York*, 7 Feb 1865 and body disembarked at Annapolis, Md and bur Ash Grove US Cem grave 321. *d* 19 June 1913.

NOBLIT, PHILIP. PVT, CO I. Age 21 (24). 5ft 9in (5ft 11½in). Hazel eyes. Black hair. Dark comp. *b* 26 Aug 1840, Chester, Pa. Farmer. Enl 28 Jan 1862, Galion, Ohio. Name appears on roster of recruits 22 Mar 1862, Cincinnati, Ohio. Mar 1862: gain. Recruit from depot 23 Mar near Raleigh, Va. May 1862: Shown on casualty list wounded 1 May 1862, Clark's Farm. Sept-Oct 1862: abs wounded in action abs in hosp. Adm USA Gen Hosp, Frederick, Md with fracture. Sent 22 Sept, Gen Hosp. Nov 1862: on duty police party. Apr 1864: on duty scout per GO from div HQ. May-June 1864: abs on det duty div scout. July 1864: abs ds with ind scouts. Aug-Dec: shown abs on ds per GO, etc. Jan 1865: mus out at Cumberland, Md by reason of exp of term of service. Brother William was killed 24 July 1864, Kernstown. *d* 18 Mar 1916, Marion, Ohio.

PRINE, JOEL. PVT, CO F. Age 21. 5ft 8½in. Gray eyes. Brown hair. Dark comp. *b* Hardin Co, Ohio. Farmer. Enr 5 June 1861, Bellefontaine, Ohio, 3 years. Mus with co 11 June 1861, Camp Jackson to date 5 June. Abs guarding prisoners May 1863, Wheeling, WVa. Mar-Dec 1864: noted abs div scout. Mus 1 Oct 1863, vet vol, Camp White. Mus out with co 26 July 1865.

PARSONS, JOHN A. PVT, CO E. Age 19. 5ft 7¼in. Gray eyes. Brown hair. Dark comp. *b* 5 Aug 1844, Canada. Stone cutter. Enr 8 June 1861, Poland, Ohio. Mus 12 June 1861, Camp Jackson to date 8 June. Mar and Apr 1862: on daily duty in QM Dept. May and June 1862: sick in camp. Wounded slightly in battle 14 Sept 1862. Apr 1863: on daily duty Pioneer. Dec 1863: abs in ds guarding prisoners, Wheeling, WVa. Jan 1864: mus 25 Mar 1864, vet vol, Charleston, WVa. Reenl 20 Jan 1864. Aug 1864: abs on ds with Blazer's Scouts. Sept 1864-Jan 1865: abs on ds with ind scouts. Wounded 18 Nov 1864, Kabletown. Ball entered posteriorly, ball entering upper part of lower third of left arm and emerging from middle third of left forearm. Mar, May, and June 1865: abs sick. May and June 1865: abs in hosp, Baltimore, Md. Jan and Feb 1865: AWOL at hosp below. Shown on list of deserters at Cuyler USA Gen Hosp, Germantown, Philadelphia, Pa. 31 Mar 1865: entered Newton University Gen Hosp 6 May 1865 for aggravation of GSW to arm. Disch for dis 28 June 1865. John may have been wounded as many as 5 times during the war and had 4 visible bullet scars on his body. Wounded in left knee 10 May 1862, Giles CH; also had GSW of left hip rec 16 Sept 1862, South Mt. Claimed to have actually been wounded twice at Kabletown, once by a carbine in the left foot and the more serious wound to his left arm. "While in my command he was always in the line of duty. . . ." Richard Blazer affidavit 8 Feb 1867. *d* 21 July 1917, Poland, Ohio.

SCOTT, DAVID E. PVT (SGT), CO D. Age 18. 5ft 6in. Blue eyes. Brown hair. Fair comp. *b* Loraine Co, Ohio. Harness maker. Enr 20 May 1861, Cleveland, Ohio, 3 years. Mus 11 June 1861 near Columbus, Ohio to date 20 May. Sept 1861: on duty prisoner guard. Oct-Nov 1861: abs sick, Camp Dennison, Cincinnati, Ohio in hosp since 7 Oct. Sept 1862: adm 12 Sept 1862, Trinity Gen Hosp, Washington, DC with wounded hand. Ret to duty 20 Sept. Oct 1863: on daily fatigue duty. Nov 1863: on daily duty at brig HQ. Mus out 14 Dec 1863 to join as vet vol to date 26 Nov 1863. Mus 14 Dec 1863, vet to date 27 Nov 1863, Charleston, WVa. Dec 1863-Jan 1864: on furl. Feb-May 1864: on daily duty scout. Appt cpl 16 July 1864. Appt sgt from cpl 12 Apr 1865. Mus out 26 July 1865, Cumberland, Md. *d* 20 Dec 1903, Harvey Co, Kans.

TAYLOR, JOHN W. PVT (SGT), CO G. Age 19. 5ft 9½in. Hazel eyes. Light hair. Fair comp. *b* Richland Co, Ohio. Student/farmer. Enr 7 June 1861, Ashland, Ohio. Mus 14 June to date 7 June 1861 near Columbus, Ohio. Dec 1862: on daily duty policing parade ground. Apr 1863: on daily duty pro mar, Charleston. June 1863: daily duty patrol, Charleston. July-Nov 1863: abs det provost guard by order of Gen Scammon 22 July 1863. Dec 1863-Feb 1864: abs ds provost guard, Charleston, WVa. 6 Apr 1863. Mar 1864: abs on ds scout, 3 Mar 1864. Morning report shows him det a scout 28 Feb 1864. Appt cpl 2 July 1864. Appt sgt from cpl 16 July 1864. July and Aug 1864: loss, MIA 24 July 1864, Winchester (Kernstown), Va. Sept 1864: gain, Cedar Creek, Va taken up from MIA. Absent POW capt by the enemy 24 July 1864. Mar 1865: loss, 15 Mar 1865, Camp Hastings, Md. POW record a shows adm 13 Dec 1864, hosp, Danville, Va. *d* 29 Dec 1864 in Rebel prison of chronic diarrhea.

TOWSLEE, GEORGE M. SGT, CO G. Age 18. 5ft 7in. Brown eyes. Brown hair. Florid comp. *b* Shenango Co, NY. Sawyer. Enr and mus 1 Sept 1862, Columbus, Ohio, 3 years. Gain 4 Sept 1862, CCO. July 1863: on duty fatigue. Nov 1863-Jan 1864: on duty at sawmill. Sept-Nov

1864: on ds scout since 1 Sept 1864 by order of Gen Crook. Dec 1864: MIA, Kabletown while acting as scout. Appt sgt from pvt 2 July 1864. Probably bur Ashland, Ohio. Tombstone was requested for cem in that city.

WEAVER, DAVID. PVT, CO H. Age 21 (64). 5ft 8in. Blue eyes. Light hair. Fair comp. *b* Utica, Ohio. Farmer. Reenl 1 Jan 1864, vet vol, Fayette CH, WVa. Mus same day, Charleston, WVa. Trans from Co E. July 1864: trans from 12th OVI. July-Oct 1864: abs ds in Cpt Blazer's Scouts by order of Maj Gen Crook. Nov 1864: abs on ds. Dec 1864: abs on ds in Blazer's Scouts. Mus out 26 July 1865, Cumberland, Md. (See 12th OVI.)

WEST, WILLIAM A. SGT, CO C. Age 20. 5ft 6½in. Blue eyes. Brown hair. Dark comp. *b* Fitchville, Ohio. Also shown Jefferson Co, Ohio. Shoemaker/farmer. Enr 20 May 1861, Cleveland, Ohio. Mus 14 June 1861 to date 20 May 1861 near Columbus, Ohio. Jan 1862: on duty on breastworks. May 1862: on duty guarding prisoners of war to CCO. Feb 1864: on daily duty scout. June 1864: loss, 11 June, Staunton, Va, disch by reason of exp of term of service. Appt cpl 24 July 1861. Also shown appt cpl 19 July 1861 by order of Col Scammon. Appt sgt 1 July 1862. Mus out by reason of exp of term of service 30 June 1864, Columbus, Ohio. Reenl 23 Feb 1864, vet vol, Newark, Ohio. Mus same date and place. Mus out 26 July 1865, Cumberland, Md.

34th OVI (Mounted)

Organized at Camp Lucas, Ohio. Moved 1 Sept 1861, Camp Dennison. Consol with the 36th OVI 22 Feb 1865. Several soldiers were just listed as "scouts" in July 1864 and may have been scouts for Gen Duffie rather than assn to Blazer. These scouts are Benjamin F. Anson, Co B; Alexander B. Pangburn, Co B; Joseph Pierce, Co C; Frederick Spotts (Spatz), Co B, and Patrick Sullivan, Co C. A full record is provided for Spotts because he was killed at a date and time of a known skirmish between Blazer's unit and guerrillas.

BARRY, PATRICK. PVT, CO H. Age 18. 5ft 5in. Blue eyes. Light hair. Fair comp. *b* 19 Dec 1844, County Cork, Ireland. Laborer. Enr 23 July 1861, Camp Lucas. Mus 7 Sept 1861, Camp Dennison. Sept-Oct 1862: wounded in the engagement 10 Sept, Fayetteville. In hosp, Gallipolis, Ohio. Rec GSW of left face. Nov-Dec 1862: abs wounded since 10 Sept 1862. Mar-Apr 1864: on ds with co of scouts. Ret to his regt by order of Lt Blazer for getting drunk 7 June 1864. July-Aug 1864: abs sick wounded 20 Sept 1864. Adm 23 July 1864, USA Gen Hosp, Cumberland, Md flesh wound of left gluteal region, rec 20 July 1864 by a musket ball. Mus out 13 Sept 1864, CCO. Also served with Co D 4th US Vet Vol Inf from Feb 1865-Feb 1866; Co C 8th US Inf from Oct 1867-Oct 1870 and Co H 18th US Inf from Dec 1870-Dec 1875 and from Dec 1875-Oct 1880. *d* 10 May 1924, Cincinnati, Ohio. Bur Calvary Cem.

BUPP, ELI. PVT, CO I. Age 22. 6ft. Black eyes. Brown hair. Dark comp. *b* Auglaize Co, Ohio. Farmer. Enr 10 Aug 1861, Wapakoneta, Ohio, 3 years. Mus 14 Sept 1861, Camp Dennison. Dec 1863: loss. 26 Nov 1863: disch by virtue of reenl as vet vol under provision of GO No 191, Series 1863, War Dept. Re-mus 2 Dec 1863. Abs on 30 day vet furl from 2 Dec 1863. Mar 1864: abs det scout since 9 Mar 1864. Sept 1864: trans to Co C. Jan 1865: abs POW capt 11 Jan 1865, Beverly, WVa. Feb 1865: trans 22 Feb, 36th OVI. Mar 1865: abs POW, CCO. Apr-May 1865: abs capt at Beverly. June 1865: par prisoner, Columbus, Ohio since Apr 1865. Mus out 12 June 1865, CCO. POW record shows him confined 21 Jan 1865, Richmond (Libby), Va brought from Staunton. Par 15 Feb 1865, Richmond, Va. Furl 1 Mar 1865, CCO and ret 2 May 1865.

CORBLY, MILTON. PVT, CO A. Age 24. 5ft 8in. Black eyes. Black hair. Dark comp. *b* Amelia, Clermont Co, Ohio. Farmer. Enr 1 Jan 1862, Camp Red House, Va, 3 years. Mus 28 Dec 1862, Fayette CH, Va. Dec 1863: Charleston, Va, disch by reenl under GO 191, War Dept. Remus 2 Dec 1863. Abs vet on furl, 30 days from 2 Dec 1863. Feb 1864: disch and reenl as vet vol. Apr-Nov 1864: abs scout since 1 Apr 1864. Shown present at mus roll of USA Gen Hosp, Chester, Pa for Sept and Oct 1864. No hosp papers in file. Possibly wounded. Mus out 20 Jan 1865, Cumberland, Md. *d* 20 Oct 1919, Nat Mil Home, Dayton, Ohio.

DAVIS, WILLIAM. CPL, CO F. Age 19. 5ft 9in. Blue eyes. Light hair. Light comp. *b* Green Co, Ohio. Farmer. Enr 25 July 1861, Xenia, Ohio, 3 years. Mus 2 Sept 1861, Camp Dennison. Oct 1862: det in provost guard, Charleston, Va since 30 Oct 1862. Jan 1864: reenl 1 Jan 1864, vet vol, Green Co, Ohio. Mus 1 Jan 1864, Charleston, Va. Abs on furl in Ohio since 26 Jan 1864. July 1864: abs without leave since 24 July 1864. Sept and Oct 1864: abs scout since 2 Sept 1864 by order of Gen Crook. Appt cpl 1 Sept 1864. Det 2 Sept 1864 in Blazer's Ind Scouts. Nov 1864: MIA 20 Sept 1864, not before reported. POW record shows him capt 20 Sept 1864 near Winchester, Va. Confined 23 Sept 1864, Richmond. Sent 24 Sept 1864, Danville, Va. Entered hosp 17 Oct 1864, Danville, where he *d* 3 Feb 1865 of GSW in left thigh. Bur Danville Nat. Cem, no 279.

FISHER, JACOB B., JR. PVT, CO B. Age 18. 5ft 4in. Black eyes. Dark hair. Dark comp. *b* Louisville, Ky (also shown Germany from descriptive book). Cooper. Enr 2 Sept 1861, Camp Dennison, Ohio and mus same day and place. July-Aug 1862: det in McMullen's battery since 17 Aug 1862. Sept and Nov 1863: abs on ds in Simmond's battery since 29 Sept 1863. Appears on returns of Cpt Simmond's Ky Lt Arty. Gain, 27 Sept, Camp Toland det from 34th regt OVMI by order Gen Duffie. Dec 1863: disch and reenl 2 Dec 1863, vet vol, Charleston, WVa. Enl 26 Nov 1863, Ripley, Ohio. Mus 22 Jan 1864. On furl, 30 days. Feb 1864: on duty scout. Mar 1864: on ds scout GO div HQ since 17 Mar 1864. Apr-May: abs ind scout for div. June-Dec: listed on duty in Blazer's Scouts. Jan 1865: des from Blazer's Scouts. War Dept notation 19 Apr 1864 Adj Gen's Dept shows application for removal of charge of desertion and for an honorable disch has been denied.

FRITH, JOSEPH. SGT, CO D. Age 23. 5ft 7½in. Gray eyes. Light hair. Light comp. *b* Huron Co, Ohio. Farmer. Enr 30 July 1861, Bellevue, Ohio, 3 years. Mus 31 July, Camp Lucas. Nov-Dec 1862: in arrest/confinement since 20 Nov 1862. Prom cpl 10 Jan (also shown 10 Feb) 1863. Jan-Feb 1863: 3 months pay deducted by order of GCM. Oct-Nov 1863: abs recruiting service since 17 Oct 1863. Dec 1863: Charleston, WVa, disch by virtue of reenl as vet vol per GO 191. Prom sgt 21 Jan 1864. Feb 1864: on duty scout. Mar-Apr 1864: on det duty with Blazer's Ind Scouts since 31 Mar 1864. Shown abs scout div/ind scout through June 1864. KIA 3 June 1864, Callihan's [Callaghan's] Station, Va. Brother George Frith served in the 123rd OVI and was mortally wounded 15 Jan 1863, Winchester.

GRIFFIN, SELAH J. PVT, CO F. Age 25. 5ft 5½in. Blue eyes. Dark hair. Light comp. *b* 12 Aug 1834, Richmond, Mo. Laborer. Enr 16 Aug 1862, Xenia, Ohio. Mus 18 Dec 1862, Fayette CH. Oct 1862: gain, 6 Oct 1862, Pt Pleasant, recruit from depot. Mar 1864: abs det scout since 19 Mar 1864. Apr 1864: abs div scout. May-June: abs ind scout. Aug 1864: abs sick at Bolivar Heights since 2 Aug 1864. Sept-Oct 1864: abs teamster since 29 Aug 1864. Jan 1865: abs POW. Capt 11 Jan 1865, Beverly, Va. POW record shows him confined at Richmond, brought from Staunton 21 Jan 1865. Par 15 Feb 1865, Richmond, Va, reported 17 Feb 1865, CGB. Sent 19 Feb, CCO. Reported 24 Feb, CCO. Furl 2 Mar, 30 days and ret 3 Apr. Sent 5 Apr, Pro Mar, Columbus, Ohio. Reported there 5 Apr and sent Wheeling, WVa same day. No mus out record. Also served in Co E 12th Regt Ind Inf. That 1 year regt was in the state service prior to 22 July 1861. *d* 1 July 1914, Hamilton, Ohio.

HAYS, DAVID S. PVT (CPL), CO I/E. Age 24. 5ft 8in. Blue eyes. Light hair. Fair comp. *b* Licking Co, Ohio. Farmer. Enr 10 Aug 1861, Wapakaneta, Ohio, 3 years. Mus 14 Sept 1861, Camp Dennison. Jan 1863: loss, 19 Jan, Fayetteville, reported as deserter. Apr 1863: gain, 7 Apr 1863, ret from desertion. July 1863: on duty teamster. Aug 1863: on duty teamster. Oct 1863: abs sick 19 Oct, Gallipolis, Ohio. May 1864: abs POW. Capt July 1863, Wytheville, Va. June 1864: abs sick leave since 25 May 1864. Sept 1864: Co E gain 3 Sept 1864, Charles Town, Va. Trans to Co E. Abs scout. Oct 1864: abs scout. Nov 1864: abs in Blazer's Scouts. Feb 1865: trans to Co I 36th OVI. Mar 1865: on duty orderly dept HQ. Prom cpl 10 May 1865. Notation as POW probably in error. No POW record supporting. *d* 30 Jan 1918, Nat Mil Home, Kans.

HEIDSCHUCK, JACOB. PVT, CO E. Age 20. 5ft 8½in. Brown eyes. Auburn hair. Light comp. *b* Germany. Teamster. Jan 1862: enl. Mus 14 Aug 1863, Camp Piatt, Va. Feb 1864: abs at Columbus, Ohio to guard recruits since 10 Feb 1864. Aug 1864: abs scout since 25 Aug 1864. Sept and Oct 1864: abs in Blazer's Scouts since 3 Sept 1864. Nov 1864: on det duty since 3 Sept 1864. Jan 1865: abs ds in Blazer's Scouts since 30 Sept 1864. Feb 1865: trans to Co E 36th OVI. Final statement shows him KIA 20 Nov 1864 near Kabletown, Va to best information. Probably bur unknown grave Winchester Nat Cem.

HOMMEL, JOHN S. PVT, CO D. Age 21. 5ft 6in. Blue eyes. Light hair. Light comp. *b* 24 Nov 1843, Brown Twp, Mifflin Co, Pa. Painter. Enl 27 July 1861 as pvt, Co D 34th OVI, Wheeling, WVa (Camp Lucas), 3 years. Mus roll dated 31 Oct 1861 abs sick at Camp Red House. Reenl 24 Nov 1863, vet vol, Charleston, WVa, 3 years. Nov 1863: on furl in Ohio since 23 Nov 1863. Dec 1863: loss, 24 Nov, Charleston, WVa disch as vet vol and re-mus under provision of GO 91. Aug 1864: abs scout. Sick in hosp, Sandy Hook, Md of jaundice, 8-11 Sept 1864. Rolls of July and Aug 1864 show him abs det on scouting party by order of Col Johnson (34th OVI), 20 Aug 1864 by order of Gen Crook. Sept 1864: abs det Blazer's Scouts since 11 Sept 1864. Oct-Nov 1864: abs scout since 20 Aug 1864. Jan 1865: abs in Blazer's Scouts per order of Gen Crook. Feb 1865: trans to 36th OVI. Mus out 27 July 1865, Wheeling, WVa.

HOOD, JOHN A. PVT, CO K. Age 21. Enr 10 Aug 1861, Camp Lucas, 3 years. Mus 12 Sept 1861, Camp Dennison. Prom cpl 3 Aug 1862. May-June 1863: listed as pvt, no reason for reduction. Mar-Apr 1864: on ds since 30 Mar (also shown as 18 Mar) by order of Gen Crook. Shown det Blazer's ind scouts through Oct 1864. Oct 1864: loss, disch 18 Sept 1864, CCO. Enl 5 Apr 1865, 5th US Vet Inf. Disch from 5th US Vet Inf 10 Apr 1866, New Haven, Conn by exp of term of service. Peter Shaffer, a comrade in Co F of the 5th noted he "was always ready to discharge a soldiers duty and was loved by all the officers and soldiers of his co." Postwar occ: farmer. *d* 19 June 1905, Butte, Mont. Bur Forest, Ill.

LIGHT, CHARLES H. PVT, CO A. Age 22. 6ft. Hazel eyes. Dark hair. Dark comp. *b* Clermont Co, Ohio. Farmer. Enr 27 July 1861, Camp Lucas, Ohio, 3 years. Mus 27 July 1861, Camp Lucas, Ohio. July 1862-Jan 1863: on duty teamster. Feb-Mar 1863: abs sick at Mt Pisgah, Ohio since 9 Feb 1863. Apr-May 1863: on duty regt teamster. June 1863: on extra duty in QM Dept. July-Aug 1863: on duty forage clerk in RQM. Sept-Nov 1863: on duty RQM. Dec 1863: disch 2 Dec 1863, Charleston, WVa by reason of reenl under provisions of GO 191, War Dept. Re-mus 2 Dec 1863. Abs vet furl since 2 Dec 1863. Aug-Oct 1864: abs scout since 1 Aug 1864. Nov 1864: abs det Blazer's Scout. Detachment mus roll for Jan-Feb 1865: present at CCO. *d* Thomasboro, Ill.

MORRIS, JAMES F. PVT, CO F. Age 18. 5ft 9in. Gray eyes. Light hair. Light comp. *b* Fairfield, Ohio. Farmer. Enl 4 Jan 1864, 3 years. Jan 1864: gain Charleston, WVa 19 Jan recruit from depot. Sept 1864: trans from Co I. Wounded 10 May 1864, Cove Gap, Va. Det Blazer's Ind Scouts

24 July 1864. Shown det through Nov 1864. Jan 1865: Capt 11 Jan 1865, Beverly, Va. Confined 2 Jan 1865, Richmond. Par 15 Feb 1865, Richmond, Va. Furl 27 Feb 1865, 30 days and ret 12 Apr 1865. No mus out card in file.

SHAFER, CHARLES. SGT, CO G. Age 23. 5ft 8in. Hazel eyes. Black hair. Dark Comp. *b* Cincinnati, Ohio. Cooper. Enr 22 July 1861, Camp Lucas, 3 years. Mus 20 Aug 1861, Camp Lucas. Mus roll for July and Aug 1862 shows him reduced to ranks by CM. No papers filed with record. July 1863: abs sick in hosp since 17 July 1863. Adm USA Gen Hosp, Pt Pleasant, WVa with a contusion. Ret to duty 18 Aug 1863. Mus 1 Jan 1864, vet vol, Charleston, WVa. May 1864: cpl. Abs sick, Charleston. Prom 1 July 1864 from cpl. Aug 1864: abs scout since 25 Aug 1864. Shown det in scouts through Jan 1865. POW record shows him capt 20 July 1864, Winchester and confined 23 Sept, Richmond, Va. Sent 24 Sept 1864, Danville. Par 2 Mar 1865, NE Ferry, NC. Shown on mus roll of par prisoners at CCO for Jan-Feb 1865. Furl 10 Mar 1865, 30 days and ret to regt 30 Apr 1865. Trans 20 Feb 1865, Co G 36th OVI. Mus vet. James G. Smith remembered he "was a most excellent soldier." *d* 28 Dec 1889, Friedley, Mont.

SLOAN, WILLIAM M. CPL, CO C. Age 22. 5ft 7in. Gray eyes. Brown hair. Fair comp. *b* Hamilton Co, Ohio. Farmer. Enr 5 Aug 1861, Camp Lucas, 3 years. Mus 15 Aug 1861, Camp Dennison, Ohio. Cpl to date from 1 Sept 1861. Mus out 20 Jan 1864 to date 1 Dec 1863. Disch by virtue of reenl as vet vol under the provisions of GO 191, Series 1863, War Dept. Jan 1864: abs on furl since 28 Jan 1864. Feb 1864: abs on furl as vet vol since 13 Feb 1864. Mar 1864: det scout since 18 Feb 1864 by order of Gen Crook 1 Mar 1864. May 1864: abs scout. June and July 1864: abs det scout since 18 Feb 1864. Oct 1864: loss, 5 Sept 1864, Berryville, Va. KIA. Final statement lists d. 3 Sept. Possibly bur Winchester Nat Cem. Cemetery records show a William Sloan buried in grave 329. "10th Ohio Inf, died 18 Nov 1864." These entries are probably in error. The 10th Ohio Inf did not serve in the Shenandoah Valley. Sloan was killed during the Myer's Ford fight on 4 Sept 1864, not Kabletown fight on 18 Nov 1864, according to the records. Asbe Montgomery indicates one man was killed in the Myer's Ford fight. This man's body was removed from Myer's Farm, which also probably held men killed in earlier fighting around Kabletown. He was probably erroneously listed among the dead at the Kabletown fight.

SMITH, WILLIAM S (FRANK S. ALLISON). PVT, CO I/B. Age 18. 5ft 10in. Blue eyes. Light hair. Fair comp. *b* Richland Co, Ohio. Painter. Enr 8 Aug 1861, Wapakaneta, Ohio, 3 years. Mus 14 Sept 1861, Camp Dennison. Mus out 23 Jan 1864 to date 29 Nov 1863. Disch by virtue of reenl as vet vol under provision of GO 191, Series 1863, War Dept. Re-mus 23 Jan, Charleston, WVa. Feb 1864: abs on vet furl. Apr 1864: abs div scout since 25 Apr 1864, SO 22. Det scout through Sept. Sept 1864: gain, Summit Point. Trans from Co I to Co B. Oct-Nov: det scout. Dec 1864: abs sick. POW record shows he was capt 20 Sept 1864, Winchester, Va. Confined 23 Sept, Richmond, Va. Sent 24 Sept, Danville. Adm 23 Feb 1865, Hosp No 3, Goldsboro, NC of scorbutus [scurvy]. Exch. Par 4 Mar, NE Ferry, NC. Adm 8 Mar 1865, Newton Hosp, Baltimore, Md from Hosp Div 1, Annapolis, Md. Sent 29 Mar, CGB, Md. Sent 2 Apr, CCO. Reported CCO. Furl 8 Apr 1865, ret 9 May 1865. See 36th OVI.

SPOTTS (SPATZ), FREDERICK. PVT, CO B. Age 24. 5ft 7½in. Dark eyes. Light hair. Light comp. *b* Germany. Farmer. Enr 2 Sept 1861, Camp Dennison. Mus 2 Sept 1861, Camp Dennison. Dec 1863: loss, 2 Dec, Charleston, WVa. Disch by virtue of reenl as vet vol under provision of GO No 191, Series 1863, War Dept. Abs vet on furl from 2 Dec 1863. Shown on mus roll dated 22 Jan 1864, Charleston, WVa mus out to date 25 Nov 1863. Mus 26 Nov, Camp Toland. May 1864: abs scout. Killed by Bushwhacker 3 June 1864, Warm Springs, Va.

STAHL, ARTHUR L (LEROY). PVT, CO K. Age 18. 5ft 10in. Blue eyes. Light hair. Fair comp. *b* 1 Oct 1843, Greenville, Darke Co, Ohio. Brother of Samuel Stahl, KIA at 3rd Winchester. Farmer. Enr 5 Aug 1862, Greenville, Ohio, 3 years. Mus 28 Dec 1862, Fayette CH. Joined co for duty 29 Aug 1862. Sept 1863: abs sick, Clarksburg, WVa since 12 Sept 1862. Jan-Feb 1864: abs with leave, 30 days from 1 Feb 1864 by order of Gen Kelley. Vet vol. July-Aug 1864: det on special duty by order of Gen Duvall. (Also shown det prov guard, but probably was for Blazer's Scouts.) Sept 1864: trans 3 Sept 1864, Co G. Sept-Nov 1864: abs div provost guard. Jan 1865: abs det Blazer's Scouts. Postwar occ: miner. *d* 3 Dec 1914, Soldiers Home, Calif.

SWARNER, MOSES. PVT, CO K/G. Age 21. 5ft 6in. Hazel eyes. Brown hair. Dark comp. *b* Montgomery Co, Ohio. Farmer. Enr 10 Aug 1861, Camp Lucas, 3 years. Mus 12 Sept 1861, Camp Dennison. May 1863-Jan 1864: on duty teamster. Nov-Dec 1863: disch by reason of reenl as vet vol under provision of GO 191, Series 1863, War Dept. Aug 1864: abs scout since 25 Aug 1864 by order of Gen Crook. Sept-Oct 1864: trans from Co K 3 Sept 1864 and det in Blazer's Scouts by order of Gen Crook. Nov 1864: abs Blazer's Scouts. Jan 1865: abs det Blazer's Scouts. Severely wounded 18 Nov 1864, Kabletown. Rec GSWs to both thighs and back. At Island USA Hosp, Harper's Ferry, WVa. Nov-Dec 1864: USA Gen Hosp, Cumberland, Md. Jan-Apr 1865: adm from the field 7 Feb 1865. Disch for dis 23 May 1865.

THOMPSON, CHARLES (BARNEY C. HENSHAW). PVT, CO G. Age 21. 5ft 11in. Blue eyes. Brown hair. Light comp. *b* 7 Mar 1841, Economy, Wayne Co, Ind. Clerk. Enr 22 July 1861, Camp Lucas, 3 years. Mus 20 Aug 1862, Camp Lucas. Mus out roll dated 23 Jan 1864 shows him mus out to date 31 Dec 1863. Disch by virtue of reenl as vet vol under provision of GO 191, Series 1863, War Dept. Re-mus 1 Jan 1864, Charleston, WVa. Jan-Feb 1864: abs on furl as vet vol, 30 days, Ohio since 31 Jan 1864. Mar 1864: abs det scout since 14 Mar 1864. Apr 1864-Jan 1865: abs det Blazer Scout by order of Gen Crook. Jan-Feb 1865: on mus roll of par prisoners at CCO dated 17 Mar 1865. Capt 20 Sept 1864, Winchester. POW record shows him confined 23 Sept 1864, Richmond, Va. Sent 24 Sept 1864, Danville, Va. Adm 23 Feb 1865, Gen Hosp No 3, Goldsboro, NC for pneumonia. Exch NE Ferry, NC, 4 Mar 1865. Reported 10 Mar 185, CCO. Furl 15 Mar 1865 and ret 4 Apr. Engaged in farming. *d* 19 Dec 1928, Garden City, Kans.

WESTFALL, JONATHAN S. PVT, CO G/K. Age 18. 5ft 4in. Gray eyes. Brown hair. Dark comp. *b* Darke Co, Ohio. Farmer. Enl 24 Feb 1864, Dayton, Ohio, 3 years. Joined as recruit from depot 20 Mar 1864. 3 Sept 1864: trans from Co K to Co G. Sept-Oct 1864: abs scout by order of Gen Crook. Nov 1864: abs Blazer's Scouts. Jan 1865: abs POW. Capt 11 Jan 1865, Beverly, WVa. POW record shows him confined 21 Jan 1865, Richmond, brought from Staunton. Par 15 Feb, Richmond, Va. Reported 17 Feb 1865, CCO. *d* 5 Feb 1880 of lung disease contracted while in prison camp.

WRIGHT, WILLIAM. PVT, CO D/I. Age 22. 5ft 5in. Gray eyes. Brown hair. Fair comp. *b* Harrison Co, Ohio. Farmer. Enl 29 Feb 1864, Lima, Ohio, 3 years. Mus same day and place. Mar 1864: recruit from depot 12 Mar 1864, Charleston, Va. Aug 1864: abs scout. Sept 1864: trans to Co D from Co I. Oct-Nov 1864: abs in Blazer's Scouts since 21 Sept, order of Col Johnson. Oct 1864: adm 3 Oct 1864, Sheridan Hosp, Winchester, Va with intermittant fever. Trans 10 Oct 1864, Mower USA Gen. Hosp, Chestnut Hill, near Philadelphia, Pa. Ret to duty 30 Nov 1864. Jan 1865: abs POW capt 11 Jan 1865, Beverly WVa. POW record shows him confined 21 Jan 1865, Richmond brought from Staunton. Par 15 Feb, Richmond, sent 17 Feb, CGB, Md. Sent 19 Feb, CCO where he reported 24 Feb 1865. Furl 2 Mar, 30 days. Ret 20 Apr 1865. Sent 25 Apr, Pro Mar, Columbus, Ohio. Reported 26 Apr, Columbus and sent to regt via Wheeling, WVa same day. *d* 6 Jan 1905.

WYNN, DAVID. PVT, CO E. Age 24. *b* 1835. Enr 1 Aug 1861, Camp Lucas, Ohio, 3 years. Mus 15 Aug 1861, Camp Dennison. Jan 1862: on duty teamster. Mar 1864: abs det on scout. Apr 1864: abs div scout. May-June: det in scout corps by order of Gen Crook. July-Aug 1864: det in Blazer's Scouts by order of Gen Crook. Sept 1864: loss, 3 Sept 1864, Charleston, WVa. Mus out by reason of exp of term of service. Cpt John D. Millard, Co E: "was a good soldier and a man of good habits and performed all duties assigned him faithfully and well." Bur Bakesto Cem, Adams Co, Ind.

36th OVI

Organized 30 July-31 Aug 1861, Marietta, Ohio. Unless otherwise noted all men mus out 27 July 1865, Wheeling, WVa.

BEATTY, WILLIAM (BILLY) E. PVT, CO B. Age 18. 5ft 6in. Blue eyes. Light hair. Light comp. *b* 9 Nov 1845, Athens, Ohio. Enr 12 Aug 1861, Vinton Co, Ohio, 3 years. Mus 26 Aug 1861, Marietta, Ohio. Adm 36th Regt hosp for a variety of complaints including bouts of pneumonia, pain, conjunctivitis, and diarrhea. Mus 14 Feb 1864, vet vol, Chattanooga, Tenn. Occ: soldier (now listed as 5ft 9in). Nov and Dec: on daily duty at HQ. May 1864: abs nurse, Charleston, WVa since 9 May 1864. Ds to date 23 Aug 1864 per SO 10, HQ 2nd div order of I. H. Duvall. Aug 1864: noted abs in Blazer's Scouts since 25 Aug 1864. Sept and Oct: abs ds in ind scouts. Nov 1864: KIA near Kabletown, Va. Brothers Thomas and James also served in Co B, 36th OVI. Bur Limerick Cem, Jackson Co, Ohio.

CLUTE, JOHN. PVT, CO E. Age 28. 5ft 10in. Black eyes. Black hair. Dark comp. *b* Richland Co, Ohio. Boatman. Enr 13 Aug 1861, Woodsfield, Ohio, 3 years. Mus 26 Aug 1861, Marietta, Ohio. Sept and Oct 1862: confined. Jan and Feb 1863: AWOL since 24 Feb 1863. Listed des 24 Feb 1863, Nashville, Tenn. Ret from des 25 May 1864, Meadow Bluff. Sept and Oct 1864 on ds. Det in Blazer's Scouts since 25 Aug 1864. Nov and Dec 1864: in arrest awaiting sentence of GCM. Killed by a pistol shot in right breast by Cpt Lintz [Link] of the 1st Md Cav in a row 31 Dec 1864, Cherry Run, Va. Clute also belonged to Co B 45th Ky Inf. Enl Mar 1863, 12 months. Des Mar 1864, Russelville, Tenn. Bur Antietam Nat Cem, grave no 1200. Originally interred at Cumberland, Md. *ROH* no XV lists grave no 36, lot B, section 1.

DARLING, DANIEL H. SGT, PVT, CO K. Age 20. 5ft 11½in. Gray eyes. Sandy hair. Ruddy comp. *b* 23 July 1841, Jackson Co, Ohio. Farmer. Enl 10 Aug 1861, Jackson, Ohio. Aug 1862: adm 36th Ohio Regt Hosp with "febris intermitt." Nov 1862: on ds, Wheeling, Va from 27 Nov. Feb 1863: loss, Louisville, Ky, des 30 Jan 1863. Shown on list of arrested deserters as having given himself up 1 Aug 1863, Jackson, Ohio. 23 Aug 1863: gained from des, Jasper, Ky. Mus 14 Feb 1864, vet, Chattanooga, 3 years. Aug 1864: abs in Blazer's Scouts since 25 Aug 1864. Sept-Dec 1864: abs in Blazer's Scouts. Feb 1865: abs with leave. Mar 1865: on daily duty cook. Appt cpl 26 Feb 1865. Appt sgt from cpl 30 June 1865. *d* 9 Oct 1916, Jackson, Ohio. "He was born in this co. and always lived here. He was a staunch Republican all his life and had many friends here." Bur Coalton Cem.

GILES, SETH W. PVT, CO H. Age 19. 5ft 7½in. Blue eyes. Light hair. Fair comp. *b* Meigs Co, Ohio. Farmer. Enr 12 Sept 1861, Harrisonville, 3 years. Recruit joined co 22 Oct 1861. Prom 1 May 1863, cpl. Reduced 21 Sept 1863. Nov 1863: abs ds nurse in hosp, Chattanooga, Tenn since 26 Nov 1863. Dec 1863-Jan 1864: ab on ds with 19th Ind Battery since 1 Nov 1863 per SO No 44, 36th OVI. Feb 1864: on duty co cook. May and June 1864: on daily duty co commissary. Aug

William Lewellen
William Lewellen (left) and his
brother Jerry.
Courtesy William Lieuellen

1864: abs Blazer's Scouts 25 Aug 1864. Sept-Dec 1864: abs ds ind scouts 25 Aug 1864. Mar 1865: on daily duty co commissary. Apr-June 1865: co clerk. Reenl 15 Feb 1864, vet vol.

HUFFORD, JOHN W (WESLEY). PVT, CO F. Age 18. 5ft 8in. Black eyes. Brown hair. Dark comp. *b* Guernsey Co, Ohio. Farmer. Enr 1 Aug 1861, Tunnel, 3 years. Mus 26 Aug 1861, Camp Putnam, Marietta, Ohio. Jan 1862: adm regt hosp with "febris typhoides." May 1862: abs sick Summerville, Va (pluritis). Oct 1863: adm 18 Oct, regt hosp for GSW of right thumb, accidental. June 1864: abs sick Charleston, WVa 30 May 1864. Aug-Dec: ds Blazer's Scouts 25 Aug 1864. Vet reenl and mus 22 Feb 1864 to date 15 Feb 1864, Chattanooga, Tenn. Listed des 24 June 1865. List of disch furnished by CMO of state under the provision of circular dated 29 June 1865. Disch furnished 7 May 1867, Columbus, Ohio. Dishonorably disch 7 May 1867 to date 27 July 1865 in compliance with Par 3 SO No 72 of 1867 Dept of the Lakes. War Dept notation dated 19 Aug 1884: "The Charge of desertion of June 24, 1865 against this man is removed. The dishonorable discharge heretofore issued to this man is canceled." *d* 11 Mar 1907, Belpre, Ohio.

LEWELLEN (LIEULLEN), WILLIAM. PVT, CO C. Age 21. 5ft 7¾in. Gray eyes. Dark hair. Dark comp. *b* 20 Aug 1840, Athens Co, Ohio. Farmer. Enr 3 July 1861, Albany, Athens Co, Ohio, 3 years. Mus 27 Aug 1861, Marietta, Ohio. June and July: abs sick Murfreesboro since 23 June 1863. Adm USA Gen Hosp, Nashville, Tenn with remittent fever. Mus 1 Jan 1864, vet, Chattanooga, Tenn. Jan and Feb 1864: abs on furl as vet vol since 28 Jan 1864. Sept-Nov 1864: abs ds ind scouts since 25 Aug 1864. Morning report shows him on ds scout at Corps HQ. Capt 18 Nov 1864, Kabletown. Confined 22 Nov 1864, Richmond brought from Gordonsville. Par 15 Feb 1865, Richmond, Va. Reported 17 Feb 1865, CGB, Md. Sent 19 Feb 1865, CCO where he reported

Charles Nowlin
Postwar photo of Charles
Nowlin from his pension file.
Courtesy National Archives

24 Feb 1865. Furl 1 Mar 1865, 30 days. Ret 14 Apr. Dec-Feb: abs sick or wounded. Wounded Annapolis. Apr 1865: abs par prisoner. May 1865: abs sick 28 Feb 1865, Annapolis, Md. June 1865: abs sick Columbus, Ohio since 28 Feb 1865. Mus out 27 July 1865, Wheeling, WVa. Mus out in compliance with GO No 77 dated 28 Apr 1865. Postwar occ: farmer. *d* 8 Feb 1922, Albany, Ohio.

NOWLIN, CHARLES. PVT, CO I. Age 23. 5ft 11in. Hazel eyes. Dark hair. Dark comp. *b* Gallia Co, Ohio. Farmer. Enr 13 Aug 1861, Chambersburg, 3 years. Mus 27 Aug 1861, Marietta, Ohio. 24 Oct 1863: MIA. Ret from MIA 1 Jan 1864. Place and dates in confinement as POW not stated . Reenl 14 Feb 184, vet, Chattanooga, Tenn. Det ind scouts per order of Col Duval commanding 2nd. Div, Army of WVa, 25 Aug 1864. 2nd Inf Div casualty list shows him wounded 18 Nov 1864, Kabletown. Morning report for 9 Dec 1864 shows him abs wounded in action since 1 Dec 1864. Shown on roll of Island USA Hosp Nov and Dec 1864. Furl approved 31 Dec 1864, 30 days due to GSW of left arm rec at Kabletown. J. D Brooks, MD requested extension of furl 28 Feb 1865. Shown sick 3 May 1865, Little York Hosp, Philadelphia, Pa. Adm 6 May 1865, Newton University Gen Hosp for treatment of GSW to left elbow. Adm from Winchester. Adm 19 May 1865, York, Pa USA Hosp for GSW to left arm caused by pistol ball. Sick 3 May 1865, no disch given. Disch per cert of dis due to GSW of left arm 16 Feb 1865, York, Pa USA Hosp per order of M. G. Cadwalader. Kin listed on hosp card: Levi Nowlin. *d* 1911.

SHAFFER, ALBERT D. PVT, CO A. Age 19. 5ft 9½in. Gray eyes. Black hair. Dark comp. *b* Washington Co, Ohio. Farmer. Enr 29 July 1861, Lowell, Ohio, 3 years. Mus 24 Aug 1861, Camp Putnam, Marietta, Ohio. Apr 1863: adm regt hosp with hepatitis. Reenl 15 Feb 1864, vet Chattanooga, Tenn. Aug 1864: abs det with Blazer's Scouts 25 Aug. Sept-Nov 1864: abs ds ind scouts 25 Aug 1864. Jan 1865: abs with leave 12 Jan 1865. Rel from ds and joined co 17 Dec 1865. Mar 1865: on daily duty wood chopper. *d* 2 Dec 1904, Peoria, Ill.

SMITH, WILLIAM S. PVT, CO I. Age 18. 5ft 9in. Blue eyes. Light hair. Fair comp. *b* Richland Co, Ohio. Painter. Enl 8 Aug 1861, Co I 34th OVI. Reenl 30 Nov 1863, Xenia, Ohio. Mar and Apr 1864: sick at Dennison USA Gen Hosp, Camp Dennison, Ohio. Apr 1864: det in Blazer's Scouts per order of Gen Crook. Capt 18 Nov 1864, place not given. Det ind scout 26 Apr 1864. 28 Feb 1865: det in Blazer's Scouts. Also shown capt 19 Oct, Cedar Creek. Jan 1865: abs POW. Mar 1865: abs POW, par CCO. Apr and May 1864: abs capt Cedar Creek. Vet mus out 12 June 1865, CCO per surgeon's cert of dis and in accordance with GO 77 War Dept dated 28 Apr 1865. Vet trans from Co B 34th OVI to Co I 36th OVI. *d* 9 Mar 1900, Cleveland, Ohio. See 34th OVI.

TOPPING, JOHN W. PVT, CO H. Age 18. 5ft 9½in. Blue eyes. Dark hair. Dark comp. *b* Meigs Co, Ohio. Stonemason. Enr 12 Aug 1861, Harrisonville, 3 years. Mus 26 Aug 1861, Marietta, Ohio. Jan 1863: AWOL from 28 Jan 1863. May 1863: gain, 18 May 1863 joined from des. Aug-Oct 1863: abs sick Cowan, Tenn since 17 Aug 1863. Adm No 19 USA Gen Hosp, Nashville, Tenn Branch 1 with scrofula. Sent 23 Sept, USA Conval Camp Hosp. Ret to duty 19 Nov 1863. July 1864: abs sick 30 July 1864, Sandy Hook, Md. Regt hosp records also show him treated numerous times for pain, diarrhea, and other ailments. Aug-Nov 1864: abs det Blazer's Scouts since 25 Aug 1864. Ds since 2 Sept 1864 order 10 HQ AWV. Reenl 15 Feb 1864, vet vol Chattanooga, Tenn. Mar 1865: abs ds Dept HQ, 26 Mar 1865. June 1865: abs ds since 3 May 1865. Postwar occ: contractor. *d* 18 Aug 1904, Huntington, WVa.

WAXLER, ARCHIBALD. SGT (CPL), CO D. Age 22. 5ft 10½in. Blue eyes. Light hair. Light comp. *b* Washington Co, Ohio. Farmer. Enr 18 Aug 1862, Marietta, Ohio, 3 years. First shown on mus roll dated 2 Oct 1862 near mouth of Antietam, Md. Appt cpl 10 Oct 1863. Mar-Apr 1864: det from 10 Mar 1864, Ringold, Ga SFO No 64, DC. May-June 1864: joined from ds 25 May 1864. Prom from cpl 26 Aug 1864. 10 Mar 1864: present sgt. Rolls for July and Aug 1864 present sgt. Ds in scouting party, no and date of order unknown. Sept-Oct 1864: abs det since 26 Aug order 10, HQ, Dept WVa. Aug-Nov 1864: det in scouts since 25 Aug 1864. Nov 1864: KIA near Kabletown while on det duty in Cpt Blazer's detachment of scouts. Probably bur unknown grave, Winchester Nat Cem.

WEST, DAVID W. PVT, CO B. Age 25. 5ft 9¾in. Blue eyes. Brown hair. *b* Gallia Co, Ohio. Farmer. Enr 20 Sept 1861, Vinton Co, Ohio. Mus 25 Sept, Parkersburg, Va. Joined co 25 Sept 1861, Summersville. 1 Jan 1863: Charleston, Va, des. Mar 1863: Carthage, Tenn, joined from des. Sept 1863-Feb 1864: on daily duty pioneer. Aug-Nov: on ds with Blazer's Scouts since 25 Aug 1864. Det per SO 10 dated HQ 2nd Div AWV 23 Aug by order of Col I. H. Duval. Dec 1864: abs sick or wounded, Danville since 18 Nov 1864. POW record shows him capt 27 Oct, Kabletown, Va and confined 22 Nov, Richmond brought from Gordonsville. Par 15 Feb 1865, Richmond and reported 17 Feb 1865, CGB, Md and sent 19 Feb 1865, CCO. Notation "Pemberton" on POW record. Mar 1865: abs sick or wounded 19 Oct 1864. Apr 1865: abs sick 18 Jan 1865, Grafton, WVa. May 1865: abs sick Baltimore, Md. June 1865: abs Columbus, Ohio since 13 Oct 1864. Mus out CCO per GO 77 War Dept. Lived in Metropolis, Ill postwar. *d* 10 Mar 1911. Also served in Co G 18th OVI.

WILLINGTON, AMOS B. PVT, CO K. Age 18. 5ft. 8¾in. Brown eyes. Brown hair. Dark comp. *b* Jackson Co, Ohio. Farmer. Enr 10 Aug 1861, Jackson, Ohio. Mus 31 Aug 1861, Marietta, Ohio. Reenl 14 Feb 1864, vet Chattanooga, Tenn. On ds per SO 10 HQ AWV with Blazer's Scouts since 25 Aug 1864. Sept and Oct: on ds ind scouts since 25 Aug 1864. *d* 19 Nov 1864 of wounds rec 18 Nov. Probably bur unknown grave, Winchester Nat Cem.

John Alexander
Courtesy Society of the Army of WVA

91st OVI

Organized 26 Aug 1862, Camp Ironton, Ohio. Unless otherwise noted all men mus out with regt 24 June 1865.

ALEXANDER, JOHN M. SGT (1ST SGT), CO A. Age 20. 5ft 6in. Gray eyes. Light hair. Light comp. *b* 17 May 1841, Delaware Co, Ohio. Carriage trimmer. Enr 15 Aug 1862, Gallipolis, Ohio, 3 years. Mus 4 Sept 1862, Ironton, Ohio as 5th sgt. July 1863: abs guarding prisoners to CCO since 24 July 1863 by SO 74 of Col Turley. Sept 1863: on duty in scouting co. Morning report for 28 Oct 1863 shows him ret to co from scouting co. Feb 1864: abs with leave on furl till 29 Feb. July-Aug 1864: abs sick left at Parkersburg, WVa 12 July 1864. Wounded 22 Sept 1864 in the Battle of Fisher's Hill. Severe GSW 2d toe of left foot. Abs wounded 23 Sept 1864, Baltimore, Md. Oct 1864: abs sick Baltimore, Md. Nov-Dec 1864: abs sick Philadelphia, Pa. Letter dated Jan-Feb 1865: abs sick Gallipolis, Ohio since 8 July 1864. Appt 1st sgt 3 Apr 1865. Ret to trade as carriage trimmer until 1874. Elected trustee of Gallia Co in 1880 and elected mayor of Gallipolis in 1883 and re-elected in 1885. He then entered the grocery business until 1889 when his business was destroyed by fire. In Apr 1890 he became president of the Gallipollis Shoe Manufacturing Co. *d* 11 Mar 1914, Gallia Co. Bur Mound Hill Cem with wife Eliza.

BAILY, JAMES. PVT, CO F. Age 26. 5ft 11½in. Blue eyes. Dark hair. Dark comp. Enr 11 Aug 1862, Green?, 3 years. Mus 7 Sept 1862, Camp Ironton, Ohio. May-June 1863: in confinement for abs without leave since 17 June 1863. Notation "des. Feb. 13, 1863 at Camp Reynolds. Ret. Apr. 9, 1863" as shown by the rolls was crossed off record. Mar-Apr 1864: abs on ds ind scout since 29 Mar 1864. Ret to regt by order of Lt Blazer for getting drunk 7 June 1864. (In this case the order may have been rescinded since he is still shown det for July-Aug.) July-Aug 1864: det scout 25 Aug 1864. *d* 10 June 1883.

BARBEE, CHARLES P. PVT (4TH SGT), CO C. Age 22. 5ft 7¾in. Black eyes. Dark hair. Dark comp. *b* 16 Sept 1839, Portsmouth, Scioto Co, Ohio. Carpenter. Enr 4 Aug 1862, Clay, Ohio, 3 years. Mus Camp Ironton, Ohio 7 Sept 1862. Sept-Oct 1863: on duty musician in scouting co. Morning report shows him det scout. Feb 1864: abs on leave with furl till 29 Feb 1864. Sept-Oct 1864: wounded slightly in hand 19 Sept 1864, Winchester, Va. Also shown with GSW of right shoulder and sent to Sandy Hook Field Hosp from the field. Abs sick in hosp, Winchester, Va since 19 Sept 1864. Nov 1864: abs sent 19 Sept, Sandy Hook Hosp, Md. Dec 1864-Jan 1865: abs sick Frederick City, Md. Mus rolls show him at Cuyler USA Gen Hosp, Germantown, Pa. Sept-Oct 1864: trans 10 Oct 1864, McClellan Gen Hosp, Philadelphia, Pa. Pvt to 22 Aug 1862. Cpl to 12 Oct 1862. Sgt till 15 Oct 1864. Appt 1st sgt, wounded 19 Sept 1864, Winchester. Surgeon J. B. Warwick remembered him as "a good soldier, always ready for duty and in line of battle always in the front line where danger was the greatest." Postwar occ: railroad carpenter.

BARTON, THOMAS A. PVT, CO A. Age 19. 5ft 6in. Gray eyes. Light hair. Light comp. *b* Meigs Co, Ohio. Farmer. Enr 11 Aug 1862, Gallipolis, Ohio, 3 years. Mus 7 Sept 1862, Camp Ironton. Sept-Oct 1863: on duty in scouting co. Morning report for 22 Feb 1864 shows him on daily duty in scouting co. Det in scouting co since 11 Feb 1864 by order of Gen Crook. KIA near Charles Town, WVa (Kabletown). Probably bur unknown grave at Winchester Nat Cem.

BISHOP, WILLIAM. PVT, CO A. Age 18. 5ft 11in. Hazel eyes. Dark hair. Dark comp. *b* Jackson Co, Va. Farmer. Enr 11 Aug 1862, Gallipolis, Ohio, 3 years. Mus 7 Sept 1862, Camp Ironton. Oct 1862: abs sick Pt Pleasant Hosp since 19 Oct. Sept-Oct 1863: on duty in scouting co. Dec 1863: morning report for 11 Dec 1863 shows him wounded in left leg in a skirmish on Big Sewell Mt between Blazer's Scouts and Thurman's bushwhackers. Report for 24 Aug 1864 shows him disch for wounds rec at Sewell Mt. In hosp, Gallipolis, Ohio Jan-June 1864. Aug 1864: disch for dis 14 July 1864. *d* 13 Jan 1911, Dallas, Tex. Bur Huntington, WVa.

BOLDMAN, SALATHIEL. PVT, CO I. Age 18. 5ft 3in. Brown eyes. Brown hair. Dark comp. *b* Adams Co, Ohio. Laborer. Enr 1 Aug 1862, Green, Ohio, 3 years. Mus 7 Sept 1862, Camp Ironton. Mar 1863: abs in arrest in confinement 1 Mar 1863, Fayetteville, Va. Apr 1863: abs in arrest sent to CCO to work for 6 months by order of GCM, GO 16, Col Toland, 19 Mar 1863. May-July 1863: abs in arrest at Charleston to work during 6 months (term of enl). Oct 1863: on duty in scouting co. Dec 1863: capt by rebels 11 Dec 1863, Big Sewell Mt. POW record shows him confined 30 Dec 1862, Richmond, Va. Sent 10 Feb 1864, Andersonville, Ga. No later record. Probably *d* Andersonville.

BROWN, MILTON W. PVT, CO G. Age 26. 5ft 8½in. Gray eyes. Light hair. Fair comp. *b* Pike Co, Ohio. Farmer. Enr 11 Aug 1862, Marion Twp, 3 years. Mus 7 Sept 1862, Ironton, Ohio. Jan 1863: on duty wood chopper. July 1863: AWOL since 27 July 1863, Ohio. Appt cpl 19 Oct 1863. Aug-Dec 1864: abs ds in ind scouting co since 8 Feb 1864 (cpl). July-Aug 1864: abs det duty scout since 25 Aug 1864. *d* 16 Nov 1921, Portsmouth, Ohio.

BROWN, MILTON. SGT (1ST LT), CO K. Age 20. 5ft 8¾in. Blue eyes. Black hair. Dark comp. *b* Jackson, Ohio. Farmer. Enr 10 Aug 1862, Jackson CH, 3 years. Mus 7 Sept 1862, Camp Ironton, Ohio, sgt. 7 Sept-31 Oct 1862: 5th sgt. Sept 1863-Aug 1864: carried on the rolls as sgt. Oct 1863: on duty in scouting co. Jan 1864: abs with leave at home in Ohio on furl. Sept 1864: loss, 23 Sept, Woodstock, Va. Appt 2d lt. Sept-Dec 1864: (2d lt) present. Prom vice John A. Hamilton, prom. Disch by order of Maj Gen Crook. Prom from sgt and assn to duty 23 Sept 1864. Jan-May 1865: (1st lt Co E) present, prom from 2d lt Co K 26 Jan 1865, joined co. Killed 28 May 1889 by a tornado at Cottonwood Falls, Kans.

BRUCE, GEORGE. PVT, CO C. Age 27. 5ft 8in. Blue eyes. Light hair. Fair comp. *b* Scioto Co, Ohio. Farmer. Enr 7 Aug 1862, Valley, 3 years. Mus 7 Sept 1862, Ironton, Ohio. July 1863: AWOL since 27 July 1863, Ohio. Sept-Oct 1863: on duty in scouting party. Morning reports show him as scout along with Sgt Charles P. Barbee, Pvts Clark Wilson, C. W. Volgamore, and Jacob Schultz. 22 Apr 1864: adm regt hosp for measles. July-Aug 1864: abs sick left at Charleston, WVa. Adm USA Gen Hosp, Gallipolis, 2 July 1864 with dysentery. Ret to duty 22 Sept 1864 "To Washington by order of Board of Examiners. Age 29." Sept 1864: abs sick hosp, Gallipolis 9 July 1864. Feb-Apr 1865: on duty in QM Dept. May 1865: abs det at HQ 1 Brig 4 Prov Div, Army of Shenandoah, Staunton, Va since 3 May 1865. Shown on a list of officers and enlisted men of the 91st Regt unfit for duty at Gallipolis Gen Hosp 10 Aug 1864. Adm 2 July 1864 for phthisis incip. [wasting]. *d* 12 Aug 1899. Bur cem near Peru, Ind.

CAIN, SAMUEL W. PVT, CO E. Age 27. 5ft 9in. Hazel eyes. Sandy hair. Sandy comp. *b* Adams Co, Ohio. Farmer. Enr 9 Aug 1862, Oliver, 3 years. Mus 7 Sept 1862, Camp Ironton, Ohio. Sept-Oct 1863: on duty in scouting co. Dec 1863: abs on furl at home in Ohio from 19 Dec-3 Jan 1864. Mus out 24 June 1865, Columbus, Ohio. *d* 2 Jan 1891.

CASTER, JAMES. PVT, CO G. Age 20. 5ft 9½in. Gray eyes. Brown hair. Fair comp. *b* 1 Oct 1844, Pike Co, Ohio. Farmer. Enr 11 Aug 1862, Marion Twp, Ohio, 3 years. Mus 7 Sept 1862, Ironton, Ohio. Sept-Oct 1863: on duty in scouting co on daily duty scout since 11 Sept 1863. July-Sept 1864: abs left sick Parkersburg, WVa. 12 July 1864: treated for diarrhea, acute. Ret to duty 27 Sept 1864. Jan 1865: abs on furl, 20 days since 27 Jan 1865. *d* 23 Apr 1923, Nat Mil Home, Ohio. Bur Greenlawn Cem, Portsmouth, Ohio.

CHERINGTON (CHERRINGTON), JAMES W (WADDEL). CPL (PVT), CO A. Age 19. 5ft 7½in (5ft 9in). Hazel eyes. Light hair. Light comp. *b* 26 Nov 1842, Centerville near Thurman, Gallia Co, Ohio. Student, farmer, and teacher. Enr 15 Aug 1862, Gallipolis, Ohio, 3 years. Mus 4 Sept 1862, Ironton, Ohio. May 1863: adm regt hosp for debility. Sent 20 May 1863, Gen Hosp. Sept 1863: (cpl) on duty musician in scouting co. Reduced to the ranks by his own request to enter regt band, GO 9, Col Turley 19 Oct 1863. Nov-Dec 1863: (pvt) on duty musician. Jan-Feb 1864: on duty in regt band. Mar 1864-May 1865: on duty musician. Postwar occ: lumber business, Cincinnati, Ohio. *d* 30 Mar 1922, Ashland, Ky.

CONNEL, THOMAS D. PVT, CO E. Age 28. 5ft 7in. Blue eyes. Light hair. Fair comp. *b* 12 Nov 1833, Adams Co, Ohio. Carpenter. Enr 7 Aug 1862, Winchester, Va, 3 years. Mus 7 Sept 1862, Ironton, Ohio. Oct-Dec 1862: abs det to artillery battery since 8 Oct 1862. Sept-Oct 1863: on duty in scouting co. Dec 1863: abs on furl at home in Ohio 19 Dec 1863-3 Jan 1864. Feb-Sept 1864: abs on ds scout since 11 Feb 1864 by order of Gen Crook GO 2. Postwar occ: carpenter. *d* 8 June 1913, Camden Co, Mo.

COOPER, JOHN. PVT, CO E. Age 20. 5ft 11½in. Hazel eyes. Dark hair. Dark comp. *b* Adams Co, Ohio. Farmer. Enr 18 Aug 1862, Monroe, 3 years. Mus 7 Sept 1862, Camp Ironton, Ohio. Sept-Oct 1863: on duty in scouting co. Morning reports show him ret to co from scouting party 15 Nov 1863. Sept 1864: abs sick 19 Sept 1864, field hosp, Winchester. *d* 2 Mar 1934, Adams Co, Ohio. "Mr. Cooper was a most robust specimen of manhood having the distinction of never needing the care of a doctor during his entire life until a few weeks ago." Listed as last surviving member of the 91st OVI.

CURRY, GEORGE D. PVT (CPL), CO A. Age 29. 5ft 8in. Blue eyes. Dark hair. Dark comp. *b* Gallia Co, Ohio. Brickmason. Enr 15 Aug 1862, Gallipolis, Ohio, 3 years. Mus 7 Sept

1862, Ironton, Ohio. Prom cpl 8 Jan 1863 vice Durea, reduced to the ranks. May 1863: adm regt hosp with "febris remitt." Sent 15 June, Gen Hosp. June 1863: (cpl) abs sick 15 June 1863, Gallipolis Hosp. Sept 1863: on duty in scouting party. Reduced from cpl by SO 94, Col Turley, 14 Oct 1863. Also shown as by order of Col C. B. White for insolence. June 1864: wounded in action 18 June 1864, Lynchburg. July-Aug 1864: abs sick left at Harper's Ferry, Va 20 July 1864. Shown attch to Hosp Div 1, USA Gen Hosp, Annapolis, Md 1 Aug 1864. Trans 14 Aug 1864, Gen Hosp, Camp Parole with febris typhoides. Trans (shown on mus roll) USA Gen Hosp, York, Pa. July-Aug 1864: adm 18 Aug 1864 as conval. Ret to duty 17 Sept 1864. Prom cpl 3 Apr 1865. *d* 24 Oct 1878, Gallipolis, Gallia Co, Ohio. Reported to be a victim of yellow fever epidemic, but this is highly unlikely considering the time of year. Bur Pine Street Cem.

CYDRUS, MERIDITH. PVT, CO G. Age 20. 5ft 6in. Blue eyes. Light hair. Light comp. *b* Gallia Co, Ohio. Farmer. Enr 11 Aug 1862, Omega PC, Ohio, 3 years. Mus 7 Sept 1862, Camp Ironton. July 1863: AWOL since 27 July 1863, Ohio. Oct 1863: on duty in scouting co since 24 Oct 1863. July 1864: AWOL since 12 July. Aug 1864: abs confined since 12 Aug 1864, Cincinnati, Ohio. Notation AGO 16 Feb 1886: des 12 July 1864, Parkersburg, WVa. Arrested 24 July 1864, Sharonville, Ohio by Pro Mar, 12th Dist of Ohio and delivered 25 July 1864, Tod Barracks, Columbus, Ohio and forwarded to regt the same day via Cincinnati. Reward $30.00. Expenses $5.95. Shown on list of prisoners in mil prison, Wheeling, WVa (aka Atheneum Prison) 25 July 1864. Sent 27 July, Cumberland. Postwar occ: farmer. Killed 23 Dec 1902, railroad accident. Interred at Sharonville, Ohio.

DAVIS, JAMES. PVT, CO E. Age 31. 5ft 6in. Blue eyes. Sandy hair. Sandy comp. *b* Brown Co, Ohio. Farmer. Enr 11 Aug 1862, Oliver, Ohio, 3 years. Oct 1863: on duty in scouting co. Morning report shows him ret to co from scouting party 15 Nov 1863. Apr 1865: on duty pioneer. May 1865: abs det at HQ, 1st Brig, 4 prov div, Army of Shenandoah, Staunton, Va since 3 May 1865. Postwar occ: farmer. *d* 26 Oct 1899.

DIETRICH, JOHN H. SGT (CPL), CO F. Age 24. 6ft. Blue eyes. Light hair. Light comp. *b* 18 Mar 1837, Alleghany Co, Pa. Farmer. Enr 11 Aug 1862, Bloom Twp. Mus 7 Sept 1862, Camp Ironton. Shown as cpl on mus Sept-Oct 1862. Oct 1863: on duty in scouting co. Feb 1864: abs with leave on furl until 29 Feb 1864. Prom sgt 18 June 1864 vice C. Stiles. *d* 22 Jan 1919, S Webster, Ohio.

ELLISON, IRA W. PVT, CO E. Age 19. Blue eyes. 5ft 6in. Black hair. Fair comp. *b* Adams Co, Ohio. Farmer. Enr 31 July 1862, Oliver, Ohio, 3 years. Mus 7 Sept 1862, Camp Ironton, Ohio. Sept-Oct 1863: on duty in scouting co. Feb 1864: abs with leave on furl until 5 Mar 1864. 26 Mar 1864: *d* of smallpox, regt hosp, Fayetteville, WVa.

EKHART, JACOB. PVT, CO K. Age 19. 5ft 7in. Gray eyes. Dark hair. Dark comp. *b* 7 Aug 1843, Jackson, Ohio. Farmer. Enr 13 Aug 1862, Jackson CH, 3 years. Mus 7 Sept 1862, Camp Ironton, Ohio. Morning report for 8 Oct 1863 shows him det scout. No notation in CSR. July 1864: wounded in action 20 July, Stephenson's Depot, Winchester, Va in right hip. July-Aug 1864: abs sick 25 July 1864, Cumberland, Md. Sept-Nov 1864: abs sick Parkersburg, WVa since 12 July 1864. Dec 1864: abs sick Parkersburg, WVa since 1 Oct 1864. Jan-Feb 1865: abs sick at home in Ohio on surgeon's cert 21 Jan 1865 with leave. Apr 1865: abs sick 3 Apr 1865, Cumberland, Md. May 1865: loss, 26 May, Cumberland, Md, disch for dis. "This soldier was wounded July 20, 1864 in action near Winchester, Va. by a musket ball which entered his right thigh and lodged." *d* 11 Sept 1916, Scioto, Ohio.

EMMONS, WILLIAM J. PVT, CO K. Age 24. 6ft. Blue eyes. Dark hair. Light comp. *b* 1837, Jackson Co, Ohio. Farmer. Enr 12 Aug 1862, Jackson CH. Mus 7 Sept 1862, Camp Ironton, Ohio. Appt 3rd cpl 22 Aug 1862. Oct 1862: abs sick Pt Pleasant Hosp since 27 Oct. Dec 1862: adm regt hosp with pneumonia. Ret to duty 24 Dec. Des 26 Jan 1863, Fayettesville, Va. Det at home on furl by sickness. Ret 3 Feb 1863. Reduced to the ranks 2 July 1863 for leaving his post while on duty and other improper and indecent conduct. Aug-Dec 1864: abs det in ind scouting co since 11 Feb 1864. Sept-Oct 1864: on det duty ind scout since 29 Aug 1864. Sept 1864: adm USA Field Hosp, Sandy Hook, Md with "febris remittant." Trans 7 Sept 1864, Gen Hosp, Frederick, Md. Appears on mus roll of USA Gen Hosp, Frederick, Md. Adm for acute diarrhea. Sept-Oct 1864: trans 22 Sept 1864, Baltimore, Md, Jarvis USA Gen Hosp. Ret to duty 6 Oct. *d* 1 July 1914, Lancaster, Ohio. Bur Jackson Co, Ohio, Byer Cem.

FRANKLIN, CHARLES. PVT, CO G. Age 25. 6ft 1 ¼in. Blue eyes. Sandy hair. Sandy comp. *b* Muskingum Co, Ohio. Farmer. Enr 8 Aug 1862, Waverly PC, Ohio, 3 years. Mus 7 Sept 1862, Ironton, Ohio. Sept-Oct 1862: on duty in scouting co since 11 Sept. Jan 1864: loss, 10 Jan 1864. Fayetteville, WVa. *d* of typhoid fever.

FERGUSON, JOHN H (ALIAS FURGISON, JOHN). PVT, CO D. Age 24. 5ft 9 ⅓in. Dark eyes. Dark hair. Fair comp. *b* Ohio. Farmer. Enr 5 Aug 1862, Unionville, Ohio. Mus 7 Sept 1862, Camp Ironton, Ohio. Dec 1862: treated at regt hosp for gonorrhea. Sent 3 Jan 1863, Gen Hosp. Jan-Apr 1863: abs sick Charleston Hosp since 6 Jan 1863. Oct 1863: on duty in scouting co. Morning report for 8 Oct 1863 shows him det scout. June 1864: abs sick left at Meadow Bluff, WVa 31 May 1864 ordered by C. White. July-Aug 1864: abs sick hosp, Sandy Hook (Harper's Ferry) since 18 Aug 1864. Adm 19 Aug from the field with GSW left hand, shown wounded at Cedar Creek. At Harper's Ferry until Oct 1864. Trans 20 Aug, Baltimore. Adm 21 Aug, Jarvis USA Gen Hosp. Trans 31 Oct, Gallipolis. Nov 1864: abs since 18 July 1864, Gallipolis, adm for GSW caused accidentally. Dec 1864-Jan 1865: abs sick Baltimore, Md (Jarvis USA Gen Hosp) since 20 Oct 1864. Shown AWOL Sept-Oct 1864, Jarvis Hosp. Shown on descr list of deserters at USA Gen Hosp, Gallipolis, Ohio. Furl 2 Nov 1864. Adm regt hosp, 91st OVI, 1 Nov 1864. Ret to duty 4 Nov 1864. Des 22 Feb 1865. Feb-May 1865: abs sick Gallipolis, Ohio. Mus out 24 July 1865, Cumberland, Md. Disch 13 June 1865, Gallipolis, Ohio in accordance with GO 77, AGO Series 1863.

GATTEN, JOSEPHUS. PVT, CO G. Age 18. 5ft 7in. Blue eyes. Brown hair. Light comp. *b* 30 Apr 1844, Barnsville, Belmont Co, Ohio (listed as Ross Co in pension). Farmer. Enr 2 Aug 1862, Omega PC (Sharonville), 3 years. Mus 7 Sept 1862, Ironton, Ohio. Jan 1863: loss, 31 Jan 1863, Fayetteville, Va, des. Abs at home when regt was paid. Feb 1863: gain, 23 Feb 1863, Fayetteville, Va. Ret from des. Sept 1863: on duty musician in scouting co. July-Aug 1864: abs under arrest since 29 July 1864. Sept 1864: wounded 19 Sept, Winchester, Va. Nov-Dec 1864: due US for transportation and arrest as deserter $35.95. AWOL from 12 July-8 Sept 1864. Ret to duty by order of Col Hayes commanding div. Arrested 24 July 1864, Circleville, Ohio. War Dept notation 23 Jan 1888 states: "He des. July 12/64 at Parkersburg, Va, was arrested July 24/64 at Sharonville, Ohio, by Pro. Mar., 12th Dist. Ohio, and delivered July 25/64 at Tod Bks., Columbus, Ohio, . . . rec. at Wheeling, W. Va. July 26/64 and sent to Cumberland, Md., July 27/64; rejoined co. Sept. 8/64. As he was subsequently ret. to duty by competent authority without trial, but upon conditions which appear to have been complied with (so far as not waived by the government) the charge of desertion no longer stand against him. . .the fact that he was absent in desertion from July 12, 1864 to July 24, 1864 cannot, however be expunged." *d* 4 May 1924, Newark, Ohio. Bur Cedar Hill Cem.

HALDERMAN (HALTERMAN), HENRY. PVT, CO K. Age 19. 5ft 5in. Black eyes. Black hair. Dark comp. *b* 26 Aug 1843, Jackson Co, Scioto Twp, Ohio. Collier. Enr 12 Aug 1862, Jackson CH, 3 years. Mus 7 Sept 1862, Camp Ironton, Ohio. Dec 1862: abs 29 Dec driving post team. July 1863: AWOL since 27 July 1863, Ohio. Sept-Oct 1863: on duty in scouting co. *d* 23 Dec 1918, Wellston, Ohio. Bur Salem Cem, Milton Twp.

HAMMONS, EDWARD J. PVT, CO K. Age 28. 5ft 8in. Blue eyes. Fair comp. Dark hair. *b* 14 Jan 1834, Jackson, Ohio. Laborer. Enr 12 Aug 1862, Jackson CH, 3 years. Mus 7 Sept 1862, Camp Ironton, Ohio. July 1863: AWOL since 27 July 1863, Ohio. Feb 1864: on duty scout. Mar-Apr 1864: abs on ds scout by GO 2 of Gen Crook 16 Feb 1864. June 1864: abs sick Gallipolis Hosp, 31 May 1864. July-Dec 1864: abs on ds in ind scouting co since 11 Feb 1864. (Name also appears as Edward J. Hammond, E. J. Hammon, and Hammonds.) *d* 17 May 1909.

HANSON, WILLIAM H. PVT, CO A. Age 24. 5ft 8in. Blue eyes. Dark hair. Light comp. *b* Columbiana Co, Ohio. Farmer. Enr 7 Aug 1862, Gallipolis, Ohio, 3 years. Mus 7 Sept 1862, Ironton, Ohio. Oct 1862: abs sick Pt Pleasant hosp since 19 Oct. July 1863: abs sick 24 July, Ashland Hosp. Ret to duty 3 Aug. Sept 1863: on duty in scouting co. Nov 1863-Feb 1864: on daily duty hosp nurse. Mar-Apr 1864: on duty in regt hosp. May-July 1864: on duty in Hosp Corps. Aug 1864: abs nurse in Gallipolis Hosp, 4 Oct 1862. *d* 23 Jan 1890, insane asylum, Wesson, W Va. Bur on the grounds of the asylum.

HEAGERTY (HAGERTY), JOHN. PVT, CO E. Age 21. 5ft 9½in. Hazel eyes. Light hair. Fair comp. *b* 8 July 1841, Washington Co, Pa. Farmer. Enr 1 Aug 1862, Oliver, Ohio. Mus 7 Sept 1862, Camp Ironton, Ohio. Sept-Oct 1863: on duty in scouting co. Feb 1864: abs with leave on furl until 5 Mar 1864. May 1864: on duty pioneer. July-Nov 1864: abs sick Cumberland, Md 20 July 1864 wounded in action, Stephenson's Depot. War Dept notation dated 27 Mar 1879. "Seriously wounded in the thigh in action at Winchester, Va. July 20, 1864 by a musket ball." Adm USA Gen Hosp, Cumberland, Md from the field 25 July. Ret to duty 8 Jan 1865. *d* 23 Aug 1918, Cherry Fork, Ohio.

HARROP, SAMUEL. CPL, CO B. Age 20. 5ft 6in. Blue eyes. Dark hair. Light comp. *b* 2 June 1842, Pittsburg, Alleghany Co, Pa. Molder. Enr 8 Aug 1862, Gallipolis, Ohio, 3 years. Sept-Oct 1863: on duty in scouting party. Morning report for Nov 1863 shows him reported for duty from scouts. Morning reports for Feb 1864 also show him on duty scout. Feb-May 1864: on det duty scout by order of Gen Crook since 21 Feb 1864. June 1864: MIA 2 June 1864, Covington, Va. Descr list shows him capt and held as a POW 2 June-8 Dec 1864. POW record shows him capt 2 June, Covington, Va, place of confinement not given (POW at Andersonville). Par 24 Nov 1864, Savannah, Ga. Adm Camp Parole USA Gen Hosp with chronic diarrhea. Trans to Washington for medical treatment. Morning report 30 Dec 1864 shows Cpl S. Harrop exch in govt insane asylum, Washington, DC since 8 Dec 1864. Disch on surgeon's cert of dis 3 Jan 1865, Washington, DC. Wife or nearest kin listed as Mary Harrop on bed card. *d* 27 Dec 1889, Quincy, Ill. Bur Woodland Cem.

JAMES, GILBERT (GILL) T (TURNER). PVT, CO G. Age 17. 5ft 6in. Black eyes. Brown hair. Light comp. *b* 29 Dec 1844, Pike Co, Ohio. Farmer. Enr 11 Aug 1862, Marion Co, Ohio, 3 years. Mus 7 Sept 1862, Ironton, Ohio. Oct 1862: adm USA Gen Hosp, Pt Pleasant, Va for "febris remittans." Ret to duty 27 Oct 1862. Feb 1864: on duty scout. Mar-Dec 1864: abs on ds in ind scouting co by order of Gen Crook since 8 Feb (also shown as 22 Feb) 1864. Postwar occ: farmer. *d* 28 Sept 1907 near London, Madison Co, Ohio.

LANE (LAYNE), JOHN G. SGT, CO H. Age 29. 5ft 10½in. Gray eyes. Light hair. Light comp. *b* 31 Dec 1832, Albany, NY. Teacher. Enr 14 Aug 1862, Upper Twp, Ohio, 3 years. Mus 7 Sept 1862, Camp Ironton, Ohio. Appt 5th sgt 22 Aug 1862. Sept 1862: abs with leave from Col Lightburn. Sept-Oct 1863: on duty in scouting co. July 1864: wounded in action (slight, in arm by buckshot) at Stephenson's Depot, Winchester, Va. July-Sept 1864: abs sick (wounded) hosp, Cumberland, Md 25 July 1864, adm 23 July. Trans 25 July, Gen Hosp, Wheeling, WVa. July-Aug 1864: shown on mus roll for USA Post Hosp, Wheeling, WVa as patient. Abs on furl 22 Aug 1864. Sept-Oct 1864: on roll of USA Post Hosp, Wheeling, WVa as patient. Ret to duty 23 Sept 1864. *d* 27 Jan 1927 at home in LaGrange, Ohio. Member of Dick Lambert Post of GAR. Bur Woodland Cem, Ironton, Ohio.

LENLEY, ANDREW. PVT, CO B. Age 33. 5ft 9in. Blue eyes. Sandy hair. Light comp. *b* Green Co, Pa. Farmer. Enr 8 Aug 1862, Cheshire, Ohio, 3 years. Sept-Oct 1863: on duty in scouting co. Morning reports Nov 1863 show him reported for duty from scouts. *d* 13 Mar 1918, Cheshire, Ohio.

LEWIS, THOMAS. PVT, CO H. Age 20. 5ft 4in. Black eyes. Black hair. Dark comp. *b* 14 Mar 1842, Monmouth Co, England. Nail cutter. Enr 22 Aug 1862, Upper Twp, Sandusky Co, Ohio, 3 years. Mus 7 Sept 1862, Camp Ironton, Ohio. Appt 7th cpl 22 Aug 1862. Sept-Oct 1863: on duty musician in scouting co. Reduced to the ranks at his own request by GO 91 of Col John A. Turley dated 19 Oct 1863. Cpl until 17 Sept 1863. Oct 1863-Jan 1864: on duty musician in regt band 17 Sept 1863 (pvt). Feb 1864-May 1865: on duty musician. *d* 20 Mar 1923, Ironton, Ohio. Bur Woodland Cem, Ironton, Ohio.

MARSHALL, FINLEY. PVT, CO H. Age 17. 5ft 8in. Gray eyes. Light hair. Light comp. Laborer. Enr 15 Aug 1862, Decauter Twp. Mus 7 Sept 1862, Camp Ironton. Oct-Dec 1862: abs det 8 Oct 1862, artillery service. Sept-Oct 1863: on duty in scouting co. June 1864: abs left sick 31 May, Meadow Bluff, WVa. Shown on mus roll of stragglers and deserters forwarded from Columbus, Ohio to Wheeling, WVa dated 4 Aug 1864 shown as straggler. Shown on list of prisoners confined in military prison, Wheeling, WVa (aka Atheneum Prison) dated 5 Aug 1864. Listed as straggler, sent 7 Aug 1864, Cumberland, Md. July-Aug 1864: abs sick 31 May, Gallipolis Hosp. Jan 1865: adm USA Post Hosp, Martinsburg, WVa from provost guard, Martinsburg with fever. Trans 9 Mar 1865, Gen Hosp, Harper's Ferry. Adm Island (Field) Hosp, Harper's Ferry with chronic diarrhea. Trans 13 Mar 1965, Gen Hosp, Frederick, Md. May 1865: abs sick 16 Mar 1865, Frederick City, Md adm 13 Mar from field with incipient phthisis pul. Indolent ulcers of face and chronic diarrhea. Trans 10 Apr 1865, Gen Hosp, Gallipolis. Disch 29 May, USA Gen Hosp, Gallipolis, Ohio for dis for chronic diarrhea and incipient phthisis pul. [wasting]. Bur Mequinn Cem, Decateur Twp, Lawrence Co, Ohio.

MASSIE, MOSES P. PVT, CO A. Age 20. 5ft 7in. Blue eyes. Light hair. Light comp. *b* Gallia Co, Ohio. Farmer. Enr 8 Aug 1862, Gallipolis, Ohio, 3 years. Mus 7 Sept 1862, Camp Ironton. Sept-Oct 1863: abs in scouting co. Jan 1864: adm regt hosp with pneumonia. Feb-June 1864: abs sick 16 Feb 1864, USA Gen Hosp, Gallipolis, Ohio as conval for pneumonia. July 1864: loss, 28 June 1864 Gallipolis, Ohio. *d* 30 May 1864 of typhoid fever.

MAY, WILLIAM. PVT (1ST SGT), CO I. Age 29. 6ft 2½in. Blue eyes. Brown hair. Fair comp. *b* Guernsey Co, Ohio. Cabinetmaker. Enr 11 Aug 1862, Winchester, 3 years. Mus 7 Sept 1862, Camp Ironton. 1st sgt from organization until 22 Oct 1862. Oct 1862: loss 22 Oct, Red House. Fell out of ranks sick. Not heard from. Nov 1862-Feb 1863: supposed to be capt by the enemy 22 Oct 1862, Red House, Kanawha Valley, Va. 10 Apr 1863: to labor 30 days and forfeit 4 months pay under sentence of GCM for abs without leave. May 1863: Fayetteville, Va. Ret from desertion. Abs in confinement 16 Mar 1863, Fayetteville, Va. Sept-Oct 1863: on duty in scouting co. June 1864: AWOL 16 June 1864. July 1864: loss 16 June, Peaks of Otter, Des. Nov 1864: gain from desertion and reported POW capt by the enemy 16 June. POW record shows him capt 15 June 1864, Liberty, Va. Escaped 12 Sept 1864 near Augusta, Ga. Reported 8 Nov 1864, Knoxville, Tenn. Sent 8-11 Nov 1864, regt. Descr book shows him capt 15 June 1864 near Lynchburg. Escaped from prison 7 Sept 1864. Rejoined for duty Dec 1864. Erroneously reported deserter. *d* 23 June 1891 at home in Winchester, Adams Co, Ohio of consumption and hemorrhaging of the lungs. Disease was contracted while a POW at Andersonville, Ga.

MCKEE, SAMUEL (L). PVT, CO I. Age 18. 5ft 8½in. Gray eyes. Black hair. Fair comp. *b* Adams Co, Ohio. Farmer. Enr 11 Aug 1862, Winchester, 3 years. Mus 7 Sept 1862, Camp Ironton, Ohio. Oct-Dec 1862: abs det for artillery service since 8 Oct 1862. Sept-Oct 1863: on duty in scouting co. June 1864: loss 17 June 1864, Lynchburg. KIA.

METCALF, ARTHUR (J). PVT (CPL), CO K. Age 19. 6ft 1½in. Blue eyes. Auburn hair. Fair comp. *b* Jackson, Ohio. Farmer. Enr 31 July 1862, Jackson CH, 3 years. Mus 7 Sept 1862, Camp Ironton, Ohio. July 1863: AWOL since 27 July 1863, Ohio. Oct 1863: on duty in scouting co. Prom cpl 16 Dec 1864. *d* 24 Apr 1908 at his house in Barton Co, Mo.

MOORE, JOHN W. PVT, CO I. Age 28. 5ft 9in. Blue eyes. Brown hair. Light comp. *b* Adams Co, Ohio. Saddler. Enr 11 Aug 1862, Winchester, 3 years. Mus 7 Sept 1862, Camp Ironton. Sept 1862: on duty butcher in QM Dept. Oct 1862: adm 10 Oct 1862, regt hosp with febris remittents. Ret to duty 15 Oct. Abs sick, Pt Pleasant Hosp with chronic diarrhea since 19 Oct. Ret to duty 4 Nov. Dec 1862-Feb 1863: abs diarrhea, Pt Pleasant Hosp since 6 Dec 1862. Mar 1863: loss 6 Mar 1863, Pt Pleasant, des from hosp. Apr 1863: Summersville, Va, ret from desertion. June 1863: on duty in regt hosp. Sept 1863: on duty in scouting co. 30 Oct 1863: morning report shows him reported for duty in co from daily duty in scouting party. Feb 1864: on duty scout. Mar-June 1864: abs on ds scout since 22 Feb 1864 by GO 2 of Gen Crook. Ret to regt by Cpt Blazer 2 Aug 1864 for "cowardice." Sept-Oct 1864: abs nurse in field hosp since 19 Sept 1864. Nov 1864: abs with leave on furl since 29 Nov. This furl was to accompany Lt C. A. Hall who had been wounded to his home. Dec 1864: on duty orderly at Div HQ. Feb-May 1865: on duty in QM Dept.

NEARY, GREEN S. PVT, CO F. Age 18. 5ft 9½in. Blue eyes. Dark hair. Light comp. *b* 12 Mar 1844, Harrisonville (now Minford), Scioto Co, Ohio. Farmer. Enr 6 Aug 1862, Harrison Twp, 3 years. Mus 7 Sept 1862, Camp Ironton. Oct 1862: abs sick Charleston hosp since 30 Oct. Sept 1863: on duty musician in scouting co. Oct-Dec 1863: on duty musician. Jan 1864: on duty in regt band 16 Sept 1863. Feb-June 1864: on duty musician. July 1864: loss 24 July 1864, Winchester. MIA Kernstown. Nov 1864: gain, taken up from MIA reported POW. Nov 1864-Mar 1865: abs POW, capt by the enemy 24 July 1864. POW record shows him adm 31 Dec 1864, hosp, Danville, Va with catarrhus. Ret 3 Feb 1865 to prison. Present there 14 Feb 1865. Brought from Danville and confined 19 Feb 1865, Richmond. Par 22 Feb 1865, James River, Va. Reported 22 Feb 1865, CGB. Sent to Hosp 2, Annapolis, Md for gen debility. Furl 4 Mar 1865, 30 days. Present. Mus for commutation of rations 24 Feb 1865 Hosp Div 2. Trans 14 Mar 1865, CCO. Reported 4 Apr 1865, Columbus, Ohio. Sent 4 Apr 1865, Pro Mar and forwarded to Wheeling the same day. Postwar occ: building turnpikes, road and bridge construction. Also operated a farm. Served as co commissioner in 1900 for 6 years. Member of Bailey Post GAR. Post cmmdr and deputy post cmmdr at time of death. Member of Manly ME Church. Masonic Lodge. *d* 29 Oct 1936. Bur Memorial Park, Portsmouth, Ohio.

NIDAY, HARVEY W. CPL, CO B. Age 23. 5ft 11in. Blue eyes. Dark hair. Light comp. *b* Gallia Co, Ohio. Farmer. Enr 22 July 1862, Gallipolis, 3 years. Mus 7 Sept 1862, Camp Ironton. Sept-Oct 1863: on duty in scouting co. Morning report for Nov1863 shows him reported for duty from scouts. Apr 1864: abs with leave by permission of Col White since 22 Apr 1864. July 1864: abs sick 30 July 1864, left at Harper's Ferry, Va. Sept 1864: loss 19 Sept, Winchester, Va. Killed by gunshot, Battle of Winchester. Effects 1 watch and $3.00 notes.

O'RORICK, JAMES. 1ST CPL (SGT), CO K. Age 27. 5ft 11in. Light eyes. Sandy hair. Light comp. *b* Jackson Co, Ohio. Farmer. Enr 27 July 1862, Jackson CH, 3 years. Appt 1st cpl 22 Aug 1862. Mus 7 Sept 1862, Camp Ironton. July 1863: AWOL since 27 July 1863, Ohio. Sept-Oct 1863: on duty in scouting co. Prom sgt 23 Sept 1864 vice Milton Brown, prom. Postwar occ: ironworker (founder), Tecumseh Furnace, Ala. *d* 14 May 1885, Tecumseh Furnace, Ala.

OLIVER, HIRAM. PVT, CO H. Age 33. 6ft 1in. Blue eyes. Dark hair. Dark comp. *b* Jackson Co, Ohio. Farmer. Enr 14 Aug 1862, Waverly, 3 years. Mus 7 Sept 1862, Camp Ironton, Ohio. Sept-Oct 1863: on duty in scouting co. Dec 1863: on furl at home in Ohio 19 Dec 1863-3 Jan 1864. July 1864: wounded in action 20 July 1864, Stephenson's Depot, Winchester, Va in arm slight. MIA 20 July 1864, Winchester and Martinsburg. Suffered contusion of left foot 22 Sept 1864, Fisher's Hill. Dec 1864: abs sick Gallipolis, Ohio since 8 July 1864. Jan-Feb 1865: abs sick home in Ohio on surgeon's cert 10 Nov 1864. Apr-May 1865: abs sick 3 Apr 1865, USA Gen Hosp, Cumberland, Md. Disch 29 May 1865, USA Gen Hosp, Cumberland, Md. *d* 28 Jan 1902. Bur Mt Zion Cem, Franklin Twp, Jackson Co, Ohio.

PARKS, JAMES H. PVT (CPL), CO F. Age 21. 6ft 1in. Blue eyes. Dark hair. Light comp. *b* 21 July 1841, Jackson Co, Ohio. Farmer. Enr 6 Aug 1862, Harrison Twp. Mus 7 Sept 1862, Camp Ironton, Ohio. Sept-Oct 1863: on duty in scouting co. Appt cpl 24 Mar 1864 vice J. H. A. Colley. July 1864: wounded in action, Stephenson's Depot, Winchester, Va. Rec GSW to the right arm at the elbow joint. Med card shows adm 23 July 1864, USA Gen Hosp, Cumberland, Md with GS fracture of right humerus caused by musket ball. July-Aug 1864: abs sick USA Gen Hosp, Cumberland, Md. Trans 27 Sept 1864, Gen Hosp, Parkersburg. Disch for dis 29 May 1865, Gen Hosp, Parkersburg. Sept 1864-Apr 1865: present USA Gen Hosp, Parkersburg. *d* 28 June 1917.

PETERS, ELISHA B. PVT, CO C. Age 18. 6ft 1in. Black eyes. Black hair. Dark comp. *b* 5 Feb 1844, Pike Co, Ohio. Farmer. Enr 8 Aug 1862, Valley Twp, 3 years. Mus 7 Sept 1862, Camp Ironton, Ohio. May 1863: abs sick 18 May 1863, Charleston Hosp. June 1863: abs sick 18 May, Gallipolis Hosp. Feb 1864: abs with leave on furl until 29 Feb 1864. Aug-Dec 1864: abs det scout in ind scouting co since 11 Feb 1864. Shown on mus roll for July-Aug 1864 det 25 Aug 1864 div scout. *d* 17 June 1867.

RICKABAUGH, JOHN H. PVT, CO K. Age 18. 6ft ½in. Blue eyes. Light hair. Fair comp. *b* Jackson, Ohio. Farmer. Enr 15 Aug 1862, Jackson CH, Ohio, 3 years. Mus 7 Sept 1862, Camp Ironton, Ohio. Sept-Oct 1863: on duty in scouting co. Apr 1864: adm 7 Apr 1864, regt hosp with measles. Ret to duty 11 Apr. Aug 1864: abs sick 19 Aug 1864, Harper's Ferry (USA Field Hosp), Sandy Hook, Md. Sept 1864: abs sick 31 Aug 1864, Annapolis, Md. Oct 1864: *d* 8 Oct 1864, Frederick USA Gen Hosp, Winchester of acute dysentery. Bur area outside hosp cem, Frederick, Md. Single at time of death. Descr book shows him "*d* Nov. 7, 1864 at Frederick, Md. Bur. Antietam Nat. Cem., Lot C, Grave 117."

ROBERTS, DAVID. PVT, CO G. Age 21. 6ft. Gray eyes. Black hair. Light comp. *b* Pike Co, Ohio. Farmer. Enr 7 Aug 1862, Omega, PCO (Sharonville), 3 years. Oct 1863: on duty in scouting co. May 1864: abs sick left in regt camp 3 May 1864, Fayetteville, Va. June 1864: adm USA

John and Elvira Sheppard
Courtesy Franklin Sheppard

Gen Hosp from Post Hosp, Charleston, W Va with measles. Ret to duty 19 Nov 1864. Furl 3 Nov 1864, readm 12 Nov 1864. May-Oct 1864: abs hosp, Gallipolis. Des 8 July 1864, readm from des 26 July 1864.

SHEPARD, JOHN. PVT, CO K. Age 23. 5ft 10in. Blue eyes. Dark hair. Fair comp. *b* Jackson, Ohio. Farmer. Enr 7 Aug 1862, Jackson CH, 3 years. Mus 7 Sept 1862, Camp Ironton, Ohio. July 1863: AWOL since 27 July 1862, Ohio. Sept-Oct 1863: on duty in scouting co. Bur New Hope Baptist Church Cem near Long Lane, Mo.

SCHULTZ, JACOB. PVT, CO C. Age 23. 5ft 6in. Blue eyes. Light hair. Light comp. *b* 4 Sept 1838, Scioto Co, Ohio. Farmer. Enr 21 July 1862, Valley Twp, 3 years. Mus 7 Sept 1862, Camp Ironton. Feb-June 1863: on duty regt teamster. July-Aug 1863: abs ds brig teamster since 1 July 1863 by order of Col White. Sept-Oct 1863: on duty in scouting co. Det scout 12 Sept 1863. Feb 1864: on duty QM Dept. Feb 1864: noted div scout. Mar-Dec 1864: abs ds in ind scouting co since 22 Feb 1864 by order of Gen Crook. Capt 19 Nov 1864, Kabletown. POW record shows him confined 22 Nov, Richmond brought from Gordonsville. Par 15 Feb 1865, Richmond, Va and sent 19 Feb 1865, CCO where he reported 24 Feb 1865. Furl 26 Feb 1865, 30 days. Ret 31 Mar 1865 and sent 5 Apr 1865, Pro Mar. John W. Overturf remembered him as "a brave and efficient soldier." He was selected to be a Blazer's Scout as "a man whose bravery and efficiency could not be questioned." *d* 7 June 1926, Lucasville, Ohio.

Jacob ("Jake") Schultz
Courtesy Tom Adkins and Helen Schultz

Lewis and Elizabeth Slagle
Postwar photo of Lewis and Elizabeth Slagle taken at the C. L. Brown Studio in LaFarge, Wisconsin.
Courtesy Helen Hagen

SKELTON, SAMUEL M. PVT, CO F. Age 18. 5ft 5½in. Blue eyes. Light hair. Light comp. *b* Lawrence Co, Ohio. Farmer. Enr 28 Aug 1862, Green Twp, 3 years. May 1863: abs sick 12 May 1863, Gallipolis Hosp. Mar 1864: abs with leave on furl at home in Ohio 28 Mar-12 Apr 1864. June-Dec 1864: abs ds in ind scouting co since 8 Feb 1864 by order of Gen Crook. Postwar occ: farmer. *d* 29 Dec 1919, Portsmouth, Ohio.

SLAGLE, JOHN. CPL, CO D. Age 33. 6ft. Gray eyes. Black hair. Fair comp. *b* 3 Feb 1829, Gallia Co, Ohio. Farmer. Enr 6 Aug 1862, Symms, Ohio, 3 years. Nov 1862-Jan 1863: on duty wood chopper. Appt cpl 1 May 1863. Sept 1863 (cpl)-Oct 1863 (pvt): on duty in scouting co. Morning report shows him det scout. Dec 1863: abs furl at home in Ohio 20 Dec 1863-11 Jan 1864 (cpl). May 1864: on duty pioneer. Mar-May 1865: abs sick 18 Mar 1865, Cumberland, Md. Mus roll also shows sick hosp, Clarysville, Md. Disch per GO 77 AGO Series 1865, Cumberland, Md 2 June 1865. Postwar occ: farmer. *d* 15 June 1914, Gallia Co, Ohio. Bur Salem, Ohio.

SLAGLE, LEWIS. CPL (PVT), CO D. Age 21. 6ft. Gray eyes. Black hair. Dark comp. *b* 23 Jan 1841, Gallia Co, Ohio. Farmer. Enr 6 Aug 1862, Symms, Ohio, 3 years. Mus 7 Sept 1862, Camp Ironton, Ohio. Sept 1863: on duty in scouting co. Oct 1863 (cpl): on duty in scouting co. Dec 1863 (pvt): abs furl at home in Ohio 26 Dec 1863-11 Jan 1864. May 1864: on duty pioneer. July-Sept 1864: abs sick 8 July 1864, hosp, Gallipolis, Ohio and adm from field 2 July 1864 with burn of right foot. Ret to duty 2 Aug 1864. Apr 1865: on duty pioneer. May 1865: abs det at HQ, 1st Brig, 4th Prov Div, Army of Shenandoah, Staunton, Va since 3 May 1865. Postwar occ: farmer. Member of GAR post La Farge. "Mr. Slagle was an honest and upright citizen, a kind and loving husband and father." *d* 4 Apr 1921, Mendota, Wis. Bur Chapel Hill Cem, La Farge, Wis.

SMITH, JOHN. PVT, CO H. Age 26. 6ft 2½in. Black eyes. Dark hair. Light comp. *b* Scioto Co, Ohio. Collier. Enr 12 Aug 1862, Washington, Ohio, 3 years. Mus 7 Sept 1862, Camp Ironton, Ohio. Nov 1863: abs with leave on furl 19 Nov-2 Dec 1863 at home in Lawrence Co, Ohio. Dec 1863 (cpl): abs sick 12 May 1863, Gallipolis Hosp. Feb 1864 (pvt): on duty scout. Mar-Nov 1864: abs ds in ind scouting co by GO 2 of Gen Crook 15 Feb 1864. Capt 19 Nov 1864, Kabletown. Dec

1864-May 1865: abs POW. POW record shows him confined 22 Nov, Richmond, Va brought from Gordonsville. Par 15 Feb 1865, Richmond, Va (Pemberton). Reported 1 Mar 1865, CCO as par POW. Furl 1 Mar 1865, 30 days. Mus out 12 July 1865, CCO by order of War Dept. Disch agreeable to GO 77 date AGO War Dept 28 Apr 1865. Entitled to 3 months extra pay per order of Sec of War dated 31 May 1865.

SNEDIGER, FRANKLIN (FRANK). PVT, CO F. Age 17. 5ft 3¾in. Blue eyes. Light hair. Light comp. *b* Scioto Co, Ohio. Farmer. Enr 2 Aug 1862, Green Twp, 3 years. Sept-Oct 1863: on duty in scouting co. *d* 20 May 1905.

SNYDER, JOHN HENRY. PVT, CO D. Age 18. 5ft 5in. Gray eyes. Dark hair. Fair comp. *b* Braxton Co, Va. Farmer. Enr 31 July 1862, Unionville, Ohio. Mus 7 Sept 1862. Oct 1863: on duty in scouting co. Morning report shows him det scout 8 Oct 1863 and ret to co 10 Nov by order of Lt Blazer. Aug-Oct 1864: abs sick 18 July 1864, Harper's Ferry, Va. Nov 1864-Feb 1865: abs sick 9 Aug 1864, Sandy Hook, Md. Mar-May 1865: abs sick 25 Aug or 26 July 1864, Harper's Ferry, Va. Claims to have been in Harper's Ferry hosp for mumps and "took cold." Moved to Sandy Hook due to overcrowding and then taken to a private home and cared for by "an old woman." Upon returning to his regt he claimed that he and two others were capt by Mosby's men and he was wounded in the leg. After 3 or 4 days he escaped and returned to the private house. Never attempted to get back to his regt. POW record shows no record subsequent to 18 Aug 1864. AG 88 Roll for Aug 64-June 65 reports "absent sick at Sandy Hook, Md." "Dishonorably disch. 1-4-68 to date June 24'65 with loss of pay. Application for removal of etc. denied." AG 93 "The dishonorable discharge was based upon a misconception & is null and void & the final record is—a deserter." Apparently never rec a pension due to record of deserter, even though many citizens testified to his status as an honorable citizen.

THOMPSON, JOHN. PVT, CO D. Age 26. 5ft 9in. Gray eyes. Light hair. Light comp. *b* 28 Sept 1832, Cabell Co, Va. Farmer. Enr 2 Aug 1862, Rome, Ohio, 3 years. Det scout by GO 2, 16 Feb 1864, Charleston, WVa. Capt 18 Nov 1864, Kabletown. Claimed horse was shot and fell on him injuring left shoulder. Exch 1 Mar 1865. Nov and Dec 1864: abs in the hands of the enemy since 18 Nov 1864. Confined 22 Nov 1864, Richmond, Va. Par 5 Feb 1865, Cox's Wharf, Va. Sent from Camp Parole, Md to CCO 16 Feb 1865 where he arrived 29 Feb 1865. Furl 23 Feb 1865, 30 days. Ret 6 May 1865. Mus out 15 June 1865, Columbus, Ohio by order of War Dept. *d* 29 Aug 1916.

TREACHNOR, GREENLEAF N. PVT, CO I. Age 19. 5ft 9½in. Gray eyes. Brown hair. Dark comp. *b* 22 Sept 1841, Adams Co, Ohio. Farmer. Enr 11 Aug 1862, Winchester, Ohio, 3 years. Mus 7 Sept 1862, Camp Ironton, Ohio. Dec 1862 (pvt) and Jan 1863 (cpl): det post teamster since 27 Dec 1862. Reduced to ranks by his own request 26 Dec 1862. Apr 1863: abs post wagoner 27 Dec 1862. Sept-Oct 1863: on duty in scouting co. *d* 29 Apr 1933, Norwood, Ohio.

VOLGAMERE (VOLGAMORE, VULGANORE), CHARLES. PVT, CO C. Age 18. 5ft 6in. Dark eyes. Dark hair. Dark comp. *b* Pike Co, Ohio. Farmer. Enr 2 Aug 1862, Valley, Ohio, 3 years. Mus 7 Sept 1862, Camp Ironton. Sept-Oct 1863: on duty in scouting co. Apr 1864: loss 18 Apr 1864, Fayetteville, WVa. *d* of typhoid pneumonia in hosp. Effects included testament, blank book, and buck gloves.

WALKER, JOHN. PVT, CO B. Age 18. 5ft 4in. Hazel eyes. Light hair. Light comp. *b* Gallia Co, Ohio. Laborer. Enr 23 July 1862, Gallipolis, Ohio, 3 years. Mus 7 Sept 1862, Camp Ironton, Ohio. July 1863: abs on ds guarding prisoners to CCO since 24 July 1863 by SO 74 of Col Turley. Sept-Oct 1863: on duty in scouting co. Morning report for Nov 1863 shows him ret from duty scout. Aug-Dec 1864: abs det in ind scouting co since 8 Feb 1864. Det 24 Aug by order of Maj Gen Crook. *d* 14 Sept 1917, Gallipolis, Ohio. "One of Cpt. Blazer's Brave Soldiers." "It is said by those who know that he was a splendid, fearless soldier." Postwar occ: cook on the river. "He was a kind-hearted man, a good friend, and a loving father and husband."

WHITE, ANDREW J. PVT, CO A. Age 27. 5ft 10in. Hazel eyes. Dark hair. Light comp. *b* Cline Co, Pa. Farmer. Enr 4 Aug 1862, Gallipolis, Ohio, 3 years. Mus 7 Sept 1862, Ironton, Ohio. Oct 1863: on duty in scouting co. Morning report for 23 Oct 1863 shows him det to scouting party. Mar-June 1864: on duty in provost guard. July 1864: loss 28 June 1864, Beverly, Va. *d* of typhoid fever.

WICKLINE, ISAAC. PVT, CO H. Age 20. 5ft 11½in. Black eyes. Dark hair. Dark comp. *b* 10 Nov 1841, Gallia Co, Ohio. Farmer. Enr 12 Aug 1862, Raccoon Island, Gallia Co, Ohio, 3 years. Mus 7 Sept 1862, Camp Ironton, Ohio. Sept 1863: on duty in scouting co. May 1864: abs sick left in regt camp 3 May 1864, Fayetteville, WVa. *d* 3 Dec 1920, Richmond Dale, Ohio.

WILLIAMS, GEORGE P. PVT, CO A. Age 18. 5ft 3½in. Blue eyes. Dark hair. Dark comp. *b* Greenbrier, Va. Farmer. Enr 9 Aug 1862, Gallipolis, Ohio, 3 years. Mus 27 Dec 1862, Fayetteville, Va. Sept 1862: gain 9 Aug. Enl in the regt. Abs from mus. July 1863: abs on ds guarding prisoners to CCO since 24 July 1863 by SO 74 of Col Turley. Sept 1863: on duty in scouting co. Morning report for 5 Oct, Fayetteville, Va shows him ret to co from scouting party. Jan.1864: on duty QM Dept as teamster. Feb-Apr 1864: on duty QM Dept. Mar and Apr 1865: on duty QM Dept.

WILSON, CLARK. PVT, CO C. Age 32. 6ft. Dark eyes. Dark hair. Dark comp. *b* Scioto Co, Ohio. Farmer. Enr 4 Aug 1862, Union, Ohio, 3 years. Mus 7 Sept 1862, Camp Ironton, Ohio. Jan 1863: loss 31 Jan 1863, des. Feb 1863: gain 25 Feb 1863, Fayetteville, Va. Ret from desertion. Abs sick at home, Scioto Co, Ohio, surgeon's cert, 25 Feb 1863. Mar-Apr: abs sick at home in Scioto Co, Ohio, surgeon's cert, 8 Jan 1863. Sept-Oct 1863: on duty in scouting co. June-Aug 1864: abs sick left 31 May 1864, Meadow Bluff. Sept 1864: abs sick 9 July 1864, hosp, Gallipolis, Ohio. Oct 1864-Jan 1865: abs sick since 9 July 1864, Gallipolis, Ohio. Mus rolls show him in Co A, Prov Battalion, composed of convals of various regts during Sept-Oct 1864. "This battalion was organized from convalescent exch. men and stragglers for guard duty by SO No. 152, dated Camp Parole July 8, 1864. It was relieved from such duty by SO No. 283, dated District of Annapolis, Md., Dec. 7, 1864, which directed the officers and men to be forwarded to their respective commands.—R. and P. 384-890." Feb-Mar 1865: abs sick, Charleston since 8 July 1864. Apr and May 1865: abs sick 25 Aug 1864, Annapolis, Md. Adm 1 Mar 1865, Camp Parole USA Gen Hosp from Camp Parole. Disch in accordance with telegram AGO Washington, DC 4 May 1865. Postwar occ: farmer.

WISEMAN, SAMUEL V (VINTON). PVT (CPL), CO D. Age 18. 5ft 7⅛in. Dark eyes. Black hair. Dark comp. *b* 24 Sept 1843, Lawrence Co, Ohio. Farmer. Enr 6 Aug 1862, Symms, Ohio, 3 years. Mus 7 Sept 1862, Camp Ironton, Ohio. Sept-Oct 1863: on duty in scouting co. Apr 1864: adm regt hosp for measles. May 1864: abs sick left 3 May 1864, regt camp, Fayetteville, WVa. Appt cpl 1 Jan 1865. Postwar occ: physician. Graduated from the Miami Medical College in 1877. "Member of F. & A.M. [Masons] and George H. Thomas Post GAR and is a Republican." *d* 3 July 1924, Cincinnati, Ohio.

WOODS, JACOB B. PVT, CO E. Age 19. 6ft. Blue eyes. Dark hair. Dark comp. *b* 4 Apr 1843, Hamilton Co, Ohio. Farmer. Enr 6 Aug 1862, Spriggs (Bentonville), Ohio, 3 years. Mus 7

Dr. Samuel Vinton Wiseman
Courtesy Dr. James Wiseman

Sept 1862, Camp Ironton. Oct 1863: on duty in scouting co. Mar 1864: abs on furl at home in Ohio 28 Mar-12 Apr 1864. May 1864: on duty pioneer. Postwar occ: farmer. *d* 6 Jan 1930, Cincinnati, Ohio.

YARINGTON, WESLEY. PVT, CO G. Age 21. (5ft 6½in) 5ft 9in. Blue eyes. Light hair. Light comp. *b* 4 Oct 1841, Carrollton, Carroll Co, Ohio. Farmer. Enr 8 Aug 1862, Waverly, Ohio, 3 years. Mus 7 Sept 1862, Ironton, Ohio. July 1863: AWOL since 27 July 1863, Ohio. Sept 1863: co morning report shows him det scout 12 Sept. June 1864: abs sick 30 June 1864, Charleston Hosp. Wounded in action 17 June 1864, Lynchburg, flesh wound of right thigh by a shell. July 1864: abs sick 2 July, Gallipolis Hosp. Aug-Oct 1864: abs sick sent to hosp, Gallipolis, Ohio prior to 8 July 1864. Mar 1865: abs sick 29 Mar 1865, Cumberland, Md. Shown on list of deserters, USA Gen Hosp, Gallipolis, Ohio dated 30 Sept 1864. Des 21 Sept 1864. *d* 21 Mar 1931, Bellflower, Ill.

2d WVa Cavalry

Organized Sept-Nov 1861, Parkersburg, WVa. Mus out 30 June 1865, Wheeling, WVa.

ABLE, JESSE. SGT, CO A. Age 27. 5ft 8in. Dark comp. Brown eyes. Dark hair. *b* Monongalia Co, Va. Enl 1 Sept 1861, Ironton, Ohio, 3 years. Prom 4th duty sgt 22 July 1862. Furnished his own horse and equipment since Jan 1864. Horse valued at $140 by a board of officers by order of Gen Crook on 13 Aug 1864. 14 Feb 1864: det to scout by order of Gen Crook. Mar 1864: abs det in ind scouting co by order of Gen Crook since 1 Mar 1864. Apr-Oct 1864: abs det in ind scouting co by order of Gen Duffie. Reported sick. On leave Nov 1864 and mus out 29 Nov 1864.

BYERS, JAMES F. PVT, CO F. Age 20. 5ft 10½in. Light comp. Blue eyes. Light hair. *b* Morrow Co, Ohio. Boatman. Enl 5 Sept 1861, Zanesville, Ohio. Aug 1862: abs under sentence of GCM for getting drunk on duty and deserting his picket post. Sentenced to serve remainder of enl without pay. Mar 1864: abs in ind scouts by order of Gen Crook since 1 Mar 1864. Apr 1864:

shown det in ind scouts. Capt 8 May 1864, Locus Lain [*sic*], Va. Casualty list shows him MIA, Big Sewell Mt. Delivered 18 Feb 1865, Charleston, SC. Mus out 30 June 1865, Wheeling, WVa as vet prisoner. *d* 15 Mar 1875 near Mt Sterling, Muskingum Co, Ohio.

DAVIS, BARTON. CPL, CO K. Age 18. 5ft 9in. Fair comp. Light hair. *b* Pleasants Co, Va. Laborer. Enl 24 Oct 1861, Parkersburg, Va. Co mus roll dated 8 Nov 1861, 3 years, Camp Toland, Va. Prom cpl 1 Aug 1863. Vet vol reenl 18 Nov 1865, Charleston, WVa. Shown on ds ind scout May 1864. Appt cpl, Co E upon consol of Co E and Co K, Martinsburg, WVa, Nov 1864. Furl to Ironton, Ohio Nov 1865 on reenl. Listed des while on a scout in det of Lt E. A. Rasser, 22 Dec 1864, Camp Russell, Va with horse and full equipment. Charge of desertion was removed per SO 119, dated HQ Middle Dept, Baltimore, Md. Erroneously listed as deserter. Value of horse and equipment $30.00. One Spencer carbine approx $25.00.

DORAN, WILLIAM. PVT, CO G. Age 26. 5ft 5in. Gray eyes. Brown hair. Light comp. *b* Indiana Co, Pa. Teamster. Enl 28 Aug 1861, Ironton, Ohio, 3 years. Oct and Nov 1862: det blacksmith. Dec 1862 and Jan 1863: det teamster. Apr and May 1863: confined Charleston since 27 Apr 1863. MIA 4 July 1863 near Fayattesville on the Raleigh Rd. Listed as des 10 Aug 1863 and par POW records show him confined until 11 July 1863, Richmond, Va. Ret from MIA 1 Oct 1863. Furl as vet vol 4 Jan 1864 to Lawrence Co, Ohio, 30 days. Feb 1864: abs furl to Ironton, Ohio, 30 days from 2 Feb 1864. Apr-June 1864: abs on ds with the ind scouting co since 1 Mar 1864. Order dated 5 Apr 1864, HQ 3rd div, Dept of War, Va to Col Powell commanding 2nd WVa directs, "You will please direct that William Doran, Co. G, 2nd Va. Cav. report without delay to Lieut. Blazer Comdg Scouts for duty blacksmith. By Command of Brig. Gen. George Crook, Jas L. Botsford Adj. gen." Nov. 1864: trans to Co E from Co G. 19 Dec 1864: at Camp Russell, Va reported as des with horse and full equipment including Spencer carbine. Ret from desertion 5 Jan, Camp Averell, Va. Forfeited one month's pay by order of CM in accordance with GO 19. Jan and Feb 1865: on det duty teamster Brig HQ by order of Col Copeland. Mar and Apr 1865: abs at Brig HQ. In hosp, Alexandria, Va 7 June 1865 with broken collar bone from a fall. Disch 20 July 1865. Mus out 15 July 1865, Washington, DC. William J. Kirkendall remembered him as "a first class soldier seldom complaining always ready for duty. Brave, prompt, but not very strong." *d* 7 May 1871, Elizabeth Twp, Lawrence Co, near Ironton, Ohio.

DUNKLE, HENRY. PVT, CO D. Age 22. 5ft 8in. Brown eyes. Black hair. Dark comp. Farmer. Enl 20 Sept 1861, McArthur, Ohio, 3 years. Nov-Dec 1861: abs sick. Jan-Feb 1862: present, was arrested for being AWOL—same to 30 June 1863. July 63: furl on surgeon's recommendation 1-29 July 1863. AWOL. Det to pioneer corps since 10 Jan 1864. Carried as pioneer on mus rolls to May 1864. Det ind scout since 1 May 1864. July 1864: on ds with pioneers. Mus for May and June 1864 show he furnished own horse and equipment since 31 Dec 1863, 152 days. Sept and Oct 1864: abs dismount camp since 1 Aug 1864. Brother Amos served in the same co. Mus out Nov 1864, Wheeling. *d* 27 Dec 1903, South Topeka, Kans. Interred Rochester Cem on GAR plot.

HARVEY, JOHN. CPL, CO G. Age 34. Gray eyes. Gray hair. Light comp. *b* Jefferson Co, Ohio. Laborer. Enl 28 Aug 1861, Ironton, Ohio, 3 years. Appt cpl Sept 1861. Reduced to ranks 25 Nov 1861. Oct 1862: confined Pt Pleasant, Va. Des from Camp Piatt 25 Feb 1863. Ret from desertion 29 May 1863. Abs confined in brig guard house, Charleston, WVa since 21 Oct 1863. Reenl 20 Jan 1864, vet vol, Fayette CH. Abs on furl as vet vol since 7 Jan 1864. Mar 1864: abs det duty in ind scouts by order of Gen Crook since 1 Mar 1864. Shown on ds through May 1864. Ret to regt by order of Lt Blazer for getting drunk 7 June 1864. Sept 1864: noted he is due for horse and horse equipment furnished by him for 6 months. Nov 1864: trans to Co E. Dec 1864: on det duty by order of Col Capehart. Jan 1865: on det duty, brig HQ. Feb 1865: abs remount camp. Mar 1865: abs brig HQ. Apr 1865: serving at brig HQ, teamster. Charge of desertion was removed by act of Congress 5 July 1884. Also served in 18th OVI. *d* 19 July 1907.

MITCHELL, JAMES B. PVT, CO C. Age 24. 5ft 5in. Blue eyes. Light hair. Fair comp. *b* Monroe Co, Ohio. Wagonmaker. Enr 30 July 1863, Camp Piatt, Va, 3 years. Mus 28 Aug 1863, Camp Piatt to date 30 July 1863. Nov-Dec 1863: furnished his own horse and horse equipment since Nov 1863.

> Station: Pittsburg, Pa.
> Date: 1 Aug 1864
> Reported 1 Aug 1864, Mil Post, Pittsburgh, Pa.

Remarks: says he left regt between Chambersburg and Shippensburg about 27 July 1864. Reported at this HQ voluntarily for return transportation. Thinks regt is at Charles Town, WVa. July-Oct 1864: appears on list of prisoners confined 1 Aug 1864, Mil Prison, Wheeling, WVa (aka Atheneum Prison). Arrested by Pro Mar, Pittsburgh, Pa. "Straggler. Sent to Cumberland, Md. Aug 2/64." Det ind scout by order of Brig Gen Crook. Jan-Feb 1865: at remount camp, Md. Mar-Apr 1865: at remount camp, City Pt, Va [also shown as Pleasant Valley, Md. This is probably correct]. Co mus out roll dated 20 Nov 1864: recruit. (Not) mus out term of enl not having expired. Jan 1864: abs vet vol furl to Monroe Co, Ohio. Dec 1864: abs sick Grafton, Va [WVa]. Co mus out roll dated 30 June 1865, Wheeling mus out to date 30 June 1865

NUNNENMAKER, JOHN (H). SGT, CO D. Age 21. 5ft 8½in. Dark comp. Brown eyes. Dark hair. *b* Vinton Co, Ohio. Farmer. Enl 15 Sept 1861, McArthur, Ohio. Mus out 2 Dec 1864 and reenl as vet vol. Abs det to ind scouts 30 May 1864. Prom cpl 1 June 1864. Killed by a shell from the enemy 28 Mar 1865, Petersburg, Va.

PRICE, DAVID. PVT, CO B. Age 32. 5ft 4in. Hazel eyes. Brown hair. Dark comp. *b* Ashville, NC. Blacksmith. Enr 20 Apr 1863, Camp Piatt, WVa, 3 years. Mus 28 Aug 1863, Camp Piatt. 5 June 1863: des at Camp Piatt. 12 July 1863: ret from desertion. Sept 1863: abs on ds since 14 Sept 1863 being sent on scout under command of Lt J. B. Carlisle to Va and Tenn Railroad by order of Brig Gen E. P. Scammon, commanding 3 div 8 Army Corps. Mar 1864: det nurse in regt hosp. (Co I, 2 WVa Cav) det ind scout by order of Gen Crook. May and June 1864: abs det in ind scouts by order of Gen Crook since Mar 1864. Jul and Aug 1864: on ds. Sept 1864: abs dismounted camp, Hagerstown, Md. Oct 1864: abs on ds. Nov 1864: Co B. Trans from Co I. Abs det ind scout. Dec 1864: abs sick Harper's Ferry . Mar 1865: abs remount camp. Apr and May 1865: abs sick hosp. Adm 25 Nov 1864, Field Hosp, Sandy Hook, Md from the field with GSW left arm rec 18 Nov 1864, Myerstown, Va. Entered Jarvis Gen Hosp, Baltimore, Md 7 Feb 1865 with GSW left shoulder. Entered gen hosp, York, Pa 18 Feb 1865 and ret to duty 26 Feb 1865. Entered gen hosp, Harper's Ferry, Va 22 Apr 1865 with inflammation of the lungs. Entered gen hosp, Cumberland, Md 25 Apr with inflammation of pleura. Mus out June 1865, Cumberland, Md. *d* 24 Feb 1908.

ROBERTSON, JOHN W. PVT (CPL), CO A. Age 18. 5ft 10in. Gray eyes. Dark hair. Dark comp. *b* Carroll Co, Ohio. Farmer. Enr 1 Sept 1861, Chester, Ohio, 3 years. Mus 8 Nov 1861, Camp Bolles. Appt cpl 1 Sept 1861. Reduced to ranks for negligence 1 May 1862. Mar 1864: shown det abs ind scout since 1 Mar 1864. May-Sept 1864: det on scout with Cpt Blazer by order of Lt Col Dove 20 Feb 1864. Nov 1864: abs det ind scout. Dec 1864: KIA 20 Nov (also given as 22 Nov) 1864. Listed KIA, Front Royal, but also merely "in the Shenandoah Valley." Reenl vet vol 5 Nov 1864, Charleston, WVa.

TATMAN, JOHN W (BILL). PVT, CO K. Age 23. 5ft 7in. Gray eyes. Light hair. Light comp. *b* Vinton Co, Ohio. Farmer. Enr 1 Sept 1861, McArthur, Ohio, 3 years. Mus 8 Nov 1861, Camp Bolles, Va. Disch 31 Dec 1863 by virtue of reenl as vet vol on roll dated 21 Jan 1864, Charleston, WVa under auspices of GO 191, Series 1863, War Dept. Nov 1863: abs vet vol furl Vinton Co, Ohio, 30 days from 23 Nov 1863. Mar 1864: abs det ind scouting co to date 1 Mar 1864 by order of Gen Crook. Shown det through Nov 1864. Literate. Co mus out roll dated 2 Dec 1864, Wheeling, WVa vet vol. Mus US service, Charleston, WVa. Mus out 30 June 1865, Wheeling, WVa. Vet stop for arms retained per GO 107 AGO 30 May 1865—saber $8.50, revolver $8.50. *d* 1 Dec 1910. Bur IOOF Cem, Alexandria, Ind.

TIMBERLAKE, LOUIS (LEWIS). PVT, CO E. Age 18. 5ft 8in. Blue eyes. Dark hair. Fair comp. *b* Morgan Co, Ohio. Farmer. Enl Sept 1861, McConnelsville, Ohio, 3 years. Mar 1864: abs det ind scouting co by order of Gen Crook since 1 Mar 1864. Apr 1864: abs det scout. Killed 9 May 1864 near Brushy Ridge by bushwhacker (this is shown as 9 June 1864 in casualty list, HQ 2nd regt Va Vol Cav, Camp Toland, WVa 6 July 1864).

WILLIAMS, JOHN. PVT, CO C. Age 18. 5ft 7in. Blue eyes. Light hair. Fair comp. *b* 10 May 1845, Plum Orchard, Fayette Co, Va. Farmer/laborer. Enl 22 Apr 1863, Camp Piatt, 3 years. Recruit. Mar and Apr 1864: det scout by order of Gen Crook. July, Aug, Sept, and Oct 1864: abs dismount camp. Trans 23 Nov 1864, Co H by reason of consol, SO 86. Worked in the coal mine of Carver Brothers on Morris Creek in Fayette Co, WVa after the war. *d* 2 Dec 1916, Powellton, WVa.

WILSON, THOMAS (TOM). PVT, CO E AND K. Age 18. 5ft½in. Blue eyes. Light hair. Fair comp. *b* Indiana Co, Pa. Laborer. Enr 1861, Ironton, Ohio, 3 years. Reenl 1 Jan 1864, Camp Toland, 3 years. Mar-Apr 1862: horse died 1 Mar 1862, Camp Paxton, Va. Sept-Oct 1862: had no horse and left 25 Oct 1862, Pt Pleasant, Va. MIA 4 July 1863, Raleigh Co, Va. Confined 11 July 1863, Richmond, Va. Par 14 July 1863, City Point, Va. Reported 15 July 1863, Camp Parole, Md. Sent 5 Aug 1863, CCO. Reported 9 Aug 1863, CCO. 14 Oct 1863: rejoined unit from MIA. Mus and descr roll not dated shows him des from US Forces at CCO; remarks. Des 15 Aug 1863 par. Mus out 31 Dec 1863, Wheeling, WVa. Reenl 18 Nov 1863, vet vol, Charleston, Va. Nov-Dec 1863: furl to Ironton, Ohio 5 Dec 1863, 30 days. Det ind scouts by order of Gen Crook, 1 Mar 1864. Shown on mus rolls for Nov 1864-May 1865 on det duty with ind scouts. Nov 1864: trans to Co K.

1st WVa Vet Vols (Formerly 5th and 9th WVA Vol Infs)

BRYAN, JOHNSON ("JOHNS"). PVT, CO G. Age 20. 5ft 11½in. Blue eyes. Dark hair. Dark comp. *b* 22 Jan 1845, Fallsburg, Lawrence Co, Ky. Farmer. Recruit. Enr 19 Jan 1862, Ceredo, WVa, 3 years. Mus same day and place. Nov-Dec 1864: det Gen Crook's ind scouts. Jan-Feb 1865: sick hosp. Bed card shows him in Grafton Gen Hosp, Grafton, WVa with skin disease. Adm 25 Feb 1865. Ret to duty 14 Mar 1865. Mus out 21 July 1865, Cumberland, Md. Book mark notation: see Gen Crook's ind scouts. *d* 27 Oct 1926, Adeline, Ky.

DANIELS, WILLIAM W. PVT (CPL), CO K. Age 20. 5ft 6½in. Blue eyes. Dark hair. Dark comp. *b* 22 Apr 1845, Johnson Co, Ky. Farmer. Enr 11 Aug 1861, Ceredo, WVa as pvt, 5th WVa Inf. Wounded 8 June 1862, Battle of Cross Keys through right thigh. Disch 18 Dec 1863 by reason of reenl vet vol. Re-mus 18 Dec 1863, Charleston, WVa, vet vol. Nov-Dec: abs ds Blazer's Scouts since 21 Nov 1864. Jan-Feb 1865: on furl. Mus out 21 July 1865, Cumberland, Md. *d* 15 May 1908, Lomansville, Ky.

Notes

The following abbreviations are used in the notes and bibliography.

CSR   compiled service record

CWTI   *Civil War Times Illustrated* collection

MIC   microfilm

NARA   National Archives and Records Administration

OHS   Ohio Historical Society

OR   U.S. War Department, *The War of the Rebellion: A Compilation of the Official Records of the Union and Confederate Armies*

RG   record group

USAMHI   U.S. Army Military History Institute

VFM   vertical file manuscript

CHAPTER I

1. Taylor Hogg, pension record, National Archives and Records Administration (NARA).

2. James Morton Callahan, *History of West Virginia, Old and New*, 2 vols. (Chicago: American Historical Society, 1923), 1:374; Frank J. Welcher, *The Union Army, 1861–1865*, vol. 1, *The Eastern Theater* (Bloomington: Indiana University Press, 1989), 1055–56.

3. Welcher, *Union Army*, 1056; T. Harry Williams, *Hayes of the Twenty-Third: The Civil War Volunteer Officer* (New York: Knopf, 1965), 59–60.

4. Williams, *Hayes of the Twenty-Third*, 74, 77.

5. Callahan, *History of West Virginia*, 1:375–77; Welcher, *Union Army*, 1:1056–57.

6. Callahan, *History of West Virginia*, 1:378–79.

7. Ibid., 382–84; Welcher, *Union Army*, 1057–65.

8. Callahan, *History of West Virginia*, 1:384.

9. Stan Cohen, *The Civil War in West Virginia: A Pictorial History* (Charleston, W.Va.: Pictorial History Publishing), 85.

10. Ibid., 85.

11. Ibid., 85–86.

12. Ibid., 86. Compiled service records (CSRs) of units such as the 9th W.Va. Inf., 12th Ohio, and 91st Ohio show increased desertion during this time. NARA.

13. Cohen, *Civil War in West Virginia*, 93.

14. Ibid., 93.

15. Ibid., 94.

16. *Kanawha Valley Star* (Charleston, Va.), April 26, 1861; Jeffrey C. Weaver, *Thurmond's Partisan Rangers and Swann's Battalion of Virginia Cavalry* (Lynchburg, Va.: H. E. Howard, 1993), 3–4.

17. Weaver, *Thurmond's Partisan Rangers*, 7, 11.

18. Ibid., 9.

19. Herman Edmond Matheny, *Wood County, West Virginia, in Civil War Times; With an Account of the Guerrilla Warfare in the Little Kanawha Valley* (Parkersburg: Trans-Allegheny Books, 1987), 43–44; regimental papers, 2nd W.Va. Cav., NARA.

20. Matheny, *Wood County, West Virginia*, 281.

21. Morning report book, Co. A, 91st Ohio Vol. Inf., NARA.

22. John T. Booth Papers, MSS 180, Ohio Historical Society (OHS).

23. Ann Gorman Condon, ed., *Architects of Our Fortunes: The Journal of Eliza A. W. Otis, 1860–1863* (San Marino, Calif.: Huntington Library Press, 2001), 219.

24. Booth Papers, OHS.

25. Charles Leib, *Nine Months in the Quartermaster's Department; or, The Chances for Making a Million* (Cincinnati: Moore, Wilstach, Keys, 1862) 126–27.

26. Ibid., 44.

27. Matheny, *Wood County, West Virginia*, 47–48.

28. Weaver, *Thurmond's Partisan Rangers*, 12.

29. Ibid., 9–10.

30. *Cincinnati Daily Commercial*, November 26, 1863, MIC 08854, OHS. A more personal version of Abraham's story is contained in Evelyn A. Benson, comp., *With the Army of West Virginia, 1861–1864* (Lancaster, Pa.: Evelyn Benson, 1974), 40.

31. Benson, *With the Army of West Virginia*, 40.

32. Ibid.

33. Ibid.

34. Ibid.

35. George Crook, *General George Crook: His Autobiography*, ed. Martin F. Schmitt (Norman: University of Oklahoma Press, 1946, 1960); John G. Bourke, *On the Border with Crook* (New York: Charles Scribner's Sons, 1891), 110–11.

36. Crook, *Autobiography*, xvi–xviii.

37. Ibid., xix–xx; Bourke, *On the Border*, 109.

38. Bourke, *On the Border,* 110.

39. Booth Papers, OHS.

40. Bourke, *On the Border,* 488.

41. Crook, *Autobiography,* 83–84.

42. Ibid., 85–87.

43. Ibid.

44. Ibid., 86–88.

45. Ibid., 88; Booth Papers, OHS. Booth also noted that no quarter was given to bushwhackers: "We never take any of their class prisoners. They have murdered our men and we have retaliated."

46. Crook, *Autobiography,* 88; Booth Papers, OHS.

CHAPTER 2

1. Philip H. Stevens, *Search Out the Land: A History of American Military Scouts* (Chicago: Rand McNally, 1969), 9.

2. Benjamin F. Taylor, *Pictures of Life in Camp and Field* (Chicago: S. C. Griggs, 1875), 218–19.

3. Stevens, *Search Out the Land,* 10.

4. RG 94, regimental order book, 91st Ohio Inf., NARA.

5. Condon, *Architects of Our Fortunes,* 180; Harrison Gray Otis, "Recollections of the War," *Santa Barbara Daily Press,* October 19, 1876; emphasis Otis's. Otis wrote a series of articles for his paper, the *Santa Barbara Daily Press,* which ran on October 19, 27, 28, 30, 31 and November 1, 2, and 3, 1876.

6. Brown County Historical Society of Georgetown, *The History of Brown County* (Chicago: W. H. Beers, 1883; reprint, Evansville, Ind.: Unigraphic, 1973), 335, 336.

7. Carr B. White, CSR, Mexican War, NARA.

8. Joseph E. Chance, *Mexico under Fire: Being the Diary of Samuel Ryan Curtis 3rd Ohio Volunteer Infantry during the American Military Occupation of Northern Mexico, 1846–1847* (Fort Worth: Texas Christian University Press, 1994), xvi, 25, 111, 128, 143, 153, 160, 202. Curtis had been adjutant general of Ohio and had been responsible for recruiting all Ohio troops for the Mexican War. Although the 1st Ohio and 3rd Ohio were separated most of the time, the regiments did occasionally meet and at one point the 1st Ohio was under Curtis's command, making it very likely that he met Carr B. White. He does not mention White in his diary.

9. U.S. War Department, *The War of the Rebellion: A Compilation of the Official Records of the Union and Confederate Armies,* series 1, no. 27, vol. 3 (Washington, D.C.: Government Printing Office, 1880–1901), 51–52 (hereafter *OR*); NARA, Telegrams Collected by the Office of the Secretary of War (unbound) 1860–1870, roll 194, frame 0523 (hereafter Telegrams Collected).

10. Stevens, *Search Out the Land,* 11.

11. Ibid., 15.

12. Ibid., 16.

13. *OR* 1, 24/31, 972; *OR* 1, 30/3, 875; *OR* 1, 34/4, 10; *OR* 1, 45/1, 1212. These *OR* entries provide a few examples. A searchable CD-ROM version of the *OR* is necessary to find terms like "independent scouts" that are not listed in the printed versions. The Guild Press of Indiana version (Carmel, 1996) was used for these searches.

14. Jesse Middaugh Papers, *Civil War Times Illustrated* (CWTI) collection, U.S. Army Military History Institute (USAMHI), Carlisle, Pa.; William Toppin, Samuel Burdett, and James Webb, CSRs, NARA; David Phillips, "The Jessie Scouts," *West Virginia in the Civil War*, <www.wvcivilwar.com>, 1997.

15. Record group (RG) 393, entry 1155 (vol. 103, W.Va.) Letters Sent, April 1863–January 1864, NARA; emphasis mine.

16. Asbe Montgomery, *An Account of R. R. Blazer and His Scouts, Operations in West Virginia and in Loudoun and the Shenandoah Valleys, Against William and Philip Thurman, and Moseby, the Great Guerrillas* (Marietta, Ohio: Registry Office, 1865), 1.

17. Roane County Family History Committee, *Roane County West Virginia Family History 1989* (printed by Walsworth Publishing, copyright Roane County Family History Committee), 324–25.

18. Montgomery, *Blazer and His Scouts,* 1; Edward Davis diary, USAMHI; Richard E. Blazer and Cy R. Blazer, papers of Capt. Richard Blazer.

19. Blazer and Blazer, papers of Capt. Richard Blazer.

20. RG 393, entry 1155 (vol. 103, W.Va.), Letters Sent, April 1863–January 1864, NARA.

21. RG 393, pt. 2, 1158, 1159 (vol. 106, W.Va.), NARA.

22. John Scott, *Partisan Life with Col. John S. Mosby,* reprint (Gaithersburg, Md.: Butternut Press, 1985); Montgomery, *Blazer and His Scouts;* Otis, "Recollections," October 30, 1876; Blazer's Scouts, pension records, NARA.

23. Frederick H. Dyer, *A Compendium of the War of the Rebellion* (Des Moines: F. H. Dyer, 1908; reprint, Dayton: Morningside Bookshop, 1978), 1501; Whitlaw Reid, *Ohio in the War: Her Statesmen, Her Generals, and Soldiers* (Cincinnati: Moore, Wilstach and Baldwin, 1868), 89–90; Dumas Malone, ed., *Dictionary of American Biography.* (New York: Charles Scribner's Sons, 1934), 7:100; Richard Connelly Miller, "Otis and His Times: The Career of Harrison Gray Otis of Los Angeles" (Ph.D. dissertation, University of California, Berkeley, 1964), 19.

24. Dyer, *Compendium,* 1664; MS, record of service, 9th W.Va. Inf., WVU Archives and Cultural Center; Education Foundation, "Raid on the 9th Infantry at Guyandotte," in *West Virginia in the Civil War* (series of sketches sponsored by Education Foundation for distribution to West Virginia newspapers, Charleston, 1958; published as *West Virginia in the Civil War* by Education Foundation, Charleston, 1963), 121–26.

25. Dyer, *Compendium,* 1537.

26. E. E. E., "The Legion of Honor: A History of That Invincible Band Known

as the Blazer Scouts," *Ohio Soldier* 2, 2 (August 25, 1888). The title of this article appears to lend credence to the existence of an organization called the Legion of Honor. However, the article cites *The Life of Colonel John S. Mosby* as a source, indicating the origin of parts of the text was a Confederate source.

27. Richard Blazer, pension record, NARA.

28. Virgil Carrington Jones, *Ranger Mosby* (Chapel Hill: University of North Carolina Press, 1944), 200; Virgil Carrington Jones, *Grey Ghosts and Rebel Raiders* (McLean, Va.: EPM Publications), 287; Jeffry D. Wert, *Mosby's Rangers* (New York: Simon and Schuster, 1990); Scott, *Partisan Life,* 364; James J. Williamson, *Mosby's Rangers.* (New York: Ralph B. Kenyon, 1896; reprint, Alexandria, Va.: Time-Life Collectors' Library), 300; Crook, *Autobiography,* 135. In 1955, Jones uses the term "hardened Indian fighter" (in *Ranger Mosby*) without a reference. In 1956 he erroneously cites George Crook's autobiography. Jeffry Wert erroneously cites Scott and Williamson as the source of the Indian fighter appellation. Perhaps Jones heard the term during one of his personal interviews with survivors of Mosby's command, but there is no documentation for this assertion. He may have also meant to refer to Blazer's boss, George Crook, who did have experience fighting Indians. Wert may have meant to cite Jones, but instead erroneously cited Scott and Williamson.

29. Richard Miller, "Otis and His Times," 5–6.

30. Ibid., 7–9.

31. Ibid., 10–11; Malone, *Dictionary of American Biography,* 7:100.

32. William R. Wilson, pension record, NARA.

33. CSRs, 9th W.Va. Inf., 12th and 91st Ohio Infantries.

34. Asbe Montgomery, pension record and CSR, NARA; Matheny, *Wood County, West Virginia,* appendix A, 471–76. Montgomery was commissioned August 24, 1861. *Rossville Reporter,* March 29, 1907, 1.

35. Adam R. Head, pension record and CSR, NARA.

36. Samuel Harrop, pension record and CSR, NARA; Nancy Morebeck, family group sheets.

37. Samuel Harrop, pension record, NARA.

38. Ibid.

39. James Ireland, diary, VFM 2304, OHS.

40. Ibid.; Richard Miller, "Otis and His Times," 19.

41. Richard Miller, "Otis and His Times," 19.

42. John McMullen, CSR and pension record, NARA.

43. *History of Roane County,* 526–27.

44. Ibid., 528–29.

45. Ibid., 528–29.

46. Stephen Glaze and Marshall Glaze, CSRs and pension records, NARA; Isaac M. Glaze, CSR, NARA; *History of Roane County,* 531.

47. Patrick Collins, pension record, NARA.

CHAPTER 3

1. Montgomery, *Blazer and His Scouts*, 3.

2. RG 94, regimental order book, 91st Ohio Vol. Inf., NARA.

3. Montgomery, *Blazer and His Scouts*, 4.

4. E. E. E., "Legion of Honor."

5. Otis, "Recollections," October 30, 1876; William S. Newton, letters, MIC 17 (Civil War Collection), roll 11, OHS (hereafter, Newton letters).

6. John McMullen, CSR and pension record, NARA; Marshall Glaze, CSR and pension record, NARA. The Glaze record contained statements by Capt. John Spencer, 9th W.Va. Inf.; Capt. James Simpson, 11th W.Va. Inf.; Eli Rogers and Jacob Argobrite, 9th W.Va. Inf.

7. RG 94, regimental descriptive book, 9th W.Va. Inf., NARA.

8. Condon, *Architects of Our Fortunes*, 162–63, 200.

9. E. E. E., "Legion of Honor."

10. Ibid.; Harrison Gray Otis, CSR, NARA; War Library and Museum of the Military Order of the Loyal Legion of the United States, Philadelphia; James M. Comly Papers, unknown author contained in Comly papers, MIC 33, roll 1, frame 596, OHS. This second use of the term "headquarters in the brush" appears to confirm that it was a play on words by the men and not a mistake of Harrison Gray Otis as to the original words in the order; Condon, *Architects of Our Fortunes*, 91–92, 199.

11. E. E. E., "Legion of Honor"; E. E. E. does not make it clear which of the Thurmonds was attacked.

12. Telegrams Collected, roll 216, frame 319.

13. Montgomery, *Blazer and His Scouts*, 6.

14. Ibid., 6.

15. Otis, "Recollections," October 30, 1876; Ireland diary, OHS.

16. Ireland diary, OHS.

17. Ibid.

18. Comly Papers, roll 1, frame 596, OHS; emphasis in original.

19. James H. Miller, *History of Summers County From the Earliest Settlement to the Present Time* (Hinton, W.Va.: James H. Miller, 1908), 206–7.

20. Ibid.

21. Ibid., 207.

22. Telegrams Collected, roll 194, frame 0478; roll 216, frames 0244, 0320.

23. Ibid., roll 216, frames 0231, 0330.

24. Montgomery, *Blazer and His Scouts*, 6.

25. Ibid., 6–7. Possibly a reference to lindens or basswoods. The bark can be twisted into mats, perhaps explaining the reference to "lynn slabs."

26. Ibid., 4–5.

27. Ireland diary, OHS.

28. Joseph Blair, Samuel Irvine, Charles G. Painter, Joseph Redden, CSRs and pension records, NARA.

29. Milton Terwilliger, CSR, NARA.

30. Warren Timberlake, CSR and pension record, NARA.

31. Adam R. Head, CSR and pension record, NARA; emphasis in original.

32. Montgomery, *Blazer and His Scouts,* 5.

33. Ireland diary, OHS; Richard Miller, "Otis and His Times," 19.

34. Ireland diary, OHS.

35. Montgomery, *Blazer and His Scouts,* 5–6; Otis, "Recollections," October 30, 1876.

36. Ireland diary, OHS.

37. Ibid.

38. Ibid.

39. Ibid.

40. Newton letters, OHS.

41. Montgomery, *Blazer and His Scouts,* 7.

42. RG 94, regimental order book, 91st Ohio Inf., NARA.

43. Otis, "Recollections," October 30, 1876. This order may be a shortened version of the actual communication. It is apparently not in the *OR* and was not in letter books available at the National Archives. The previous order cited is extant at the National Archives, which supports the authenticity of these documents cited by Otis.

44. Ibid. Otis confuses the timing of events in the Lewisburg campaigns, but his facts are probably correct. The Scouts were officially disbanded after the first Lewisburg action, not before. They were reconstituted under special orders for the second Lewisburg campaign in December 1863. The combination of all sources available make this clear. RG 393, pt. 1, entries 5683, 5694; Telegrams Sent, August 1863–March 1864 and August–December 1864; Telegrams Received, July 1863–October 1865 (nos. 18, 19), W.Va., NARA.

45. RG 393, pt. 1, entries 5683, 5694, Telegrams Sent August 1863–March 1864 and August–December 1864. A portion or perhaps the entire telegram was in code.

46. Ibid.; RG 94, regimental order book, 91st Ohio Inf., NARA.

47. Ireland diary, OHS. There is no further information on the identity of "Lin."

48. Ibid.; William Bishop, Salathiel Boldman, Henry Fisher, CSRs, NARA.

49. Stephen P. Drake, "Letter from S.P. Drake," *Ironton Register,* microfilm 17266, OHS, January 7, 1864, 1.

50. Weaver, *Thurmond's Partisan Rangers,* 37.

51. Ireland diary, OHS.

52. Otis, "Recollections," October 30, 1876.

53. Newton letters, OHS.

54. Montgomery, *Blazer and His Scouts,* 7.

55. Newton letters, OHS.

56. RG 393, pt. 2, entries 1158, 1159 (vol. 106, W.Va.), NARA.

57. Possibly William Addison Witcher, colonel, 21st Regiment Virginia Volunteers. Montgomery refers to Charles Canterbury of Co. C, 45th Bn., Va. Inf., formerly 1st Regt. Cav., Virginia State Line. This company began as Capt. James R. Cook's company. Canterbury was elected September 7, 1863. He formerly commanded Co. G of the 2nd Regt., Virginia State Line. Lee A. Wallace Jr., *A Guide to Virginia Military Organizations, 1861–1865*, rev. 2d ed. (Lynchburg, Va.: H. E. Howard, 1986), 103, 126.

58. Montgomery, *Blazer and His Scouts*, 8.

59. RG 393, pt. 1, entry 5691, Letters Received, Dept. of W.Va., 1863–1865, NARA.

60. RG 393, pt. 2, entry 1155 (vol. 103, W.Va.), Letters Sent, April 1863–January 1864, NARA.

61. Telegrams Collected, roll 232.

62. RG 393, pt. 1, entries 5683–5694, NARA.

63. RG 393, pt. 1, entry 5695, telegrams received by Dept. of West Virginia and subordinate commands, 1863–1865, NARA.

64. Ibid. General Averell requested ammunition for Linder carbines by telegraph.

CHAPTER 4

1. CSRs, 23rd Ohio Inf., NARA.

2. Dyer, *Compendium*, 1507. Williams, *Hayes of the Twenty-Third*, 11–16; T. Harry Williams and Stephen E. Ambrose, "The 23rd Ohio," *Civil War Times Illustrated*, May 1964, 22–25; Reid, *Ohio in the War*, 160–61; CSRs, 23rd Ohio Vol. Inf., NARA.

3. Reid, *Ohio in the War*, 223–27; CSRs, 34th Ohio Vol. Inf., NARA. Recently acquired unattributed sketch of a drummer in the 34th Ohio.

4. Reid, *Ohio in the War*, 223–27.

5. Dyer, *Compendium*, 1665.

6. Ibid., 1665–66.

7. Dyer, *Compendium*, 1656–57; *Zanesville Courier*, March 25, 1864, microfilm 21109, OHS.

8. Tobias Haught, letter, pension record, NARA.

9. Jesse Able, CSR, NARA.

10. W. L. Curry, *Four Years in the Saddle: History 1st Regiment Ohio Volunteer Cavalry, War of the Rebellion 1861–1865* (Columbus, Ohio: W. L. Curry, 1898; reprint, Jonesboro, Ga.: Freedom Hill Press, 1984), 20, 23.

11. Sylvester Keith, letter, Barboursville, Va., November 27, 1863, NARA.

12. Jesse Middaugh, letter, Pemberton Co., Va., May 10, 1862, CWTI, USAMHI.

13. Dan Pelfrey, email received May 1, 2000; Ann Brotherton, "Family History (of the VanHoose and Middaugh families) as written down by Ann Brotherton at the Request of Dorothy McNamara," typescript, n.d.; Jesse Middaugh, CSR, NARA.

14. Jesse Middaugh, letter from Camp Copperhead, near Strasbourg, Shenandoah Co., Va., June 25, [1862]; letter, Camp near Woodville, Rappahannock Co., Va., July 29, 1862, CWTI, USAMHI.

15. Jesse Middaugh, letter, Ceredo, Wayne Co., Va., December 29, 1862, CWTI, USAMHI.

16. Jesse Middaugh, letter, Camp Reynolds, Fayette Co., W.Va., March 9, 1864; Brotherton, Middaugh history. Ann Brotherton writes that Jesse came home at one point with other soldiers. He was disguised so that even Mary Ann did not recognize him, but his daughter did "as soon as she saw his eyes."

17. Jesse Middaugh, letter, Camp Gauley, Fayette Co., W.Va., October 2, 1863, CWTI, USAMHI. This scout is nearly concurrent with the operations of the Independent Scouts under Blazer and Otis. The 5th W.Va., however, is in a different brigade than the 9th W.Va. and 12th and 91st Ohio Infantries.

18. RG 393, pt. 2, entries 1158, 1159 (vol. 106, W.Va.), NARA.

19. William Wass, pension record, NARA; Kathy Turner, "Centenary Celebration, Interesting Reminiscences of Prominent Ritchie County Family," a Ritchie County newspaper, September 6, 1940.

20. Turner, "Centenary Celebration"; Kathy Turner, unattributed obituary of William Wass, probably from a Ritchie County newspaper, n.d.; Mary Lucille DeBerry, "Bethany Homecoming—August 20, 1993," *Traditions: A Journal of West Virginia Folk Culture and Educational Awareness* 4 (1996): 6.

21. Turner, "Centenary Celebration"; DeBerry, "Bethany Homecoming."

22. William Disbro, unpublished paper on William Wass; Margaret Wilson, telephone interviews, January 24, March 13, April 27, 1997; March 8, 1998.

23. Leggett, Conaway and Company, *The History of Wyandot County, Ohio* (Chicago: Leggett, Conaway, 1884), 696–97.

24. RG 94, muster rolls, returns, and letters, 13th W.Va. Inf., NARA.

25. *Cincinnati Commercial,* November 20, 1863.

26. Ibid.

27. James E. D. Ward, *Twelfth Ohio Volunteer Infantry* (Ripley, Ohio: J. E. D. Ward, 1864).

28. Thomas Connell, CSR, NARA; emphasis Connell's as interpreted by the transcribing clerk.

29. Telegrams Collected, roll 232, frame 0761.

30. Montgomery, *Blazer and His Scouts,* 8–9.

31. Telegrams Collected, roll 232, frame 0472.

32. Montgomery, *Blazer and His Scouts,* 9.

33. Telegrams Collected, roll 232, frame 0473.

34. RG 393, entry 1155 (vol. 103, W.Va.), Letters Sent, April 1863–January 1864, NARA.

35. Montgomery, *Blazer and His Scouts,* 9–10.

36. RG 393, pt. 2, 1158, 1159 (vol. 106, W.Va.); James Ewing, CSR, NARA.

37. Montgomery, *Blazer and His Scouts*, 10.

38. Ibid., 10–11.

39. *Wheeling Intelligencer*, June 8, 1864, repeating dispatches from the *Cincinnati Commercial*.

40. Montgomery, *Blazer and His Scouts*, 10; E. C. Arthur, "The Dublin Raid," *Ohio Soldier* 2 (January 5–April 13, 1889); Howard Rollins McManus, *The Battle of Cloyd's Mountain: The Virginia and Tennessee Railroad Raid, April 29–May 19, 1864* (Lynchburg, Va.: H. E. Howard, 1989) 8. McManus incorrectly cites the 5th W.Va. as the 8th and fails to mention the participation of Blazer's unit in this operation.

41. Otis, "Recollections," October 31, 1876.

42. Montgomery, *Blazer and His Scouts*, 11–12.

43. Ibid.; Andrew J. Long, 13th W.Va. Inf., Manassas Steel, 13th W.Va. Inf., James Byers, 2nd W.Va. Cav., and Louis Timberlake, 2nd W.Va. Cav., CSRs, NARA; *Zanesville Courier* 19, 123 (June 1, 1864).

44. Montgomery, *Blazer and His Scouts*, 12.

45. Ibid., 12.

46. Ibid., 12–13.

47. Ibid., 13.

48. Ibid., 14.

49. Montgomery, *Blazer and His Scouts*, 14–15.

50. Ibid., 15. Interview, Richard E. Blazer, late grandson of Captain Blazer, 1996.

51. Montgomery, *Blazer and His Scouts*, 15.

52. Otis K. Rice, *A History of Greenbrier County* (Lewisburg, W.Va.: Greenbrier Historical Society, 1986), 296 (Rice cites *OR* 1, 37/1:9–10); Mason Mathews to J. W. Mathews, May 12, 1864, Roy Bird Cook Collection, box 9, 1:232, West Virginia and Regional History Collection, West Virginia University Libraries, Colson Hall.

53. Milton W. Humphreys, Bryan's Battery, Kings Artillery, CSA, *Military Operations 1861–1864, Fayetteville, W.VA. And Lynchburg Campaign,* pamphlet collection, no. 3, MIC P6422, West Virginia Civil War Pamphlets, West Virginia University.

54. Montgomery, *Blazer and His Scouts*, 15.

55. Ibid., 15.

56. RG 94, regimental order book, 91st Ohio Vol. Inf., NARA.

CHAPTER 5

1. Montgomery, *Blazer and His Scouts*, 14.

2. James J. Wood, diary, manuscript collection, Bowling Green State University.

3. Montgomery, *Blazer and His Scouts*, 14–15.

4. *Point Pleasant Register*, June 23, 1864, 2.

5. Montgomery, *Blazer and His Scouts*, 16.

6. Wood diary.

7. *Norwalk (Ohio) Reflector,* July 26, 1864, 3.

8. *Point Pleasant Register,* June 23, 1864; Andrew Stairwalt, diary, Hayes Presidential Center, Fremont, Ohio.

9. James Z. M'Chesney, "Scouting on Hunter's Raid to Lynchburg, Va.," *Confederate Veteran* 27, 5 (May 1920): 173.

10. Ibid., 173. The term Jessie Scouts is attributed by William Gilmore Beymer to a group of scouts serving under General Fremont in the early days of the war in the Valley. They were Fremont's favorites and wore rich uniforms laced with velvet. He named them after his wife. Long after Fremont and his scouts had left the Valley, the "name lingered in the minds of citizens and soldiery, and at last it came to be attached to those Federal scouts who wore the gray uniform." Beymer, *On Hazardous Service: Scouts and Spies of the North and South* (New York: Harper and Brothers, 1912), 25.

11. M'Chesney, "Scouting on Hunter's Raid," 173.

12. Ibid., 173.

13. Ibid., 175.

14. Ibid.

15. Ibid.

16. Ibid., 175–76; Ohio Roster Commission (Cincinnati), *Official Roster of Soldiers of the State of Ohio in the War of the Rebellion,* 12 vols. (Akron: Warner Company, 1896), 7:127.

17. Montgomery, *Blazer and His Scouts,* 16–17.

18. Ibid., 17.

19. Ibid.

20. *Cincinnati Daily Gazette,* July 1, 1864. The *Cleveland Morning Leader* also carried this story in its July 2 edition.

21. William L. Harris, CSR and pension record, NARA.

22. E. E. E., "The Ninety-First Ohio at Gallipolis," *Ohio Soldier,* August 25, 1888.

23. Montgomery, *Blazer and His Scouts,* 17–18.

24. Ibid., 17–18; Williams, *Hayes of the Twenty-Third,* 195.

25. Montgomery, *Blazer and His Scouts,* 18.

26. Ibid.

27. Ibid.

28. This is the only indication of what the Scouts may have done after the main battle lines were engaged. Falling back to the rear, they would aid the provost guards with prisoners and help the musicians and others with the wounded. Also, they were probably a deterrent to stragglers.

29. *Wheeling Intelligencer,* July 19, 1864 (citing correspondents of the *Cincinnati Gazette*); emphasis in original.

30. Montgomery, *Blazer and His Scouts,* 19–20.

31. "Narrow Escapes, Interesting War Experiences, No. 72," *Ironton Register,*

March 29, 1888. Chambers states that they were in the advance at the time. However, Buford's Gap was clearly a rear guard action.

32. Ephraim Helm, CSR and pension record, NARA.

33. Montgomery, *Blazer and His Scouts*, 20–21.

34. Scott-Palmer Papers (A&M 1423), diary of Maj. T. W. Turner, 36th Ohio Vol. Inf., West Virginia and Regional Collection, West Virginia University Libraries.

35. Ibid.; George W. Slade, pension record, 12th Ohio Vol. Inf.; Vada Zickafose, daughter of Samuel Spencer, 9th W.Va., telephone interview, January 6, 1997 (Zickafose related the story of her father and his comrades eating dogmeat); Otis, "Recollections," November 1, 1876.

36. Correspondents of the *Cincinnati Gazette,* "From West Virginia: The Butler County National Guard," *Cincinnati Gazette,* July 8, 1864, 3.

37. Donald E. Markle, *Spies and Spymasters of the Civil War* (New York: Barnes and Noble, 1994), 136–37.

38. Montgomery, *Blazer and His Scouts*, 21.

39. *Cincinnati Gazette,* July 9, 1864.

40. Montgomery, *Blazer and His Scouts*, 21.

41. Ibid.; Wallace, *Virginia Military Organizations.* Asbe Montgomery does not give enough specifics to identify "White." He is probably referring to Lt. Col. Elijah Viers White of the 35th Bn., Virginia Cav.

42. Thomas A. Lewis, *The Shenandoah in Flames* (Alexandria, Va.: Time-Life Books, 1987), 89; *OR* 1, 37/2, 9, 18, 392, 400–401; Montgomery, *Blazer and His Scouts,* 21.

43. *New York Times,* September 17, 1864, 1.

44. Montgomery, *Blazer and His Scouts*, 22.

45. *OR* 1, 43/1, 860.

46. Regimental papers, 34th Ohio Vol. Inf., NARA; Art Frith, letter and photo.

47. Montgomery, *Blazer and His Scouts*, 22.

48. Ibid., 22–23.

49. Ibid., 23.

50. Ibid., 23–24.

51. "The Shenandoah Valley," *New York Times,* September 5, 1864; E. A. Paul, dispatch, Berryville, Va., Thursday, September 1, 1864.

52. Montgomery, *Blazer and His Scouts,* 23–24.

53. Ibid., 24.

54. Ibid.; roster, 9th W.Va. Inf., copy from microfilm, West Virginia Cultural Center; James Montgomery, CSR, NARA.

55. Montgomery, *Blazer and His Scouts,* 25.

56. Ibid.

57. Ibid., 25–26.

58. Ibid., 26–27.

59. Ibid., 27; Asbe Montgomery, CSR and pension record, NARA.

60. Williamson, *Mosby's Rangers*, 229–30.

61. *Philadelphia Inquirer*, September 7, 1864, 1.

62. Ibid., Associated Press dispatches; emphasis mine. Roster Commission, *Roster of Ohio Soldiers*, vols. 3, 8.

63. *OR* 1, 43/1, 615.

CHAPTER 6

1. Capt. John Truesdale, comp., *The Blue Coats: And How They Lived, Fought and Died for the Union* (Philadelphia: Jones Brothers, 1867), 365–82; Joseph Brown, "Fighting Them Over; What Our Veterans Have to Say about Their Old Campaigns; Captured by Mosby" (letter to the editor), *National Tribune*, October 31, 1889. The first telling of this story was probably in *Harper's Weekly*, January 21, 1865, 43; *Cincinnati Daily Commercial*, November 12, 1864, 1; *Mahoning Register* (Youngstown, Ohio), microfilm 24466, OHS, December 1, 1864, 1; James E. Taylor, *The James E. Taylor Sketchbook* (Dayton: Western Reserve Historical Society, 1989; printed by Morningside House), 461. Truesdale, *Blue Coats*, erroneously gives W. W. Badger as the name. Taylor gives Badger's unit as the 3rd New Jersey Cav. However, Capt. Nicholas D. Badger served with the 8th Ohio Cav. according to a Taylor footnote and confirmed in the *Roster of Ohio Soldiers* and his compiled service record. The *Mahoning Register* account provides Captain Badger's full name, but differs markedly from the accounts of Badger and Brown. It is not sourced and may be more camp hearsay than fact.

2. Nicholas Badger and Joseph Badger, CSRs, NARA. Joseph's record contains letters that indicate William W. Badger of the 19th Corps was the brother of Nicholas and Joseph. It is interesting that the publisher of *The Blue Coats* lists the author as W. W. Badger. Could W. W. have picked up on the story of his brother and sold it as his own?

3. Hugh C. Keen and Horace Mewborn, *43rd Battalion Virginia Cavalry, Mosby's Command*, 2d ed. (Lynchburg, Va.: H. E. Howard, 1993), 290, 382; George McCauley, pension record, NARA; John N. Opie, *A Rebel Cavalryman with Lee, Stuart, and Jackson* (Chicago: W. B. Conkey, 1899; reprint, Dayton: Morningside Bookshop, 1972), 273–74; Taylor, *Sketchbook*, 461.

4. Truesdale, *Blue Coats*, 365.

5. Ibid., 366.

6. Carlisle F. Whiting is listed in Mosby's roster as a private. He had served in the 1st Va. Cav. and was wounded in action at First Manassas. From September to October 1864 he was noted "absent on scout for General T. L. Rosser." Keen and Mewborn, *43rd Battalion*, 382. David Neuhardt, emails, January–February 2000. Mr. Neuhardt is a student of the 8th Ohio Cav. and provided me information from the archivist at Antioch College.

The discrepancy between Badger's account and the roster of the 43rd Battalion may be from Badger's embellishment of the account. However, he plausibly makes the case that Whiting is certainly more than a mere private, since he is leading a significant group of Mosby's men. John N. Opie, in *A Rebel Cavalryman*, relates that several men of the "Clarke" Cavalry, 6th Va., had been detailed for "secret service" in the lower Shenandoah Valley: Sgt. Philip Swan and Pvts. Calmes, Crow, and Whiting. Opie's story differs even more dramatically from the accounts of Badger and Joseph Brown. Opie's book was written in 1899 and this account appears to be considerably distorted in comparison with the two other accounts. However, the names of Whiting and Crow are consistent with the other accounts.

7. Ibid., 368. The Greek cross was the symbol of the 6th Infantry Corps. The badge also would not have been yellow, but red, white, or blue to indicate to which division in the Corps the man belonged.

8. Joseph Brown, "Captured by Mosby." Brown gives the date of his capture as October 4, 1864. James E. Taylor's chronology places these events in early October. However, the other accounts, the correlation with the hanging of Custer's men, and the dates of the deaths of the Confederates put this incident in early November. Nearly all the other men were captured in the vicinity of Winchester. Brown erroneously puts his capture considerably to the east. The other men captured are verified through Brown's account, Taylor's *Sketchbook*, and pension records.

9. Brown, "Captured by Mosby." Brown may mean Bentonville, which is in the area in which he was captured.

10. Curtis McIntosh, pension record, NARA.

11. Major Palmer, letter, *Marietta Register*, microfilm 39487, OHS, December 8, 1864, 3; August Warseke, August. "Captured by the Enemy," *West Virginia Journal*, December 21, 1864, 3; Stephen P. Drake, CSR, NARA.

12. Truesdale, *Blue Coats*, 368.

13. Ibid., 369.

14. Ibid.

15. Ibid., 370–72.

16. Brown, "Captured by Mosby."

17. Ibid.; Michael P. Musick, *6th Virginia Cavalry* (Lynchburg, Va.: H. E. Howard, 1990), 108. "Jim Crow" is Pvt. John Thomas Crow of Co. D, 6th Va. Cav.

18. Truesdale, *Blue Coats*, 372.

19. Ibid., 373; Palmer, *Marietta Register;* Warseke, "Captured by the Enemy," *West Virginia Journal;* George McCauley, pension record, NARA. The accounts are fairly consistent in reporting that ten to twelve men were captured by various of Mosby's parties that morning and gathered together for the trip south as prisoners.

20. Truesdale, *Blue Coats*, 373; Brown, "Captured by Mosby."

21. Ibid., 373; Wert, *Mosby's Rangers.* 244–47. The date of the hanging of the Union men in retaliation for the execution of Mosby's men by Custer is well established. The timing of this episode is somewhat uncertain. Most accounts put Badger's

capture on November 1 or 2. Badger, however, indicates that only a day had passed since the hanging of the Union men, thus putting the date of capture on the 5th.

22. Truesdale, *Blue Coats*, 374.

23. Brown, "Captured by Mosby."

24. Truesdale, *Blue Coats*, 374; emphasis mine.

25. Ibid., 374.

26. Ibid.

27. Brown, "Captured by Mosby."

28. Truesdale, *Blue Coats*, 375.

29. Ibid., 375–76.

30. Ibid., 376.

31. Ibid.

32. Ibid., 377.

33. Ibid.

34. Ibid.

35. Brown, "Captured by Mosby."

36. Ibid. The guard was composed of Carlisle Whiting, John Thomas Crow, Marquis Calmes, and "McKinsley." Whiting, Crow, and Calmes are identified in the rosters of the 6th Va. Cav. Whiting also appears on the roster of Mosby's command.

37. Truesdale, *Blue Coats*, 378.

38. Ibid.

39. Ibid.

40. Ibid., 378–79.

41. Ibid., 378; Brown, "Captured by Mosby."

42. Truesdale, *Blue Coats*, 379.

43. Ibid.

44. Ibid., 379–80.

45. Ibid., 380.

46. Ibid.

47. Badger may be embellishing the account by indicating that the two scouts either were not familiar with the Spencer rifles or had not used them. At some point in their capture, probably early on, they would have told Badger that the Spencers belonged to them.

48. Truesdale, *Blue Coats*, 380–81. Badger's account may be on the mark. Three of the men were killed: Whiting, Marquis Calmes, and "McKinsley." John Thomas Crow was severely wounded but escaped.

49. Brown, "Captured by Mosby."

50. Ibid.

51. Ibid. The second man shot was probably Marquis Calmes, not "Jim Crow," as Brown relates. Over the years Brown may have confused these two men.

52. Ibid.

53. Ibid.

54. Truesdale, *Blue Coats*, 381.

55. Ibid.

56. Ibid., 381–82.

57. Ibid., 382.

58. Brown, "Captured by Mosby."

59. Ibid.

60. Ibid.

61. Ibid.

62. Ibid.

63. Ibid.

64. Ibid.

65. Ibid.

66. Palmer, letter, *Marietta Register*, December 8, 1864, 3.

67. George McCauley, pension record, NARA.

68. Francis H. Heitman, *Historical Register and Dictionary of the United States Army from Its Organization, Sept. 29, 1789, to March 2, 1903* (Washington, D.C.: Government Printing Office, 1903).

CHAPTER 7

1. Montgomery, *Blazer and His Scouts*, 27; *Philadelphia Inquirer*, September 9, 1864, 1; Dennis E. Frye, "John S. Mosby as a Factor in the 1864 Valley Campaign," in *Struggle for the Shenandoah: Essays on the 1864 Valley Campaign*, ed. Gary W. Gallagher (Kent, Ohio: Kent State University Press, 1991), 119; *OR* 1, 43/2, 315.

2. Montgomery, *Blazer and His Scouts*, 27.

3. Ibid.; NARA, M935, RG 935, Inspection Reports and Related Records Received by the Inspection Branch in the Confederate Adjutant and Inspector General's Office, Microfilm Roll 9, report M-40, beginning frame 825.

4. Montgomery, *Blazer and His Scouts*, 28.

5. *OR* 1, 43/1, 615–16.

6. George Nottingham and Barnett Locy, CSRs and pension records, NARA.

7. Richard Fuller, James Webb, Robert F. Defoe, Ulysus Mason, Charles Shafer, William S. Smith, Charles Thompson, CSRs and pension records, NARA.

8. Numerous newspaper accounts during the summer of 1864 report this method of operation by Mosby's men. See *New York Times*, August 25, 1864, 1; "Mosby's Game," *New York Times*, September 20, 1864, 1.

9. "Mr. Francis H. Long's Dispatches," *New York Herald*, November 7, 1864.

10. "Narrow Escapes No. 2," *Ironton Register*, November 25, 1886.

11. Williamson, *Mosby's Rangers*, 23. Accounts of Mosby's men being dressed in Union uniform are numerous. The story of how Captain Badger was "gobbled up" is a very typical account of Mosby's operations, particularly in the area just north of Winchester, toward Charles Town. For evidence of this method, see: "Mosby's Game,"

New York Times, September 20, 1864, 1; E. A. Paul, "Today, five of Mosby's men were brought in—two of them dressed in citizen's clothing," *New York Times,* September 10, 1864, 1. *New York Herald,* November 10, 1864, 1; *New York Herald,* November 12, 1864, 1.

12. Sylvester Keith, "Camped four miles from Winchester," letter, November 14, 1864, Pension Record, NARA.

13. Scott, *Partisan Life,* 363–64; Williamson, *Mosby's Rangers,* 299–300.

14. Scott, *Partisan Life,* 363–64; Williamson, *Mosby's Rangers,* 299–300; L. M. L., "Col. Edward Bridill's Fate," *Confederate Veteran* 2, 10 (October 1894): 311.

15. Scott, *Partisan Life,* 363–64.

16. Ibid.; L. M. L., "Bridill's Fate," 311.

17. William Leaf, CSR, NARA.

18. Jesse Middaugh, letters, USAMHI. Dan Pelphrey states that Frederick was a twin brother. Pelphrey, email, May 2, 2000.

19. Nelson W. Evans, *A History of Scioto County, Ohio, Together with a Pioneer Record of Southern Ohio,* 2 vols. (Portsmouth, Ohio: Nelson W. Evans, 1903), 2:681–82.

20. James Ewing and Thomas K. Coles, CSRs, NARA; Evans, *History of Scioto County,* 1:252–53.

21. Dyer, *Compendium,* 1501; Theodore F. Lang, *Loyal West Virginia from 1861 to 1865* (Baltimore: Deutsch Publishing, 1895), 254, 272. Reid, *Ohio in the War,* 226; CSRs, 12th and 23rd Ohio Infantries and 5th and 9th W.Va. Infantries, NARA.

22. Benjamin Killam and Albert Logan, CSRs, NARA.

23. John H. Alexander, *Mosby's Men* (New York: Neale Publishing, 1907; reprint, Gaithersburg, Md.: Old Soldier Books, 1987), 116.

24. Scott, *Partisan Life,* 365.

25. Taylor, *Sketchbook,* 464; Wallace, *Guide to Virginia Military Organizations,* 48; Maj. Harry W. Gilmore was formerly commander of a company of the 7th Va. Cav. He was captured by the Scouts, led by Henry Young.

26. Taylor, *Sketchbook,* 464.

27. Scott, *Partisan Life,* 365.

28. Margaret Wilson, telephone interviews, January 24, March 13, April 27, 1997; March 8, 1998; "Narrow Escapes No. 2," *Ironton Register,* November 25, 1886.

29. Scott, *Partisan Life,* 365–66; Williamson, *Mosby's Rangers,* 302.

30. Williamson, *Mosby's Rangers,* 302; Margaret Hopkins Funkhouser, comp., "Richard Hopkins and Mosby's Command," *Reflections: A Publication of the Great Falls Historical Society,* 1994–1996, 11; Keen and Mewborn, *43rd Battalion,* 331. The roster in this book lists Hopkins in Co. D, where his brother John E. also served.

31. Williamson, *Mosby's Rangers,* 302.

32. Alexander, *Mosby's Men,* 119–20; Scott, *Partisan Life,* 366–67; Williamson, *Mosby's Rangers,* 302–3.

33. Scott, *Partisan Life,* 368; emphasis mine. Alexander, *Mosby's Men,* 121; John W. Munson, *Reminiscences of a Mosby Guerrilla* (New York: Moffat, Yard, 1906; reprint,

Olde Soldier Books), 121–23; email, Tom Evans, 3 March 2001. Tom Evans, a Mosby historian living in the Washington area, remembers the late Virgil Carrington Jones telling about listening to Mosby Rangers as a boy. One of these was John Puryear, who Jones says had very visible rope burns on his neck. Jones never published anything about this personal experience.

34. Scott, *Partisan Life*, 367; "Narrow Escapes," *Ironton Register*, November 25, 1886.

35. Scott, *Partisan Life*, 367; Williamson, *Mosby's Rangers*, 304; Munson, *Reminiscences*, 23. Munson states, "Contrary to a popular impression we did not carry carbines at any time during the war." This is contradicted by testimony of Blazer's men that they were struck by carbine shots during the Kabletown engagement and other encounters with Mosby's men. Also, it is common knowledge that Confederate cavalrymen often used shotguns as well. The shotgun also would have been an effective weapon in close in fights.

36. Scott, *Partisan Life*, 367–68; Munson, *Reminiscences*, 120; Williamson, *Mosby's Rangers*, 304.

37. Brown, "Captured by Mosby"; William Wass, 14th W.Va. Inf., affidavit, in John G. Lyons, pension record, NARA; Montgomery, *Blazer and His Scouts*, 23; *New York Herald*, November 6, 1864. The *Herald* reports a prisoner from Loudoun County captured by Mosby's command said that Mosby's, White's, and McNeill's battalions had united in raiding Union posts.

The *Cincinnati Daily Commercial* quotes one of its sources: "Mosby's force of mounted robbers have received considerable accessions of late. . . . many of his recruits are fellows who have served their time out in the old Maryland line." *New York Herald*, November 13, 1864; quoted in *Cincinnati Daily Commercial*, microfilm 08856, OHS, November 14, 1864. The *Cincinnati Commercial* most likely reprinted the *New York Herald* stories. The *Herald* notes these regiments were ones whose time had expired. Mosby was also reported by Union accounts to have four regiments totaling between 1,500 and 2,000 men. These numbers are almost certainly too high. J. Marshall Crawford, *Mosby and His Men: A Record of the Adventures of That Renowned Partisan Ranger* (New York: G. W. Carleton, 1867; reprint, Decatur, Mich.: Invictus, 1968), 169. Crawford reports that captives taken by Blazer on the morning of November 18 included three men from Brig. Gen. Lunsford Lomax's command.

38. "Mosby Ambushes a Party of Union Cavalry," *Zanesville Ohio Signal*, December 1, 1864, 1. This account must have come from one of the survivors of the fight.

39. "Narrow Escapes No. 2," *Ironton Register*, November 25, 1886.

40. Ibid.; Funkhouser, "Richard Hopkins," 11.

41. "Narrow Escapes No. 2," *Ironton Register*, November 25, 1886.

42. Ibid.

43. Ibid.; Evans, *History of Scioto County*, 1:252. Lieutenant Coles was hit by one bullet that entered his left side and came out under his right shoulder. This wound

probably would have been mortal. The trajectory indicates the lieutenant was probably leaning forward on the neck of his horse. The second wound was in his neck and was probably the one witnessed by Henry Pancake after Tom Coles had fallen. These wounds were most likely documented during embalming in preparation for sending Coles's body back to Ohio.

44. "Narrow Escapes No. 2," *Ironton Register*, November 25, 1886.

45. Scott, *Partisan Life*, 369–70; "Williamson, *Mosby's Rangers*, 305; Wert, *Mosby's Rangers*, 256; Richard Blazer, pension record, NARA. If Captain Blazer had been knocked from a horse at full gallop by a blow to the head, he most likely would have received injuries that would have made him seek a government pension, despite his being "too independent to take money from the government." Unlike in Hollywood, getting hit with a pistol or falling from a horse will probably result in injuries with lifelong effects. Falls and injuries caused by horses were a primary reason for many pensions among Blazer's men. There were no affidavits in Richard Blazer's pension file indicating he ever had head or other injuries resulting from the fight at Kabletown. Blazer's pension claims were entirely for the effects of confinement in Confederate prisons. However, relatives of his claim he did have a scar on his head that may have resulted from this encounter.

46. Funkhouser, "Richard Hopkins," 11. The distance (3.6 miles) from Myerstown to the Hefflebower House, where Blazer surrendered, is within the range of a good-blooded horse running full out. Steeplechase horses can run up to four miles. However, the riders would have had to slow their horses on the uphill portions of the ride.

47. "Mosby's Latest Exploit," *Philadelphia Inquirer*, November 28, 1864, quoting the *Charlottesville Chronicle*, November 21, 1864.

48. Ibid.

49. Ibid.

50. Ibid.

51. Tobias Haught, regimental descriptive book, 13th W.Va. Inf.

52. Moses Swarner, CSR, NARA.

53. William Wass, pension record, NARA.

54. Ibid.

55. John G. Lyons, pension record, NARA.

56. Charles Nowlin, John Parsons, and David Price, CSRs, medical records, and pension records, NARA.

57. Williamson, *Mosby's Rangers*, 305; John Smith, CSR, NARA; Keen and Mewborn, *43rd Battalion*, 327.

58. Williamson, *Mosby's Rangers*, 306. Williamson reports that the so-called Farrell was a deserter from his regular regiment. Besides the unlikely case that Captain Blazer would have tolerated such a man in this unit, it is totally unclear how Williamson could have found out this information.

59. Ibid., 307–9.

60. Ibid., 309; Evans, *History of Scioto County,* 1:252. Thomas Coles's wounds were probably analyzed by the surgeons and embalmer, which is probably the reason there is such a detailed account of them in Evans.

61. "Narrow Escapes No. 2," *Ironton Register,* November 25, 1886; U.S. Government, War Department, Quartermaster General's Office, *Roll of Honor,* vol. 15, *Names of Soldiers Who Died in Defense of the American Union, Interred in the National Cemeteries* (Washington, D.C.: Government Printing Office, 1868), 234–36; Cy R. Blazer, interview, February 28, 1999. A "colored" is listed in the *Roll of Honor* with a death date of November 18, 1864. The Blazer family reports that the captain was very disturbed at the murder of this little boy, who may have been as young as nine or ten. This story, along with Henry Pancake's account, and the burial in a place of honor in a national cemetery, are strong evidence that this unarmed boy was simply murdered. His identity will probably never be known. The Jefferson County, W.Va., courthouse has no death records between 1861 and 1865.

62. "Narrow Escapes No. 2," *Ironton Register,* November 25, 1886.

63. Ibid.

64. *OR* 1, 43/2, 648.

65. Ibid., 650. The last two cited messages from the *OR,* plus press dispatches, have been the basis for the assumption that most of Blazer's command were killed or captured.

66. *OR* 1, 43/2, 654.

67. Comly Papers, roll 1, frame 434, OHS. A version of Rutherford B. Hayes's diary contained in these papers differs from the published version. The published version omits Hayes's comments about Blazer's command.

68. "Narrow Escapes No. 2," *Ironton Register,* November 25, 1886; *Jackson (Ohio) Standard,* December 4, 1864, microfilm 08761, OHS; Richard M. Brown, oral history of the return of William's body to Limerick, Ohio.

69. "Narrow Escapes No. 2," *Ironton Register,* November 25, 1886; Opie, *Rebel Cavalryman,* 278; *Roll of Honor,* 236. Fifteen of Blazer's men are buried at Winchester National Cemetery and three, possibly four, bodies were removed to Ohio. Appendix B is a complete list of those killed.

70. Philip Noblitt, pension record, NARA.

71. Ibid.

72. Archibald Waxler, letter, pension record, NARA.

73. George Lamaster, letter, pension record, NARA.

74. Thomas K. Coles, CSR, NARA.

75. Evans, *History of Scioto County,* 1:252–53; *Portsmouth (Ohio) Times,* December 10, 1864, 3.

76. RG 393, pt. 1, entry 5699 (vol. 21, W.Va.), NARA.

77. RG 393, pt. 1, entry 2420 ("Sheridan's Scouts"), NARA. Contains clothing account, lists roster. Lists of men furnished equipment, etc., and receipts of Colonel

Young for money received by him for his scouts. Philip H. Sheridan, *Personal Memoirs of P. H. Sheridan*, 2 vols. (New York: Charles L. Webster, 1888), 2:1–2.

78. RG 393, pt. 1, entry 2420 ("Sheridan's Scouts"), NARA.

79. Crook, *Autobiography*, 135–36; emphasis mine.

80. Ibid., 134.

CHAPTER 8

1. CSRs, 12th and 91st Ohio and 9th W.Va. Infantries, NARA.

2. Stephen Glaze, CSR, letters, pension record, NARA.

3. Ibid.; George A. Otis and D. L. Huntington, *The Medical and Surgical History of the Civil War* (Wilmington, N.C.: Broadfoot Publishing, 1992), 10:541.

4. Stephen Glaze, letters, pension record, NARA.

5. David Albaugh, pension record, NARA; Arthur, "Dublin Raid," 2, 21 (January 5, 1889), 371.

6. CSRs, 12th Ohio and 91st Ohio Regts., NARA.

7. Otis, "Recollections," November 2, 1876.

8. RG 94 regimental order book, 91st Ohio Vol. Inf., NARA; Otis, "Recollections," November 2, 1876; Roger D. Hunt and Jack R. Brown, *Brevet Brigadier Generals in Blue* (Gaishersburg, Md.: Olde Soldier Books, 1990), 665.

9. Richard Miller, "Otis and His Times," 23–24.

10. Ibid., 24.

11. Samuel Spencer, pension record, NARA; Vada Zickafose, daughter of Samuel Spencer, telephone interview, January 6, 1997.

12. Adam R. Head, pension record, NARA.

13. Ibid.

14. Ibid; emphasis in original.

15. William May, pension record, NARA.

16. Albert D. Richardson, *The Secret Service, the Field, the Dungeon, and the Escape* (Hartford, Conn., American Publishing, 1865), 425, 428–29; Richard Fuller and Barnett Locy, CSRs and pension records, NARA.

17. Richardson, *Secret Service*, 451.

18. Ibid., 461–67.

19. Richard Fuller, CSR, NARA.

20. Barnett Locy and Robert Defoe, CSRs and pension records, NARA; *OR* 2, 7 (Prisoners of War, etc.), 1268. Union prisoners, unlike those Confederate prisoners who joined the Union army and were sent out west to fight Indians, were notoriously difficult to "galvanize." One group of these men at Savannah "deserted in large numbers, and finally mutinied, and were narrowly prevented from going over in a body to the enemy. The ringleaders were shot and the remainder sent back to prison. These men were selected with great care, and were principally foreigners, and this is, there-

fore, a fair test of such troops. I recommend that all authority to organize similar commands be revoked." This message was sent by W. J. Hardee from Charleston, S.C., December 24, 1864.

21. Richard Fuller and Barnett Locy, CSRs and pension records, NARA; "Dreadful Fire at Sea," *New York Times*, April 3, 1865, 4–5; *Portsmouth (Ohio) Times*, April 8, 1865, 2; Charles Dana Gibson and F. Kay Gibson, comps., *Dictionary of Transports and Combatant Vessels, Union Army 1861–1865*, The Army's Navy Series (Camden, Maine: Ensign Press, 1995), 128. The screw steamer *General Lyon* should not be confused with the gunboat of the same name.

22. *New York Times*, April 3, 1865, 5.

23. Ibid.

24. Ibid.

25. Ibid.

26. Ibid.; Robert Defoe, pension record, NARA.

27. *New York Times*, April 3, 1865, 5. Barnett Locy, pension record, NARA.

28. Barnett Locy, pension record, NARA; *New York Times*, April 3, 1865, 4–5. Richard W. Lawrence, email, December 15, 2000. Lawrence is Unit Head, Underwater Archaeology Branch, Office of State Archaeology, Division of Archives and History, North Carolina Department of Cultural Resources.

29. Patrick Collins, CSR, NARA.

30. Samuel Harrop, CSR, NARA.

31. Samuel Harrop, *Memorials and Poems of Samuel Harrop*, ed. William H. Collins (Quincy, Ill.: Cadogan-Hatcher Manufacturing, 1899), 53–54.

32. Ibid.; Samuel Harrop, CSR and pension record, NARA.

33. Samuel Harrop, pension record, NARA.

34. CSRs and pension records, NARA; H. H. Hardesty, *The Military History of Ohio, Illustrated, Special Local Department in Editions by Counties, Lawrence County, Ohio* (New York: H. H. Hardesty, 1888), 281.

35. *New York Times*, September 8, 1864, 3. The Negros mentioned here were most likely slaves assigned to menial work in the prisons.

36. William Lewellen and David West, pension records, NARA.

37. Hardesty, *Military History of Ohio*, 281; John G. Lyons, pension record, NARA.

38. CSRs, Blazer's Scouts captured at Kabletown, NARA; Robert E. Denney, *Civil War Prisons and Escapes: A Day-by-Day Chronicle* (New York: Sterling Publishing, 1993), 342. The escape mentioned here has been passed down in the oral history of the Wass, Shultz, and Lieuellen families. All three men were from different regiments and lived in different parts of the country. There is no documentary evidence that any of Blazer's men escaped from the Richmond area prisons. However, some of these men may have escaped and made it to parole points where they merely mingled with other parolees and were listed as such in POW records. Also, it is possible that the North and South may not have wanted to publicize any escapes since this was a sensitive time, just

after the exchange system had been reinstated. Two of the families' oral histories have their men crossing or swimming a river in winter. Jake Shultz was reported to have had bad teeth from chewing his way through the bars of Libby Prison. A close examination of the bars on the upper stories of Libby shows that the bars appear to be made of wood, not iron or steel, making this story plausible.

39. Harry C. Burns, "Prison Life in Pemberton, Concluded," *Ohio Soldier* 1, 46 (June 30, 1888), 725.

40. Ibid.

41. Ibid.

42. William J. Emmons, CSR, NARA.

43. Ibid.

44. 91st Ohio Infantry, order book, NARA; Sec. War, Telegrams Collected, roll 342, frames 0664, 0665–0668, NARA.

45. Samuel Burdett, CSR, NARA; *Ironton Register,* October 8, 1863, microfilm 17265, OHS; RG 393, pt. 2, 1158, 1159 (vol. 106. W.Va.), NARA.

46. John Clute, CSR, NARA.

47. Daniel Link, court martial record, NARA.

48. Ibid.

49. Ibid.

50. Ibid.

51. Ibid.

52. Ibid.

53. Ibid.

54. Ibid.; personal observation; Quartermaster General's Office, *Roll of Honor,* vol. 15, p. 54: Clute is listed as no. 1845, grave 36, lot B, section 1. John Clute is buried at grave marker 1200, marked Jno. Clute. Grave numbers on stones differ from entries in the *Roll of Honor.*

55. Jesse Middaugh, letters, CWTI, USAMHI.

56. Brotherton, *Middaugh History; Gallipolis Dispatch,* March 3, 1865.

57. Special order 2, May 24, 1864, Meadow Bluff; RG 393, pt. 2, 1158, 1159 (vol. 106, W.Va.), NARA; Jesse Middaugh, CSR, NARA; C. Mitchell Hall, *Jenny Wiley Country: A History of "Jenny Wiley Country" and Genealogy of Its People Up to the Year 1972,* vol. 2 (Kingsport, Tenn.: Kingsport Press, 1972), 562. This genealogy directly links the names Middaugh and Meadows: "N. Anna Van Hoose—married a Middaugh (Meadows)"; "Craig Middaugh of Auxier and a brother John Middaugh, sons of Jack Middaugh (Meadows)."

Brenda Fields relates oral history from Dan Pelphrey that Jesse was killed in the final days of the Civil War because he was suspected of being a spy for the Union. Fields, email, August 9, 1999.

58. T. Harry Williams, *Hayes of the Twenty-Third,* plate xi.

CHAPTER 9

1. Richard Blazer, pension record, NARA.

2. Ibid.; *Cincinnati Commercial,* weather reports, August–November 1878. Daytime high temperatures after mid-September rarely exceeded 50 degrees. Jo Ann Carrigan, *The Saffron Scourge: A History of Yellow Fever in Louisiana, 1796–1905* (Lafayette: Center for Louisiana Studies, University of Southwestern Louisiana, 1994), 116. Khaled Bloom, *The Mississippi Valley's Great Yellow Fever Epidemic of 1878* (Baton Rouge: Louisiana University Press, 1993), 10–11, 280. Carrigan provides a good general study of the history of yellow fever and Bloom's book is an excellent study of the 1878 epidemic. Both books explain in detail the transmission of yellow fever.

3. Eugene F. Ware, *The Indian War of 1864* (Topeka: Crane, 1911; reprint, Lincoln: University of Nebraska Press, 1994), 4–5.

4. Ibid., 126.

5. Otis, "Recollections" October 30, 1876.

6. Chance, *Mexico under Fire,* 143, 202; Ware, *Indian War,* 115–16; Dyer, *Compendium,* 1345; Thomas W. Dunlay, *Wolves for the Blue Soldiers* (Lincoln: University of Nebraska Press, 1982), 44, 149. Dunlay gives a detailed account of the organization of the Pawnee scouts and the white officers associated with them.

7. Time-Life Books, *Scouts,* 85.

8. Dunlay, *Wolves for the Blue Soldiers,* 46–47.

9. Crook, *Autobiography,* 163.

10. Charles F. Lummis, *General Crook and the Apache Wars,* ed. Turbese Lummis Fiske (Flagstaff, Ariz: Northland Press, 1966), 17; emphasis in original; Bourke, *On the Border,* 142–44.

11. Society of the Army of West Virginia, *Proceedings of the Eighth Annual Reunion of the Society of the Army of West Virginia held at Cumberland, Md. September 2, 3 and 4, 1884* (Cumberland, Md.: Daily News Printing Office and Bindery, 1885), WVU microfilm 955.

12. Lummis, *Crook and the Apache Wars,* 17; Crook, *Autobiography,* 213–14; Dunlay, *Wolves for the Blue Soldiers,* 89.

13. Crook *Autobiography,* 193–97. Most sources put the number of combatants either as about equal or as the Indians outnumbering Crook's force by several hundred, not three to one. See Angie Debo, *A History of the Indians of the United States* (Norman: University of Oklahoma Press, 1970), 237.

14. Ibid., 213–14.

15. Ibid., 245, 255.

16. Ibid., 259, 263–64.

17. Ibid., 263–65.

18. Malone, *Dictionary of American Biography,* 7:100.

19. Harrison Gray Otis, volunteer service record, NARA.

20. Ibid.

21. Ibid.

22. Malone, *Dictionary of American Biography,* 7:100.

23. Ibid.

24. David Halberstam, *The Powers That Be* (New York: Dell, 1980), 137, 148.

25. Harrison Gray Otis, volunteer service record, NARA.

26. Ibid.; William Page, secretary of San Francisco Building Trades Council, telegram, May 5, 1989; "An Unpopular Appointment," *San Francisco Call,* n.d.

27. Otis, volunteer service record, NARA.

28. Ibid.

29. Ibid.

30. *Los Angeles Times,* July 31, 1917, pt. 2, 1, 7.

31. Ibid.

32. Stanley Karnow, *In Our Image* (New York: Random House, 1989), 182; David Haward Bain, *Sitting in Darkness: Americans in the Philippines* (Boston: Houghton Mifflin, 1984), 9.

33. Brian McAllister Linn, *The U.S. Army and Counterinsurgency in the Philippine War, 1899–1902* (Chapel Hill: University of North Carolina Press, 1989), 70.

34. Frederick Funston, *Memories of Two Wars: Cuban and Philippine Experiences* (New York: Charles Scribner's Sons, 1911), 315–16.

35. Stevens, *Search Out the Land,* 126.

36. Ibid.; Funston, *Memories,* 297–383.

Selected Bibliography

Numerous county and local histories were consulted. Newspapers included the large eastern newspapers, major regional newspapers, and numerous local newspapers.

MANUSCRIPTS

Bowling Green State University, Center for Archival Collections, Bowling Green, Ohio

Wood, James J. Diary, May–October 1864.

National Archives and Records Administration, Washington, D.C.

Record Group 94, compiled service records.

 12th, 23rd, 34th, 36th, 91st Ohio Infantries.

 Microfilm:

  5th, 9th, 13th, 14th West Virginia Infantries.

  2nd West Virginia Cavalry.

  1st West Virginia Veteran Infantry.

Record Group 94. Regimental book records. Descriptive books, letter books, order books, company morning report books, company order books, muster rolls, returns, and letters.

————. Entry 534. Records of the Adjutant General's Office, carded medical records, volunteers, Mexican and Civil Wars, 1846–1865.

————. Entry 652. Records of the Adjutant General's Office, 1780s–1914; records relating to the sick and wounded, 1814–1919; regimental casualty lists, Civil War.

Record Group 98. Records of military departments, Dept. of West Virginia, books 20, 21, 106.

Record Group 110 (Provost Marshal General's Office). Scouts, guides, spies and detectives, two or more names, 1861–1865.

Record Group 393. Part 1, entry 2420. Sheridan's Scouts. Contains clothing account, list of names, list of men furnished equipment, etc., and receipts of Col. Young for money received by him for his scouts.

―――. Pt. 2, entry 1155 (vol. 103, W.Va.). Letters sent April 1863–January 1864.

―――. Entries 1158, 1159 (vol. 106, W.Va.).

M-504, telegrams collected by the Office of the Secretary of War (unbound), 1860–1870.

Record Group 935. Inspection reports and related records received by the inspection branch in the Confederate Adjutant and Inspector General's Office. Microfilm roll 9, report M-40, beginning frame 825.

Pension records of men in Blazer's Scouts.

Ohio Historical Society, Columbus

Ireland, James. Diary. VFM 2304, 12th Ohio Volunteer Infantry Regiment.

Newton, Dr. William. MIC 17, roll 11, letters and documents.

John T. Booth Papers, MSS 180 (36th Ohio Vol. Inf.) Notes of Chas Ward diary and notes for 36th OVI history.

James M. Comly Papers, MIC 33, roll 1.

Rutherford B. Hayes Presidential Center, Library, Fremont Ohio

Anonymous soldier, 23rd Ohio. Diary.

Stairwalt, Andrew. Diary.

United States Army Military History Institute, Archives, Carlisle Barracks, Pennsylvania

Civil War Times Illustrated Collection

Middaugh, Jesse. Letters.

Civil War Miscellaneous Collection

Edward Davis Papers (9th West Virginia Infantry Regiment). Diary.

West Virginia and Regional History Collection, West Virginia University Libraries, Colson Hall

Scott-Palmer Papers, A&M 1423, 1458.

Society of the Army of West Virginia. *Proceedings of the Eighth Annual Reunion of the Society of the Army of West Virginia held at Cumberland, Md. September 2, 3 and 4, 1884.* Cumberland, Md.: Daily News Printing Office and Bindery, 1885. West Virginia University microfilm no. 955.

Milton W. Humphreys Bryan's Battery, Kings Artillery C.S.A. *Military Operations, 1861–1864, Fayetteville, WVA. And Lynchburg Campaign.* MIC P6422, West Virginia Civil War Pamphlets, no. 3.

PUBLISHED SOURCES

Alexander, John H. *Mosby's Men.* New York: Neale Publishing, 1907. Reprint, Gaithersburg, Md.: Old Soldier Books, 1987.

Arthur, E. C. "The Dublin Raid." *Ohio Soldier* 2, 21 (January 5, 1889).

——. "The Dublin Raid." *Ohio Soldier* 2, 27 (March 30, 1889).

——. "The Dublin Raid." *Ohio Soldier* 2, 8 (April 13, 1889).

Bain, David Haward. *Sitting in Darkness: Americans in the Philippines.* Boston: Houghton Mifflin, 1984.

Beymer, William Gilmore. *On Hazardous Service: Scouts and Spies of the North and South.* New York: Harper and Brothers, 1912.

Bishop, William H. *A History of Roane County, West Virginia, 1774–1927.* Spencer, W.Va.: Spencer Publishing, 1927.

Bourke, John G. *On the Border with Crook.* New York: Charles Scribner's Sons, 1891.

Brotherton, Ann. "Family History (of the VanHoose and Middaugh families) as written down by Ann Brotherton at the request of Dorothy McNamara." Typescript, n.d.

Brown County Historical Society of Georgetown. *The History of Brown County [Ohio].* Reprint ed. of original Chicago: W. H. Beers, 1883. Reprint, Evansville, Ind.: Unigraphic, 1973.

Brown, Joseph. "Fighting Them Over; What Our Veterans Have to Say about Their Old Campaigns; Captured by Mosby." Letter to the editor, *National Tribune,* October 31, 1889.

Burns, Harry C. "Prison Life in Pemberton, Concluded." *Ohio Soldier* 1, 46 (June 30, 1888).

Callahan, James Morton. *History of West Virginia, Old and New.* Vol. 1. Chicago: American Historical Society, 1923.

Chance, Joseph E. *Mexico under Fire: Being the Diary of Samuel Ryan Curtis 3rd Ohio Volunteer Infantry during the American Military Occupation of Northern Mexico, 1846–1847.* Fort Worth: Texas Christian University Press, 1994.

Cohen, Stan. *The Civil War in West Virginia: A Pictorial History.* Charleston, W.Va.: Pictorial Histories Publishing, 1976.

Condon, Ann Gorman, ed. *Architects of Our Fortunes: The Journal of Eliza A. W. Otis, 1860–1863.* San Marino, Calif.: Huntington Library Press, 2001.

Crawford, J. Marshall. *Mosby and His Men: A Record of the Adventures of That Renowned Partisan Ranger.* New York: G. W. Carleton, 1867. Reprint, Decatur, Mich.: Invictus (P.O. Box 317), 1968.

Crook, George. *General George Crook: His Autobiography.* Ed. Martin F. Schmitt. Norman: University of Oklahoma Press, 1946. Reprint, 1960.

Dornbusch, C. E. *Military Bibliography of the Civil War.* New York: The New York Public Library, 1961.

Dunlay, Thomas W. *Wolves for the Blue Soldiers.* Lincoln: University of Nebraska Press, 1982.

Dupuy, Trevor N., Curt Johnson, and David L. Bongard. *The Harper Encyclopedia of Military Biography.* New York: HarperCollins, 1992.

Dyer, Frederick H. *A Compendium of the War of the Rebellion.* Des Moines: F. H. Dyer, 1908. Reprint, Dayton: Morningside Bookshop, 1978.

E. E. E. "The Legion of Honor; A History of That Invincible Band Known as the Blazer Scouts." *Ohio Soldier* 2, 2 (August 25, 1888).

Evans, Nelson W. *A History of Scioto County, Ohio, Together with a Pioneer Record of Southern Ohio.* 2 vols. Portsmouth, Ohio: Nelson W. Evans, 1903.

Funkhouser, Margaret Hopkins, comp. "Richard Hopkins and Mosby's Command." *Reflections: A Publication of the Great Falls Historical Society,* 1994–1996.

Funston, Frederick. *Memories of Two Wars: Cuban and Philippine Experiences.* New York: Charles Scribner's Sons, 1911.

Gallagher, Gary W., ed. *Struggle for the Shenandoah: Essays on the 1864 Valley Campaign.* Kent, Ohio: Kent State University Press, 1991.

Gibson, Charles Dana, and F. Kay Gibson, comps. *Dictionary of Transports and Combatant Vessels, Union Army 1861–1865.* The Army's Navy Series. Camden, Maine: Ensign Press, 1995.

Halberstam, David. *The Powers That Be.* New York: Dell, 1980.

Hardesty, H. H. *History of Gallia County.* New York: H. H. Hardesty Publishers, 1882.

———. *The Military History of Ohio, Illustrated; Special Local Department in editions by Counties: Lawrence County, Ohio.* New York: H. H. Hardesty Publishers, 1888.

Harrop, Samuel. *Memorials and Poems of Samuel Harrop.* Ed. William H. Collins. Quincy, Ill.: Cadogan-Hatcher Manufacturing, 1899. Published for the benefit of the Reference Room of the Free Public Library, Quincy, Ill.

Jones, Virgil Carrington. *Ranger Mosby.* Chapel Hill: University of North Carolina Press, 1944.

Karnow, Stanley. *In Our Image.* New York: Random House, 1989.

Keen, Hugh C., and Horace Mewborn. *43rd Battalion Virginia Cavalry, Mosby's Command.* 2d ed. Lynchburg, Va.: H. E. Howard, 1993.

Leggett, Conaway and Company. *The History of Wyandot County, Ohio.* Chicago: Leggett, Conaway, 1884.

Leib, Charles. *Nine Months in the Quartermaster's Department; or, The Chances for Making a Million.* Cincinnati: Moore, Wilstach, Keys, 1862.

Linn, Brian McAllister. *The U.S. Army and Counterinsurgency in the Philippine War, 1899–1902.* Chapel Hill: University of North Carolina Press, 1989.

L. M. L. "Col Edward Bridill's Fate." *Confederate Veteran* 2, 10 (October 1894).

Lummis, Charles F. *General Crook and the Apache Wars.* Edited by Turbese Lummis Fiske. Flagstaff, Ariz.: Northland Press, 1966.

Malone, Dumas, ed. *Dictionary of American Biography.* 12 vols. New York: Charles Scribner's Sons, 1934.

Markle, Donald E. *Spies and Spymasters of the Civil War.* New York: Barnes and Noble, 1994.

Matheny, Herman Edmond. *Wood County, West Virginia, in Civil War Times; With an Account of the Guerrilla Warfare in the Little Kanawha Valley.* Parkersburg: Trans-Allegheny Books, 1987.

M'Chesney, James. "Scouting on Hunter's Raid to Lynchburg, Va." *Confederate Veteran* 27, 5 (May 1920): 173–76.

Merry, Capt. L. E. "Company 'D' Thirty-Fourth O.V.I. Regiment." *Firelands Pioneer,* September 1876.

Miller, James H. *History of Summers County: From the Earliest Settlement to the Present Time.* Hinton, W.Va.: James H. Miller, 1908.

Miller, Richard Connelly. "Otis and His Times: The Career of Harrison Gray Otis of Los Angeles." Ph.D. dissertation, University of California, Berkeley, 1964.

Montgomery, Asbe. *An Account of R. R. Blazer and His Scouts, Operations in West Virginia and in Loudoun and the Shenandoah Valleys, Against William and Philip Thurman, and Mosby, the Great Guerrillas; by Asbe Montgomery, One of the Scouts and Belonging to Captain Blazer's Company, Marietta, Ohio.* Marietta, Ohio: printed at the Registry Office, 1865. (Marietta College Library and WVU Library.)

Munson, John W. *Reminiscences of a Mosby Guerrilla.* New York: Moffat, Yard and Company, 1906. Reprint, Gaithersburg, Md.: Olde Soldier Books.

Musick, Michael P. *Sixth Virginia Cavalry.* Lynchburg, Va.: H. E. Howard, 1990.

Opie, John N. *A Rebel Cavalryman with Lee, Stuart, and Jackson.* Chicago: W. B. Conkey, 1899. Reprint, Dayton: Morningside Bookshop, 1972.

Otis, Eliza Ann. *"Where Sets the Sun": The Writings of Eliza A. Otis.* Comp. Harrison G. Otis. Los Angeles: Times-Mirror, 1903.

Otis, Harrison Gray. "Recollections of the War." *Santa Barbara Press,* October 19, 27, 28, 30, 31, November 1, 2, 3, 1876.

Phillips, David. "The Jessie Scouts." *West Virginia in the Civil War.* <www.wvcivilwar.com>, 1997.

Portsmouth Area Recognition Society. *A History of Scioto County Ohio, 1986.* Portsmouth, Ohio: Portsmouth Area Community Exhibits, 1986. Printed by Taylor Publishing, Dallas.

Reid, Whitlaw. *Ohio in the War: Her Statesmen, Her Generals, and Soldiers.* Cincinnati: Moore, Wilstach and Baldwin, 1868.

Rice, Otis K. *A History of Greenbrier County.* Lewisburg, W.Va.: Greenbrier Historical Society, 1986.

Richardson, Albert D. *The Secret Service, the Field, the Dungeon, and the Escape.* Hartford, Conn.: American Publishing, 1865.

Ritchie County Historical Society. *The History of Ritchie County, West Virginia to 1980.* Ritchie County Historical Society, 1980. Printed by Taylor Publishing, Dallas.

Roane County Family History Committee. *Roane County West Virginia Family History, 1989.* Roane County Family History Committee, 1989. Printed by Walsworth Publishing.

Scott, John. *Partisan Life with Col. John S. Mosby.* Reprint. Gaithersburg, Md.: Butternut Press, 1985.

Sheridan, Philip H. *Personal Memoirs of P. H. Sheridan, General United States Army.* 1888. Reprint, New York: Da Capo Press, 1992; introduction by Jeffry D. Wert.

Shetler, Charles. *West Virginia Civil War Literature.* Morgantown: West Virginia University Library, 1963.

Society of the Army of West Virginia. *Report of the Proceedings of the Eighth Annual Reunion of the Society of the Army of West Virginia, Held at Cumberland, Md. Sept 2, 3, and 4, 1884.* Cumberland, Md.: Daily News Printing Office and Bindery, 1885.

Stevens, Philip H. *Search Out the Land: A History of American Military Scouts.* Chicago: Rand McNally, 1969.

Taylor, James E. *The James E. Taylor Sketchbook.* Dayton: Western Reserve Historical Society, 1989. Morningside edition of the original *With Sheridan Up the Shenandoah Valley in 1864.*

Truesdale, Capt. John. *The Blue Coats: And How They Lived, Fought and Died for the Union.* Philadelphia: Jones Brothers, 1867.

U.S. War Department. *The War of the Rebellion: A Compilation of the Official Records of the Union and Confederate Armies.* 128 vols. Washington, D.C.: Government Printing Office, 1880–1901.

Wallace, Lee A., Jr. *A Guide to Virginia Military Organizations, 1861–1865.* Rev. 2d ed. Lynchburg, Va.: H. E. Howard, 1986.

Ward, James E. D. *Twelfth Ohio Volunteer Infantry.* Ripley Ohio: J. E. D. Ward, 1864.

Ware, Captain Eugene F. *The Indian War of 1864.* Topeka: Crane, 1911. Reprint, Lincoln: University of Nebraska Press, 1994.

Weaver, Jeffrey C. *Thurmond's Partisan Rangers and Swann's Battalion of Virginia Cavalry.* Lynchburg, Va.: H. E. Howard, 1993.

Welcher, Frank J. *The Union Army, 1861–1865.* Vol. 1, *The Eastern Theater.* Bloomington: Indiana University Press, 1989.

Wert, Jeffry D. *Mosby's Rangers.* New York: Simon and Schuster, 1990.

Williams, T. Harry. *Hayes of the Twenty-Third: The Civil War Volunteer Officer.* New York: Knopf, 1965.

Williamson, James J. *Mosby's Rangers.* New York: Ralph B. Kenyon, 1896. Reprint, Alexandria, Va.: Time-Life Collectors' Library, 1981.

Index

Page references in italic type designate illustrations.